EDUCATIONAL PERSPECTIVES IN LEARNING DISABILITIES

Educational Perspectives in Learning Disabilities

Edited by
DONALD D. HAMMILL and NETTIE R. BARTEL

JOHN WILEY & SONS, INC.
New York • London • Sydney • Toronto

Library of Congress Catalogue Card Number: 70–165948

ISBN 0–471–34725–6

Printed in the United States of America.

10 9 8 7 6 5 4 3 2 1

Preface

In a field as diverse as that of learning disabilities, there are many competent professionals who maintain divergent points of view regarding pertinent issues and practices. Up to the present time, discussions of the positions of these individuals (especially individuals who are comparatively new to the field) have been available only in the multitude of journals and convention proceedings of the several disciplines interested in this type of child. This volume brings together, in a systematic way, representative statements on several of the major educational issues confronting the field today.

From the considerable material published on the subject of learning disabilities in recent years, thirty-three articles have been carefully selected for inclusion in this book. Generally, the selection process was governed by three criteria: (1) only articles published since 1965 were included; (2) only articles with a definite educational orientation were considered; and (3) not only did each article have to be timely and educational but it also had to make a unique contribution to the education of children with learning disabilities—as a result, needless overlap among the articles was kept to a minimum.

Because of the acceleration in the development of the learning disabilities area in recent years, we arbitrarily included only articles published since 1965. Our intent was to provide the reader with an overview of current points of view toward learning disabilities rather than with a historical review. In fact, learning disabilities as an integrated, vital movement in American education probably predates 1965 by only several years. Prior to that date the field seems to have been fragmented into a multitude of groups, each with its own parochial interest in a specific problem area—for example, perceptual-motor deficits, reading difficulties, and language disorders. During this pre-1965 period, Cruickshank, Kephart, Kirk, Orton, Lehtinen, Fernald, Myklebust, and Strauss, among many others, were laying the foundation on which today's learning disability approach is based. The post-1965 period has witnessed (1) the proliferation of agencies and professional groups devoted to the child with learning disabilities, (2) the availability of federal and state support for research, teacher training, and service to this child, (3) the refinement of approaches developed by the foundation people, and (4) the development of new directions in rationale, assessment, and management. The articles included here reflect these trends. Readers who desire a historical perspective are referred to the publications of the persons mentioned above and to the anthology edited by Frierson and Barbe, which will provide them with significant articles from the 1950's and early 1960's.

We have included only the articles that contribute to an educational orientation toward learning disabilities. This decision is not meant to minimize the contribution of medicine or psychology to the total management of children evidencing learning disorders. It reflects, instead, the opinion that a volume with a specifically educational point of view is preferable to one that calls for the multidisciplinary approach and that spells out the roles and functions of various disciplines relating to learning disorders in children.

There is an adequate anthology edited by Myklebust that is devoted to detailed discussions of the medical (especially pediatric, neurologic, and psychiatric) aspects of learning disability. While promoting a general understanding of learning disabilities, the information provided in the books edited by Hellmuth, by Tarnopol, by Cruickshank, and by Bortner is only occasionally relevant to teachers, speech and reading therapists, school psychologists, and other school personnel, mostly because of the lack of an intervention focus and because of the heavy emphasis on clinical and etiological aspects. However, the teacher and serious student will find considerable profit in reading these works and we encourage them to do so.

Our purpose in preparing this volume was to acquaint the reader with some of the current, major unresolved educational issues in the learning disabilities area. These issues involve questions of definitions, conceptual orientations, the use of labels, the role of neurological symptomatology, and approaches to evaluation and to school management. This book is not designed as a text in educational methodology. Readers who desire a review of basic instructional approaches are referred to the recent books by Myers and Hammill and by Johnson and Myklebust.

We were careful not to duplicate either the articles or the orientation of previously published anthologies. To our knowledge, the contributions of Dunn, Valett, and Hewett are the only exceptions to our stated criteria, since these articles have been republished previously or predate 1965. This book concentrates on educational matters—that is, on school-related matters—and thereby makes a unique contribution to the study of learning disabilities. Because of its special focus, the book should be of primary interest to school personnel and teachers-in-training, and it should be of secondary interest to professionals in related disciplines who want to become acquainted with the educational aspects of learning disabilities.

DONALD D. HAMMILL
NETTIE R. BARTEL

Contents

Part I

Background and Overview to Learning Disorders

Johnny is a nine-year-old boy who doesn't, can't, or won't read. The teacher believes that his reading achievement would be substantially improved if he would "settle down" and concentrate on the assignments. In fact, Johnny rarely attends to the lesson for more than a few minutes at a time; instead, he bothers his classmates repeatedly, talks incessantly, and is in and out of his seat a great deal. He appears to be distracted by the sights and sounds around him and most of all by his fellow pupils. Johnny's intelligence is average and his motor coordination seems normal except for a noticeable degree of awkwardness.

Classroom teachers have recognized children like Johnny for many years—that is, children with obvious learning difficulties who are too bright to be considered mentally deficient and too reality-oriented to be considered emotionally disturbed. Nevertheless, until recently, many of these children were placed in classes for children labeled "mentally retarded" or "emotionally disturbed" because they seemed to benefit little from instruction in the regular grades.

In the past ten years, an explosion of interest in this type of child has developed, though concern has been mounting steadily since Strauss and Lehtinen set forth their educational principles in 1947. Even though their concepts have been enlarged with time and the terms used to describe these children have changed, the child with specific learning difficulties and concomitant behavioral characteristics is still recognized as distinct from other groups of exceptional children and as needing particular special educational services.

Professionals have by no means been unanimous in hailing the discovery of yet another type of exceptional child as representing some kind of educational progress. Among the objections raised to the reification of an additional category of special children are (1) the recognition of commonly shared behavioral learning characteristics of groups of children invariably leads to their being christened with a label; (2) no matter how neutral the label is intended to be, it will rapidly acquire a stigma; (3) negative labels may reduce teacher expectations and demands from these students, thus further depressing their opportunities for achievement; (4) it is easy to use labels as causes for conditions that the label is supposed to describe—a kind of tautological thinking in which one can reason that the child is not learning to read because he has a learning disability, and he must have a learning disability because he is not learning to read; and (5) these children differ so widely on intellectual, perceptual, motor, and behavioral traits that a common label—and more importantly, a common treatment—is meaningless and impossible.

Conversely, some individuals argue that (1) if we ever want to effectively treat this type of child, we will have to accurately describe and agree on his characteristics, remediation being impossible without evaluation; (2) a label can be useful in providing a frame of reference for individuals concerned with these children; (3) it is necessary to think in terms of categories for purposes of training personnel, lobbying for legislation and appropriation of funds, and administration of special services; and (4) it is impossible to conduct meaningful research or disseminate and implement findings without clear notions, however oversimplified, of the nature of the population with which we are dealing.

Whatever the merits of the two points of view, it is clear that special educators are now cognizant of another discernable group of children in need of special services. The authors included in this anthology represent both orientations, and as of the present, the issue is far from resolution.

Among the authors who have been concerned with questions of labels and definitions are Kass, McCarthy, Kirk, and Maietta. Their discussions, which follow, are actually keynote-type presentations dealing broadly with many substantive issues in special education in general and learning disabilities in particular.

1. INTRODUCTION TO LEARNING DISABILITIES

CORRINE E. KASS

The effects of continuing failure on the human being, especially when it is recognized by the person himself, has been well documented in psychiatry, psychology, and educational psychology. The phenomenon of failure in learning disabilities is well known. The child who is not achieving as expected is frustrated and is puzzling to those adults responsible for his welfare. Experts from a number of disciplines are increasingly reaching a consensus regarding the antidote to failure: successful learning. Educational management then becomes paramount in importance, with ancillary aids given when necessary by the medical and mental health professions.

Basic to an understanding of the area of learning disabilities within special education are several assumptions: (1) that there are children with a handicapping condition who can be so labeled; (2) that, although services for these children are scarce now, both public and private programs are growing in number; (3) that, while the understanding of learning disabilities is complex, behavioral science research indicates that the child with learning disabilities has psychological process deficits and that the usual educational manipulation of the environment is not ade-

SOURCE. Reprinted from *Seminars in Psychiatry*, 1969, 1, 240–244. By permission of the author and publisher.

quate for remediation purposes; and (4) that the handicapping condition known as learning disabilities can be diagnosed educationally and psychologically and that specialized remedial education programs can be prescribed.

LABELING

The question of labeling generally precedes definition. Special educators have been going through a period of transition regarding labeling children according to the traditional categories. In their efforts to revise and improve, many have snatched at the term learning disabilities as a catch-all educational phrase to liberate special education from medical models. After all, who can deny that all handicapped children have problems of learning in normal ways? By casting categories aside, some have felt it would be possible to group children with varying handicaps together with a "generalist" special educator. While this view has not gained widespread approval among special educators, it has served to improve communication among the category specialists and will undoubtedly lead to improved services for all children with handicaps.

In contrast to special education's attempt to erase category lines is the general public's propensity for creating labels. It is amazing with what alacrity laymen and professionals alike have applied such labels as "dyslexia," "minimal brain dysfunction," "interjacent child," "hyperkinetic child," "brain-injured," "invisibly crippled," and "shadow children" without having more than a superficial list of characteristics, all of which can probably be found to some extent within the normal population. As a result, labels become misused. "Learning disabilities," too, as a label, is being misused rather generally. Under the Federal Elementary and Secondary Education Act, money is available for supplementary services to school children. Many of these projects use the term learning disabilities to refer to behavioral, social, and achievement problems with only vague reference to treatment services.

DEFINITION

The responsibility for the definition of a word lies with the labeler. I believe it is safe to say that in no other area of special education has so much effort and controversy gone into the refinement of a definition which would characterize those children who come within the responsibility of special education and require special methods and techniques. Over time, definitions have evolved through the efforts of various groups. Following are five such definitions given in chronological order.

(1) 1962. The following definition appeared in a textbook on exceptional children:[5]

"A learning disability refers to a retardation, disorder, or delayed development in one or more of the processes of speech, language, reading, spelling, writing, or arithmetic resulting from a possible cerebral dysfunction and/or emotional or behavioral disturbance and not from mental retardation, sensory deprivation, or cultural or instructional factors."

(2) 1966. A task force on terminology and identification of the "child with minimal brain dysfunction" was cosponsored by the National Society for Crippled Children and Adults, Inc., and the National Institute of Neurological Diseases and Blindness of the National Institutes of Health.

"The term 'minimal brain dysfunction syndrome' refers to children of near average, average, or above average general intelligence with certain learning or behavioral disabilities ranging from mild to severe, which are associated with deviations of function of the central nervous system. These deviations may manifest themselves by various combinations of impairment in perception, conceptualization, language, memory, and control of attention, impulse, or motor function.

"Similar symptoms may or may not complicate the problems of children with cerebral palsy, epilepsy, mental retardation, blindness, or deafness."[7]

(3) 1967. At the 1967 conference, the Association for Children with Learning Disabilities, a national parent organization adopted the following definition formulated by professionals and a group of executives of the organization:

"A child with learning disabilities is one with adequate mental ability, sensory processes, and emotional stability who has a limited number of specific deficits in perceptual, integrative, or expressive processes which severely impair learning efficiency. This includes children who have central nervous system dysfunction which is expressed primarily in impaired learning efficiency."[1]

(4) 1967. A further clarification of learning disabilities for the educator was suggested at an Institute for Advanced Study which was planned collaboratively by Northwestern University (Institute for Language Disabilities) and the Unit on Learning Disabilities Division of Training Programs, Bureau of Education for Handicapped, U. S. Office of Education. This meeting took place in August 1967, at Northwestern University. The 15 invited special educators agreed on the following definition:

"A learning disability refers to one or more significant deficits in essential learning processes requiring special educational techniques for its remediation.

"Children with learning disability generally demonstrate a discrepancy between expected and actual achievement in one or more areas, such as spoken, reading, or written language, mathematics, and spatial orientation.

"The learning disability referred to is not primarily the result of sensory, motor, intellectual, or emotional handicap, or lack of opportunity to learn.

"Deficits are to be defined in terms of accepted diagnostic procedures in education and psychology.

"Essential learning processes are those currently referred to in behavioral science as perception, integration, and expression, either verbal or nonverbal.

"Special education techniques for remediation require educational planning based on the diagnostic procedures and findings."[8]

(5) 1968. The National Advisory Committee to the Bureau of Education for the Handicapped, Office of Education, provided the following definition as a guideline to the Office of Education for its present program:

"Children with special learning disabilities exhibit a disorder in one or more of the basic psychological processes involved in understanding or in using spoken or written language. These may be manifested in disorders of listening, thinking, talking, reading, writing, spelling, or arithmetic. They include conditions which have been referred to as perceptual handicaps, brain injury, minimal brain dysfunction, dyslexia, developmental aphasia, etc. They do not include learning problems which are due primarily to visual, hearing, or motor handicaps, to mental retardation, emotional disturbance or to environmental deprivation."[6]

SERVICES AND PERSONNEL

Educational services for children with learning disabilities run the gamut from itinerant tutoring through resource rooms to special classes. In reality, education can be no better than the personnel providing the services, and marketable skills in the specialty of learning disabilities are extremely important. Several institutions of higher learning are presently engaged in guiding graduate students in their acquisition of specialized skills and knowledges. For a description of some of these programs, the reader is referred to Kass and Chalfant.[4] (1968).

The following skills and knowledges gained from a program in learning disabilities is submitted as a portrait of the special education "specialist:"

The specialist will have a basic foundation or introduction to both the behavioral and physical sciences, with grounding in the humanities. This is generally accomplished in the first two years of a college education. Basic information regarding sensory functioning, classic research in perception from both the physiological and psychological areas, and experience with communication through the written word are steps toward becoming well educated in learning disabilities.

The specialist will acquire advanced knowledge at the graduate level as new discoveries are made concerning human learning. The neural basis of memory, for example, is constantly being clarified as research progresses. The student of learning disabilities learns to interpret and utilize information from discoveries about other facets of human learning as well as memory.

The specialist will be skilled in diagnosis and remediation of process deficits within the child. Testing skills require the incorporation of the principles of individual testing and the technical mastery of testing procedures. Remediation skills require understanding of the deficits revealed by tests, and mastery of the application of appropriate pedagogy. The gap between diagnosis and remediation can be bridged through the *understanding* of learning deficits. One understanding of the specialist is the distinction among developmental, corrective, and specialized teaching. Developmental learning occurs in the majority of the population when environmental conditions and psychological characteristics follow the normal growth patterns. Corrective teaching is necessary when there has been a gap in a child's education due to such factors as absence from school. Specialized teaching is remedial instruction, which is defined by English and English as "teaching that is designed to remove, where possible, specific causes of lack or deficiency."[2] Corrective teaching can be given by the child's regular teacher with information about the level of achievement. Specialized teaching must be given by specialists trained in the diagnosis and remediation of learning disabilities. A programmed sequence by itself is not a remedial program.

The specialist will have practicum or internship experiences before having specialist status. At the present time, graduate students in learning disabilities enter the field from a variety of backgrounds. This factor has revealed identification problems. Students come from positions in remedial reading, elementary education, psychology, counseling and special education. The programs in learning disabilities are located within departments of special education. During their practicum experiences, graduate students must find identity within the entire area of special education, as well as within the category of learning disabilities. The number of "specialists" in the category of learning disabilities is relatively small at the present time. Qualifications and professional standards have yet to be established on a nation-wide basis. Practicum experiences range from private settings to public school programs. Some hospital or institutional settings may also be used. The university center seems most reasonable during the identification transition. The university staff in learning disabilities provides the most rapid identification with the concept of the learning disability specialist.

The specialist will be able to work with an interdisciplinary team. With the characteristics listed above, the graduate of a learning disability program would be confident of the data he would carry to an evaluation team and thus would inspire the confidence shown in a professional who is an "expert." A feeling of security about one's own expertise reflects itself in more effective team problem-solving.

The specialist will be able to carry out research. The research in learning disabilities appears to be in a transitional stage.[3] Students at the doctoral level in learning disabilities are expected to evaluate this transition and to help formulate imaginative research questions and methodology.

The specialist will be able to communicate with teachers. Consultants are to be found in the schools in increasing numbers. Over the years, the professional consultants who could not or would not communicate with teachers produced reports which were ignored. One of the major objectives for children with learning disabilities is to leave them in the regular classroom, if possible, while giving individualized tutoring, or to return them to the regular classroom as soon as possible. This means that the teacher must know what the child's learning disabilities are, what the specialist is doing about the disabilities, and what her role is to be in transferring remediated skills to everyday learning.

The specialist will develop a personal philosophy or structure as the basis of specialist status. With the explosion of knowledge in all disciplines, much confusion can result from a vague eclectic approach to learning disabilities. A structure encompasses the major factors in the human organism which relate to learning disabilities. The student will find such structures or theories in the literature and, through scholarship and synthesis, will incorporate and develop existing theories into expanding and more valid structures. The behavioral science procedures for the analysis of input-feedback-output processes may be the place to begin.

CONCLUSION

An introduction to learning disabilities, of necessity, begins with the label itself. No one profession has a premium on a label, however, and the use of a label without a definition is professional irresponsibility. In this paper, both labeling and definitions were considered. Professional training programs in the area of learning disabilities can be found throughout the country. A portrait of the specialist who graduates from such programs was presented. The challenge of the field of learning disabilities is enhanced by the pressure for services from both parents and professionals.

References

1. Association for Children with Learning Disabilities. Annual conference, New York City, meeting of executives of the organization and selected professionals, 1967.
2. English, H. B., and English, A. C.: A Comprehensive Dictionary of Psychological and Psychoanalytical Terms. New York, David McKay, 1958.
3. Kass, C. E.: Learning disabilities. Rev. Educat. Res. February, 1969, (in press).
4. Kass, C. E., and Chalfant, J.: Training specialists for children with learning disabilities. In Hellmuth, J. (Ed.): Learning Disorders, Vol. III. Seattle, Special Child Publications, 1968.
5. Kirk, S. A.: Educating Exceptional Children, Boston, Houghton Mifflin, 1962, p. 263.
6. National Advisory Committee on Handicapped Children. First Annual Report, Special Education for Handicapped Children. Washington, U.S. Department of Health, Education, and Welfare, Office of Education, 1968.
7. National Society for Crippled Children and Adults, Inc., and the National Institute of Neurological Diseases and Blindness, of the National Institutes of Health: Minimal Brain Dysfunction in Children. Washington, D.C., U. S. Department of Health, Education and Welfare, NINDB Monograph 3, 1966.
8. Northwestern University and U. S. Office of Education. Unpublished proceedings of the conference on Learning Disabilities and Interrelated Handicaps, Evanston, Ill., August 8, 1967.

2. LEARNING DISABILITIES: WHERE HAVE WE BEEN? WHERE ARE WE GOING?

JEANNE McRAE McCARTHY

Seldom has a concept burst upon the educational scene with such cataclysmic force as the concept of special learning disabilities. Although the early impetus of the published work of Strauss and Lehtinen with the brain injured dated from the late 1940's and early 1950's, and the work of Orton and the dyslexia group dated from the 1920's and 1930's, the educational scene remained quite unruffled as late as the early 1960's. With the possible exception of some isolated research and practice in childhood aphasia and related language disturbances in such centers as Syracuse University, Northwestern, Purdue, the University of Illinois, and Bellevue Hospital, activity in the area which we now call learning disabilities was largely subliminal or limited to abortive excursions into new methods of remedial reading or new approaches to psychiatric or child guidance practice with children whose nonlearning was seen as a hostile response to parental pressure or rejection.

State legislatures had not yet been bombarded by parental pressure groups to enact enabling legislation. The USOE was blissfully unaware of what was about to erupt. Universities, with rare but notable excep-

SOURCE. Reprinted from *Selected Convention Papers*, Council for Exceptional Children Convention, Denver, Colorado, April, 1969, 33–39. By permission of the author.

tions, had no courses on the books to train personnel either to diagnose a learning disability or to teach the child who had one. Nor were there any plans afoot to initiate such training programs. Even The Council for Exceptional Children, the professional organization devoted to the education of children with special needs, at their annual convention in 1960 had not one program or paper which addressed itself to the topic under any of the various aliases which have been used to describe the child who cannot learn.

It is probably safe to say that in 1960 there were no public school classes for these children except for remedial reading programs. In Illinois in 1959 and 1960, we were able to bootleg service to a limited number of children by christening them "multiply handicapped"—the most common combination of handicaps being educational retardation, emotional disturbance, and brain damage. With the children thus labeled and documented, the public schools could legally initiate an educational program to teach them.

There were few parent groups organized to serve these children in 1960. I believe the New York Association for Brain Injured Children, the California Association for Neurologically Impaired Children, and the Fund for Perceptually Handicapped Children were the only ones in existence.

In a very few years since 1960, when all was relatively quiet on all fronts, until now, a great deal of progress has been made in all areas. Both federal and state legislation has been enacted to provide funds to train professional personnel as well as to provide the structure within which public school districts may initiate services and programs. At least 13 states now have within their education code a term which relates to LD. Parent groups have been organized at the national level, at the state level, and at the local level. There are now over 200 local and state affiliates of the Association for Children with LD. Many universities now have a sequence of courses leading to a masters degree or a doctorate in learning disabilities. There are many summer workshops or institutes in which a classroom teacher may enroll in order to upgrade her skills in meeting the needs of children with learning disabilities. Programs to train speech correctionists are collaborating with other disciplines to provide services for these children. Guidance counselors, particularly at the elementary level, are looking at learning, or nonlearning, as an essential part of their training and practice. Psychological diagnosis, as well as the training of clinical or school psychologists, has taken a decided turn away from an emphasis on the dynamics of psychosexual development to an emphasis on learning as a modifiable behavior, and on perception and cognition rather than concentrating on emotional responses to environmental pressures. The total involvement of the field of medicine, whether in a positive or negative way, is everywhere apparent, whether it be in the obvious fields of pediatrics, neurology, and psychiatry, or in the less obvious fields of endocrinology, obstetrics, ophthalmology, otology, or genetics.

What meaning does all of this activity have to you as you attempt to integrate these new concepts into your established body of knowledge, into the organizational structure of your school system—whether you direct a program in New York, Florida, Wisconsin, Utah, or California? In simplest terms, it means that your job will be infinitely easier in this year of 1969 than it would have been at any other time. This is not to suggest, however, that your job will be easy. However, you do have some models—some other programs which have been started in public schools —from which you can learn a great deal. You do have a body of research theory and practice from which you can build a source program for children with learning disabilities. You also have a series of mistakes and blind alleys to assist you in plotting an educationally sound program.

In looking closely at where we have been and where we are going it seems safe to say that we seem to have come full circle and to have arrived again at what Binet in 1909 described as "mental orthopedics"— or the concept of the educability of intelligence. Binet, who predicted that era of mental measurement which spawned the notion that intelligence was hereditary, constant, and essentially unmodifiable, was committed to the belief that each specific function of intellect could be improved with training, and that "the same was true of the ensemble as of the elements"—that intelligence itself could be improved and increased with specific training. The same attitude was apparent in the early work of Samuel Orton and Marian Monroe. However, with the influence of the Freudian school of psychology, educators became involved in several decades of viewing learning problems as psychogenic manifestations of inner conflict in the child or as due to "poor motivation." Thus, the "child who cannot learn" was seen as the "child who would not learn," because nonlearning served a conscious or unconscious role in his struggle with forces which impede ego development. During this era of an essentially psychodynamic conception of learning problems, educators found themselves encouraging parents to involve the child in extensive periods of psychotherapy in an effort to resolve the inner conflicts which were causing or contributing to the inability to learn. Child development specialists emphasize the need of the child for success experiences, praise, and a relaxed, pleasant approach to school learning tasks. After several decades of often fruitless efforts at manipulating the child's attitude toward learning, it became apparent to many psychiatrists, psychologists, and social workers, that tender loving care, or a deeper understanding of his own motivation, could at best produce a child who was comfortable, albeit euphoric, with his nonlearning. It began to occur to some psychiatrists that someone was going to have to teach him to read. Pioneer research at this point was begun in a variety of facilities, among them at Hawthorne Center by Ralph Rabinovitch, who found that the greatest number of emotionally disturbed children who recovered were among those who were being tutored as part of the therapy.

During the waning days of the psychodynamic approach to nonlearning, another thread of research and practice began to make an impact on the educational scene, the work of Alfred Strauss, Laura Lehtinen, and Newell Kephart and that of Rosa Hagin and Archie Silver with brain damaged children. The concept of brain damage as a cause of nonlearning was apparently a welcome change from the more nebulous, more abstract concepts derived from Freudian psychoanalysis. However, the "brain damaged" era began slowly, with the publishing of Strauss and Lehtinen's book in 1947, and did not emerge full blown until the early 1960's, as a many labeled concept embodying elements derived from a variegated heritage. As a body of theory and research has developed over the past decade involving the child who does not learn, it seems apparent that strands from many disciplines are coalescing in the emergence of special learning disabilities as a significant educational concept.

Each year, I have attempted to delineate trends and issues in the field of learning disabilities which seem to be evolving from year to year. By far the most important issue in the field today is that of definition. In some areas there is still a serious question in the minds of special education over the very existence of learning disabilities. Are we just talking about "dumb kids," as one notable educator suggested to me last week? Is the child with special learning disabilities just the MR kid in the suburbs? Is this not just another label for the emotionally disturbed child? As we look at the trends in definitions, it becomes apparent that the early medical emphasis is being replaced with an educational emphasis. The early emphasis on etiology is being replaced by an emphasis on remediation. The six or seven current definitions which seem acceptable to the majority of practitioners in the field, including the Task Force I definition, the Task Force II definition, the ACLD definition, Kirk's early definition, the definition of the Northwestern Conference, or the National Advisory Committee definition, all have two concepts in common: the first is the intact clause, the second is the discrepancy clause. Most definers seem to agree that the child with special learning disabilities is basically an intact organism. This concept of intactness is expressed differently in different definitions. Some follow Dr. Gallagher's comment in St. Louis at the CEC meeting, when a small group were attempting to formulate a definition acceptable to all factors, "whenever you start to define a horse, you first have to define a nonhorse." Thus, the "nonhorse" part of the definitions may be more specific than the definition of what a learning disability is. We seem to be quite sure that the learning disability is not "primarily due to visual, hearing or motor handicaps, to mental retardation, emotional disturbance or to environmental disadvantage." These are basically intact children.

However, "the discrepancy clause" seems to be somewhat less specific. The National Advisory Committee describes the children with special learning disabilities as those who "exhibit a disorder in one or more of the basic psychological processes involved in understanding or in using spoken or written language." These may be manifested in disorder of listening, thinking, talking, reading, writing, spelling, or arithmetic.

This definition seems to be one upon which a sound educational program can be based. You will notice that there is no statement of possible etiology in this definition. We seem to have outgrown our need for a medical model around which we can build an educational program. We have learned from the experience of those programs which have included a medical diagnosis of organicity that the neurological examination or the EEG provides a tenuous base upon which to build an educational program. For those of you who are saddled with legislation or a program which includes some statement of physical disability before these children can be served, I highly recommend that you read, in the February issue of *Journal of Special Education*, Roger Freeman's article entitled: "Special Education and the Electroencephalogram: A Marriage of Convenience." After reviewing the extensive research involving the EEG, Dr. Freeman recommends that special education consider at least a trial separation from neurology and the EEG.

My reason for spending this much time on the evolution of a viable definition is that I am convinced that the most important decision you will make is that of the definition—because your definition will dictate for you the terminology to be used in your program, the prevalence figures your selection criterion, the characteristics of your population, and the appropriate remedial procedures.

I would like to point out that this emphasis on definition seems to be of more intense concern in the area of learning disabilities than in any other area of handicap.

The question of incidence, or more correctly prevalence, is one that is causing a great deal of difficulty at the present time. "Guesstimates" of how many children there are with special learning disabilities range from 1 to 40 percent of the total school population. Prevalence is determined directly by the definition used. Dr. Myklebust, in discussing the question of "how many children are there," has said, "Tell me how many you want to find, and I'll write you a definition that will find that many." Using the National Advisory Committee definition, there is some evidence to suggest that learning disabilities exist in varying degrees in children. While the milder learning disabilities may profit from the individualization of instruction in the regular classroom, the more severe problems require special remedial procedures. An extremely conservative estimate of the latter group would include 1 to 3 percent of the total school population, according to the Report of the National Advisory Committee.

Regardless of which guesstimate you elect to use in your program, be assured that you will find that there are too many children with learning disabilities which require educational modifications to be served by special class placement or to be individually diagnosed by trained specialists.

You will also find that learning disabilities come in all shapes and sizes. The varying degrees of learning disabilities in children require varying degrees of intensity of service in the schools. To describe an "exemplary program" for all children with learning disabilities, as if any one type program will serve all children, is to oversimplify an extremely complex problem.

To summarize progress to date is to come to grips with the possibility that we are going around in circles rather than making progress:

Methodologically, we started with visual perception, then went to sensorimotor training, then to ocular pursuit, then to the establishment of cerebral dominance, then to stimulus reduction, then to auditory perceptual or language training, then to multisensory training, then to integration of sensory stimuli, then to an analytic approach, and then to behavior modification. Academically, we have gone from Orton to Fernald to Gillingham to Spaulding to SRA to BRL, to Phonovisual, to the Language Master, to ITA, and now to any reading method which has a decoding emphasis. The focus of remediation has been passed from the social worker to the pediatrician to the psychiatrist to the psychologist to the neurologist to the endocrinologist and now back to the teachers.

So much for where have we been! It is much more difficult to discuss where are we going! I am indebted to Dr. Samuel Kirk and Dr. Masland for confirming some of my ideas about the future in the speeches they made at the recent ACLD conference in Fort Worth. I am also indebted to Alice Thompson for sharing some of her ideas in a paper she presented to the California CASE group last year. By pooling these expert opinions, I have gathered the courage to make some predictions about the future.

I predict the special learning disabilities will continue to gain prestige as a respected category of special education.

As learning disabilities stabilizes, so should those areas which seem to be clouding the picture at the present time: language problems, aphasia, dyslexia, remedial reading slow learners, and some emotionally disturbed and mentally retarded children.

It seems quite clear that the National Advisory Committee definition includes children with developmental aphasia. Thus, a district with a program for children with learning disabilities would automatically include aphasic children in such a program.

My second prediction involves a proliferation of new programs and services for children with special learning disorders. Pressure from parents will continue to keep pace with the demands of society. As administrators it is urgent that you come to grips with some of the pressure points involved in the program, and plan carefully to avoid the booby traps. By all means plan programs of varying degrees of intensity to match the varying degrees of severity of learning disabilities in the children. You will need (a) consultants to regular classroom teachers, either on an itinerate basis or on a one consultant per building basis; (b) you will need some resource room teachers, where children are bused to the school to spend a portion of each day in the regular class and a portion in the special class; (c) you will need some self contained classes for the most severely involved children where the major emphasis in the self contained classroom should be on return to a resource room program in the school in which the child "belongs" since research and experience indicate that the farther a child is removed from the normal educational program, the more difficult it becomes to return him to the mainstream. Major emphasis needs to be placed on the individualization of instruction for most children with learning disorders within the regular classroom. I cannot conceive of the pressure in one of our states for residential schools for these children. And yet, this was the major thrust of both parents and educators. And why? Because the legislation was written in such a way as to reward residential placement, but not to support public school classes. If your state is faced with the problem, roll up your sleeves and become involved in rewriting the legislation, but don't subscribe to the notion of packing these children off to boarding—or hospital—schools.

By the same token, the best prevalence figures we have suggest that most districts would have enough children to start a class in their own district, rather than as part of a joint agreement or cooperative arrangements. To bus most children with special learning disorders to a special school run by a cooperative, as I have seen done in N.G. is to compound an already complex problem. It may be necessary to provide diagnostic services on a cooperative basis, but major emphasis on programs needs to be placed at the local district on local building level. The reunifications for preservice and inservice training are monumental. We need to work toward a drastic change in attitude on the part of regular classroom teachers from the current "He doesn't belong in my class" to an attitude of "What can I do to help him?"

My third prediction in answer to where are we going involves early identification of these high risk children and a complete change in attitude toward our interest in and responsibility for preschool children. There is no question that these children can be identified in kindergarten. Many of them could be identified and served at four. The current trend toward mandatory education at age three is one that I believe will continue to gain support at all levels. Impetus for this will come from the one hundred demonstration programs funded under PL 90–538, the Handicapped Children's Early Education Assistance Act.

This also suggests that speech correctionists will begin to become more directly involved in the limited disorder program, that the division of labor between DCCD and DCLD might well be reexamined.

Dyslexia will be viewed as a subset of learning disabilities. Severely disabled readers will be programed just as severely disabled learners of any other type. It is probable that remedial reading populations are now made up of some children who have special learning disabilities and some whose failure to learn is due to causes outside of the child. Thus, care will need to be taken by administrators to avoid duplication of services, without cutting out needed services to children with corrective reading problems. It is probably safe to say that the current practice of some districts of having parallel programs serving the same child will be discontinued.

It seems well within the realm of probability that the National Advisory Committee on Dyslexia and Related Reading Disorders will, in their final report due in June, help to clarify the relationship between limited disorders and dyslexia, thus providing a base for better articulation between reading specialists and limited disorder specialists at the national, state, university, and public school levels. Limited disorder may be the bridge which will increase communication and articulation between elementary education and special education, since most children with SLD will not need a self contained special class, but will remain in a regular class for part of the day.

The current furor over "an IQ of 90 or above" seems quite likely to dissipate rather quickly, as psychologists and educators continue in their disenchantment with the IQ as a measure of function in children. We are now aware that IQ's in many children respond to programs aimed at training intelligence, and are unstable enough to warrant careful matching to performance in and out of the classrooms. The number of hours of expensive professional time being wasted on trying to decide whether a child with an IQ of 79–81 is mentally retarded with a learning disability or merely a limited disorder should reduce sharply, as classes for mentally retarded children begin to individualize instruction and utilize the concepts of clinical teaching commonly found in limited disorder classes (requisitions and ordering).

In the immediate future, I predict that little or no valuable time will be wasted trying to decide whether a child is primarily emotionally disturbed or learning disabled. In the normal school population, the child with a LD will stick out like a sore thumb. The fact that he also has emotional problems is a *given*. Psychotic, schizophrenic and autistic children will also stick out like sore thumbs, and obviously need to be programed differently than the child with minor adjustment problems. Between these two extremes lies a large group of conduct problem learning disabled children who can profit from a carefully structured, purposeful, learning focused classroom atmosphere, regardless of the label for the condition.

If you do not have a program, I heartily recommend that you start with early identification and programing at the kindergarten or first grade level. This is a difficult place to start, since awareness of failure on the part of the child has not yet hit his parents or his teachers. You will also be fighting a large segment of kindergarten teachers who still subscribe to the "leave them alone and they'll come home" philosophy. At the very least, begin to reexamine your entrance policies for high risk children and design a program to serve them rather than sending them home for another year in an environment which already has them behind their peers.

My fourth prediction involves the relationship between learning disabilities and cultural deprivation—or between special education and compensatory education, if you will. We have already excluded culturally deprived children from the learning disability population by definition, but this does not solve the practical problems for you. I am not too hopeful that learning disability concepts are going to have a great deal of impact on the problems of the culturally deprived. I am quite convinced that the answers to these problems will need to involve total societal involvement, of which special education is a small part. There is no question that massive changes must take place in the community, in the home, and in the school system before we begin to find answers to these learning problems. But let us not fail to provide for the smaller number of children with special learning disabilities of unknown etiology, while we wait for answers to the much larger problem of cultural deprivation.

My fifth prediction involves our current concept of the diagnostic process. At the present time diagnosis is primitive, time consuming, expensive, and frought with problems of validity and reliability. Our instruments for diagnosis and prediction are at best rudimentary. Test constructors will continue in their efforts to provide valid microscope measures of cognition. As psychologists become more disenchanted with the traditional tools of their trade and as a new breed of psychologists replaces those left over from the Rorschach days of their Veterans Administration training, you will begin to see more creative use of some of the good diagnostic instruments available to your school psychologists.

My sixth prediction involves remedial methods. We seem to have tried all the global approaches to remediation that can be conceived. Now we are ready to begin differentiating the teaching methods so that we will see the emergence of real clinical teaching, where the goal is a precise match between the cognitive style of the learner and the cognitive demands of the task. We will be seeing emphasis placed on the diagnostic role of the teacher, as well as the training of specialists who are both psychoeducators, diagnosticians, and clinical teachers.

In the foreseeable future I suspect that such neuropsychologists as Karl Pribram will be able to tell us something meaningful about the chemistry of learning in human children. At the present time, they are quite knowledgeable about earthworms, rats, pigeons, and even chimpanzees, but not about children. I am not willing to sit around and wait for the "pill" which will prove to be the panacea that will solve all of the problems of children who do not learn. In the meantime I hope that you will be as aware as I that children who do not learn do not do so for an infinite variety of reasons. For some of these it is because of a special learning disability. For these, we can and should provide special educational programs.

3. LEARNING DISABILITIES: THE VIEW FROM HERE

SAMUEL A. KIRK

The term learning disabilities has been introduced widely in educational circles to indicate an area which includes different kinds of specific disabilities that inhibit a child's ability to develop in a normal fashion. These disabilities do not include the general categories of physical, mental, or emotional handicaps. Although the term was originally designed to include specific disabilities primarily in the communication process, other definitions have been formulated. The most recent one that seems to be the most acceptable is the one formulated by the National Advisory Committee for the Handicapped in the United States Office of Education. This definition states:

"Children with special learning disabilities exhibit a disorder in one or more of the basic psychological processes involved in understanding or in using spoken or written language. These may be manifested in disorders of listening, thinking, talking, reading, writing, spelling, or arithmetic. They include conditions which have been referred to as

SOURCE. Reprinted from *Selected papers on learning disabilities. Progress in parent information, professional growth, and public policy.* Sixth annual conference of the Association for Children with Learning Disabilities, Fort Worth, Texas, March 1969, 21–25. By permission of the author and publisher.

perceptual handicaps, brain injury, minimal brain dysfunction, dyslexia, developmental aphasia, etc. They do not include learning problems which are due primarily to visual, hearing, or motor handicaps, to mental retardation, emotional disturbances, or to environmental disadvantage."[1]

HISTORICAL BACKGROUND

Beginning as early as 1819, authorities, such as Gall, followed by Hughlings Jackson, Henry Head, and James Hinschelwood, discussed the problems of disorders in thinking, speaking, listening, reading, and other specific disorders of the communication process in relation to brain dysfunction. Much of the work in these areas has been conducted with adults who lost their abilities in communication, speaking, reading, etc. as a result of brain injury. The concentration of the physicians was understandably on the discovery of the relation between brain function and behavior. They were particularly interested in discovering the etiological factors in disorders in communication. This interest continues to the present day. The assumption is that if the etiological factors can be discovered, it may be possible either to prevent the disorder, or to correct it through surgery, drugs, or other means.

In terms of neurological dysfunction, the problems are more difficult to diagnose in children. Furthermore, with the exception of a small number of cases, surgery or medicine has not altered the child's learning disability. As yet, drugs have not been discovered which will assist the child who is not talking or isn't learning to read. It is possible, however, that in the future the molecular biologist will make these discoveries.

Since medicine has not yet been able to solve all the problems of children with developmental defects of this kind, education and training had to enter the scene. The term learning disability is an outgrowth of this educational emphasis in contrast to the more biological terms of alexia, dyslexia, apraxia, aphasia, acalculia, agraphia, and others, each of which implies some brain dysfunction.

The emphasis on education for the learning disabled today is not different from the emphasis on education for other kinds of handicapped children. If a child is born deaf, it is of scientific and preventive interest to discover whether the child became deaf because of meningitis, con-

[1] National Advisory Committee. In *Notes and Working Papers Concerning the Administration of Programs Authorized under Title VI of Public Law 89-10, Elementary and Secondary Education Act, As Amended: Education of Handicapped Children for the Subcommittee on Education of the Committee on Labor and Public Welfare United States* (Washington, D.C.: U. S. Government Printing Office, 1968), p. 14.

genital factors, or other etiological factors related to deafness. Although there are some surgical techniques, such as the fenestration operation, which may restore hearing, the majority of deaf children are deaf for life. Ordinarily, we request the otologist to restore hearing in a child. When the otologist tells us that he cannot restore hearing through surgery or medicine, we then introduce educational techniques for the child that will develop speech by artificial means—lip reading, reading through the visual channel, or other techniques. There is, in many instances, no relationship between the teaching of a deaf child and the etiology of his deafness. In other words, the first stage in any handicapping condition is to do what can be done medically, and then, when medicine reaches its limits, education begins.

The same condition prevails in the field of learning disabilities. If a child has a developmental deficit, a disorder in one of the communication processes, and the condition cannot be corrected, ameliorated, or cured through surgery or medicine, then psychoeducational diagnosis and remedial education begin. The educational diagnosis and remediation generally have little relationship to the assumed etiology.

FUTURE DEVELOPMENTS

I should like to make some predictions on the future developments in this field in the next five to ten years. If my historical sketch has any merit, I predict that the main responsibility for the remediation of learning disabilities in children will fall upon the schools. The sooner the public schools assume the responsibility for the analysis of these children —their identification and their remediation—the sooner the problem will be solved for many of them.

I make this statement because I believe that when a problem is everybody's business it is nobody's business. Because of the concern of parents, we have arising in our midst a great number of procedures, promises, and unscientifically oriented cures for all kinds of problems for children with learning disabilities. There is no point in criticizing these procedures. The best way to eliminate quackery is to give the necessary services to children. The agency which has been organized in our society to teach and to remediate deficits in children is the public school. Hence, the public, and legitimate private schools, must assume the responsibility for the assessment and remediation of school-age children with learning disabilities.

I have another prediction. The analysis and so-called diagnosis of children with learning disabilities, from a psychoeducational standpoint, has been—and probably still is—based on superficial tests and observations.

For many years, we have given psychometric tests, such as the Rorschach tests, Bender-Gestalt tests, Stanford-Binet Intelligence Scale, Wechsler Intelligence Scale (WISC), and others.[2] These tests do not lead to hypotheses for remediation. They are, of course, necessary steps in the diagnosis. We use our current intelligence tests, such as the Binet, to tell us whether the child is retarded, average, or superior. A general reading test tells us whether the child is up to grade, below grade, or above grade. What has evolved in the last several decades, and what appears to be a more promising approach, is the more microscopic type of test, such as, Wepman's Auditory Discrimination Test, Illinois Test of Psycholinguistic Abilities, Frostig Developmental Test of Visual Perception, Purdue Perceptual-Motor Survey, a series of diagnostic reading tests, and other similar tests. In the field of cognitive development, L. L. Thurstone and others have attempted to break up general intelligence into its parts so that we can tell whether the child is developing normally in all functions, or has deficits or abilities in some areas.

I feel that the current analytical or diagnostic tests bring us closer than we have ever been to providing help in writing a prescription for teaching. I believe we are on the right track in that approach, but I also believe that we are currently in the stage of infancy in the use of these kinds of measurements, which help us evolve a hypothesis for remediation. My prediction is that these kinds of tests will multiply and through research will finally provide reliable and valid measures of abilities and disabilities in children, described by the test results in such a way that hypotheses for adequate remediation or prescription can follow.

A third prediction has to do with the adequate development of methods and materials for the remediation of special deficits. Currently, we are experiencing an influx of methods and materials for teaching children with learning disabilities. I shall not name these methods here, because many of them are applicable to some children and are useless for others. At the present time, many teachers are learning about one method, or one set of materials, and are using these with all children labeled "learning disabilities," without too much reference to whether the method or materials apply to a particular child. I believe that we will refine our diagnostic techniques and devise corresponding remedial materials and methods for each of the specific deficits found in children with learning disabilities. We will then come closer to what I call scientific pedagogy or what Binet called "mental orthopedics."

A fourth prediction is as follows: Today we are beginning to train people in psychoeducational diagnosis and remediation. In the past we have relied on the doctor to make the medical examination, the psycholo-

[2] See references at the end of this article for sources of tests.

gist to administer the mental test or other tests, the social worker to give a history, and then when this team has determined that a learning disability in a child does exist, the child is referred to a remedial teacher to organize the program for him. This procedure has not worked too well, since the individuals who assess the child and determine his eligibility for a program have few specific suggestions for the teacher who is going to conduct the remediation. What we really need are people with interdisciplinary training who can give the psychoeducational diagnosis, evolve the remedial hypotheses, and organize the remedial program for the child. Currently, I believe this type of training will require approximately a two-year graduate program over and above an undergraduate program in one of these fields. This training would give the student the skills in diagnostic techniques, and the ability to organize a remedial program for different kinds of disabilities.

Until we have such a psychoeducational remediationist who is the responsible agent for a child with a learning disability, we will continue to flounder from one profession to another. I predict that a position for a person with interdisciplinary training will evolve in our schools, perhaps entitled "Diagnostic-Remedial Specialist." This individual will serve as the responsible agent for the child—responsible for adequate diagnosis, evaluation or assessment, and for the remediation or the organization of remediation for a child with a learning disability. All personnel involved in the assessment of the child—doctors, psychologists, and social workers —will report their findings and interpretations to this diagnostic-remedial specialist. She, or he, will be responsible for the collation and interpretation of information, for remediation, or for the prescription for remedial education. The diagnostic-remedial specialist will function somewhat as the family physician does—as the responsible agent for obtaining information from other specialists and for prescribing treatment.

In the past, children with learning disabilities have been identified primarily during the school-age period. In the future, an attempt will be made to identify these children at the preschool level. Identification procedures—especially for those who have psychological deficits that will inhibit their ability to learn in school—are being developed, and remedial procedures to prevent failure in reading or other school subjects will be organized. The goal will be to identify these children at an early age, diagnose the specific deficits, and institute remedial education. A universal application of this approach may tend to prevent the majority of learning disabilities at an older age.

The remedial programs in the schools will be itinerant programs with resource rooms, primarily. Classes for a heterogeneous group of children labeled "learning disabilities" will probably be abolished. The goal of remedial education will be to correct or ameliorate the disability and to integrate the child in the class with his age group.

References

Bender, Lauretta. *Visual-Motor Gestalt Test*. New York, N.Y.: American Orthopsychiatric Association, Inc., 1946. Clawson, Aileen. *Bender Visual-Motor Gestalt Test for Children*. Beverly Hills, Calif.: Western Psychological Services, 1962. Koppitz, Elizabeth M. *Bender Gestalt Test for Young Children*. New York, N.Y.: Grune and Stratton, 1964.

Frostig, Marianne, with D. Welty Lefever, John R. B. Whittlesey, and Phyllis Maslow. *Marianne Frostig Developmental Test of Visual Perception*. Third edition. Palo Alto, Calif.: Consulting Psychologists Press, Inc., 1961–1964.

Kephart, N. C., and Eugene B. Roach. *Purdue Perceptual-Motor Survey*. Columbus, Ohio: Charles E. Merrill, 1966.

Kirk, Samuel A., James McCarthy, and Winifred Kirk. *Illinois Test of Psycholinguistic Abilities*. Urbana, Ill.: University of Illinois Press, 1968.

Rorschach, Hermann, and Hans Huber. *Psychodiagnostic Plates* (Rorschach Tests). New York, N.Y.: Grune and Stratton, 1954.

Terman, E. Lewis, and Maud A. Merrill. *Stanford-Binet Intelligence Scale*. Boston, Mass.: Houghton-Mifflin, 1961.

Thurstone, L. L. *Primary Mental Abilities*. Chicago, Ill.: Science Research Associates, Inc., 1952–1963.

Wechsler, David I. *Wechsler Intelligence Scale for Children* (WISC). New York, N.Y.: Psychological Corporation, 1949.

Wepman, J. *Auditory Discrimination Test*. Chicago, Ill.: Language Research Associates, 1958.

4. CURRENT HALLOOS
CONFRONTING SPECIAL LEARNING DISABILITIES

DONALD F. MAIETTA

Not long ago, Dunn took the position that "a large proportion of this so-called special education in its present form is obsolete and unjustifiable from the point of view of the pupils so placed. . . . We are not arguing that we do away with our special education programs for the moderately and severely retarded, for other types of more handicapped children, or for the multiply handicapped. The emphasis is on doing something better for slow learning children who live in slum conditions, although much of what is said should also have relevance for those children we are labeling emotionally disturbed, perceptually impaired, brain-injured, and learning disordered."[4]

As progenitors of the modern movement of education and remediation of children and youth with special learning disabilities, Strauss and Lehtinen, in a text complete with philosophy, evaluation, education, and remediation, summarize their 20 years of work with "those children, physically handicapped or physically sound, who show intellectual and personality aberrations as a result of injury to the brain substance." They define the "brain-injured child" as "a child who, before, during, or after

SOURCE. Reprinted from *Seminars in Psychiatry*, 1969, 1, 245–252. By permission of the author and publisher.

birth has received an injury to or suffered an infection of the brain. As a result of such organic impairment, defects of the neuromotor system may be present or absent; however, such a child may show disturbances in perception, thinking, and emotional behavior, either separately or in combination. These disturbances can be demonstrated by specific tests. These disturbances prevent or impede a normal learning process. Special education methods have been devised to remedy these specific handicaps."[14]

In the intervening span of 22 years since the published work of Strauss and Lehtinen, many disciples, protagonists, antagonists, converts, opportunists, and revisionists have emerged. Currently, no area of education or special education has become more controversial or is receiving more publicity than special learning disabilities. To what extent these exhortations are reflections of a profession's growing pains and to what extent they reflect serious challenges or changes in the direction of national efforts to provide quality education for our children is not fully known or understood by most activists of this movement. Certainly, if we were to examine *Education for the Professions*, published by the United States Office of Education,[1] comparable developmental patterns in more than 30 professions could be detected when service is the central focus of comparison.

There is a familiar historical ring to concerns about administration and preparation of personnel, recruitment and availability of trained personnel, university and college programs of teacher education to meet the needs and interests of the community, effects of emphasis on research or clinical services on scientific image and attainment, and the delicate issue of professional "intrusion."

Although many professional organizations prefer to wink at the special learning disabilities movement, anticipate its rapid decay or decline, or simply dismiss the existence of children identified by various labels implying brain dysfunction, the unalterable fact faces society that too many children in and out of schools have ways of learning that do not respond to the usual methods utilized in most current educational settings. The problem has become of sufficient magnitude, as identified by improved scientific instruments for measurement and educational programming, to command the attention of federal and state agencies.

In its annual report to the U. S. Commissioner of Education (on special education for handicapped children) the National Advisory Committee on Handicapped Children maintained that "the problem of special learning disabilities should be considered as part of a larger issue of the classification of handicapped children. . . . a federal study, sponsored jointly by the National Institute of Neurological Diseases and Blindness, the

National Society for Crippled Children, and the Office of Education, is now in progress to attempt to define more clearly the nature and extent of these problems, and to provide a basis for the planning of more effective programs of research and service."[11]

Such prominent national personalities as Benton, Bryant, Carroll, Chall, deHirsch, Haring, Masland, Smith, and Strother have been invited by HEW to serve as a panel to study problems of dyslexia and related reading disorders.[6] The panel of experts have the expressed charge of examining the state of research, diagnosis and evaluation, teacher preparation, and corrective education.

Although factors and forces that have stirred our nation's interest in assisting our school-age population affected by special learning disabilities are too numerous and too complex to recite, important major issues are emerging and are worthy of serious study and action. These may be identified according to definition, clinical preparation of teachers, assessment and methodology, and research and change.

DEFINITION

The field of special education's approaches to the definition of learning disabilities are as varied and confusing as attempts at definition have been in other professions. Perhaps the generic inability of modern science to understand fully the nature of learning, intelligence, and behavior serves as the source of our dilemmas. Damaging scars to children with learning disorders have been caused by labels attached to children and their problems. Publications and operational definitions have been directed toward children with dyslexia, perceptual impairment, educational retardation, hyperkinesis, psychoneurological impairment, brain-injury, cerebral dysfunction, emotional disturbance, sensory impairment and many other clinical labels. Confusion has not been reduced by contributions from medicine, education, or the para-medical and para-educational professions. Compounding the problems are the vested interests of many professional groups anticipating loss of power or prestige if their causes and definitions are not constantly kept before the eyes of the public and those with special influence. To define a child as having a learning disability only if he has average intellect, no motor or sensory deficit, no emotional disturbance or environmental deprivation, may cause the definers more headaches than solutions. Is it possible that the definition formulated by the National Advisory Committee on the Handicapped reveals an initial attempt to carve out a recognition of children in need of special services not currently receiving a just and adequate education because of their exclusion from special classes for emotionally disturbed, mentally retarded, speech and hearing handicapped, visually impaired, or environmentally disadvantaged?

"Children with special learning disabilities exhibit a disorder in one or more of the basic psychological processes involved in understanding or in using spoken or written languages. These may be manifested in disorders of listening, thinking, talking, reading, writing, spelling, or arithmetic . . . They do not include learning problems which are due primarily to visual, hearing, or motor handicaps, to mental retardation, emotional disturbance or to environmental disadvantage."

An alarming increase of research evidence raising serious questions about the efficacy of special day classes for handicapped children, including those labeled emotionally disturbed,[12] points to our need for immediate review of patterns of special education classes of all types. Separating the child with special learning disabilities from similar children identified by other arbitrary or special labels can be just as disastrous for the movement as separating the special child from other children in his school, community, or neighborhood. When it comes to what is best for society and our children, wishful thinking that children with learning disabilities will disappear is as unsound as rationales defending vested interests and other classifications or placements by professional groups through their power, influence, and image. Do we, through this movement, have a fresh opportunity to examine our collective professional consciences, and use our interrelated efforts to significantly change the role and course of special services in educational settings? Can we afford the luxury of thinking that mentally retarded children with auditory-perceptual disorders, or deaf children with visual-perceptual problems are having their needs adequately met in existing programs and really represent a type of child with educational needs different from children who have auditory or visual-perceptual problems who happen to be normal in intelligence?

CLINICAL PREPARATION OF TEACHERS

From problems of definition, it follows that any preparation of teachers will reflect in one way or another either highly specialized or generalized programs related to classifications given those children. Forces which limit imagination and innovation toward programs of preparation for teachers or specialists in universities and colleges readily can be attributed to: federal regulations and patterns for awarding fellowships and traineeships; state certification requirements by areas of handicap such as mental retardation, deafness, blindness, speech handicaps and others; departmental administrative and philosophical patterns hardened into highly specialized areas; influence of professional groups and memberships; and already existing specialized training programs with historical roots in a highly concentrated area of special learning disabilities.

Spiraling tuition costs, coupled with a great deal of prestige and power attached to receiving federal funds in a number of specified areas, condition universities and colleges to resist a fresh approach that cuts across specialty areas, particularly with full knowledge that federal funds are simply not too plentiful for innovative approaches, and the likelihood of receiving a greater amount of federal funding by submitting applications revealing a freshly revised innovative approach to learning disorders is significantly a greater financial risk than applying for funds established for several existing areas of specialization. Federal funds for special learning disabilities essentially are now tapped from well-established professional areas of specialization and tapped with high resentment from other professionally ingrained groups. Yet ". . . a large proportion of this so-called special education in its present form is obsolete and unjustifiable from the point of view of pupils so placed."[11] Some encouragement and relief may be forthcoming from Congress if recommendations from the National Advisory Committee are heeded by legislators: ". . . funds appropriated for research and training programs for children with special learning disabilities should be substantially increased. Such additional funds, necessary to define and explore this area, should not be allocated at the expense of the pressing program needs in established areas."[11]

Although actions of state departments of education traditionally have lagged behind research evidence pointing to change in certification requirements, competence, and in quality programs, exciting opportunities for change present themselves to state directors of special education through various titled funds such as ESEA Title III and ESEA Title I (P.L.89–10).* Remarkable progress in some states in breaking through supposedly hardened and unchangeable categories of special education

* Among the many programs of federal money administered by the U.S. Office of Education for fiscal year 1969 are Title III of the Elementary and Secondary Education Art which supports supplementary educational centers and services with 15 per cent of $164,876,000 specifically designated for handicapped children. Local education agencies apply directly to state education agencies.

ESEA Title I (P.L. 89–10) has several types of assistance available to local school districts through state education agencies. To meet special educational needs of educationally deprived children, $1,078,000,000 has been appropriated; to develop special education programs for migratory children, $45,000,000 has been allocated; to improve the education of delinquent and neglected children in local and state-operated institutions, $27,000,000 is available.

is being made with direction and support of state and local administrators of these programs, not only because of the availability of financial resources but as a result of federal pressure encouraging experimentation and development of exemplary and innovative programs. Are universities and colleges willing and able to participate with state departments of education in a grand design for change?

Another important problem facing this newly branching professional movement is lack of central organization and structure. Current influence and pressure for change seem to emerge through centrally rooted professional groups while acknowledging that certain benefits can accrue from a permissive and multi-faceted structure. It is conceivable that an organization such as the American Association On Special Learning Disabilities would generate more solutions than problems and at the same time weed out opportunism. On the other hand, maybe the time is ripe for all specialized professional groups to meet seriously to establish guide lines for creation of a hybrid professional organization geared to the educational needs of children and youth with learning disabilities and capable by its nature to yield more significant service, professional preparation, and research than any existing group can muster. Is it possible that over-specialization and fragmentation of special services will lead to the extinction of specialized efforts, labels, and programs?

Within modern universities in tune with community interests and needs, growing uneasiness and restiveness are present among faculties active in the education of teachers of handicapped children and youth. While many factors have facilitated dissatisfaction with ongoing graduate and undergraduate programs of teacher preparation,[13] a major concern has its roots in the sterility of theories, philosophies, curricula, detachment of subject matter and teaching from communities and children, and from a gnawing recognition that what is being offered, although eloquently expressed in professional conferences, conventions, and publications, is little more than educated speculation on what is valid. Emphasis at Boston University on a full-year program of systematic observation of variously labeled handicapped children coupled with observational seminars planned as a core feature of curricula for all undergraduate and graduate students in special education is a striking attempt to remove children's labels and to develop astute powers of teacher observation related to ongoing daily dynamic behavior of children in a variety of environmental and educational settings.[13] Broadened perspectives and perceptions among clinically prepared teachers and specialists participating in these seminars in the coming decade should provide an important breed of special educators having rich sources of observational data and tools for research and service.

ASSESSMENT AND METHODOLOGY

The rigidity or flexibility with which special learning disabilities are defined will critically affect not only administrative organization and content of undergraduate and graduate programs but will shape attitudes and practices concerned with evaluations and services offered children. Assumptions, rationales, dictates, highly directional programs and methods are in abundance. Although vehicles for assessment and service are more scientific than in the past, this movement, as in so many other professional areas, has more sound than fury, more unanswered questions than solutions, more ambiguity than direction, more clinical "guesstimates" than researched postulates, more room for growth and development than self-righteousness and complacency, and undoubtedly more inappropriate than appropriate services. Despite the persistent contentions of Delacato and his colleagues about the merits of patterning to neurological organization,[3] of Frostig about the value of her training program for visual-perceptual problems,[5] of Johnson and Myklebust that auditory perceptual deficits are not appreciably responsive to phonetic approaches to teaching reading,[7] of Cruickshank that specific physical arrangements and structure facilitate learning of the brain-injured,[2] and of Kirk about the importance of carefully programmed and sequenced materials and learning environments,[9] the efficacy of these and other theories, hypotheses, and methodologies are in need of rigorous evaluation and research. This is not to say that they are not useful or critically needed by children with special learning disabilities. The message emerging from these theories or points of view and their highly specialized methods attaches a new reverence and posture to the importance of accurate assessments before interventions with specific and individualized educational and remedial programs. Improved scientific techniques and materials for assessment and interventions offer bright promises to educators seeking to keep pace with scientific knowledge. While a number of traditionally or intuitively oriented educators, para-educators, psychologists, and medical professionals are quick to point up the dangers of individualized prescriptions and programs as "Mickey Mouse, cookbook" or "cafeteria-style" approaches, solid evidence inherent in individualized education now sweeping the nation demands scientific orientation and direction in programs of teacher preparation. There is little consolation for intuitive approaches insisting that no single test or method is superior to all others. What is crucially important is that modern philosophy and programs of clinical preparation of teachers and specialists build into our future educators competent knowledge and skills to know which tests and interventions are appropriate for special learning disabilities at a given time and circumstance.

Much of the material released for publication today stresses importance of structure and sequence to learning and achievement. Any professional worker who has rolled up his sleeves and interacted with children having special learning disabilities knows that external structure and careful sequencing are required to a greater extent and intensity with these children than with other children enrolled in regular educational programs. This strategy is particularly useful as the severity of the learning disability detracts from a child's potentials. Much systematic observation and evidence are needed to reveal whether or not the structure should be isolated or in small-group learning environments; tutorial versus special class arrangements; initial sequencing of interventions and materials from general and gross levels to specific and highly minute levels as the child's learning patterns approach normal expectancy levels; whether the body teaches the mind[8] or whether the mind teaches the body or learns independently; whether perception can be learned and can be taught as a separate and distinct entity from concept formation and cognitive development.

While the child with special learning disabilities may have been a part of mankind since his beginnings and while various professional groups have attempted to label, assist, or educate him in part or in some combination of his total needs, his problems belong basically to the educator and psychologist, particularly the educator. Improved techniques in research and methodology offer the child of today the most optimistic promise ever. Results of current efforts to educate him and to remediate his problems, for all their known scientific shortcomings, show meaningful progress and change, with ready acceptance and support from parents and legislators throughout our communities and levels of government.

RESEARCH NEEDS

Many areas of special learning disabilities need immediate and long-range research and evaluation. The character and life-flow of this newly established movement depend on the relevance and scope of scientific and clinical explorations. We have already mentioned several areas needing inquiry regarding definition, assessment, methodology, and professional preparation, but perhaps the single most important priority for professional workers is systematic study of the current image and practices of special services and education to determine how much of our efforts justify what is being offered these children and the public and how much of these efforts require change. Efficacy studies on handicapped children point to current successes of regular class placements for education of mild to moderately handicapped children regardless of disability label. Should special educators take a second and more objective look than heretofore at what modern programs of preparation are doing for teachers of children in regular elementary and secondary schools? Is the message we are receiving saying clearly that modern teachers and methods do not see children as handicapped or special to the point of isolating them from other children in community day schools? Does education need a new breed of specialists capable of coping with the multi-faceted demands of class and school in the entire school program and not just in special classes? Since increasing numbers of our children labeled as handicapped are now being integrated with children in regular classes, should we be concerned with efficient ways to prepare supportive personnel to work with specialists, professional workers, and teachers?

The roles of instructional materials centers for the handicapped and their learning needs have received continued federal emphasis since their inception several years ago.[10] Will research of instructional materials and their demonstration with handicapped children support the belief that teachers can be significant developers and innovators in the area of instructional materials? What should be the relation of materials to instruction? Are materials useful to children with learning disabilities and other handicaps equally beneficial to the nonhandicapped and vice versa? Can these centers become more than libraries for teachers and specialists?

One of the questionable outgrowths of present practices and regulations regarding special classes is the restriction imposed on these children by a definition that excludes related handicaps. Careful research is needed to determine if children of normal intelligence coming from white, middle-class environments taught by middle-class teachers or methods are a unique population of learners. That these children need help, not currently being programmed for them in other special classes, cannot be denied. That they have a right to equal educational opportunity as other groups designated as mentally retarded, speech handicapped, deaf, and blind, cannot be ignored or refuted. If problems that confront them are similar to learning problems confronting other handicapped children, grave moral, ethical, and professional issues face us in the types of educational programs being developed for teachers and specialists, in the types and quality of services extended our children and youth, and in the types of research and directions created for future generations.

Educators cannot afford the luxury of believing that modern medicine and biochemistry will in the immediate future provide our children with a pill or an injection that will abruptly correct and normalize their handicaps and destiny. While promising strides are reported in the laboratory and literature from para-educational sources, the basic responsibility for change and promise for children of today and tomorrow rests with educators in commitments that soon will involve other professional workers and groups and extend from birth to death instead of the brief journey from kindergarten through grade twelve.

As education, psychology, psychiatry, medicine and other professions use their joint interests to provide services and develop research into the pre-school years of children, opportunities to work out significant differences in background and orientation into translatable communication from each other's professional jargon should reach a new high toward understanding and helping children with special learning disabilities. Federally funded early childhood educational projects such as Head Start, Community Mental Health Centers, and others from the Department of Health, Education, and Welfare should go a long way toward changing the image and scope of education and special education.

References

1. Blauch, L. E.: Education for the Professions. Washington, D.C., Office of Education, U. S. Department of Health, Education and Welfare, 1955.

2. Cruickshank, W. C.: A Teaching Method for Brain-Injured and Hyperactive Children, Syracuse, N. Y., Syracuse University Press, 1961.

3. Delacato, C. H.: Neurological Organization and Reading Problems. Springfield, Ill., Charles C Thomas, 1966.

4. Dunn, L. M.: Special education for the mildly retarded—Is much of it justifiable? Exceptional Child. 35:5–25, 1968.

5. Frostig, M., and Horne, D.: The Frostig Program for the Development of Visual Perception. Chicago, Follett, 1964.

6. HEW appoints blue-ribbon panel to study problems of dyslexia. Washington Sounds 2:4, 1968.

7. Johnson, D. J., and Myklebust, H. R.: Learning Disabilities: Educational Principles and Practices. New York, Grune & Stratton, 1967.

8. Kephart, N. C.: The Slow Learner in the Classroom. Columbus, Ohio, C. E. Merrill, 1961.

9. Kirk, S. A., and McCarthy, J. J.: Illinois Test of Psycholinguistic Abilities. Urbana, Ill., University of Illinois Press, 1961.

10. McCarthy, J. J.: Educational materials for the mentally retarded: A quandary. Exceptional Child. 1:24–32, 1966.

11. National Advisory Committee on Handicapped Children: First Annual Report, Special Education for Handicapped Children. Washington, D.C., U. S. Department of Health, Education and Welfare, Office of Education, 1968.

12. Rubin, E. J., Senison, C. B., and Betwee, M.: Emotionally Handicapped Children in the Elementary School. Detroit, Mich., Wayne State University Press, 1966.

13. Sarason, S. B., Davidson, K., and Blatt, B.: The Preparation of Teachers: An Unstudied Problem. New York, John Wiley and Sons, 1962.

14. Strauss, A. A., and Lehtinen, L.: Psychopathology and Education of the Brain-Injured Child. New York, Grune & Stratton, 1947.

Part II

Educational Implications of Cerebral Dysfunction

Educators in the area of learning disabilities have apparently recovered from their long period of intoxication with the concept of brain injury and pseudomedical terminology. In part this change of attitude has been in response to the development within special education of a sense of its own identity based squarely on educational and behavioral principles rather than on anatomic or etiologic considerations.

This shift has been facilitated by the recognition of the fact that knowledge of the presence or absence of cerebral dysfunction (real, presumed, or imagined) is not very useful to the teacher who must design a program for an individual child. In practice, an educational program is prepared **37** by the teachers in response to the individual child's educational needs and behaviors, and not in response to any diagnostic label the child may carry.

The fundamental reason for this is that at present there is no empirically validated program for the education of children with cerebral dysfunction. Techniques exist for developing auditory, visual, and tactile perception; for enhancing motoric integration and balance; for perfecting syntax, grammar, reading, speech, arithmetic, spelling, and writing; and for controlling hyperactivity, perseveration, and inattention, but no educational techniques treat or cure brain injury. The techniques work well when used with children who require training in percepto-linguistic-behavioral areas regardless of the presence or absence of neurological handicaps. Clinicians, teachers, and researchers have consistently noted that many children who do not suffer from brain injuries or dysfunctions evidence specific learning disabilities, while large numbers of apparently brain-injured cases manifest no learning disabilities whatsoever.

To be sure, all children with educationally defined learning disabilities should have a thorough medical examination to rule out progressive pathology, to consider the desirability of drug therapy or surgical intervention, and to determine the child's general health condition. But the decision-making policies concerning the choice of class placement and the selection of teaching strategies are school matters and are best left to school personnel.

It is interesting that some educators and psychologists are more entranced with the organic approach to instruction than are many physicians. A number of physicians have long noted that teachers of children with learning disabilities cannot expect much help from them in the active instruction of such children.

Yet since many children with specific learning disabilities do evidence apparent or equivocal signs of cerebral disturbance, a wealth of material has been written that focuses on the neurological aspects of educational inadequacy. In the main these contributions have dealt with such non-instructional topics as (1) psycho-medical assessment, (2) characteristics, and (3) possible causes of brain dysfunction in children with learning disability. Such discussions are valuable to the teacher in that they contribute to a comprehensive understanding of the child and his problem, but tend to have limited application to educational evaluation and the resultant instruction.

With these considerations in mind, the four articles included in this section were selected. They provide the reader with a basic and realistic overview of relevant aspects pertaining to educational and organic interactions. In addition, the authors repeatedly advise caution in making instructional decisions based essentially on physical and/or neurological findings.

Freeman discusses the uses and limitations of the EEG as a medical procedure and reviews the relationship of the EEG tracings to epileptic equivalents, headache, migraine, and reading disability. The association of abnormal brain-wave patterns with minimal cerebral dysfunction and behavior disorders are discussed also. Paine, Werry, and Quay have studied the relationship among neurological, electroencephalographic, behavioral, intellectual, and historical findings. Money and Bobrow present a case study of a child with severe birth defects and apparently no associated intellectual, perceptual, or learning disorder whatsoever. The literature that pertains to the teaching of reading to brain-damaged children is thoroughly reviewed by Reed, Rabe, and Mankinen, and their article provides an apt conclusion to this chapter. One may conclude from reading these articles that teachers and other professionals should be circumspect in making assumptions about a particular child's learning patterns, potential, or needs, that are based on his physical or neurological characteristics.

5. SPECIAL EDUCATION AND THE ELECTROENCEPHALOGRAM: MARRIAGE OF CONVENIENCE[1]

ROGER D. FREEMAN

Timmy was 7 when he was referred by his school for neurological evaluation because of his short attention span and disinhibited behavior in the classroom. The school specifically requested an electroencephalogram (EEG). When after the neurologist's examination an EEG was not recommended, the school informed the clinic that if one was not done the case would be referred elsewhere.

An unusual case? No. In the experience of the writer and his colleagues, there is an increasing tendency for educators to request an EEG to establish the cause or category of a pupil's difficult behavior. Educators have become more sophisticated recently in dealing with IQ scores, realizing both the limitations of the method and the attractiveness of a concrete number in a field where certainty is rarely possible. However,

SOURCE. Reprinted from *The Journal of Special Education*, 1967, **2**, 61–73. By permission of the publisher.

[1] This study was supported by U. S. Children's Bureau Grant #416, Personnel Training Grant for Handicapped Children. The author would like to acknowledge his indebtedness to Henry W. Baird III, M.D., for increasing his appreciation of the complexities of the EEG as it relates to neurological and behavioral disorders.

41

in some parts of the country an "abnormal" EEG has been made a legal requirement for admission to special education classes for the "brain damaged" or "neurologically impaired."

This paper will attempt to clarify some of the limitations of the EEG and the controversies surrounding its use. This will be done in a critical and perhaps iconoclastic spirit that is not, however, meant to detract from the valid clinical usefulness of this instrument.

LIMITATIONS OF THE EEG

General Problems of Methodology

There have been many efforts to correlate brain phenomena and behavior; they have met with limited success. Although many investigators pay lip-service to the mind-body unity, one still finds in practice dichotomizations between the "functional" (often used as equivalent to "psychogenic") and the "organic." The gap between the understanding of molecular events in the neuron and molar aspects of behavior is extremely wide. Henry (1965) has suggested that the primitive bio-electric functions of the brain cannot be directly correlated with the complex and phylogenetically recent development of human personality. He questions whether even gross personality and behavior typologies are amenable to EEG studies. Thus, while the criteria of abnormality chosen for such studies are crucial (Bergman & Green, 1956), they vary tremendously from one report to another.

On what basis should brain-injured and non-brain-injured groups be selected? A history of possible or probable trauma, for example, does not indicate whether the damage was transient or is still having an effect (Graham & Berman, 1961). Neurological examination for purposes of defining criterion groups in children is limited by the wide range of normal variation, the lack of cooperation of many children, high levels of anxiety that confounds results, and insufficiently precise standards of norms.

Does an "unusual" EEG record indicate an abnormality? Not necessarily. There are large areas of overlap in records of groups obviously brain damaged and apparently normal. The control groups of children that are sought for comparison purposes are less accessible for study than are adults, and those used in many studies cannot be considered representative (Graham & Berman, 1961). If *strict* criteria of abnormality are used, 45% of patients with undisputed seizures will produce normal EEG's (false negatives) according to Bergman & Green (1956), which will reduce the number of false positives, while the loosening of criteria will reverse this relationship. On this basis alone many studies are difficult to compare or replicate.

Abnormal brains may generate normal brainwaves. Bergman and Green (1956) found that in some cases seizure states induced by electroshock did not alter the EEG, even in the presence of obvious transient "neurological signs." On the other hand, the reported incidence of "abnormal" EEG's in the general population varies from close to 10% to more than 20%, depending on the criteria used.

Many people do not realize how subjective the interpretation of the EEG is (Bray, 1964). In some ways, the question of normality or abnormality in relation to an individual's EEG record is analogous to the same question in relation to a person's height. When does tallness or shortness become "abnormal" and to what extent can the extremes be correlated with organic disease? There are undoubtedly nutritional, hereditary, ethnic, endocrine, orthopedic, and even emotional factors involved. Similarly, anyone reviewing the significance of EEG findings in non-epileptic individuals will become trapped in a morass of conflicting reports. A multitude of positive factors have been accumulated, but they are "so utterly contradictory that their algebraic sum is almost nil" (Gastaut, quoted in Henry, 1965, p. 15). In our own experience, children with grossly abnormal EEG records may show a full range of variation in behavior from no abnormality to complete incapacitation.

To further complicate an already confusing mass of data, Gibbs, Gibbs, Carpenter, and Spies (1959) reported that common childhood infectious diseases (measles, German measles, scarlet fever, mumps) without signs of encephalitis produce a high percentage of abnormal EEG's during the acute and postacute periods. They concluded that perhaps these diseases, usually considered benign, are responsible for more central nervous system disease than was previously supposed. (It should be noted that these changes were not simply due to febrile reactions.)

EEG records are *summations* of millions of individual neuronal discharges (Knott, 1960). This fact, too, makes differential assessment and correlation extremely difficult. Goldensohn (1963) aptly summed up a review of these difficulties:

"Are there predictable scalp EEG correlates for consciousness? It appears not. For interference with memory? It appears not . . . When does a seizure start? When does it end? The scalp EEG frequently does not tell us. The answers to these questions are generally negative because the attenuated post-synaptic potentials that are found at the cortex are only approximate and incomplete indications of the underlying cerebral dysfunction (p. 312) . . ."

Psychiatric classification schemes which are used in EEG studies of children are based upon the adult model and are generally believed to be grossly inappropriate. Many psychiatric "diagnoses" are arrived at through a history taken from the parents and office evaluation of the child. Particularly with young or handicapped children, extrapolation of results from an atypical "clinical" setting to the classroom or home is hazardous (Freeman, 1967). The significance of behavior in a child, normal or abnormal, cannot be established without reference to both organismic (intrapsychic and organic) and environmental factors, all of which are difficult to specify.

Technical Problems

An excellent general discussion of the technique of recording the EEG can be found in Hess (1966). Summated electrical potentials are recorded from the scalp and amplified about 1,000 times. Recently there has been an attempt to standardize the placement of electrodes (Bray, 1964). There is heated argument over whether monopolar recordings (measuring the potential difference between a scalp electrode and the interconnected ears, the latter as a reference point) or bipolar recordings (scalp to scalp) are superior. There are numerous artifacts that creep into the record, both from the instrument and from patient movement, requiring expert interpretation. Electrical changes occurring in deep structures may never reach the surface of the brain or pass through to the scalp, and there are only a limited number of ways in which abnormalities can be expressed in the recording (Bray, 1964). Gross abnormalities recorded directly from the exposed cortex at operation (electrocorticograms) may not appear in the EEG at all.

Some authors who have reported changes which have not been corroborated by others have asserted that the lack of replication was due to inadequate technique. Some advocate special locations for the electrodes (nasopharyngeal, anterior temporal, etc.). Special procedures may also be used to evoke "latent" abnormalities not present in the normal waking record: sleep, photic stimulation (flickering light), hyperventilation, and certain drugs, among others. But even here there is considerable variation from one laboratory to another, and the electroencephalographer must, in the final analysis, depend upon his experience and subjective interpretation.

Reliability. No adequate study of the reliability of EEG interpretations in children was found in a review of the literature. However, in a study with ten adult patients and five electroencephalographers, Blum (1954) reported a very low degree of agreement. The cases were assessed on two dimensions: (a) normal, borderline, or abnormal tracings; and (b) diffuse or focal abnormalities. There was 40% agreement on the presence or absence of pathology, 30% on whether changes were focal or diffuse, and when both dimensions were combined, *the concordance was only 10%.* "This low reliability of judgments by five experienced neurologists suggests caution in accepting electroencephalographic validity" (Blum, 1954, p. 145). One possible criticism of this study, however, is that the EEG's were read in isolation from the clinical history and other neurological findings.

Correlations With Learning and Behavior. Paine (1965) discussed the "attractive hypothesis" that sudden, subclinical EEG changes might represent interferences in the continuity of thinking or attending and concluded that:

". . . the existing studies . . . generally provide conflicting evidence. It has to be stated at present that subclinical electroencephalographic discharge sometimes interferes with learning in some children and appears not to do so on other occasions in the same children, or in other children . . . It must be acknowledged that at present we are in general unable to make correlations between the location of electroencephalographic abnormalities and the nature of children's difficulties in learning (pp. 17–18)."

Grossman (1966) stated that many attempts had been made to relate EEG deviations to abnormal learning and behavior,

". . . but it would appear that each investigator has approached the phenomenon somewhat differently and there is no consensus . . . Thus far, there does not appear to be any specific electroencephalographic abnormality that correlates with a specific aberration in learning and/or behavior (p. 64)."

The following sections of this paper will discuss some of the areas in which conflicting results have been obtained in attempts to establish some of these correlations.

AREAS OF CONTROVERSY

Epileptic Equivalents

Perhaps because of the anatomical and functional ramifications of the nervous system, it has been implicated in the etiology of a vast number of poorly-understood conditions. The term "epileptic equivalent" usually refers to episodic symptoms, not obviously convulsive, with a variety of manifestations, frequently involving the autonomic nervous system and/or subcortical structures. Two reviews of this subject (with a "biological" bias) are those of Kellaway, Crawley, and Maulsby (1965) and Snyder (1958). A good example of the mind-body dichotomy can be found in the former.

"Recognition of subtle disturbances of cerebral function revealed by electroencephalography is important because the attitude of physician, parent, and teacher is changed by the realization that the child has an organic cerebral disorder. Thus the usual techniques of punishment and reward for performance are ineffective in such children (Kellaway et al, 1965, p. 42) . . ."

The writer would question why "organicity" would necessarily make these techniques ineffectual. Changed attitude toward "organic" children as indicated by the authors might be helpful or harmful, depending upon individual factors. Furthermore, the "usual techniques of punishment and reward" are not always successful with "normal" children.

In the brief descriptions that follow it will be apparent that many writers have used the term "dysrthythmia," referring to certain EEG abnormalities in rhythm, as synonymous with certain "clinically" observable states, a practice which can only confuse the issues even more.

Headache and Migraine. Snyder (1958) reported that half the children brought to a pediatric clinic for recurrent headaches showed a "paroxysmal cerebral dysrhythmia" responsive to anticonvulsant medication and felt that this was an indication of a true epileptic sensory fit. Halpern and Bental (1958) described similar cases but reported less dramatic improvement with medication. More recently Barolin (1966) did an extensive study and concluded that there was no direct connection between migraine headaches and epilepsy, though 50% of patients with migraine had abnormal EEG's. "Neither faints, nor abnormal EEG's, nor focal signs can prove an epileptic etiology" (p. 64). Whitehouse, Pappas, Escala, and Livingston (1967) reviewed the literature and particularly the "14- and 6-per-second positive spike" (to be discussed below), and concluded that migraine is a convulsive equivalent, the 14- and 6-per-second positive spike pattern (PSP) being evidence of an autonomic dysfunction. Yet they issued the caveat that clinical evaluation is more important than EEG abnormality.

All these studies are complicated because the vascular changes that accompany migraine may *produce* transient neurological abnormalities rather than being caused by them. In addition, headaches are common in many "normal" people and subjective in nature.

Abdominal Epilepsy. There have been many reports of children with episodic abdominal pain, nausea, or vomiting responding to anticonvulsant medication in a more or less dramatic manner. Snyder (1958) gives an interesting case description along these lines. However, this "diagnosis" is often too readily employed in the presence of unusual EEG patterns without alterations in consciousness or the occurrence of motor phenomena. As with headaches, such symptoms are frequent in childhood, can result from a variety of causes, and may occur in relation to many kinds of environmental stress. In our experience many children to whom this term is applied have questionable EEG abnormalities which have lulled the clinician into a false sense of diagnostic certainty, precluding search into often quite disturbing and complex family problems.

Nightmares. Snyder (1958) mentions that non-convulsive spells occurring during sleep may be confused with simple nightmares and discusses the differential diagnosis. Some children have seizures only at night, especially during the stage of light sleep (Gastaut & Tassinari, 1966).

Reading Disability. Oettinger, Nikonishi, and Gill (1967) investigated 19 children with reading disability and found that in five of them the reading process seemed to activate EEG abnormalities which then resulted in alterations of consciousness or unpleasant symptoms leading to inhibition (or possibly aversive conditioning) of the reading. They diagnosed these cases as "subclinical reading epilepsy." Although this report has not yet been corroborated by others, it should be pointed out that there is an entity known as "reading epilepsy" in which seizures may be produced *only* by reading. This is one of a variety of unusual and intriguing forms of epilepsy involving very discrete functions. An excellent review of the various types of epilepsy has been provided by Gastaut and Tassinari (1966).

Other Symptoms. Fever, personality changes, and pains in parts of the body other than the head and abdomen have all been reported (Snyder, 1958). Personality disorders will be discussed later.

In summary, while there is good reason to believe that convulsive and subconvulsive phenomena can be protean in their manifestations and may mimic many other conditions, the EEG cannot necessarily be regarded as decisive in the differential diagnosis.

The 14- and 6-Per-Second Positive Spike Pattern (PSP)

A large and controversial literature has failed to fully clarify the nature of this peculiar finding. Gibbs and Gibbs (1951) suggested that it originates in the thalamus and hypothalamus and is a distorted form of the normal sleep pattern. Some of the patients studied had a history of attacks of apparently unprovoked rage, pain, or symptoms attributable to the autonomic nervous system. It was reported in 2% of control subjects and 6% of patients with "epileptiform disorders." Gibbs and Gibbs felt it might disappear with maturity and that it was relatively benign in the absence of other abnormal findings. Poser and Ziegler (1958) agreed generally with Gibbs and Gibbs, finding the highest incidence of the PSP in children, adolescents, and young adults, with the peak in adolescence. They reported an association with behavior disorders and episodic symptoms of the types previously mentioned. In a rather poorly designed but frequently quoted study, Schwade and Geiger (1960) interpreted 73% of the records of patients with severe behavior disorders as abnormal because of the PSP, relating it to lack of impulse control and unpredictable violence, though declining to label the disorders "epileptic." In an extensive review, Henry (1963) stated:

"As of this writing the real clinical significance of this pattern, *if there be any*, is anything but clear. There is a surfeit of possible clinical relationships, too often resulting from uncontrolled studies, but almost nothing is known of the basic neurophysiological substrate that might produce such an unorthodox discharge (p. 326)."

He suggested that the PSP might represent an underlying physiological stress which results in symptoms only with the concurrent stress of environmental factors. Small and Small (1964) compared 25 adult patients with PSP and 25 matched controls. They found few significant differences and concluded—"the reported significance of this EEG signal in psychiatry has not been confirmed in this study" (p. 650).

Finally, Lombroso, Schwartz, Clark, Muench, and Barry (1966) reviewed the history of the PSP and the more than 200 papers already written on the subject. Many previously enthusiastic investigators had become more cautious in interpreting this finding as abnormal. The reported incidence in the general population had risen from 2% to 20–21%. The crucial factors in these studies seemed to be (a) the criteria for selection of "normal" groups and (b) the duration of sleep necessary before reporting negative results. Lombroso's group tried to cope with these two factors by studying a healthy group of students at a New England prep school with prolonged sleep recordings. They found that 58% showed a clear-cut PSP if sleep was as long as 30 minutes. The case material was then blindly analyzed to determine whether there were correlations with the complaints usually reported to be associated with this pattern, but none were found. They concluded that in this age group caution is necessary in interpreting the PSP as pathological.

In summary, the PSP appears to be quite common in young, asymptomatic subjects. Yet it has been inappropriately linked with a very wide variety of behavioral and medical phenomena. This can often be a disservice to the patient, though it may spare the clinician much thought, time, and energy in searching for alternative explanations and adequately investigating the patient's life circumstances and feelings.

Minimal Brain Damage or Dysfunction (MBD)

There are many terms, some overlapping, which have been applied to children who are not by most definitions retarded, psychotic, cerebral palsied, or epileptic yet demonstrate one or more behavioral, learning, perceptual, or minor neurological findings. The "typical" brain-damaged child is usually described as hyperactive, distractible, perseverative, impulsive, clumsy, and socially inept, with a short attention span and figure-ground difficulties. This stereotype persists despite growing recognition that there is no *one* syndrome of brain damage in children. The history of the development of this concept will not be reviewed here, as it has been well covered elsewhere (Bax & MacKeith, 1963; Birch, 1964; National Institute of Neurological Diseases and Blindness, 1966; Pincus & Glaser, 1966; Rapin, 1964; Schulman, Kaspar, & Throne, 1965). There has been a tendency recently to avoid the term "damage" and replace it with "dysfunction" because of the acknowledged lack of proven anatomical pathology.

Since the EEG has been used as one of the major props for this currently popular appellation, some discussion of the means of diagnosis and the validity of the concept of MBD is necessary. The following brief review is somewhat broader than the use of the EEG alone, but is offered here in order to document the position that correlations between the different areas of diagnosis (EEG, neurological signs, history, and psychological tests) are poor.

EEG Studies. Taterka and Katz (1955) found no relationship between EEG abnormalities and specific aspects of behavior such as hyperactivity. Anderson (1963) reported that 26 out of 30 hyperkinetic children had abnormal EEG's by his standards, but the study was limited because 13 children had a history of at least one convulsion and seven children (or approximately 25%) were being treated as presumed epileptics. Schulman *et al* (1965) felt that normal subjects could be distinguished from abnormal but that there was much overlap. Paine, Werry, and Quay (1967) stated:

". . . we believe that routine EEG's are of limited value in the context of this type of child. Even if normal, they seldom change the diagnosis arrived at on other evidence and if abnormal, they seldom alter the plan of management and may, in fact, aggravate the situation by distressing the parents."

Neurological Signs. Minor, equivocal, or "soft" neurological signs are usually regarded as one component of the MBD syndrome. But the age norms for clumsiness, tremor, awkward gait, and associated movements in children are not well established. Furthermore, many of these "signs" are aggravated (if not produced) by high levels of anxiety. Only a few papers are reviewed here because of space limitations.

Kennard (1960) felt that equivocal signs are true neurological signs but do not show any consistent correlation with EEG type and, unlike some other writers, she found no clear association with reading disability. Schulman *et al's* conclusions included the statement that "One of the most interesting substantive findings . . . concerns the lack of relation between the neurological and the EEG" (1965, p. 82). Grossman (1966) stated:

"Actually, there is no syndrome, no aggregate of neurological signs, that can be correlated with any specific learning and/or behavior disorder. Indeed, many youngsters with profound aberrations of motor function do well in school, in their studies and in their interpersonal relationships (p. 63)."

Werry (1967) gave little credence to the presence of such neurological findings in children while Isom and Copple (1967) report a high incidence of "soft" neurological signs in normal and gifted children, including mixed and confused dominance.

Such findings and opinions at least allow the conclusion that there are many "normal" children with minor neurological signs and that while it may be eventually demonstrated conclusively that children with certain types of learning and behavioral disabilities have a higher incidence, the overlap between normal and abnormal groups is substantial. Correlations of neurological signs with the EEG seem to be low at best.

Psychological Tests. There is a large and confusing literature on the various tests used to assist in the diagnosis of brain damage. Diller and Birch (1964) pointed out that test data are contaminated and that the only way a test could be said to be diagnostic of brain damage would be to compare indisputably brain-damaged with normal populations at a given age and then show that no other factors could produce such findings; this has never been done successfully. Although Hanvik, Nelson, Hanson, Anderson, Dressler, and Zarling (1961) felt that the EEG correlated well with psychological test findings, Silverman and Harris (1954) had reported earlier that only 68% of patients with focal EEG abnormalities (supposed to be most indicative of anatomical pathology) had abnormal psychological findings and concluded that both methods were fallible. Chorost, Spivack, and Levine (1959) disputed previous reports of a relationship between rotations on the Bender-Gestalt and EEG abnormalities.

To sum up the MBD problem the author concurs with a statement by Haywood (1967) regarding the validity of the concept.

"I would guess that the syndrome is artifactual—that a diagnosis of neurological impairment, perceptual handicap, or minimal brain damage is frequently rendered by exclusion; i.e., the behavior cluster does not fit readily into any existing diagnostic category, hence it is an artifact of our own ignorance and lack of solid descriptive research (p. 8)."

The implications of the EEG for the diagnosis of such a vagary as minimal brain damage are obviously most questionable.

Delinquency and Sociopathy

Categorical statements about the contribution of organic factors in murders have been publicized in recent years, most notably in relation to Jack Ruby. Bergman and Green (1956) stated that the EEG was of no value in criminal cases, but Schwade and Geiger (1960) felt that dysrhythmias are a significant factor in sudden antisocial behavior of the "irresistible impulse" type. Low and Dawson (1961) were unable to establish a correlation between temporal lobe (psychomotor) seizures and delinquency, but Dietze and Voegele (1964) strongly advocated the organic point of view. Wiener, Delano, and Klass (1966) found no significant differences between 80 delinquent and 70 non-delinquent adolescents with regard to EEG abnormalities, including the PSP. Bonkalo (1967) has reviewed this field and concludes that there is a relatively high incidence of abnormal EEG's among the criminal and delinquent population, but that the latter is without any specific type of abnormality.

Finally, Loomis, Bohnert, and Huncke (1967) studied the EEG patterns of 100 institutionalized delinquent girls, concluding that:

"There is no observable increase in the general incidence of EEG disturbances in this delinquent group . . . the role of such abnormalities in the etiology of continuing delinquent behavior is probably less than has often been suspected (p. 496)."

We are thus left with a conflicting mass of data, probably partly because of poor selection of control subjects and inadequate age norms.

Behavior Disorders and Learning Disabilities

In 1955, Taterka and Katz reported that 79% of schizophrenic children and 73% of children with "primary behavior disorders" had abnormal

EEG's, which they regarded as evidence of a "defect or developmental retardation in the cerebral structure" (p. 70). Bradley (1955) stated that the incidence of abnormal EEG's is higher in maladjusted children but that there is no one-to-one correlation (p. 100). Bergman and Green (1956) criticized the methodology of most such studies, expressing the opinion that "unusual" EEG records are no more common in psychiatric patients than in a normal population. Weir and Anderson (1958) studied the 5% of children who failed in a public school system and interpreted 76% of the EEG records as abnormal. Hughes, Giaturco, and Stein (1961) reported a higher incidence of PSP and other EEG abnormalities in impulsive behavior disorders and attributed the cause to head injury in a substantial number of cases. Gibbs, Gibbs, Spies, and Carpenter (1964) described behavior disorders as a consequence of encephalitis but admitted there was no direct correlation between EEG abnormality and symptomatology.

In 1965, Bennett came to the questionable conclusion that behavior disorders are "presumably epileptiform" if the EEG shows seizure discharges and described personality and mood characteristics which bear a striking resemblance to the overworked "epileptic personality."

It must be emphasized that the majority of patients with clinical seizures do *not* manifest psychiatric disturbances or the MBD syndrome. Some writers have expressed the dubious idea that patients with seizures are better adjusted than those with "subconvulsive dysrhythmias" because they discharge their aggression or other drives via the seizure, whereas the latter must do it in their behavior.

On the other side of the issue, Hess (1966) speculated that "we must probably accept that emotional disturbances influence the EEG and result in unusual records which, once the child has recovered its equilibrium, return to what is common for the age group" (p. 131). Small and Small (1967) found no significant differences between subjects and controls in incidence of psychiatric disorders, history, physical and neurological signs, or family history of epilepsy in 134 matched, non-epileptic patients who were divided into normal and abnormal EEG groups. Recently, Aird and Yamamoto (1966) reviewed attempts to attribute behavior disorders to convulsive phenomena or "cerebral dysmaturation." Some writers feel that both the reported EEG abnormality and the disturbed behavior have immaturity as the common denominator.

Some of the problems in any studies of this kind are: groups of children with behavior disorders are heterogeneous, their difficulties are closely related to environmental and social circumstances, many problems are transient and age-specific, and adequate normal or control groups are difficult to provide. EEG abnormalities in psychiatric patients *may* represent underlying organic pathology, but the latter in most cases can only be presumed to constitute predisposing, but not sufficient, factors in causation, while in other situations they may be coincidental or related to extraneous factors already discussed.

Head Injury and the Post-Concussion Syndrome. Opinions have varied regarding the cause of behavioral and personality aberrations following moderate to severe head injury. Bergman and Green (1956) felt there was no correlation between the EEG and symptoms of the post-concussion syndrome. As previously mentioned, Hughes *et al* (1961) attributed 40% of their cases of PSP to head trauma, and most of these were said to have behavior disorders or autonomic symptoms. In 1961, Dillon and Leopold investigated the post-concussion syndrome in children and reported that the EEG changes in the children's records reverted to normal much more rapidly than their behavior. These results they felt were related to interference with normal emotional development in the children by the realization of previously fantasied bodily damage. Injury was seen by the children as jeopardizing ego controls. Thus, we find again conflicting opinions as to both the etiology of the behavior disorder and the significance of the EEG.

DISCUSSION AND CONCLUSIONS

Psychogenesis versus organicity, mind or body—these dualisms are still very much in evidence. The EEG appears to be regarded with more awe than it deserves. It is not very reliable, and there are many technical problems in its use with children, yet our electronic age, with its admiration for gadgets and the paucity of knowledge in the behavioral sciences, lends to this instrument a certain mystique. Furthermore, unusual records are obtained often enough (unlike blood, urine, or X-ray studies in these children) to make speculation seem worthwhile. The EEG is also painless for the child (though he may not believe it!)—a not inconsiderable factor supporting its use.

The influence of the EEG among educators may possibly be due to the inundation of the literature with poorly done papers describing children with supposed minimal brain damage. Perusal of any state medical society journal will probably reward the patient reader, if he be so inclined, with at least one such report. This type of study, along with initial uncontrolled drug reports, has become a favorite way to "get a paper published."

The marriage of convenience between the EEG and special education has never been a very happy one. The available evidence suggests that until more definitive information is available a trial separation, or at least a Platonic relationship, would be more appropriate.

Medical diagnosis in any case has only limited application to educational diagnosis, and the physician has generally not been trained in providing an appropriate recommendation for special education (Grossman, 1966, pp. 64 & 66).

Professional workers should recognize that the fantasy often expressed by parents and children that the EEG in some way tells what is going on inside one's head, or even what one is thinking, is generally only a fantasy, and they should not reinforce it.

Finally, on the more positive side, the EEG does have value when used in conjunction with a multi-faceted evaluation and full recognition of its limitations. There are a few conditions in which the recorded pattern correlates well with a clinical disorder, such as the 3-per-second spike and wave of petit mal epilepsy and the hypsarhythmia of infantile myoclonic seizures. It also may be useful in following the course of a seizure disorder, helping to decide when to terminate anti-convulsant medication in the seizure-free patient, in the diagnosis of some children with gross brain lesions, and in clinical research.

In closing, there is a selection which the writer feels he cannot improve upon and therefore wishes to quote. It may help to stimulate greater caution on the part of those who deal with disturbed and handicapped children.

"The tranquillizing effect on a profession of the application of some distinguished label and accompanying description such as schizophrenia, infantile autism, or minimal brain injury is too well known to require extended comment. These terms describe extraordinarily vague entities, explain nothing, and lead to no clear prescription as to what should be done. They provide only a false sense of order and knowledge. The relief that is obvious at a case conference once one of these labels is convincingly pinned on the child is evidence that all tend to seek certainty and security, sometimes at the expense of broadening professional wisdom (Gallagher, 1966, p. 27).

References

Aird, R. B., & Yamamoto, T. Behavior disorders of childhood. *Electroencephalography and Clinical Neurophysiology*, 1966, 21, 148–156.

Anderson, W. W. The hyperkinetic child: a neurological appraisal. *Neurology,* 1963, 13, 968–873.

Barolin, G. S. Migraines and epilepsies: a relationship? *Epilepsia,* 1966, 7, 53–66.

Bax, M., & MacKeith, R. (Eds.) *Minimal cerebral dysfunction.* Little Club Clinics in Developmental Medicine No. 10. London: William Heinemann, 1963.

Bennett, A. E. Mental disorders associated with temporal lobe epilepsy. *Diseases of the Nervous System,* 1965, 26, 275–280.

Bergman, P. S., & Green, M. A. The use of electroencephalography in differentiating psychogenic disorders and organic brain diseases. *American Journal of Psychiatry,* 1956, 113, 27–31.

Birch, H. G. *Brain damage in children: the biological and social aspects.* Baltimore: Williams & Wilkins, 1964.

Blum, R. H. A note on the reliability of electroencephalographic judgments. *Neurology,* 1954, 4, 143–146.

Bonkalo, A. Electroencephalography in criminology. *Canadian Psychiatric Association Journal,* 1967, 12, 281–286.

Bradley, C. Organic factors in the psychopathology of childhood. In P. Hoch & J. Zubin (Eds.), *Psychopathology of childhood.* New York: Grune & Stratton, 1955. Pp. 82–104.

Bray, P. F. Electroencephalography. In *Brennemann-Kelley practice of pediatrics.* Vol. 4. Hagerstown, Md.: W. F. Prior, 1964, Chapter 2, Pp. 21–36.

Chorost, S. B./Spivack, G./Levine, M. Bender-Gestalt rotations and EEG abnormalities in children. *Journal of Consulting Psychology,* 1959, 23, 559.

Dietze, H. J., & Voegele, G. E. Juvenile delinquency and organic brain impairment. *Pennsylvania Psychiatric Quarterly,* 1964, 4, 3–12.

Diller, L., & Birch, H. G. Psychological evaluation of children with cerebral damage. In H. G. Birch (Ed.), *Brain damage in children: the biological and social aspects.* Baltimore: Williams & Wilkins, 1964. Pp. 27–45.

Dillon, H., & Leopold, R. L. Children and the post-concussion syndrome. *JAMA,* 1961, 175, 86–92.

Freeman, R. D. The home visit in child psychiatry: its usefulness in diagnosis and training. *Journal of the American Academy of Child Psychiatry,* 1967, 6, 276–294.

Gallagher, J. J. Children with developmental imbalances: a psychoeducational definition. In W. M. Cruickshank (Ed.), *The teacher of brain-injured children.* Syracuse: Syracuse University Press, 1966. Pp. 23–43.

Gastaut, H., & Tassinari, C. A. Triggering mechanisms in epilepsy: the electroclinical point of view. *Epilepsia,* 1966, 7, 85–138.

Gibbs, E. L., & Gibbs, F. A. Electroencephalographic evidence of thalamic and hypothalamic epilepsy. *Neurology*, 1951, 1, 136–144.

Gibbs, F. A./Gibbs, E. L./Carpenter, P. R./Spies, H. W. Electroencephalographic abnormality in "uncomplicated" childhood diseases. *JAMA*, 1959, 171, 1050–1055.

Gibbs, F. A./Gibbs, E. L./Spies, H. W./Carpenter, P. R. Common types of childhood encephalitis. *Archives of Neurology*, 1964, 10, 1–11.

Goldensohn, E. S. EEG and ictal and postictal behavior. In G. H. Glaser (Ed.), *EEG and behavior*. New York: Basic Books, 1963. Pp. 293–314.

Graham, F. K., & Berman, P. W. Current status of behavior tests for brain damage in infants and preschool children. *American Journal of Orthopsychiatry*, 1961, 31, 713–727.

Grossman, H. J. The child, the teacher, and the physician. In W. M. Cruickshank (Ed.), *The teacher of brain-injured children*. Syracuse: Syracuse University Press, 1966. Pp. 59–67.

Halpern, L., & Bental, E. Epileptic cephalea. *Neurology*, 1958, 8, 615–620.

Hanvik, L. J./Nelson, S. E./Hanson, H. B./Anderson, A. S./Dressler, W. H./Zarling, V. R. Diagnosis of cerebral dysfunction in children. *American Journal of Diseases of Children*, 1961, 101, 364–375.

Haywood, H. C. Perceptual handicap: fact or artifact? *Child Study*, 1967, 28, 2–14.

Henry, C. E. Positive spike discharges in the EEG and behavior abnormality. In G. H. Glaser (Ed.), *EEG and behavior*. New York: Basic Books, 1963. Pp. 315–344.

Henry, C. E. Electroencephalographic correlates with personality. In W. P. Wilson (Ed.), *Applications of electroencephalography in psychiatry*. Durham, N. C.: Duke University Press, 1965. Pp. 3–18.

Hess, R. *EEG handbook*. Sandoz Monograph, 1966. No address given: Sandoz Ltd.

Hughes, J. R./Giaturco, D./Stein, W. Electro-clinical correlations in the positive spike phenomenon. *Electroencephalography and Clinical Neurophysiology*, 1961, 13, 599–605.

Isom, J. B., & Copple, P. Effect of individual differences and motivation on school performance. Presented at the American Academy of Pediatrics Postgraduate Course on School Problems, Portland, Oregon, August 24, 1967 (To be published).

Kellaway, P., Crawley, J., & Maulsby, R. The electroencephalogram in psychiatric disorders in childhood. In W. P. Wilson (Ed.), *Applications of Electroencephalography in Psychiatry*. Durham, N. C.: Duke University Press, 1965. Pp. 30–53.

Kennard, M. A. Value of equivocal signs in neurologic diagnosis. *Neurology*, 1960, 10, 753–764.

Knott, J. R. EEG and behavior. *American Journal of Orthopsychiatry,* 1960, 30, 292–297.

Lombroso, C. T./Schwartz, I. H./Clark, D. M./Muench, H./Barry, J. Ctenoids in healthy youths: controlled study of 14- and 6-per-second positive spiking. *Neurology,* 1966, 16, 1152–1158.

Loomis, S. D./Bohnert, T. J./Huncke, S. Prediction of EEG abnormalities in adolescent delinquents. *Archives of General Psychiatry,* 1967, 17, 494–497.

Low, N. L., & Dawson, S. P. Electroencephalographic findings in juvenile delinquency. *Pediatrics,* 1961, 28, 452–457.

National Institute of Neurological Diseases and Blindness. Minimal brain dysfunction in children. NINDB Monogr. No. 3. Washington, D. C.: U. S. Printing Office, PHS Publ. No. 1415, 1966.

Oettinger, L., Jr./Nikonishi, H./Gill, I. G. Cerebral dysrhythmia induced by reading (subclinical reading epilepsy). *Developmental Medicine and Child Neurology,* 1967, 9, 191–201.

Paine, R. S. Organic neurological factors related to learning disorders. In J. Hellmuth (Ed.), *Learning disorders.* Vol. 1. Seattle: Special Child Publications, 1965. Pp. 1–29.

Paine, R. S./Werry, J. S./Quay, H. C. A study of "minimal cerebral dysfunction." Unpublished manuscript, 1967.

Pincus, J. H., & Glaser, G. H. The syndrome of "minimal brain damage" in childhood. *New England Journal of Medicine,* 1966, 275, 27–35.

Poser, C. M., & Ziegler, D. K. Clinical significance of 14 and 6 per second positive spike complexes. *Neurology,* 1958, 8, 903–912.

Rapin, I. Brain damage in children. In *Brennemann-Kelley practice of pediatrics.* Vol. 4. Hagerstown, Md.: W. F. Prior, 1964. Chapter I, Pp. 1–52.

Schulman, J. L./Kaspar, J. C./Throne, F. M. *Brain damage and behavior: a clinical-experimental study.* Springfield, Ill.: Charles C Thomas, 1965.

Schwade, E. D., & Geiger, S. G. Severe behavior disorders with abnormal electroencephalograms. *Diseases of the Nervous System,* 1960, 21, 616–620.

Silverman, A. J., & Harris, V. W. Electroencephalography and psychometric testing in brain-damaged patients. *Journal of Nervous and Mental Diseases,* 1954, 120, 31–34.

Small, J. G., & Small, I. F. Fourteen- and six-per-second positive spike. *Archives of General Psychiatry,* 1964, 11, 645–650.

Small, J. G., & Small, I. F. EEG spikes in non-epileptic psychiatric patients. *Diseases of the Nervous System,* 1967, 28, 523–525.

Snyder, C. H. Epileptic equivalents in children. *Pediatrics,* 1958, 21, 308–318.

Taterka, J. H., & Katz, J. Study of correlations between

electroencephalographic and psychologic patterns in emotionally disturbed children. *Psychosomatic Medicine,* 1955, 17, 62–72.

Weir, H. F., & Anderson, R. C. Organic and organizational aspects of school adjustment problems. *JAMA,* 1958, 166, 1708–1710.

Werry, J. S. The diagnosis, etiology, and treatment of hyperactivity in children. In J. Hellmuth (Ed.), *Learning disorders,* Vol. 3. Seattle: Special Child Publications, 1967, in press.

Whitehouse, D./Pappas, T. A./Escala, P. H./Livingston, S. Electroencephalographic changes in children with migraine. *New England Journal of Medicine,* 1967, 276, 23–27.

Wiener, J. M./Delano, J. G./Klass, D. W. An EEG study of delinquent and non-delinquent adolescents. *Archives of General Psychiatry,* 1966, 15, 144–150.

6. A STUDY OF "MINIMAL CEREBRAL DYSFUNCTION"[1]

RICHMOND S. PAINE, JOHN S. WERRY,
and HERBERT C. QUAY

INTRODUCTION

Despite the large literature on minimal brain dysfunction (Clements 1966), few studies have attempted to use statistical techniques to analyse the clinical syndrome. The exceptions are Rodin *et al.* (1964), Lucas *et al.* (1965) and Werry *et al.* (1967), who used factor analysis to examine the association between a variety of historical, neurological, electroencephalographic, perceptual-cognitive and behavioral measures.

An advantage of factor analysis is that, given an adequate number of subjects, a meaningful within-group analysis can be made, which, as Rodin *et al.* pointed out, should provide hypotheses for future research. However, without a normal control group the technique cannot indicate whether the observed clinical findings are peculiar to children with minimal brain dysfunction, or whether they reflect general developmental functions which are perhaps deviant in a patient population.

Rodin *et al.* found that in their group of 72 children referred by school

---

SOURCE. Reprinted from *Developmental Medicine and Child Neurology*, 1968, **10**, 505–520.

[1] Presented in part at the 1966 Annual Meeting of the American Academy for Cerebral Palsy, New Orleans, U.S.A.

authorities because of behavior or academic problems there were several apparently independent clinical dimensions. The first was motor inco-ordination and was comprised mostly of neurological signs of impaired sensorimotor co-ordination. Others were related to intelligence, matura-tion, abnormal electroencephalography, hyperactivity and anti-social behavior. In general, the analysis revealed a disappointing lack of rela-tionship between abnormal history, neurological, electroencephalographic, intellectual and behavioral findings. They concluded that the clinical picture observed in a child was most probably the result of a unique combination of causes, including innate, traumatic, psychological and social. There was thus little evidence that the syndrome of minimal brain dysfunction was a single homogeneous syndrome or that it reflected, as is commonly assumed, a single cause, namely "minimal brain damage."

In a study of 100 chronically hyperactive children of normal intelli-gence, Werry *et al.* (1967) confirmed, with minor differences, the findings of Rodin *et al.* both in terms of factor structure and particularly in the lack of relationship between neurological, electroencephalographic, be-havioral, intellectual, and historical findings.

Schulman *et al.* (1965), using the technique of cluster analysis, also failed to find any relationship between neurological, electroencephalo-graphic, psychometric, behavioral and psychophysiological measures, and concluded that there was no such thing as a brain damage syndrome. Though the children studied were retarded, the findings are nevertheless relevant, since many of the subjects showed evidence of minimal brain dysfunction as it is ordinarily diagnosed. The study is also remarkable for its sophisticated methodology and thoughtful discussion of brain damage and behavior.

In view of the paucity of studies utilizing statistical analysis of the clinical symptoms of the minimal brain dysfunction syndrome, and of their conflicting findings, it was decided in this study to subject the data to correlational and factor analytic methods, in addition to the usual descriptive analysis.

METHODS

Subjects

These were selected from a group of 97 children referred because of suspicion of minimal organic cerebral dysfunction. It was often difficult to pinpoint a single reason for referral since multiple complaints were usually involved. Hyperactivity at school and at home, or nonachievement at school despite normal IQ on psychometric testing were the commonest reasons. Other cases were primarily medical referrals, usually because of the pediatricians' suspicion of the diagnosis on the basis of clumsiness or hyperactivity. In some instances, the referral was made because of the psychologist's detection of irregularities of the "organic pattern" on the Wechsler Intelligence Scale for Children or other tests. Of the original 97 children, 83 were finally considered to fit the diagnostic criteria established (Table I). The other 14 had diagnoses such as mild cerebral

TABLE I
Diagnoses for 97 Referrals

Mental Retardation	5
No Disease	3
Mild Cerebral Palsy	2
Psychiatric Problems Only	2
Epilepsy	1
Specific Dyslexia	1
"Minimal Cerebral Dysfunction"	83

palsy, epilepsy, familial dyslexia without other irregularities of learning or behavior, or psychiatric problems. Those with IQ's below 80 were excluded from the study.

The minimum criteria for inclusion were any one of the following:

1. Abnormal neurological signs on physical examination (beyond mere clumsiness).
2. An abnormal EEG.
3. Psychological findings of the type seen in organic encephalopathies *plus* either excessive clumsiness or an abnormal EEG.

Background data on the 83 patients are given in Table II. As in most similar studies, boys considerably outnumbered girls, by almost 3 to 1 in this instance. The mean age was $8 \cdot 4$ years $\pm 2 \cdot 6$. All the children were seen either as private patients or in a special neurological clinic which had a relatively high income ceiling for admission, and all were examined by the same physician (R.S.P). This weights the sample in a socio-economic sense which was inevitable if material from one examiner was to be used, but chiefly because the diagnosis is not coded in the Standard Nomenclature of Diseases and Operations and such cases are therefore difficult to obtain from hospital out-patients records. The parents were thus mostly in social classes I and II in the classification of the British Registrar General. The high proportion of Jews (21 out of 83) probably reflects the emphasis on education in this socio-cultural sub-group, which leads to prompt and full investigation of learning problems, rather than

TABLE II
Background Data on 83 Patients with M.C.D.

Boys	62
Girls	21
Mean Age: 8·4 years; SD: 2·6 years	
Jewish	21
Negro	0
Other	62
Adopted	12
Referral: Medical	19
Behavioral	16
Educational	40
Miscellaneous	8
Mean IQ: 96·3; SD: 17·0	

any ethnic genetic factor. Twelve children were adopted, a high proportion compared with the general population, but this again may reflect
the greater concern of parents about any suggestion of abnormality in
an adopted child.

The reasons for referral have already been commented on above.
Nineteen were listed as "medical" in that the pediatrician or general
practitioner was the first to arrange the referral, but in some instances
this may have been initiated at school. The 30 children described as
"educational" referrals were seen at the instigation of school authorities
but in each case the approval of the pediatrician was first obtained. All
children lived in the District of Columbia or in Maryland or Virginia,
and the group did not include any of the patients previously reported by
Paine in 1962.

History and Neurological Examination

A complete medical history was taken, with emphasis on any potential
prenatal, perinatal, or subsequent cerebral insults. Detailed review of
obstetrical records was not made routinely, however, if the patient's
mother and referring physician gave no indication of any abnormality.
The limitations on the value of retrospective data in studies of this type
are just as great as in those of cerebral palsy or mental retardation, but
a prospective study was not feasible under the circumstances, and
retrospective data were evaluated for whatever they might prove to be
worth. A complete neurological examination was performed in the usual
way, with emphasis on tests of co-ordination, praxis and gnosis. These
include such items as construction of a three-dimensional figure of logs
to match a sample presented by the examiner, or the assembly of plastic

puzzles composed of geometrical shapes. These have been previously standardized on a group of normal children. Language functions were appraised in terms of the child's ability to speak, to name objects and to describe actions, both aloud and in writing if old enough. The child's ability to identify objects in pictures as named by the examiner and to describe actions out loud or in writing was also examined. Tests such as the copying of designs or assembly of block designs, which a physician might "borrow" from clinical psychologists, were seldom used because each child had psychological tests. Co-ordination was appraised in a necessarily subjective manner throughout the entire examination, and by specific tests, such as imitation of movements and postures of the examiner, use of pencil and paper, walking, running and hopping. Having the child hold the upper limbs extended in front of the body with the fingers spread often brought out minor degrees of choreoathetosis, although this is admittedly difficult to distinguish from normal fidgeting. In the absence of quantitative normal standards of what is summed up as "co-ordination," the subjective impression of the examiner had to be relied on as to whether a certain child was excessively clumsy compared with others of his own age or of his mental age.

Electroencephalography

EEG's were not done routinely on all patients. This may have excluded some who would have qualified for retention, although all of the 14 referrals who were excluded from the study were excluded because of another positive diagnosis. Some patients had had EEG's done at other centers, but these were included in the analysis only if the original EEG could be reviewed in its entirety.

We believe that routine EEG's are of limited value for this type of child. Even if normal, they seldom change the diagnosis arrived at on other evidence, and if abnormal they seldom alter the plan of management, and may even aggravate the situation by distressing the parents. Most of the abnormalities detected were minor and their effect on the children's difficulties was doubtful.

Psychological Tests

While all children had had psychological tests, the data were included in the computer analysis only if a complete report could be obtained from the testing psychologist, including the subtests of the WISC if used, and if it appeared that co-operation and other circumstances were good enough to permit a fair evaluation. Data of this type were available for 56 of the 83 children. In 34 instances the test used was the WISC and in the remainder, usually younger children, the Stanford-Binet. The

Stanford-Binet yields only one IQ score, but the WISC yields a total of 15 scores—the full scale, verbal and performance IQ's and 12 subtests. Subtest scores were analyzed separately in view of the emphasis which has been given in the past to the contribution of specific subtests, such as block design and object assembly, to the diagnosis of brain damage. Herbert (1964), in an extensive review of the subject, concluded that psychological tests are generally of little value in this respect. Also, in deference to common belief of the importance of the relationship between the Verbal and Performance IQ's (Clements and Peters 1962), we added two others, the ratio of Verbal IQ to Performance IQ and a qualitative split of either Verbal IQ > Performance IQ or vice versa. In addition, where applicable, psychologists' reports were scanned for five measures: irregularity of the subtests, difficulty with abstraction, perseveration, dyscalculia and short attention span during testing. This information was available for both WISC and Binet tests.

Behavior Rating. This was assessed by utilizing 58-item checklist of common behavior problems originally developed by Peterson (1961). This checklist has been subject to a series of factor analyses (Quay and Quay 1965, Quay 1965, Quay et al. 1966) and refinements. The value of this method of assessing behavioral status is also enhanced by the fact that a certain amount of normative data at various age levels in the two sexes is available, though, unfortunately, it does not span the complete age range of children in the present study. The form of the checklist used here yields scores on three of the factor analytically derived dimensions; conduct problems, neurotic problems and immaturity-inadequacy.

Unfortunately, these data were not available in the records and mothers were therefore contacted by mail and asked to complete the enclosed checklist with reference to how the child was approximately at the time of examination. Of the 83 children, 70 (82 percent) were finally rated thus.

DATA ANALYSIS

All data were transferred to IBM cards and processed in the IBM 7094 computer at the University of Illinois. An initial frequency count of items was made and those which occurred in less than 10 percent of cases were discarded from subsequent analyses. Then an initial intercorrelation of neurological and historical variables was carried out and those which yielded such high correlation coefficients as to suggest part-whole relationships or equivalence were deleted. This left 33, or approximately 35 percent of the original demographic, historical and neurological variables, for the factor analysis.

Because not all data were obtainable on all Ss, correlations between any two variables were computed over those Ss for which data on the two variables were present. This procedure resulted in a matrix of inter-correlations, most of which were obtained over different numbers of Ss. However, only in the case of the IQ and EEG variables were the correlations based on such comparatively small numbers of Ss as to be of concern in the performance of the subsequent factor analysis. Since this study was primarily exploratory in nature, the factor analysis of correlations based on unequal numbers of cases was felt to be justified.

Factor analysis was carried out by the principal axis method using the highest absolute value of r as the communality estimates. Factoring was stopped when the eigenvalues fell below unity. The principal axis factors were then subjected to a varimax rotation to ensure maximal simplicity of factor structure.

The final data analysis consisted of a correlation between individual scores on the above factors (estimated by assigning a unit weight to individual items and summing across those items loading on the factor to a degree greater than $0 \cdot 40$), factor scores on the Peterson problem checklist, the intelligence test scores and the psychologists' comments about the testing.

RESULTS AND DISCUSSION

Historical Data. Tables III, IV, V and VI give the number of patients with historical prenatal, perinatal, or subsequent cerebral insults as evaluated from the available history. Little information was available concerning adopted children and these were not included in the Tables. In each of the four categories of prenatal, perinatal, and post-natal insults and neonatal evidence of distress, more than half the children had no historical abnormality.

Evidence of "brain damage" was considered in relation to the probability of a known historical cerebral insult followed by at least temporary derangement of cerebral function in terms of signs and/or symptoms at the time. No such factors appeared to be known in 37 of 81 children (46

TABLE III
Prenatal Cerebral Insults

Infections	4
Hemorrhages	5
X-radiation	1
Miscellaneous	15
None	54

TABLE IV
Perinatal Cerebral Insults

B.W. < 3½lb.	1
B.W. 3½–5½lb.	11
Abruptio Placentae	2
Placenta Praevia	1
Prolonged Labor	6
Breech Extraction	4
Delayed Resuscitation	4
High- or Mid-forceps	3
Emergency Cesarean section	2
Other	18
None	41

TABLE V
Neonatal Abnormalities

Apnoeic spells	4
Convulsions	1
Jittery baby	2
Depressed baby	8
Cyanosis	4
Poor cry	5
Poor feeding	2
Respiratory distress syndrome	1
Other	8
None	62

TABLE VI
Postnatal Cerebral Insults

Trauma	12
Fever > 105°	2
Encephalitis	1
Anoxia	1
Other	2
None	65

percent), and suggestive or definite evidence was obtained in 21 and 11 percent respectively (Table VII). This is somewhat greater than would be expected in an unselected population; Rogers *et al.* (1955) reported a frequency of approximately 70 percent uncomplicated prenatal, perinatal and neonatal histories in a white population from Baltimore. In

TABLE VII
History of "Brain Damaging" Events

None	37	(45·7%)
Equivocal	18	(22·2%)
Suggestive	17	(21·0%)
Definite	9	(11·1%)

the present study the criteria for diagnosis of abnormality were more stringent than those of Rogers *et al.* The proportion with abnormalities is, however, rather less than usually encountered in studies of the population of cerebral palsy clinics.

Neurological Findings. Table VIII summarizes the abnormal neuro-

TABLE VIII
Overall Neurological Abnormality

None	0	(0%)
Minor signs only	30	(43%)
Probable major abnormality	35	(50%)
Definite major abnormality	5	(7%)

logical signs.

One group of findings, perceptual difficulties (Table IX), involves a

TABLE IX
Perceptual and Conceptual Disabilities

Pattern	71
Size	45
Assembly of parts into whole	68
Space	43
Body image	40
Right-left orientation	25
None	4

synthesis of psychological test reports and the physician's own impression. There was very rarely any significant disagreement between the two. The overall final impression was in no case of complete normality but 30 (43 percent) of the children had no abnormal physical signs other than what was felt to be excessive clumsiness for mental age. Clumsiness was the abnormal sign most frequently encountered, but many such patients also had choreoathetosis, tremor, hyperreflexia, extensor plantar reflexes or other signs which would scarcely be labelled "soft." Possible tactile inattention, extinction or perseveration were sought by the methods described by Bender (1952), but definite abnormality was never confidently diagnosed. This is probably because of the children's ages, at which tactile inattention for the hand in the case of double simultaneous stimulation of face and hand would be normal for most. The factor of attention is very important and since a low span of concentration characterized most of the children studied, this type of sensory testing was more often than not unsatisfactory.

EEG Findings. 59 percent of the patients had no detectable abnormalities in the electroencephalogram. Of those which were abnormal, the most frequent finding was irregular slowing or irregularity of background activity. Seizure discharges were seen in approximately one-third of the abnormal tracings and other focal abnormalities in 40 percent (Table X). This may suggest that two populations are being studied, if the

TABLE X
EEG's In MCD Study

Normal	59%	
Abnormal	41%	
Rate (slowing)	70%	of abnormals
Irregular background activity	70% "	"
Voltage	60% "	"
Focal ability (other than sz.)	40% "	"
Seizure discharges	33% "	"
Exaggerated build-up on O.V.	22% "	"

electroencephalogram itself is taken as evidence of organic cerebral dysfunction. Some correlations of the electroencephalographic findings with antecedent history and psychological items were found and will be discussed, but there was no correlation with abnormal physical neurological signs.

Psychological Test Findings. The mean IQ for the group was 96.3 with a standard deviation of 17·0 (see Table II). Though the standard deviation—i.e., the spread—approximates to that expected in any large number of children, the mean IQ is probably about 10 to 20 points lower than would be expected in a group of children coming from this superior socio-economic background. Of the 55 children for whom this information was available 95 percent were described as having irregularity of the subtests on psychological testing; 43 percent showed difficulties in abstraction, 10 percent perseveration, 31 percent dyscalculia, and 57 percent short attention span. It is difficult to evaluate the significance of these findings since the terms are vague, no normative data are available and, as Herbert (1964) has pointed out in his extensive review, their actual neurological diagnostic value scarcely warrants the respect they seem to be accorded. However, one measure, the discrepancy between the verbal and performance IQ's, is capable of accurate assessment since norms are available (Field 1960).

In Table XI the results of the present study have been compared with

TABLE XI

WISC Verbal/Performance IQ Discrepancies Compared with Norms for 7½ and 10½ Year Levels[a]

Points Difference	Observed No. (N=34)	Expected No.	Observed Percentage	Expected Percentage
9·0+ (8·0+)	21 (22)	17·0	62 (65)	50
15·4+ (13·8+)	14 (17)	8·5	41 (50)	25
22·0+ (10·7+)	6 (8)	3·4	17 (23)	10

[a] Number in whom V > P, 21; V = P, 1; V < P, 12.

normative data for the two age levels (7½ and 10½ years) which approximates most nearly that of the present group (8·4 years). Though the discrepancy is clearly greater than normal, in terms of actual number of children, the excess is relatively small. It is interesting to note that the criteria of significant abnormality for children with minimal brain dysfunction set out by Clements and Peters (1962), namely a discrepancy of 10 to 15 points between verbal and performance IQs, would, according to Field, be expected to occur in excess of 25 percent of normal children.

Behavioral Ratings. Though the available normative data do not cover the full age range of the present group of children, the mean scores and standard deviations of behavior factors covered in this group suggests that in this respect subjects were essentially normal (Table XII). This

TABLE XII

Behavior Ratings on Peterson Problem Checklist (N = 70)

	Mean	S.D.
Conduct Factor	5·30	4·10
Personality Factor	3·80	2·56
Immaturity Factor	1·72	1·38

is consistent with the reason for referral for the majority of the children (it was behavioral in only 16 or about 20 percent of the total) and with the field of the examiner (neurologist rather than psychiatrist).

The factor analysis of historical and neurological data yielded seven clusters or symptom-complexes. These are set out in Appendix A and have been named according to the items loading on them. The names should not be taken too literally since they represent intuitive guesses as to what dysfunctions they might represent; they are given in terms of their abnormal, rather than their normal, pole—*e.g.*, incoordination rather than ordination. Four clusters seem to be primarily reflections of current CNS status (I. Perceptual Deficits; II. Motor Incoordination; IV. Abnormal EEG; VII. Abnormal Reflexes). Of these, the first two are overwhelmingly the most accurate and important. Not surprisingly perhaps, since it is difficult to test perception without motor performance, apraxia and motor signs appear in Cluster I. Apparently too, the diagnosis of abnormal overall neurological status is most often a reflection of sensorimotor incoordination which itself decreases with age. In general, abnormalities in history do not appear in any of the neurological clusters (except the EEG) but are found in two separate clusters (III. Abnormal Perinatal History; VI. Abnormal Prenatal History). Just as historical items do not appear in neurological clusters, neurological items do not appear in the historical clusters except with negative loadings. The nature of Cluster V is not clear, but it has some relationship with later birth order or an older mother. It may represent a brain damage factor since three of the four variables loading on it are supposed to be related to the propensity for, or presence of, brain damage.

In summary, the factor analysis reveals that there is not one but four patterns of neurological abnormality, each unrelated to the others. These neurological patterns or symptom-complexes are in turn independent of the two abnormal historical syndromes. Thus, for example, abnormality of the EEG is not related to motor incoordination, to perceptual deficit, or to abnormal peri- or pre-natal history. The absence here of behavioral syndromes noted by Rodin *et al.* (1964) is due to the absence of behavioral measures in the history and neurological examination (see below).

A final analysis attempted to ascertain the degree of relationship, if any between the various historical-neurological factors, the intelligence test scores, psychologist's observations and behavioral measures.

The total number of correlation coefficients thus produced was 467, of which 46 or about 10 percent were at the $p = 0.05$ level of significance for the associated N. In such a large number of correlation coefficients, the number which would be expected to be significant at the

5 percent level by random fluctuation would be approximately half that actually observed. Thus, the degree of meaningful relationship between the various neurological factors, behavioral, and psychological variables is rather small.

1. Neurological-Historical Factors

The perceptual deficit factors, like the two historical factors, bore few important relationships to any other measures. Motor incoordination had two significant relationships: the first with a behavioral measure, a high neurotic score, which is perhaps surprising in view of the widely held belief (except Jenkins 1966) that this is more commonly related to conduct problems such as hyperactivity; the second with the WISC Verbal-Performance, which suggests that as might be expected, clumsy children have relatively lower performance IQs.

The abnormal EEG factor showed the greatest number of relationships to behavioral and intellectual measures of any of the neurological-historical factors. It was positively correlated with a high neurotic score (again contrary to common belief), with difficulties in abstraction, irregular subtests and with impaired WISC performance IQ.

The later birth order factor seems to be related to generally impaired intelligence, which perhaps reflects the increasing risk of brain damage associated with increasing birth order or maternal age. The abnormal reflexes factor had only one very small correlation, with the absence of neuroticism. In general, the relationships between the neurological-historical factors and behavioral and psychological test measures are few in number and minimal in degree.

2. Behavior Ratings

As noted above, the neuroticism score tends to yield more relationships with neurological and historical variables than the conduct score, which includes most of the behavioral items (such as hyperactivity) usually attributed to "brain damaged" children. This may be an artifact of the fact that the majority of children in this study were behaviorally normal. The immaturity factor's correlations (all from that of the psychologists' observations) are of interest in that the nature of this factor is not yet fully understood (Quay 1965). The present findings suggest that it reflects chronological immaturity, since all the features described are characteristic of younger children.

3. Psychologists' Observations

Not surprisingly, most correlation occurred with the intelligence tests, the primary source of the psychologists' observations. Of the five items, only two, difficulties in abstraction and irregularity of the subtests, bear any relationship to the neurological-historical factors, though these are perhaps the most likely to bear such a relationship. It is difficult to know whether the psychologist is influenced to some extent in the interpretation, as opposed to the scoring, of his results by the history which is ordinarily available to or taken by him. In general, the psychologists' observations bear most relationship with the content of their tests and with behavioral measures, particularly immaturity.

4. Psychological Tests

Most of these findings have already been commented on but two measures of relationship between the verbal and performance IQs deserve special mention. In this study, this relationship, whether quantitative (ratio) or qualitative (V P, P V), proved an unrewarding way of looking at the psychological tests, since each revealed only one relationship. We were thus unable to confirm the utility of these particular criteria of diagnosis, a conclusion also reached by Herbert (1964) in his review.

In summarizing the relationship between neurological-historical syndromes, behavior rating, psychological tests, and psychologists' ratings, it may be said that these relationships are disappointingly infrequent and minor. When present, the findings are often contrary to common belief.

CONCLUSIONS

This study has outlined some of the clinical and psychological factors present in 83 white upper-middle-class children seen by a pediatric neurologist chiefly for learning problems, and diagnosed as having minimal brain dysfunction. Only one-third of the group gave strong evidence of a history suggesting brain damage. None of the children appeared normal on neurological examination; 57 percent had definite or probable significant abnormality but 43 percent had only minor abnormalities of uncertain significance. Thirty of the 83 children were clumsy but had no other abnormal neurological signs. The behavior ratings of the children by mothers showed them to be essentially normal, which suggests that the diagnosis of minimal brain dysfunction does not necessarily imply behavioral disturbance, especially when the children are seen primarily by other than psychiatrists or psychologists.

The group's mean IQ, though normal (96·3), was lower than that expected in upper-middle-class children, and was consonant with the commonest problem of school difficulties. This might reflect cerebral damage but it might also be simply a sign of increased concern about the less intelligent child in a competitive subculture. The relationship between the verbal and performance IQs on the WISC showed that these children differ, though not dramatically, from normal children in an increased frequency of discrepancies greater than 9 points. However, this measure did not prove particularly meaningful in subsequent analyses, despite its current popularity.

A factor analysis indicated that most of the neurological abnormality could be accounted for by two symptom-complexes—perceptual deficits and motor incoordination. There were two additional factors, electroencephalographic and reflex abnormalities. Abnormal history appeared in two discrete factors—abnormal pre- and abnormal peri-natal history. A final factor was related to both order and maternal age and may reflect increased fetal risk. Because of the nature of factor analysis, the dimensions underlying these seven symptom-clusters are necessarily independent and unrelated. Some of this lack of relationship may be due, particularly in the case of history (Wenar 1963) to some inherent unreliability of present methods of assessment. Nevertheless, the high degree of interrelatedness between abnormal history, neurological and electroencephalographic abnormalities, as observed in children with major neurological abnormalities, cannot necessarily be extrapolated to children with minimal brain dysfunction.

Correlations between the estimated scores of the subjects on the neurological examination-history and electroencephalographic-symptom-complexes were, except in the case of the latter, generally infrequent and small in degree, so they too appear largely independent of neurological and historical symptom-complexes.

There are probably certain potential cerebral insults which are not yet recognized and which might show correlations with subsequent neurological, psychological, or electroencephalographic findings but the correlations appear minimal in the work done so far. It is also probable that more subtle diagnostic methods might identify more children as abnormal, and thus increase the apparent correlations with previous history. However, this would be more a matter of finding individual physical signs or special tests which would correlate better with past events, and not of an overall diagnosis of neurological abnormality classifiable as "minimal cerebral dysfunction," since this diagnosis was, in fact, reached in all but 14 of the 97 children in the original group. A crucial question, too, is to what extent the behavior of the child and even his nonsuccess on certain neurological and psychological tests could be due to adverse experience and to emotional factors, which often coexist.

Some of the more subtle abnormal neurological signs may even be due in some cases to psychological factors, and not necessarily be signs of *physical* etiology. Pincus and Glaser (1966) have recently pointed out that both organic and environmental factors are probably involved, and the latter would include both the child's difficulty in reacting to and coping with his environment and his response to the pressures applied to him.

Thus, minimal cerebral dysfunction is not a homogeneous diagnostic entity, but rather a way of describing a variety of unrelated minor dysfunctions, some neurological, some behavioral and some cognitive, which may put a child in difficulties with his social and familial environment. This group of highly discrepant children does exist and they are usually better managed by recognizing the varying problems which are involved in each individual child, and which need to be taken into account in planning his schooling, management at home, treatment with amphetamines or other drugs, psychotherapy, or behavior therapy.

A single hypothetical underlying dimension accounting for the relationships among the neurological, behavioral and cognitive abnormalities, which the concept of "minimal brain damage" implies, is not borne out by this study and it seems likely that the pattern of abnormalities observed in individual children reflects a complex matrix of underlying dimensions, some innate, some traumatic, and some psychosocial (Rodin *et al.* 1964). One suspects that the overall group of children referred to would merge imperceptibly into the normal population at one end of the scale, and at the other into more obvious ones of brain damage, such as cerebral palsies or mental retardation. The data available do not, however, support the contention of Pasamanick and Knobloch (1960) that they are a part of "a continuum of reproductive casualty" with more severe results such as cerebral palsy, neonatal death and stillbirth.

The results of this study support the essentially similar findings of Rodin *et al.* (1964), Schulman *et al.* (1965), and Werry *et al.* (1967). They are also consistent with the poor intercorrelations of medical-psychological electroencephalographic findings in Hanvik's study of children in a child guidance clinic (1961). A conference at Oxford in 1962 reached as its most important conclusion the consensus that the term "minimal brain damage" ought to be abolished (Bax and Mac Keith 1963). At the least, professional persons working with these children should be more circumspect in hypothesizing about cerebral status, and instead place emphasis on adequate psycho-educational assessment and rehabilitative programs, guided by assessment of each child's demonstrated assets and liabilities.

SUMMARY

This paper reports the study of 83 children with a diagnosis of "minimal cerebral dysfunction." Minimum criteria for inclusion in the study were any one of the following:

1. Abnormal neurological signs.
2. Abnormal EEG.
3. Psychological findings of the type seen in organic encephalopathies, plus either excessive clumsiness or an abnormal EEG.

Data collected included full medical history with neurological examination, EEG study, psychological tests and behavior ratings. Although there are interesting correlations within each class of data collected, there was a disappointing lack of correlation between the data collected under different headings. The study suggests that the pattern of abnormalities observed in individual children reflects a complex matrix of underlying dimensions, some innate, some traumatic and some psychosocial. Professionals should be circumspect in hypothesising about cerebral status in individual cases and concentrate on adequate psychosocial and educational assessment and rehabilitative programs.

References

Bax, M., Mac Keith, R. (Eds.) (1963) Minimal Cerebral Dysfunction. London: Spastics Society/Heinemann.

Bender, M. B. (1952) Disorders in Perception. Springfield, Ill.: Thomas.

Clements, S. D. (1966) Minimal Brain Dysfunction in Children. NINDB Monograph No. 3, U.S. Department of Health, Education and Welfare.

Clements, S. D., Peters, J. E. (1962) 'Minimal brain dysfunction in the school-age child.' Arch. gen. Psychiat, 6, 185.

Field, J. G. (1960) 'Two types of tables for use with Wechsler's Intelligence Scales.' J. clin. Psychol. 16, 3–7.

Hanvik, L. J. et al. (1961) 'Diagnosis of cerebral dysfunction in children as made in child guidance clinic.' Amer. J. Dis. Child. 101, 364.

Herbert, M. (1964) 'The concept and testing of brain-damage in children: A review.' J. Child Psychol. 5, 197.

Hermann, K. (1959) Reading Disability. Springfield, Ill.: Thomas.

Jenkins, R. L. (1966) 'Psychiatric syndromes in children and their relation to family background.' Amer. J. Orthopsychiat. 36, 450.

Lucas, A. R., Rodin, E. A., Simson, C. B. (1965) 'Neurological assessment of children with early school problems.' *Develop. Med. Child Neurol.* 7, 145.

Paine, R. S. (1962) 'Minimal chronic brain syndromes in children.' *Develop. Med. Child Neurol.* 4, 21.

Pasamanick, B., Knobloch, H. (1960) 'Brain and behavior: Symposium 1959. 2. Brain damage and reproductive casualty.' *Amer. J. Orthopsychiat.* 30, 298.

Peterson, D. R. (1961) 'Behavior problems of middle childhood.' *J. consult. Psychol.* 25, 205.

Pincus, J. H., Glaser, G. H. (1966) 'The syndrome of "minimal brain damage" in childhood.' *New Engl. J. Med.* 275, 27–35.

Quay, H. C. (1964) 'Personality dimensions in delinquent males as inferred from the factor analysis of behavior ratings.' *J. Res. Crime Delinq.* 1, 33–37.

Quay, H. C., Morse, W. C., Cutler, R. L. (1966) 'Personality patterns of pupils in special classes for the emotionally disturbed.' *Except. Child.* 32, 287.

Quay, H. C., Quay, L. C. (1965) 'Behavior problems in early adolescence.' *Child Develop.* 36, 215.

Rogers, M. E., Lilienfeld, A. M., Pasamanick, B. (1955) Prenatal and paranatal factors in the development of childhood behavior disorders. *Acta psychiat. scand.* Suppl. 102.

Rodin, E., Lucas, A., Simon, C. (1964) 'A study of behavior disorders in children by means of general purpose computers.' *Proc. Conf. Data Acquis. Proc. Biol. Med.* Oxford: Pergamon, 115.

Schulman, J. L., Kaspar, J. C., Throne, F. M. (1965) Brain damage and behavior: A clinical-experimental study. Springfield, Ill.: Thomas.

Wenar, C. (1963) 'The reliability of developmental histories.' *Psychosom. Med.* 25, 505.

Werry, J. S., Weiss, G., Douglas, V. (1967) 'Minimal cerebral dysfunction: An empirical analysis.' Paper presented to the Annual Meeting of the American Psychiatric Association, Detroit, Michigan.

Appendix A

Factor Analysis of History and Neurological Data
Cluster I (Perceptual Deficits)

Variable	Varimax Factor Loading
Misconception of space	0·70
Perceptual deficits	0·66
Imperception of assembly into whole	0·66
Imperception of size	0·62

Variable	Varimax Factor Loading
Imperception of patterns	0·56
Misconception of body image	0·54
Dyspraxia	0·52
Motor signs	0·39
Higher socio-economic class	0·42

Cluster II (Motor Incoordination)

Clumsiness—small movements	0·60
Choreoathetosis	0·57
Poor penmanship	0·51
Clumsiness—large movements	0·50
Younger age	0·43
Motor signs	0·44
Walked at later than 18 months	0·42
Overall neurological status	0·39
No misconception of R–L orientation	0·39

Cluster III (Abnormal Paranatal History)

Perinatal insults	0·67
Neonatal problems	0·64
History of brain damage	0·61
No tremor	0·43

Cluster IV (Abnormal EEG)

Abnormal EEG	0·69
Post-natal insults	0·60
History of brain damage	0·49

Cluster V (Later Birth Order)

Age of mother at birth	0·60
Birth order	0·58
Walked at	0·46
Hyperreflexia	0·39

Cluster VI (Abnormal Prenatal History)

No 'other neurological signs'	0·43
Prenatal insults	0·41

Cluster VII (Abnormal Reflexes)

Extensor plantars	0·43
Hyperreflexia	0·41

Appendix B

Significant (P < ·05), Correlations Between Subjects'
Scores on Neurological-Historical Syndromes, Behavior Ratings,
Psychological Tests and Psychologists' Ratings

* *these variables were also intercorrelated with each other*
N ranges from 83 to 25   Total number of R's = 467
                          Total number of significant r's = 46

1. Neurological-Historical Factors

    I. Perceptual-Deficit: None
    II. Motor Incoordination: Neurotic score (− ·25), WISC v/p (·40), Digit span s.t. (·43)
    III. Abnormal Paranatal History: Similarities s.t. (− ·44), Coding s.t. (− ·41)
    IV. Abnormal EEG Score: Neurotic score (·37), Difficulties in abstraction (·33). Subtests irregular (·37), WISC performance IQ (− ·37), Similarities s.t. (− ·53), Vocabulary s.t. (− ·42), Picture completion s.t. (− ·46), Block design s.t. (− ·40), Object assembly s.t. (− ·43)
    V. Later Birth Order: WISC performance IQ (− ·53), WISC verbal IQ (− ·38), Vocabulary s.t. (− ·45)
    VI. Abnormal Prenatal History: Subtest irregular (·29)
    VII. Abnormal Reflexes: Neurotic score (− ·26)

2. Behavior Ratings

    I. Conduct Score: Comprehension s.t. (·44)
    II. Neurotic Score: Motor incoordination (·25), Abnormal EEG (·37), Abnormal Reflexes (− ·26), Irregular subtests (− ·34), Digit span s.t. (·48)
    III. Immaturity Score: Short attention span (·37), Dyscalculia (·32)

3. Psychologists' Observations

    I. Short Attention Span: Immaturity score (·37), Similarities s.t. (− ·50), WISC v > p (− ·37)
    II. Dyscalculia: Immaturity score (·32), Difficulties in abstraction (·40), WISC verbal IQ (− ·42) Arithmetic s.t. (− ·69), Similarities s.t. (− ·57), Vocabulary s.t. (− ·48), Coding s.t. (− ·42)
    III. Perseveration: None
    IV. Difficulties in Abstraction: Abnormal EEG (·33), Immaturity score (·38), Dyscalculia (·40), Negatively

with all s.t.'s except Block Design and
Object Assembly

V. Subtests Irregular: Abnormal EEG (·37), Abnormal prenatal history
(·29), Neurotic score (− ·34)

4. Psychological Tests (subtests omitted)

I. Full Scale IQ: Difficulties in abstraction (− ·52)

II. WISC Verbal IQ: Later birth order (− ·38), Difficulties in abstraction (− ·53)

III. WISC Performance IQ: Abnormal EEG (− ·44), Later birth order
(− ·53), Difficulties in abstraction (− ·56)

IV. WISC V/P Ratio: Motor incoordination (·40)

V. WISC V > P: Short attention span (− ·37)

7. BIRTH DEFECT OF THE SKULL AND FACE WITHOUT BRAIN OR LEARNING DISORDER: A PSYCHOLOGICAL AND PEDAGOGICAL REPORT

JOHN MONEY and NANCI A. BOBROW

There are many sources and causes of learning disability and impaired school achievement requiring special educational services. Nonetheless, educators and psychologists tend to drift into an attitude of mind whereby learning disability becomes a diagnostic term in itself, referring to a specific syndrome. Learning disability is, in fact, a symptom and not a syndrome. As a symptom, it may be a manifestation of several different syndromes. The world of learning disability and special education rather urgently needs an accumulation of detailed studies of children with special disabilities—studies in which the relationship, or nonrelationship, between specific impairments and educational achievement or failure is documented. Only in this way will educators accumulate the necessary body of knowledge that puts special education for children with learning disabilities on a scientific basis.

The purpose of this paper is to document, in detail, the psychological findings in an exceptionally rare case of a severe congenital deformity on the left side of the face and skull, so that these findings may be used to evaluate: (a) whether the cosmetic effects of the deformity may ad-

SOURCE. Reprinted from *Journal of Learning Disabilities*, 1968, 1, 9–17. By permission of the authors and publisher.

versely affect school achievement; and (b) whether the brain may be directly implicated, either currently as a result of diagnostic testing or, years from now, should the brain ever come to autopsy.

The case was selected for presentation because it is uniquely rare. It throws light on the indirect and secondary emotional effects of a birth defect on learning, in addition to ruling out a possible primary neuropsychologic effect of direct brain involvement.

CASE REPORT

Name:	Ernest _____
JHH Number:	104–62–36
Date of Birth:	8/12/54
Dates of Testing:	(See Below)
Chronological Age:	13 years, 1 month
Examiner:	Nanci A. Bobrow

Reason for Referral: The patient was referred for psychological evaluation from the plastic surgery clinic, with reference to the ongoing program of plastic surgical repair to his congenital left facial deformity, and by way of the pediatric endocrine clinic in relation to his retarded statural and pubertal development.

Medical-Chart Excerpts: The left external ear and left eye were congenitally absent (Figure 1). There were multiple bony abnormalities, namely, of the left maxilla (the bone above the mouth), zygoma (cheekbone), and mandible (jawbone). The skull was asymmetrical with flattening of the left frontal region accompanied by increased convexity of the left parietal area, above and to the rear of the missing ear, and flattening of the left posteroparietal area. This condition persists. The boy had a cleft palate that has been repaired surgically. The history of increased indistinctness of speech following adenoidectomy suggests, however, some degree of nasopharyngeal insufficiency. The palate moves symmetrically in the production of speech, but the tongue projects to the left with limited side-to-side movements. Testing of the right eye reveals that the right pupil is regular and it reacts to light and accommodation. Visual acuity is 20/30–20/20, or from just beyond to within the normal range. The facial appearance remains peculiar despite the plastic surgical procedures so far carried out in 18 different operations. There is clinical evidence of a heart murmur which has not interfered with the surgical history. The second and third toes on each foot are joined together, and an inward curvature of both fifth fingers is evident.

All the deformities are of prenatal origin. No complications of birth

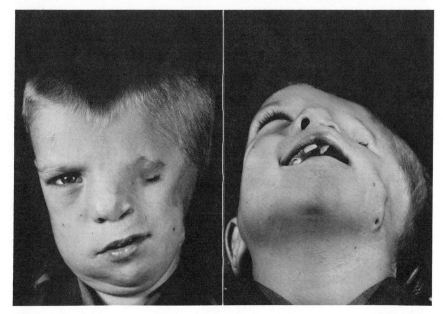

FIG. 1. *Two views of the patient at age 8 after completion of cleft-palate surgery, but before the beginning of plastic reconstruction of the remaining facial deformity. That the patient gave his explicit consent to the use of these photographs is a measure of his self-esteem and absence of self-defeating shame.*

were recorded. The labor was 4½ hours. The child reached the developmental milestones at the normal times. He had measles at the age of 4½. The EEG findings at age 8 showed relative depression of the fast frequencies on the left hemisphere and increased theta activity. No seizure discharges were present. Clinically, there has been no history of seizures.

A current endocrine and laboratory work-up has revealed that the boy has no human growth hormone. The etiology of this deficit and the resultant short stature are still unexplained. It could represent a primary hypothalamic-pituitary defect or a secondary, functional hormonal deficit similar to the type reported in dwarfs by Powell, Brasel and Blizzard (1967).

School Report: At present, the boy is in the eighth grade, which is the appropriate grade level for a 13-year-old boy. He has attended three different schools in the last three years: a grammar school, a high school in Maryland where he lived with his father and mentally disturbed stepmother, and a high school in West Virginia where he now lives with his paternal grandparents. Despite this change of schools and long absences due to hospital admissions for surgery, the boy has maintained good academic achievement. His final grades for the seventh grade, last year, were: marks of B for English, reading and general math, and marks of C for general science, physical education, and arts and crafts. In spite of an absence of approximately one month this year, he has managed to keep abreast of his school assignments. His grades for the first six weeks were B's for music and physical education and C's for math, literature, history and science. In English, he missed spelling tests which were not made up in time for him to receive a grade.

His current teachers report that he participates in class discussion and does not hesitate to volunteer to contribute. According to them, he works hard, is polite and responsive, expresses pride in his high test scores and reacts with pleasure to their praise. He is not a behavior problem. The teachers' comments indicate that the other children generally avoid seeking the boy's friendship, but they accept him and he is able to get along with them. The teachers all note a minimum of teasing observed in the classroom.

Schedule of Psychologic Examination

September 21, 1967
WISC, Verbal, (except vocabulary); Interview.

September 25, 1967
WISC, Vocabulary and Performance; Harris Tests of Lateral Dominance; Draw-A-Person; Wepman Auditory Discrimination Test (Form I); Gray Oral Reading Test (Form A); Interview.

September 26, 1967
Ishihara Tests for Color Blindness; Sacks Sentence Completion; Benton Visual Retention Test—(Form C); Bender Visual-Motor Gestalt Test; TAT; Interview.

October 3, 1967
Road-Map Test of Direction Sense; Test of Smell; Interview.

October 6, 1967
Interview—Dr. John Money; Interview with Father—Dr. John Money.

October 13, 1967
Interview, sex education and history.

Results of Psychologic Examination

Wechsler Intelligence Scale for Children

Verbal IQ	97
Performance IQ	101
Full IQ	99

Verbal Scaled Scores

Information	8
Comprehension	10
Arithmetic	9
Similarities	10
Vocabulary	13
Digit Span	8

Performance Scaled Scores

Picture Completion	9
Picture Arrangement	11
Block Design	12
Object Assembly	12
Coding	7

According to the Wechsler norms, an IQ between 90 and 109 is rated as average and places a person between the 25th and 75th percentiles. An IQ of 99 ranks a person between the 40th and 50th percentiles.

There is a range in subtest scores from 9 to 13 (which is unremarkable), except for Digit Span 8, and Coding 7. A Cohen factorial-based analysis shows discrepancies as follows:

Verbal Comprehension Factor (Mean of Inf. + Comp. + Sim. + Vocab.)	10.25
Perceptual Organization Factor (Mean of Bl.Des. + Obj. Ass.)	12.0
Freedom from Distractibility (Mean of Arith. + Dig. Span)	8.5

There is an orderly sequence of passes and failures on items within subtests and there are no unusual responses. All answers were brief and appropriate to the questions. It was necessary to repeat many of the questions for the arithmetic subtest. Because the boy's speech is characteristic of a patient with a repaired cleft palate, he was difficult to understand, and it was necessary for him to repeat many of his responses to establish effective communication.

The examiner believed the results of this test to be representative of

9

the patient's level of functioning at the time of testing. During the initial testing session, three days postoperatively, though he said he was in no pain, the patient was too fatigued to complete all the subtests. He was attentive and cooperative throughout the second testing session.

Gray Oral Reading Test (Form A)

Grade Equivalent Score: 9.7

Types of Errors:

gross mispronunciation
partial mispronunciation
repetition

Observations on Quality of Reading Performance:

poor phrasing
lack of expression
monotonous tone
pitch too high
voice too soft
poor enunciation
disregard of punctuation
head movement
finger pointing

At school the boy is in the eighth grade, therefore he functions adequately according to the standards of this test, despite the fact that when reading an eighth grade selection his score is not absolutely perfect and his reading is not absolutely fluent.

Last year, while in the seventh grade, the boy was tested at school with the Durrell-Sullivan Reading Test and earned a grade equivalent score of 7.2.

The figure drawn first is a male, which reveals adequate gender-identity. This is a "pirate and convict" shown full face, and sketched with long flowing lines. The second drawing, of a pirate woman, is also shown full face and the same drawing technique is used. The Harris (1963) scoring methods rate them highly, as seen above.

The male figure is the largest of the drawings, filling nearly the entire length of the page. In the self-and-friend drawing, while the patient was reluctant to draw himself, he portrayed the self figure as the taller. The friend is David, his hospital roommate of one day. The patient was not sure if David was taller than himself and did not know David's age. Again reluctant to draw himself in his family drawing, the patient asked if the figures could be small. The figures are exceedingly small, ranging from 1 to 2 inches. The boy and his sister, identified by name labels, are drawn the same height with a notation that Sharon, his 12-year old sister, is the taller. It is unusual for a child to depict his own relative height inaccurately. It may be interpreted as pathognomonic of personality disturbance relative to this issue.

The male "pirate and convict" of the first drawing has a hook instead of a left hand. He is a menacing figure which, given a double role, represents strength and power exceeding the patient's own. This is the boy's only projected sign of aggression or hostility. He has drawn this figure with an obvious deformity, the hook for the left hand. Other deformities seen in the drawings are as follows. The female figure has four toes on both feet and four fingers on the left hand. The self is drawn, both times, with only the left, (not the right, as in the patient's case) eye and ear. Also on the right side there is a patch, perhaps a bandage over the ear region; the ear is simply omitted in the self with the family. A right eye patch is present in both. Also, the self and friend and family drawings are crowded to the extreme left of the page. Finally, while the father is drawn with two ears and the patient with only one, Kevin, the younger brother, is drawn with none.

Sacks Sentence Completion Test

No numerical scoring criteria are employed on this test. The items offering insight into the patient's emotions and character are included below. (The given stimuli have been italicized to contrast with the patient's ensuing reply.)

I know it is silly but I am afraid of needles.
I believe that I have the ability to learn.
Most of my friends don't know that I am afraid of everything just about.
I don't like people who pick on me.
I wish I could lose the fear of being afraid.
If I had sex relations I don't know what that means.
I feel that my father is pretty good for a father.
My sex life I don't know anything about sex.

Finally, of special interest was:

People who play with me usually play nicely sometimes. Tease me sometimes, but I can take it. "If I couldn't (take it), they'd tease me more," the boy then said in a spoken addendum.

Some idiosyncratic behavior was manifest here. The patient worked silently for a long time and then announced that he was finished; only

TABLE I
Draw-A-Person Test

	Figure	Raw Score	Standard Score	Percentile
Point Scale	Male	52	113	81
	Female	51	114	82
Quality Scale	Male	M-9	121	92
	Female	W-10	135	99

half the items had been answered. He expressed worry and concern about who would see the record form, and I feel that the written and oral answers do not express the totality of his true feelings.

Bender Visual-Motor Gestalt Test

The designs are reproduced exactly and are quite precise. They are placed on the left side of the paper one below the other to the bottom; the last two are on the right side. According to the scoring manual by Koppitz (1964) the performance merits a perfect (zero) score.

There are no rotations or reversals and no signs of motor and/or integrational disturbance. The patient is left-handed, which indicates dominance of the right hemisphere of the brain, the right side of the head being the one unaffected by deformity.

Benton Visual Retention Test (Form C)

Administration A: 10-second exposure and immediate reproduction
Correct reproductions: 7
Erroneous reproductions: Designs V, VII, and X

For a 13- to 14-year old child with an average IQ, the expected number of correct reproductions is between 7 and 8. There is, therefore, no evidence of any specific disability in visual memory or visuomotor function. This conclusion is further supported by a comparison of the 13- to 14-year old average IQ, expected-error score of 4 and the patient's observed error score of 3.

Harris Tests of Lateral Dominance

Hand Dominance   Moderate Left
   (items 2–6)
Foot Dominance   Strong Left
   (items 7–8
Eye Dominance   Patient has only right eye

	Dominance
Subtests	*Ratings*
1. Knowledge of left and right	Normal
2. Hand Preferences	Strong Left (100%)
3. Simultaneous Writing	Moderate Left
4. Handwriting	Mixed
5. Tapping	Strong Left
6. Dealing Cards	Moderate Left
7. Kick	Strong Left
8. Stamp	Strong Left

Road-Map Test of Direction Sense

Number of Correct Turns: 27
Number of Incorrect Turns: 5
Percentile Rank for Age: 50th
Turn-Type Pattern: no recurrent type of error

This test was administered to observe the patient's orientation for right and left simultaneously with coming and going in space. The normal age for developing this skill in right-left direction sense is between 11 and 15. The patient, aged 13, therefore evidences no unusual difficulty.

Wepman Auditory Discrimination Test (Form I)

Errors when stimuli were identical: 3 out of 30
Errors when stimuli were different: 0 out of 10

This test was administered to determine the patient's ability to recognize fine differences between phonemes used in English speech. According to the norms, inadequate development for 8 years and older, is indicated by more than three errors. The patient's score, therefore, falls within the adequate range.

Test of Smell

Aromatic oils were presented to the patient. He identified, by name, peppermint oil ("mint") and creosol ("disinfectant"), and distinguished others as being different. Thus, there was no evidence of anosmia.

Ishihara Tests for Color Blindness

Type of Response	*Plate Numbers*
Indicating normal color vision	1, 3, 16, 38
Indicating red-green deficiency pattern	2, 4–15, 17–25, 26–37

According to the Ishihara manual, the patient's record fits the pattern of red-green deficiency. Further, on plates 22 to 27, his responses fit the pattern of the deutan type, which means that he has trouble distinguishing greens and grays. Purple-red, the complementary color of green, also appears as gray.

During the test, the patient reported that his sister said, "Moss is green" but he knew that it was "red". He could not elaborate any further on this statement. He further indicated that the line traced in plates 34 and 35 was "green" when, in fact, it connected bluish-green and purple dots.

The boy seemed a bit amused by the idea of being color-blind. He asked if I thought he was color-blind, but looked bewildered when I returned his question. He did not indicate any knowledge of this condition, nor awareness of any difficulties relating to color perception. The evidence of the strength of social learning is clear. When I asked the father if his son was color-blind, he answered with a definite negative answer.

Interview. Extensive interview material was recorded and transcribed. There are two outstanding points that need to be brought to light. One is the boy's fear of needles. He is preoccupied with needles in any discussion of the hospital or medication. A prime example is his panicky reaction to how he would have to take hormonal medication to help him to grow. If it will be with needles, he is against it. In this context, his needle phobia is in conflict with one of his most crucial desires, as expressed in his three wishes test and elsewhere, namely, to grow.

The second point is the boy's expression of his desire to grow taller and be six feet like his father. He states that he is teased because he is the smallest one in his class. At school he is in the eighth grade with his own age group. He said he plays mostly with boys his size who are 9 or 10 years old. It is apparent that his small size is another vehicle of ridicule used by his age-mates to reject him, as if his deformity were not sufficient. He elected to wait at least another year for the decision to begin sex hormone therapy when it was explained that he had a better chance for an ultimately greater height if he could wait. He was encouraged to cultivate friendships within his own age group. He was singularly ignorant in sex education which kept him socially further apart from his teenage group. To aid him with his social adjustment, he was given sex information to which he acted with a mature interest.

Comments and Impressions After Testing: It is not known whether the brain itself, like the left face, is in any part hypoplastic. One purpose of the present battery of psychological tests was to ascertain whether any psychoneurologic deficits might be present and, if so, whether they might suggest a brain defect, even though the latter might not be confirmable at the present time.

In actual fact, the tests show the boy to be apparently free of major brain defect. Color-blindness, the major deficiency in his psychologic functioning, need not be attributed to any malformation of the brain itself. According to Dr. Louise Sloan of the Wilmer Eye Clinic of The Johns Hopkins Hospital, the boy may be considered simply as one among 8% of males with a red-green color vision deficiency.

The findings that may be related to the congenital hypoplastic phenomenon pertain not to deficits in brain function, but lateralization. The boy is left-handed and it therefore appears that the right hemisphere of the brain is the dominant one. Further evidence to support such a conclusion is the high Cohen factorial score for Perceptual Organization on the WISC. The right parietal lobe of the cerebral cortex is generally believed to be dominant over the left parietal lobe in the organization of visuoconstructional and visual-perceptual functioning. While his speech is mechanically indistinct, language function, which is normally dominant in the left temporal lobe, in right-handed people, is not impaired in this boy. Either the left hemisphere is intact for language, but not for handedness, or, from birth onward, the right side took over the control of language. The latter is a good possibility, in view of the boy's left-handedness.

At the present time there is no demonstrated relationship, either primary or secondary, between the patient's facial deformity and his statural growth failure. Empirically, it has been confirmed that the boy has no human growth hormone. Theoretically then, a cranial involvement could, in a primary way, directly affect the pituitary gland whose hormones control growth. Alternatively, the relationship could be as a derived and secondary response to, and a function of, his life's dilemma of congenital deformity and maternal abandonment. This mechanism may resemble the one already mentioned as having been observed in certain dwarfs by Powell and co-workers (1967). Whereas, at first glance, the boy seems to cope with this deformity in a realistic manner, in actual fact it is more likely that he manifests a benign exterior and is reluctant or unable to express his emotions, as is evident in his Sentence Completion responses and in parts of the transcribed interviews. There is obviously more to the story than meets the eye, if one judges by the intensity of the boy's phobia for injection needles. His fear of needles is disproportionate and exaggerated. Indeed, all of his medical and hospital fears seem to have been displaced and focalized onto needles.

Recommendations After Psychologic Testing

1. Return for psychologic follow-up on subsequent outpatient visits and inpatient admissions.
2. Delayed sex-hormonal therapy for at least one year, in order not to prematurely interrupt additional growth in height, at which time psychologic evaluation can be repeated.
3. Further counseling on problems of adjustment relative to dwarfism (Money, 1967) and pubertal delay

DISCUSSION

At the present time, we do not know if this boy's brain is abnormally formed as his face and skull are. If the brain is affected, then the present test findings are remarkable for their normalcy. Should some of the left hemisphere of the brain be defective or missing, then it must be assumed that the right hemisphere has compensated completely for the defect. It is known that such a compensation is possible when one hemisphere is damaged or even totally removed in earliest infancy, whereas, after the acquisition of speech, recovery is at best only partial with some residual neuropsychologic symptoms always remaining. Geschwind (1962) pointed out that while fairly restricted lesions in the left hemisphere of an adult may cause severe disability in the area of language, even total destruction of the left hemisphere in early infancy does not usually prevent the acquisition of language. Hécaen and Ajuriaguerra (1964) summarized the findings on left hemispherectomy of infant epileptics and hemiplegics. These findings show that the nondominant hemisphere can, by itself alone, take over all the functions of the missing dominant hemisphere, provided the operation is done in infancy, before the critical developmental period of brain plasticity has expired.

Obviously, the only way to settle the issue in this particular case will be to obtain a report on the brain itself. We may have to wait 50 or 60 years for the conclusion of a normal life span before such a report is obtainable. As remote as that time seems, it is signally important for the advancement of knowledge, regarding brain structure and learning ability, that plans be made so far ahead. If teachers and physicians wish to understand the limitations of brain damage—and so-called minimal brain damage—on learning ability, then they have no alternative than to examine brains and correlate brain findings after the cessation of life with learning and performance during life.

This case, then, illustrates the desirability of an administrative machinery that will permit psychological test findings and observations in life to be correlated with autopsy findings on the brain years later. This administrative machinery could be similar to Medic-Alert, an organization with a membership of people with medical histories which must be brought to the immediate attention of a physician at the time of an emergency. An identification bracelet with the Medic-Alert number and the type of disorder is worn by the patient at all times. By calling the emergency number, the physician is apprised of the pertinent facts of the case in the form of a brief abstract. Recommendations for the patient's care also may be included. He is then, quickly and completely armed with the knowledge needed to relate the present treatment to the past findings.

In the present case there should be a device for alerting the physician who signs the death certificate that there is information in a test record to be retrieved and that the brain should be submitted to autopsy. Then it will be possible to match brain findings with the test data retrieved. By keeping a permanent file of their academic and test data, school teachers and psychologists become important collaborators with medical people in the advancement of knowledge of the relationship between the brain and learning.

Meantime, during life and at the beginning of the teenage years, the value of psychologic testing has been the demonstration that the boy is not severely handicapped intellectually as a result of his birth defect. His education does not need to be planned in the uncertainty of suspecting he has so-called minimal brain damage. He doesn't.

ACKNOWLEDGEMENTS

Supported by Research Grant #MD-00325 and Research Career Development Award #MD-K3-18,635, The National Institute for Child Health and Human Development, The United States Public Health Service.
We wish to thank Dr. Robert Blizzard of the Pediatric Endocrine Clinic and Dr. Milton Edgerton of the Plastic Surgery Department for referring this patient to us.
We also wish to thank Dr. Louise Sloan for her consultation regarding the boy's color-vision deficiency.
Department of Psychiatry and Behavioral Sciences and Department of Pediatrics, The Johns Hopkins University School of Medicine.

Glossary

Anosmia: A loss of the sense of smell. It may be essential or true, due to lesion of the olfactory nerve; mechanical or respiratory, due to obstruction of the nasal fossae; reflex, due to disease in some other part or organ; functional, without any apparent causal lesion.

Gender-Identity: The sameness, unity and persistence of one's individuality as male or female (or ambivalent), in greater or lesser degree, especially as it is experienced in self-awareness and behavior; gender identity is the private experience of gender role, and gender role is the public expression of gender identity.

Hypoplasia: A condition of arrested development in which an organ or part remains below the normal size or in an immature state.

In vivo: In the living body; referring to vital chemical processes etc., as distinguished from those occurring in the test tube.

Nasopharyngeal: Rhinopharyngeal; relating to the nasal cavity and the pharynx or to the nasopharynx; denoting also a slight groove marking the separation of the nasal cavity from the pharynx.

Parietal lobe: The part of the cortex of the brain that lies approximately above the ear between the temple and the back of the head.

Pathognomonic: Characteristic or indicative of a disease, denoting especially one or more typical symptoms.

Bibliography

Geschwind, N., The Anatomy of Acquired Disorders of Reading. In Reading Disability: Progress and Research Needs in Dyslexia (J. Money, ed.). Baltimore, Johns Hopkins Press, 1962.

Harris, D., Children's Drawings As Measures of Intellectual Maturity, New York, Harcourt, Brace and World, 1963.

Hécaen, H. and de Ajuriaguerra, J., Left-Handedness: Manual Superiority and Cerebral Dominance. Translated by Eric Ponder. New York, Grune and Stratton, 1964.

Koppitz, E. M., The Bender Gestalt Test for Young Children. New York, Grune and Stratton, 1964.

Money, J., Dwarfism: Questions and Answers in Counseling. Rehabilitation Literature, 1967, 28, 134–138.

Powell, G. F., Brasel, J. A. and Blizzard, R. M. Emotional Deprivation and Growth Retardation Simulating Hypopituitarism. New England Journal of Medicine, 1967, 276, 1271–1278.

8. TEACHING READING TO BRAIN-DAMAGED CHILDREN: A REVIEW*

JAMES C. REED, EDWARD F. RABE,
and MARGARET MANKINEN

The evidence that retarded readers with brain damage require special methods of instruction is extremely meager. The lack of evidence stems from a paucity of studies which directly address the question of differential instruction as a function of brain damage. Studies that have attempted to investigate this problem suffer from an inadequate experimental design and a failure to specify the criterion information used in the diagnosis of brain damage.

In this paper the experimental studies on brain damage and reading which have appeared in the literature between January 1960 and July of 1969 were reviewed. The purposes were to examine the evidence for not only (1) the effectiveness of various instructional methods for teaching brain injured children to read, but also, and primarily (2) to assess the quality of the criteria used in the documentation of brain damage, and then (3) to make recommendations concerning standards to be employed in future investigations of remedial techniques for the brain-damaged.

SOURCE. Reprinted from *Reading Research Quarterly*, 1968, 1, 289–298. By permission of the author and publisher.

* This paper was supported in part by Research and Training Grant #7, Social and Rehabilitation Service.

Does the fact of brain damage itself make a difference? If one views the number of instructional programs and special classes for the perceptionally handicapped, the hyperactive child, the child with minimal cerebral dysfunction, etc., the answer can only be given in the affirmative. The scientific evidence, however, is lacking. As Birch (1964) has pointed out, the "brain-damaged" child may or may not have damage of the brain. Cruickshank (1966) stated that there is no agreement on the meaning of the term. Others have implied that the characteristics of these children are well known and that it is immaterial whether or not there is damage to the brain. There are flaws in this line of reasoning. First, such a statement shows little respect for the value of scientific investigation and the rules of evidence which permit advances in knowledge. Second, if one assumes that it is immaterial whether or not there is damage to the brain, one has indeed made a diagnosis, namely, that damage, if present, is *chronic* and *non-progressive*.

Knowledge of neurological deficits may or may not help in planning an educational program. One will never know unless rigorous experimentation is done, and such experimentation must include a clear delineation of the criterion information by which brain damage is specified. Possibly children with lesions primarily involving the left cerebral hemisphere would indeed profit more from a teaching regime designed to promote language skills than would children with lesions primarily involving the right cerebral hemisphere. The validity of this statement can never be judged unless formal experimentation is done in accordance with commonly accepted criteria of good experimental design.

In order to provide a background for the review of the studies pertaining to brain damage and reading, it will be necessary to consider (1) some of the problems in identifying the brain-damaged child, (2) the procedures involved in a neurological examination, and (3) the limitations of various neurological criteria information. In the section which follows, the use of psychological tests for inferring cerebral dysfunction is not discussed. If one uses psychological tests to infer neurological deficit, the criterion becomes the psychological tests and there are the attendant problems not only of the reliability but also of the validity of the classification. Psychological tests can be used to describe the ability deficits, the emotional characteristics, or the perceptual handicaps of children with brain damage, but to do so, there must be evidence independent of psychological tests for the fact of damage, otherwise, the prophecy becomes self-fulfilling. It is, for the purpose of this discussion, meaningless to ask whether psychological tests are better than neurological tests for identifying brain damage, because if the criterion is neurological information, the procedure cannot be better than the criterion.

LIMITATIONS OF NEUROLOGICAL EVIDENCE

Problems in Specifying Brain Damage

A major difficulty in studying the relation between brain damage and reading abnormality is one of definition. The term "brain damage" by strict definition implies a "loss due to injury." Loss may imply loss of brain (neurones, glia, and blood vessels) and if sufficient brain cells are lost, there is an associated loss of specific function, or deterioration in the quality of an existent function. Neuronal loss is irreplaceable and the associated functional deficit would therefore be permanent. On the other hand, "loss due to injury" may imply another thing, i.e., loss of function. Thus, a patient with a post infectious meningoencephalitis[1] may have diffuse brain pathology involving the meninges, the subpial and subependymal, and peri- and paravascular gray and white matter. This pathology may be accompanied by loss of consciousness and a diffusely slow electroencephalogram (EEG). Within weeks, consciousness can return, the EEG frequencies become normal, and the patient can function as before. This sequence represents a transient loss of function by a large part of the brain due to reversible pathology. There need not, in such instances, be permanent evidence of functional or structural loss. In summary, brain damage may imply cellular loss and an anatomical change which, if large enough, will produce clinical symptoms. Depending upon the anatomical site of the structural change there may be focal or diffuse signs of malfunction which are permanent. On the other hand, brain damage may imply functional loss with an anatomical change which is reversible and thus a loss of function which is similarly reversible.

The basis of the discussion so far is the assumption that specific symptoms and signs are consistently associated with pathological change and malfunction at the cellular or ionic level of a particular level of the brain. This is so to a usable degree when one is involved with "classical" neurology. Thus, if a ten-year-old child suddenly has convulsions involving the right face, arm, and leg, and following recovery from the seizure has a permanent right hemiparesis, mild dysarthria, and persistent total awareness with no evidence of brain stem dysfunction, one knows that the patient has a lesion involving the left precentral gyrus and posterior frontal lobe or the white matter tracts emanating from these areas and going through the left internal capsule. Further investigation must be undertaken in order to determine the nature and extent of the lesion and whether or not it is due to focal inflammatory disease (abscess), vascular

---

[1] This and other technical terms are defined in the *Glossary of terms* which follows the text.

disease (occlusion of a branch of the middle cerebral artery by vasculitis, emboli, or a rupture of a vascular abnormality), tumor growing within the brain substance (glioma), or upon the surface of the brain (meningioma, chronic subdural effusion). The delineation of the lesion causing the signs of pathology will necessitate the use of a number of ancillary techniques including a lumbar puncture, electroencephalography, echoencephalography, contrast studies of the brain vascular system and/or brain ventricles, and radioisotope encephalography (Toole, 1969). Despite the use of all of these and the delineation specifically of abnormality of electrical discharge from the involved area, abnormal permeability of the vascular system in a focal area by radioisotope distribution, abnormalities of displacement of the midline structures by echoencephalography, and displacement of vessels by arteriography or of the ventricles by air contrast studies, the precise nature of the lesion may have yet to be determined by surgical exploration and microscopic examination of removed tissue.

Unfortunately, signs of neurological dysfunction associated with reading problems in children are either absent or when present are not examples of classical neurology. Instead, the signs are those of mild brain dysfunction. These signs are so difficult to classify that they have been the subject of several national task forces which have undertaken to define and describe their existence under the heading of the syndrome of minimal brain dysfunction (Clements, 1966, Task Force II Report, 1969). As presently understood the syndrome consists of children with near average, average, or above average intelligence who present learning and/or behavior disabilities associated with deviations of function of the central nervous system. These deviations are manifested by various combinations of impairment of perception, conceptualization, memory, language, motor coordination, and control of attention and impulse. The neurological signs of this syndrome[2] are highly variable and include some combination of the following: abnormalities of eye movement, head-eye dissociation, articulation, alternating supination and pronation of the extended arms and hands, serial apposition of fingers, heel-shin tapping, walking on heels and toes, hopping on one foot, and tandem walking. In addition, short attention span, easy distractability, and difficulties with visual-motor tasks can be found. These disabilities have several qualities; first, they are often classifiable as disabilities only when compared with a rough age dependent standard, i.e., the seven-year-old may perform like a four- or five-year-old; second, as the child grows

[2] These signs are the so-called "soft signs," a term the present authors find objectionable.

older, abilities to perform tests of integration of movement improve; third, there is no known brain pathology associated with these aberrations and none can be implied by correlation with knowledge of "classical" neurology; and finally, some children have behavior or learning disabilities without these signs and some children with poor performance in the motor tests have no clear learning or behavior abnormalities.

Although the syndrome has been carefully defined as that of minimal brain dysfunction (MBD) it is an habitual tendency to regard these children as having brain damage despite the lack of evidence for structural damage. This is done because of an uncritical tendency to equate poor psycho-motor function with a damaged brain. Another reason why this group of children has been labeled brain damaged stems from an early and widely accepted concept of Strauss and Lehtinen (1947) that children who behaved in a specific fashion and have a history of antecedent disease which could have produced brain damage had a syndrome of behavior due to brain damage. At the same time, similarly behaved children who do not have a history of antecedent disease which could have produced brain damage but behaved in a similar manner have also been labeled as children having the "brain damage syndrome." The problem boils down to the fact that children with minimal brain dysfunction syndrome have evidence by examination of abnormal neurophysiology, principally in tests of motor integration, impulse inhibition, maintenance of attention, and learning abilities. Whether the basis of this abnormal function lies in a delay of brain maturation, in an as yet undescribed tissue or chemical pathology, or some other factor, is not presently known.

Assuming that cases of classical neurological syndromes associated with the common types of reading problems in children cannot be found consistently, what kind of information should be sought in the study of children with reading problems which might define the potential for, or existence of, concomitant brain damage or neurological dysfunction? What is the value of each piece of information and what is its significance?

Specific Neurological Tests

The most frequently used pieces of evidence to determine the existence and possible cause of brain dysfunction are patient history, physical and neurological examination, electroencephalography, and neuropsychological tests. Contrast studies of brain vasculature and brain ventricles (arteriography, pneumo- or ventriculoencephalography) or isotope encephalography can show very specific evidence of abnormalities of structure and, by inference, brain damage, but these studies are used principally in the instance when the nature of the disease may be one which should be treated to prevent further damage or when repair of existing pathology is possible. Since this situation rarely exists in the type of patients under discussion these tests are rarely used. Since the use of neuropsychological tests is discussed elsewhere, the value of history, neurological examination, and electroencephalogram in the investigation of patients with a reading problem will be discussed here.

Historical data providing evidence of possible value in relating reading problems to evidence of brain dysfunction include items in the family, gestational, paranatal, developmental, and other past history. In using these data, one must be aware of their limitations. For example, a history of a well documented incidence of developmental dyslexia in a male uncle who went through college but with great effort and using as many auditory input crutches as possible (tape recorder, discussion with classmates) is one thing, but a history of an aunt who read poorly and dropped out of seventh grade at age 18 years, is another. A history of vaginal bleeding intermittently during the first trimester of pregnancy or of a full-term, four-day-old infant with a serum bilirubin of 18 mgs. percent which was untreated are both pieces of evidence which increase the likelihood of the infant in one instance having congenital encephalopathy at birth and in the other, developing bilirubin encephalopathy. However, neither guarantees the cause and effect relationship between the event and the finding later in life of reading difficulty or signs of minimal brain dysfunction. A history of delayed onset of respiration at birth, of treated bacterial meningitis at age three years, or of brief unconsciousness following a fall from a table at 20 months of age are all examples of statistics, which if coupled with another observation, may have possible relevance to the subject at hand. Minimal brain syndrome or abnormalities of reading may be related to such antecedent events, but when the past history lists items that have a statistical possibility but not an absolute chance of causing MBD or reading problems, the limitation of information must be stated.

The ability of one to deduce from the neurological examination evidence of structural brain damage or of neurological dysfunction without evidence of clear structural damage has been previously described. Several points need emphasis, however. First, since a classical neurological syndrome which implies damage to a particular area of the brain will be an uncommon finding in children with reading problems and since evidence of neurological dysfunction of varying severity and region of involvement will be common, it would be best in reporting these data to describe the tests used and to grade the level of dysfunction. The second point is that since the signs and symptoms of dysfunction change in severity with age, these data should be grouped according to age and the change in severity of the signs and symptoms from one time period to another for each individual should be documented.

The ability of the EEG to determine the existence of brain damage or neurological dysfunction is limited. Some of these limitations are unique to this test and some are similar to those of the neurological examination. It is rare that the brain wave test could be used alone to determine the existence of brain damage in a structural sense. If one assumes a certain wave form is an abnormal one and that this type of electrical discharge indicates disordered electrophysiology, hence functional damage, a further point to be determined is the significance of this finding for the patient. To put these problems in perspective, the subject will be reviewed briefly.

The electroencephalograph is an electrical amplifier attached to an oscilloscope which measures the frequency and voltage of oscillating potentials derived from pairs of electrodes placed on the surface of the scalp. The electrical potential originates from the electrical activity of the brain beneath. The normal frequencies and voltages vary with the age of the patient, the stage of consciousness, and the area of the brain being measured. Electrodes placed over the surface of the scalp cover only one third of the total brain surface and it is unclear how much of the total brain electrical activity is measured because of the spatial limitation. Furthermore, it is unclear how much of the electrical activity of the brain at great distances from the surface electrode is measured at the scalp. This situation probably accounts in part for the problem posed by patients who have gross pathology such as intracerebral hemorrhage, deeply situated tumors, or a discharging electrical focus in the amygdala, and a normal EEG (Glaser, 1963).

Interpretation of the EEG is difficult. Standards of normality vary according to the patient's age and state of consciousness. The detection of abnormalities may depend upon the recording technique, for certain abnormalities may be recognized only in monopolar not bipolar tracings, and in drowsiness and sleep and not when the patient is awake. Some wave forms are seen much more frequently in sleep than wakefulness. Because of the large number of variables to be considered in the interpretation of the EEG, the readings may be biased according to the experience and emphasis of the interpreter.

The significance of abnormalities in the EEG which are clearly established is not always easy to determine even in the light of clinical data. For example, a patient with grand mal epilepsy or brain tumor may have a normal EEG. On the other hand, a patient with 14 and 6/second positive spikes may have no symptoms, severe behavior problem, recurrent attacks of headache, vomiting and sleep, or a blatant seizure disorder (Gibbs & Gibbs, 1964). A negative spike discharge occurring in the EEG, especially when repeated, and from one locus, is thought to indicate an abnormally discharging area of the cortex. Such a negative spike focus can occur in a child who has suffered brain trauma in the past with resultant focal cortical damage. Historical and clinical evidence of brain injury is thus available. Under such circumstances, the focal discharge is presumed to derive from the area between the scar tissue, replacing damaged brain, and the surrounding normal brain. However, similar spike foci in the EEG can be seen in children who have seizure disorders and no history of antecedent disease leading to brain damage or concomitant neurological abnormality on examination. Furthermore, repeated EEG tracings over a period of years reveal in some of these children that the spike focus moves from one area of the brain to another and finally disappears altogether (Gibbs, Gillen, & Gibbs, 1954). The occurrence of shifting spike foci in children with seizure disorders is thus evidence that the cortically evoked abnormal discharge is not a sign of structural brain damage but rather evidence of abnormal cortical electrophysiology, the molecular basis of which is not yet known.

The difficulties encountered in relating EEG abnormalities to a dysfunction which includes reading problems are illustrated by one study of electroencephalography and learning disabilities (Hughes, 1968). Among 66 children who were studied, 62 percent had abnormal EEGs. The most frequent EEG abnormality was posterior slowing and 14 and 6/second positive spikes. An attempt was made to correlate the EEG findings with 22 psychological test functions. Relations between various combinations of EEG abnormality and psychological test abnormality were discovered only after grouping and regrouping the two sets of data. It was concluded that relationships between EEG and psychological function in a population of learning disorders could be obtained with multivariate techniques using the aid of a digital computer and that more than univariate analysis was necessary to obtain significant results. However, the significance of these results is quite puzzling and at present merely raises more questions than it answers. The complexity of translating this type of data into practical formulation is enormous. Such studies are clearly dependent, whatever one may think of their implications, upon precisely defined terms and there is no room for issue clouding ones such as "brain damage" to explain the results.

In conclusion, the EEG serves best in studies of children with reading disabilities if it is regarded as an instrument that can reflect a sign of disordered electrophysiology. The EEG sign must be clearly defined, its relation to other parameters must be described, and cognizance taken of the fact that this sign can change with time and is not in itself an indication of structural brain damage. In itself, the EEG can neither diagnose MBD syndrome, reading problems, learning disorders, nor brain damage.

The contribution of the neurologist and his techniques of history taking, patient examination, and the use of the electroencephalogram to studying the relation between brain damage and reading disability can be a significant one. It is based mainly upon insistence that the methodology, implications, and limitations of each of the techniques used be clearly known and described. It insists upon the recognition of the implications of the term "maturation" in studying a population of children. Constant insistence upon the need to apply these principles will certainly increase the volume of reliable conclusions derived from future studies attempting to relate reading problems to real brain damage or the more common neurological dysfunction.

REMEDIAL READING PROCEDURES FOR THE BRAIN DAMAGED

With the foregoing knowledge of what constitutes adequate neurological information, some of the specific studies which pertain to the question of brain damage and reading will now be examined.

In selecting articles for this presentation, the standard bibliographical references were used—*The Psychological Abstracts,* the *Readers Guide to Periodical Literature,* and the annual Summaries of Investigations Relating to Reading by Helen Robinson, *et al.* If the title of the article contained terms such as "dyslexia," "perceptually handicapped child," "brain injured child," "minimal cerebral dysfunction," or one of the multitudinous synonyms, the article was included for review. In all, 101 articles were chosen. Thirty-six of these were position or discussion papers on dyslexia, learning disabilities, and brain damage. There were 23 articles which were descriptive studies of dyslexic and/or brain-damaged children. That is, the studies were concerned with the psychological characteristics or the ability deficits of children who had been diagnosed as dyslexic or brain-damaged. The actual number of articles appearing in the foregoing categories during the 1960's was much larger but many were eliminated from consideration because they were primarily tangential to the purposes of this paper. Forty-two articles pertained to educational and remedial methods for the brain-damaged child and of these 42, 33 described teaching procedures but gave no evidence of their merit. Only nine, (representing seven studies) were honest efforts at experimental investigation of the efficacy of a particular method or methods of instruction.

Research Articles

These seven studies were selected for review, and criticisms have been limited to descriptions of the sample employed and the quality of the neurological criterion information. Some may view this as a rather restricted task. Many of the studies described could also be criticized and, perhaps more severely, for inadequate statistical analysis, the lack of an appropriate control group, or the failure to employ randomization. The aspect of the neurological criterion information was taken as a focus because many researchers in reading lack training in the neurological sciences and are unaware of the merits and limitations of diagnostic neurological information. They do not know what constitutes acceptable evidence to neurologists. In addition, even if the study were otherwise adequately designed and analyzed, failure to provide satisfactory criterion information would restrict the generalizations which could be drawn. Indeed, it is of questionable benefit to know that teaching method A is more effective for group Y, while teaching method B is more effective for Group Z, if one cannot describe how Y and Z differ. Finally, if one accepts the truism that the purpose of scientific experimentation in education is to generalize to the "not here" and the "not now," there is a need to scrutinize the factual basis for such generalizations by critically examining, from a neurological point of view, the investigations on brain damage and reading in order to determine just who was studied.

A major study and one of the more conscientious attempts to investigate specific teaching procedures was reported by Cruickshank, Bentzen, Ratzeburg, and Tannhauser (1961). They listed the psychological characteristics of the brain-injured child as distractibility, motor dysinhibition, dissociation, disturbance of figure ground, perseveration, and poor self concept and body image. Their sample consisted of forty subjects divided into two diagnostic groups: (1) those clinically diagnosed as having neurological and medical evidence of brain damage, and (2) those with behavior patterns typical of the brain-damaged group, but no evidence of brain damage on medical examination or history. For each subject, the authors listed the results of the clinical neurological examination. They also presented perinatal data. Unfortunately, the authors did not indicate the specific criteria for brain dysfunction but they did state which of the subjects were diagnosed as having neurological deficits, and the careful reader, by scrutinizing the results of the clinical neurological examination, can form an independent opinion as to whether the information was adequate. In the experiment, the authors had two experimental groups and two control groups, and each experimental and each control group contained an equal number of brain-damaged and non-brain-damaged subjects. The authors did not report the results according to brain damage vs. non-brain damage so there is no way to judge the efficacy of their procedures for brain-damaged children. However, the authors are to be complimented on the care with which they presented neurological criterion information. One may not agree with the adequacy of the information, but the data are sufficient so that one has a basis for disagreement.

Talmadge, Davids, and Laufer (1963) studied experimental methods for teaching emotionally disturbed, brain-damaged retarded readers. They studied a group with reading impairment due to central nervous system dysfunction, subcortical or cortical, which interfered with the ability to retain and reproduce visual, auditory, or motor cues as well as inducing behavior syndromes of hyperactivity, distractibility, perseveration, and a lack of abstraction and generalization. From 42 children, they selected 24 who were found to be at least two years retarded in reading on the California Achievement Test. These 24 were tested for brain damage by a neuropsychiatrist who used the following methods: (1) case history, (2) neurological examination, (3) EEG, and (4) photometrazol tests. Eight of the subjects were found to have cortical dysfunction, six were questionable, and ten showed no evidence of cortical dysfunction. This study had the advantage of specifying the procedure used to determine brain damage but it is limited in that specific neurologic findings were not presented and the subclassifications were not given. For example, in how many subjects was there positive evidence from all four diagnostic procedures? Or, if positive evidence was obtained by one procedure, were the other procedures employed? It is not clear whether the authors were using the terms "dysfunction" and "damage" interchangeably. The answers to questions such as these have the potential for changing rather nebulous classifications to well-documented neurological impairment which might lead to some understanding of brain-behavior relationships.

Miller (1964) reported on an attempt to teach an emotionally disturbed brain-injured child. Using a single case has its limitations. Although generalizing from an n of 1 is dangerous, that is not the main weakness of this study. In fact, much might be learned from a single patient where there is an accurate description of teaching procedures and good documentation of the brain injury which would include type and site of lesion, age of onset, premorbid history if possible, together with neurological information used in making the diagnosis. In this study, however, the patient was described as chronological age eight, having normal appearance with a history of early illness with a high fever. (The degree and length of time the fever lasted were not specified.) The patient had an I.Q. of 80 (tests not specified) with the verbal I.Q. much lower than the performance I.Q. The patient had a poor attention span and poor concentration. There appeared to be diffuse organic impairment. Behavioral symptoms included disorganized and impulsive behavior, drooling, and poor directional orientation. (The name of the test for directional orientation was not given.) The foregoing description was followed by the unusual statement that the EEG and neurological examination were inconclusive but indicated brain damage. No further details were given. The limitation of this study is that the behavioral symptoms cannot be taken as synonymous with brain damage. The fact that the verbal I.Q. was lower than the preformance I.Q. is irrelevant as far as providing diagnostic information about the brain. If the EEG and neurological examination were indeed inconclusive, it is questionable whether they indicated brain damage. In other words, on the basis of the descriptive information listed for this case, the reader cannot determine whether brain damage was present. It is not only impossible to generalize to other children, it is almost impossible to know what the particular characteristics of this child were.

Hagin, Silver, and Hersh (1965), Silver, Hagin, and Hersh (1967), and Silver and Hagin (1967) reported a long term experiment on the treatment of children with specific reading disabilities. Subjects were forty boys divided into two groups with each boy paired in terms of chronological age, intelligence quotient, psychiatric diagnosis, and neurological status. The neurological status was determined from the classical neurological examination plus right-left discrimination, a measure of handedness, eyedness, footedness, and an extension test. These studies represent a well organized attempt to evaluate specific teaching procedures, i.e., stimulation of deficit perceptual areas; however, too little information is given concerning the findings on the neurological examination. One is unable to determine the relation of neurological impairment to improvement in reading, albeit this was not the author's purpose in doing the study.

Hewett, Mayhew, and Rabb (1967) attempted to develop a basic sight vocabulary in neurologically impaired, mentally retarded, and severely emotionally disturbed children. There were a total of 26 subjects, eight of whom were neurologically impaired. The neurological impairment was based on a history of convulsions, perceptual-motor difficulties, and cerebral palsy. A technical point in this study which is frequently overlooked by non-neurological specialists is that convulsions or a seizure disorder alone is not necessarily diagnostic of brain damage, even in the presence of abnormal EEG tracings. It is true that many types of damage to the brain will result in seizures, focal or generalized, but the mere presence of seizures cannot be used to justify a diagnosis of brain damage. A seizure may result from an electrical disturbance where there is no evidence of damage. Indeed, as a consequence of a severe febrile condition, an otherwise normal patient may have a convulsion. What needs to be specified in the study of brain damage is a condition which would result in the seizure.

Willson (1968) reported on the effectiveness of three clinical techniques applied to children for whom the most probable cause of reading retardation had been determined. Three groups of male dyslexics consisting of 6, 5, and 6 subjects respectively, were studied, one group of which included the dyslexics with evidence of neurological disorders. No data were presented on how the neurological disorders were identified.

Weiner (1969) reported on the effectiveness of resource rooms for children with specific learning disabilities. There were 72 subjects screened on the Wechsler Intelligence Scale for Children, the Bender-Gestalt, Draw-A-Person, Vineland, a neurological, and a psychiatric examination. These subjects displayed classic symptoms of neurologic impairment: hyperactivity, dissociation, figure background reversals, distractibility, perseveration, and behavioral disorders. All were in the I.Q. range of 90–130, chronological age 7–12, grade in school 1–6. No other information concerning the nature of the group was reported. In spite of the fact that a neurological examination was given, how the findings were used was not explained. The diagnosis of neurological impairment was apparently based on behavioral symptoms and, as was stated previously, in classical neurology there is no known pathology which results only in such a syndrome. A suspected limitation with respect to inferring dysfunction at the level of the cerebral hemispheres can be found in the reported I.Q. range of 90–130. It is very difficult to compose a group of brain-damaged children where the mean I.Q. will fall well into the average range for the general population. One of the results of damage, that is, actual tissue destruction at the level of the cerebral hemispheres, is a general lowering of intellectual ability (Reed & Reed, 1967; Reed & Fitzhugh, 1966; Reed, Reitan, & Kløve, 1965). Weiner did not actually state that he was studying brain-damaged children; rather, his concern was children who had specific learning disabilities. Nevertheless, from his description of the sample, one could easily infer that he was interested in children with cortical involvement.

These seven studies represent experimental efforts that were made to investigate the relation of brain damage to reading. Another series of reports did not deal directly with children who were brain damaged; nevertheless, this series does have implication for those interested in modifying instructional procedure as a consequence of neurological findings. Certain books have appeared describing procedures which may be used for teaching brain-injured children and these procedures represent either the wisdom of experts or the accumulated folklore of history, depending upon one's point of view.

Theories and Opinions

Delacato (1966) summarized his theory of neurological organization as it pertained to reading and presented a series of studies which reported on the efficacy of his training methods. Glass and Robbins (1967) reviewed these studies with respect to meeting the criteria of sound experimentation. The training procedures may or may not be effective but in view of present knowledge, the development of the child from a neurological point of view does not provide justification for Delacato's methods. No known neurological evidence supports either (1) Delacato's stages of neurological organization or (2) use of his procedures as pedagogical devices for the improvement of reading.

Certain other writers (Ebersole, Kephart, & Ebersole, 1968; Kephart, 1966; Orton, 1966) employ a vocabulary which smacks of neurological sophistication but which, in fact, might be quite misleading with respect to understanding how the condition of the brain may be related to reading or how teaching procedures may be differentially employed with brain-damaged youngsters. Orton, for example, theorized that certain reading disabilities were due to physiological variation related to the establishment of a normal unilateral dominance in the visual language area of the brain. There is no scientific evidence for such a theory. It further implies that there is agreement that areas of the brain can be pinpointed and their functions specified. Such is not the case. Kephart (1966, pp. 171–80), emphasizing the concepts of space-time structures and the perceptual-motor match, described three major principles which must be followed in teaching brain-injured children. These principles include (1) developmental teaching from motor to perceptual to conceptual levels; (2) emphasis on the development of generalizations at all levels; and (3) establishment of veridicality in the already existing body of the child's information, e.g., it ". . . is desirable to use the strongest area of activity as the basis for establishing veridicality" (Kephart, p. 177.) Such statements with their esoteric vocabulary imply more knowledge than actually exists. Like Spanish doubloons and pieces of eight, the scientific basis for such remarks is difficult to locate. Indeed, no studies have been undertaken where the concepts were even put to a test. These and other writers do describe procedures which may prove to be effective for an individual child. However, the effectiveness of the method may be quite separate from what the authors theorize as the justification for it. Above all, there is no empirical basis for recommending certain pedagogical procedures over other ones for use with brain-injured children as opposed to non-brain injured children who also may have a learning disability.

Cruickshank (1966) summarized and edited a book entitled *The Teacher of Brain-Injured Children: A Discussion of the Bases* for *Competency* whose scope went far beyond the teaching of reading alone. However, the experimental evidence for many of the expressed points of view is almost nonexistent. Although the contributions of this volume may represent expert opinion and may represent effective programs of educational management, in general, the procedures are not grounded in sound experimental evidence. It is difficult to see, and perhaps unrealistic to try to see, how these methods and procedures represent unique programs for the brain-damaged child.

SUMMARY AND RECOMMENDATIONS

To change position from that of destructive critics to constructive critics, the following remarks are offered. Principals, curriculum supervisors, and teachers concerned with the education of brain-injured children, rather than proceeding on mere faith, should be quite critical of procedures which involve major reorganization of existing facilities, such as the restructuring of physical space, the dislocation of the individual child, or the purchase of large, space-occupying training materials. The recommendations for teaching brain-injured children offered in this paper are only recommendations and little evidence exists for their support. If a child with a reading problem has suffered brain damage, and this damage has resulted in a neurological condition which is chronic and static in course, there is little, if any, evidence to suggest that the teaching procedures for such a child should differ materially from those used for another child with a reading problem of similar extent and degree but without brain damage. Perhaps it is better to concentrate on developing aptitudes for reading rather than using procedures which essentially duplicate the teaching methods employed in the classroom and by which the child has already experienced failure. This is a question quite apart from the presence or absence of chronic cerebral dysfunction.

From the standpoint of research, it may well be that the classroom is not the appropriate laboratory or forum for experimentation or for clarification and elucidation of brain-behavior relationships. If significant advances are to be made in teaching procedures for the brain-injured child, if programs are to be effectively planned to meet individual differences, and if such programs are to be evaluated precisely, then during the next ten years more definitive experiments will have to be done than were performed during the decade of 1960 to 1970. An educational climate which produces so many recommendations and which leads so many to engage in behaviors for which there is little experimental evidence is indeed worthy of sociological investigation. Good experiments on instructional procedures are extremely hard to design. Unravelling the effect of differential methods of instruction and relating these effects to the type and site of lesion may not in fact be possible because of the moral restrictions imposed in experiments with human beings and because of the difficulties in studying any chronic disease of long duration. However, no progress can be made unless there is acute awareness of the necessity to provide adequate criterion information on the group studied.

One of the purposes stated at the start of this paper was to examine the effectiveness of methods used to teach reading to brain-injured children. This purpose was not achieved because of (1) the few number of experiments directed toward the problem, and (2) the inadequacy of the neurological information used to document brain damage. To determine whether children with organic cerebral neurological impairment, static in course, require or will benefit from specially adapted teaching procedures, carefully designed experiments will have to be performed. Brain damage should be the independent variable and rate of progress or achievement level should be the dependent variable. Brain-damaged subjects will have to be studied along with non-brain-damaged subjects as controls.

The following recommendations are given:

1. The diagnosis of brain damage ought to be limited to those cases where there is strong reason to believe that tissue change has occurred. In any event, the detailed basis for group composition must be specified.
2. If the findings are based on the clinical neurological examination, the exact criteria specifying the abnormality should be stated. If more than one finding is present, the number and percent of the children showing each pathological sign should be specified.
3. When ancillary tests are used, the kind and type of test should be clearly stated; thus, if contrast studies were employed, the number of children for whom this procedure was used and the details of the contrast studies should be given. If EEG was done, all details of the technique must be reported. If the information results from neurosurgical findings, the exact findings should be listed.
4. If groups heterogeneous with respect to brain damage are studied, the type of each neurological condition should be identified, and the

number of children having this condition be specified. For example, in a group of ten children, four might have a documented history of head trauma, three might have suffered from an inflammatory disease, and three suffered from acute infantile hemiplegia. The age when the event occurred is necessary.

5. Anamnestic information is weak, but if it must be used, the specific criteria for acceptance or rejection should be delineated. It is not enough to say there was prolonged labor; in addition, the time interval should be given. Reporting only a history of high fever is useless. If hospital charts are used for information it should be recognized that they are highly unreliable and a careful evaluation and reading of the chart must be done.

6. For the purpose of research, results from psychological tests cannot be accepted as evidence for brain damage in the present state of knowledge. The effects of brain lesions on psychological testing can vary with type and size of lesion, chronicity and acuteness, age of onset, and a host of other variables too numerous to outline here. Furthermore, if a neurologist makes use of psychological test findings in the neurological examination, this fact should be specified. It is permissible to study the relation of teaching procedures to distortion of Bender-Gestalt drawings. To report distortions in Bender-Gestalt drawings as evidence for brain damage is naive and reveals a lack of appreciation for the complexities of obtaining neurological criterion information.

7. The selection of appropriate control subjects is an extremely complicated but an extremely crucial matter in a well designed study. There are many specialized diagnostic procedures which the physician may not employ to rule out the presence of brain damage. Theoretically, it is desirable to use the same tests to rule out brain damage that are used to determine brain damage. In practice, this cannot be done. When control subjects are used, careful histories should be taken and perhaps the clinical neurological examination can be given. If there is no reason to suspect cerebral dysfunction either from the history or from the clinical examination, the subjects can be legitimately included as controls. However, it should be remembered that "absence of evidence is not evidence for absence."[3]

The foregoing recommendations are somewhat more strict than those advocated by the task force. Following them may result in the advancement of knowledge. To carry out the foregoing recommendations, the

[3] A comment made by Hans-Lukas Teuber, Ph.D., at a conference on The Late Effects of Head Injury, Washington, D.C., March, 1969.

scientific investigator in reading will require the active cooperation of someone trained in the neurological sciences. The neurologist, the neurosurgeon, or the neuropathologist is the handmaiden who must provide the information and data concerning the condition of the brain and, of equal importance, give the limitations of such data. The rigorous criterion information provided by well executed contrast studies is no better than the man who interprets the roentgenogram. Knowledge of brain damage and reading will advance in proportion to the care exercised in specifying the criterion. A problem may well confront the investigator who does not have available the resources of a neurological laboratory, but who sincerely wishes to investigate or experiment on the effectiveness of teaching methods for brain-damaged children. There is one recommendation. Don't.

Glossary of Terms

Amygdala: A localized group of neurones forming a structure within the brain, located at the tail of the caudate nucleus.

Anamnestic information: Information which is obtained by case history and is dependent upon memory.

Dysarthria: A disturbance of speech which may be due to abnormal brain function.

Echoencephalography: A diagnostic procedure utilizing sound waves, as in sonar, which when projected through the skull harmlessly localizes anatomic structures of the brain. It is used to locate lesions in the brain.

Encephalopathy: Any disease of the brain.

Glia: The supportive or connective tissue of the central nervous system, which is non-neuronal.

Gyrus: A convolution of the brain.

Hemiparesis: A partial paralysis on one side of the body due to a disease of the central nervous system.

Infantile hemiplegia: A term used to describe profound motor dysfunction on one side of the body usually occurring during the first three years of life. It is symptomatic of a wide variety of pathological states of the brain.

Internal capsule: An important part of the white matter of the brain composed of axons derived from neurones over a large part of the cerebral cortex. It connects these neurones with others in the cerebellum, brain stem, and spinal cord.

Lumbar puncture: A puncture into the spinal subarachnoid space for the purpose of obtaining specimen of cerebrospinal fluid.

Meninges: Two membranes (pia and arachnoid) which cover the brain and spinal cord.

Meningoencephalitis: An inflammatory disease concomitantly involving the meninges and the brain.

Neurones: The basic cellular unit of the nervous system, i.e., the nerve cell with its processes, collaterals, and terminations.

Perivascular: In the subarachnoid space surrounding the blood vessels.

Paravascular: Surrounding the blood vessels outside the subarachnoid space, in the brain substance.

Photometrazol tests: Tests for susceptibility to abnormal electrical discharge from the brain induced by stroboscope stimulation of the retina while the patient is under medication with metrazol.

Roentgenogram: The developed x-ray film.

Serum bilirubin level: The concentration in the serum of bilirubin, a substance derived from the breakdown of red blood cells by the reticulo-endothelial system, and transported as a soluble salt in blood serum to the liver, from which it is excreted.

Subependymal: The area beneath the ependyma, a thin membrane lining the ventricles of the brain.

Subpial: The area beneath the pia, a thin membrane immediately covering the brain and spinal cord.

References

Birch, H. G. (Ed.) *Brain damage in children: the biological and social aspects.* Baltimore: Williams and Wilkins Co., 1964.

Clements, S. D. Minimal brain dysfunction in children. *NINDB Monograph No. 3.* Washington, D. C.: U.S. Dept. of Health, Education, and Welfare, 1966.

Committee on Medical and Health Related Sciences, Minimal Brain Dysfunction, Task Force II. *Unpublished report.* NINDB, Washington, D. C., U. S. Dept. of Health, Education, and Welfare, Public Health Service, July, 1969.

Cruickshank, W. M. (Ed.) *The teacher of brain-injured children: a discussion for the bases of competency.* Syracuse: Syracuse University Press, 1966.

Cruickshank, W. M., Bentzen, F. A., Ratzeburg, F. H., & Tannhauser, M. T. *A teaching method for brain-injured and hyperactive children.* Syracuse: Syracuse University Press, 1961.

Delacato, C. *Neurological organization and reading.* Springfield: Chas. C. Thomas, 1966.

Ebersole, M., Kephart, N. C., & Ebersole, J. B. *Steps to achievement for the slow learner.* Columbus: Chas. E. Merrill, 1968.

Gibbs, E. L., Gillen, H. W., & Gibbs, F. A. Disappearance and migration of epilectic foci in children. (Rev.) *American Journal of Diseases in Children*, 1954, 88, 596.

Gibbs, F. A., & Gibbs, E. L. Neurological and psychiatric disorders. In *Atlas of electroencephalography, Vol. III.* Reading: Addison-Wesley Publications, 1964. P. 136.

Glaser, C. H. The normal EEG and its reactivity. In C. H. Glaser (Ed.), *EEG and behavior.* New York: Basic Books, 1963. Pp. 3–23.

Glass, V., & Robbins, M. P. A critique of experiments on the role of neurological organization in reading performance. *Reading Research Quarterly*, 1967, 3, 5–52.

Hagin, R. A., Silver, A. A., & Hersh, M. F. Specific reading disability: teaching by stimulation of deficit perceptual areas. In J. A. Figurel (Ed.), Reading and inquiry. *Proceedings of the International Reading Association*, 1965, 10, 368–70.

Hewett, F. M., Mayhew, D., & Rabb, E. An experimental reading program for neurologically impaired, mentally retarded, and severely emotionally disturbed children. *American Journal of Orthopsychiatry*, 1967, 37, 35–48.

Hughes, J. R. Electroencephalography and learning. In H. R. Myklebust (Ed.), *Progress in learning disabilities. Vol. 1.* New York: Grune and Stratton, 1968.

Kephart, N. C. The needs of teachers for specialized information on perception. In W. Cruickshank (Ed.), *The teacher of brain-injured children.* Syracuse: Syracuse University Press, 1966. Pp. 169–80.

Miller, N. Teaching an emotionally disturbed, brain-injured child. *Reading Teacher*, 1964, 17, 460–65.

Orton, J. L. The Orton-Gillingham approach. In J. Money (Ed.), *The disabled reader.* Baltimore: Johns Hopkins Press, 1966. Pp. 119–46.

Reed, H. B. C., & Fitzhugh, K. B. Patterns of deficits in relation to severity of cerebral dysfunction in children and adults. *Journal of Consulting Psychology*, 1966, 30, 98–102.

Reed, H. B. C., Reitan, R. M., & Klove, H. The influence of cerebral lesions on psychological test performances of older children. *Journal of Consulting Psychology*, 1965, 29, 247–51.

Reed, J., & Reed, H. B. C., Jr. Concept formation ability and non-verbal abstract thinking among older children with chronic cerebral dysfunction. *Journal of Special Education*, 1967, 1, 157–61.

Silver, A., Hagin, R. A., & Hersh, M. F. Reading disability: teaching through stimulation of deficit perceptual areas. *American Journal of Orthopsychiatry*, 1967, 37, 744–52.

Silver, A., & Hagin, R. A. Specific reading disability: an approach to diagnosis and treatment. *Journal of Special Education*, 1967, 1, 109–18.

Strauss, A. A., & Lehtinen, L. E. *Psychopathology and education of the brain-injured child.* New York: Grune and Stratton, 1947.

Talmadge, M., Davids, A., & Laufer, M. W. A study of experimental methods for teaching emotionally disturbed, brain-damaged, retarded readers. *Journal of Educational Research,* 1963, *56,* 311–16.

Toole, J. F. (Ed.) *Special techniques for neurological diagnosis. Contemporary Neurology Series.* Philadelphia: F. A. Davis, 1969.

Weiner, L. H. An investigation of the effectiveness of resource rooms for children with specific learning disabilities. *Journal of Learning Disabilities,* 1969, *2,* 223–29.

Willson, M. F. Clinical teaching and dyslexia. *Reading Teacher,* 1968, *21,* 730–33.

Part III

Assessment for Educational Purposes

In the schools, children are evaluated primarily for three reasons: to classify the learner, to justify placement, and to assist in planning an educational program for the pupil. When *classifying* youngsters, the attempt is made to determine whether a child is mentally retarded, brain injured, emotionally disturbed, or whatever. Traditionally, this goal of assessment has been met by the employment, in school systems, of nonteaching professional examiners who frequently carry titles such as psychologist, psychometrist, or guidance counselor. Often this type of testing is engaged in by school personnel to determine the prevalence of certain types of exceptionalities, to assist in the planning of special services, and/or to determine whether the child needs additional help such as medical attention or psychiatric care.

A second purpose of the assessment of children is to initiate or justify the administrative *placement* of children. Federal, state, and local subsidies are available for exceptional children if it can be evidenced that these children have been "appropriately" placed in special schools, special classes, or resource rooms. Justification for the placement of children in such programs is almost invariably based on the performance of the children on tests of intelligence, personality, achievement, and the like.

A final purpose of evaluation is to assist the classroom teacher in *planning* an appropriate *instructional program* for a child. Little attention is paid to the question of what "type" the child represents—rather, the emphasis is on a specific delineation of what the child knows or does not know, and/or what he can or cannot do. For example, the desired goal of this type of assessment is not a grade equivalent or a percentile score in a basic school subject, but is, for example, a precise profile or inventory of a child's reading skills, such as the following: Does he know the vowel sounds? The consonants? Consonant blends? Digraphs? Diphthongs? Which ones and how well? Can he use the sounds he knows in attacking new words?

To take another example, an IQ is considered to be of limited value for classroom instruction. Apart from indicating a general level and rate of performance, the IQ sheds no light as to what skills, abilities, or content needs to be taught. Nor does it indicate readily the state of a child's information processing system. For example, can the child process visual information? Auditory information? If auditory processing is apparently defective, what kinds of auding problems does the child have—sound discrimination, blending, acuity, word comprehension? Can he retain such information? Can he integrate newly acquired information with material that was learned in a prior situation?

Clearly, a child's educational success depends in part on all three types of assessment. We feel that in the past, assessment for instruction—the most directly and educationally relevant assessment—has been largely ignored. For this reason, we express a frank interest in promoting the more widespread and intelligent employment of assessment for instruction. This bias on our part is expressed in Hammill's article "Evaluation for Instructional Purposes," which heads up our series of articles on assessment. Hammill delineates more precisely, and in a somewhat different manner, some of the points that have been made here.

The remaining papers emphasize the utility of both formal and informal assessment procedures. Frostig's article describes the formal testing program utilized by the Frostig Center of Educational Therapy.

Four standardized tests, described in the article, serve as the basis for assessing children with learning disabilities at this center.

The role of the teacher in assessing children for instruction is described by Johnson. She delineates an analysis procedure by which teachers are able to ascertain the extent to which students are able to master given subaspects of a task, such as responding in the appropriate sensory modality. She goes on to point out the natural relationship of this type of assessment to a program of remediation.

McGrady states that diagnosis implies treatment or remediation, but laments the fact that many diagnoses are filed in bureau drawers and never affect the child's education in any manner. To ameliorate this diagnosis-remediation gap, McGrady makes several suggestions for the better preparation of teachers and psychologists.

A close relationship between assessment and remediation is implicit in the behavioral approach described by Lovitt. In this approach, assessment is not a once-and-for-all task, but is an ongoing process that constantly modulates and modifies the instructional program of the child. Performance is gauged against the child's earlier baseline behavior rather than against standardized norms. The major assessment technique is direct observation of behaviors such as reading, computation, or listening and speaking.

Smith's article serves the dual purposes of systematically ordering in a hierarchical manner the various types of assessment procedures that can be engaged in by the classroom teacher, and in providing guidelines to teacher-training programs concerning the types of evaluative activities in which teachers should be trained.

The systematic observation of reading behaviors is the topic of the article by Johnson and Kress. They state that the purposes of such observation are the appraisal of reading level, determination of specific strengths and weaknesses, and the evaluation of progress. In addition, they go on to delineate the criteria by which the various reading levels are established, the materials to be used, and the procedures to be followed. Instructions for scoring and recording are also included. A thorough and sensible discussion relating to the prediction of reading failure is provided by Adelman and Feshbach, who suggest that comprehensive assessment must go beyond the measurement of perceptual and linguistic abilities by probing socioemotional and environmental factors as well.

Many observers believe that most reading problems (and other achievement problems) could be circumvented, if children having potential difficulty could be identified at very early stages of their school careers. Haring and Ridgway report an attempt to find predictors that will identify learning-disabled children at the kindergarten level. They conclude that teachers can be trained to play a key role in the identification of such children, indeed, that individual behavior analyses done by teachers may well be a more effective procedure than group testing. This conclusion parallels nicely the emphasis given to informal versus formal assessment in this section.

9. EVALUATING CHILDREN FOR INSTRUCTIONAL PURPOSES

DONALD D. HAMMILL

To ensure the most successful instruction of children with learning disabilities, the teacher must have considerable understanding of each pupil's psychoeducational strengths and weaknesses. No superficial overview of a child's performance will suffice. Knowledge of IQ, reading grade level, or neurological status, while interesting, does not provide enough information with which either to establish appropriate goals or to construct a reality-based training program for a specific child. Therefore, the implementation in the schools of an effective, educationally oriented evaluation program is of the utmost importance for a successful instructional experience for children with learning disorders.

THE TOTAL EVALUATION

All activities that contribute information or data to the teacher's knowledge of the child and his problem constitute the total evaluation process. It is this information that is synthesized and used to formulate an appropriate instructional intervention for a particular child. The ele-

---

SOURCE. Reprinted from *Academic Therapy*, Volume VI, No. 4, 1971. By permission of the author and the publisher.

ments of the total evaluation fall naturally into two divisions: the administration and interpretation of standardized tests (the formal evaluation) and the use of informal diagnostic techniques (the informal evaluation). While the teacher may administer an occasional test, he is more likely to depend upon the informal approaches to assessment, leaving the bulk of the formal testing to other school personnel.

The aims of the total evaluation are (1) to identify children who are likely to have trouble in school; (2) to refer children for medical or psychiatric attention when needed; (3) to isolate specific areas of difficulty, such as perceptive and motoric disabilities, language disabilities, academic deficiencies, and mild concomitant emotional behaviors; and (4) to probe in depth the parameters of these particular problems. Therefore, because of the breadth of the information needed, it is highly unlikely that a single individual will possess the necessary skills or time to manage the total evaluation. Instead, ideally, the total evaluation should be a joint venture to which the school psychologist, teacher, speech therapist, remedial-reading specialist, and auxiliary personnel, such as the physician, optometrist, social worker, etc., contribute their unique abilities. Unfortunately, in actual school practice, even where the team approach is used, the total evaluation rarely reflects an educationally relevant focus and often is accomplished for the sole purposes of labeling, placing, or referring youngsters who fail in school. While these are essential functions, in today's schools, they are nonetheless of extremely limited value to the teacher who must prepare a daily program for the child.

If the information that is acquired during the total evaluation process is ever to be translated into instructional action, the teacher must be recognized by the school as a primary contributor to, and interpreter of, the assessment results. It must be kept firmly in mind that where a particular child's educational problem is concerned, the teacher observes more of his learning behavior than anyone else. Therefore, it is reasonable for the teacher of learning-disabled children to participate in a meaningful way in the evaluation process. Where the major assessment effort does not contribute *directly* to better instruction for children, the total evaluation concept does not exist.

Let there be no mistake concerning this position: I do not maintain that teachers should administer IQ tests or other batteries, such as the *Wechsler Intelligence Scale for Children* (WISC),[1] the *Illinois Test of Psycholinguistic Abilities* (ITPA), or projective instruments—although this is not an unheard-of idea. I do suggest that teachers learn to incorporate the findings of such measures with the much more important data

[1] See References for sources of tests mentioned in this article.

obtained through their own critical, diagnostic teaching. I have reached the conclusion that the teacher of learning-disabled children must assume responsibility for a considerable portion of the total diagnostic effort; and, that it is unreasonable to expect the school psychologist to write an "educational prescription," which the teacher dutifully implements in the classroom. Few psychologists possess teaching experience in learning disabilities, nor do they have familiarity with the wide variety of potential intervention strategies, nor do they see the child long enough to identify with surety subtle aberration of educationally significant behavior—all of which are fundamental to the preparation of a viable "prescription."

If assessment results that are meaningful for school use are to evolve from the total evaluation, the teachers and others charged with the diagnostic function must recognize that instruction and evaluation are not separate worlds, but that they are inseparably meshed. Successful teaching, namely, teaching where the child learns, is, in itself, a reflection of a series of effective teacher assessments. This point of view is essential if the child is to be helped in a maximal fashion in the classroom.

THE FORMAL EVALUATION

The formal evaluation is that part of the total diagnostic process (1) that is characterized by the use of standardized tests, (2) that is administered by specially trained persons, (3) and that is usually made in settings other than the classroom. The information acquired is of a decidedly quantitative nature and tends to compare a given child's performance with national or regional normative data. The results, therefore, are often reported in terms of quotients, scaled scores, grade equivalents, or percentiles. In general, an attempt is made in the formal evaluation to assess many areas of mental function, including intelligence, language, academic achievement, speech, perceptual-motor skill, and social-emotional development. For this purpose, the following are examples of the most commonly used tests in the schools: intelligence— WISC, *Stanford-Binet Intelligence Scale* (revised), *Slosson Intelligence Test for Children and Adults;* language—ITPA, Mecham *Verbal Language Development Scale;* achievement—group achievement batteries, such as the *California Achievement Tests, Metropolitan Achievement Tests,* and *Stanford Achievement Tests,* as well as individual achievements tests, such as the *Wide-Range Achievement Test, Durrell-Sullivan Reading Capacity and Achievement Tests, Gates Reading Readiness Scales;* speech—tests of articulation, such as *The Templin-Darley Tests of Articulation;* perceptual-motor—the popular and ubiquitous Bender *Visual-Motor Gestalt Test, Marianne Frostig Developmental Test of Visual Perception, Wepman Auditory Discrimination Test,* Graham-Kendall *Memory for Designs Test,* or *Benton Visual Retention Test.*

In school practice, the psychologist usually collects the results of the tests, which he or others have administered, and integrates them into a report for teacher and parents. As you know, this report will vary widely in educational relevance. At best, the findings will (1) eliminate or confirm the presence of mental deficiency, (2) point out general areas and levels of failure in such subjects as reading, spelling, and arithmetic, (3) indicate possible areas of language deficit, (4) demonstrate modality strengths and weaknesses, (5) identify patterns of disruptive and undesirable behavior, (6) recommend areas for diagnostic teaching, and (7) request feedback from the teacher.

At worst, the formal evaluation is instructionally useless and will (1) demonstrate the obvious, namely, dwell at length on what is already vividly apparent to the teacher, (2) stress excessively etiological factors, such as brain dysfunction, which are of no value to the teacher, or (3) dwell at length on the interpretation of minimal and dubious evidence.

During my second year of teaching, I recall being extremely frustrated by a nine-year-old youngster who could not or would not read. In spite of the fact that he was apparently of normal intelligence, I had completely failed in my efforts to teach him even the fundamentals of the reading process. Naturally, he was referred for a formal evaluation. As the district, during those years, did not provide comprehensive psychoeducational services, the pupil was sent to a private diagnostic clinic in the community. Two months (and fifty dollars) later the report arrived. The contents can be summarized into two salient points: the pupil was diagnosed as (1) "dyslexic" and (2) "brain injured." As the original complaint specified reading as the problem and as the pupil was rather obviously a spastic hemiplegic, the report was useless.

Fortunately, most reports are of considerably more educational value. This is especially true when the reports are interpreted by the examiner or reinterpreted by the teacher into an education framework. However, no matter how exhaustive the formal testing of a child has been, the teacher will need additional information. This need arises from numerous factors, most of which are inherent in the formal-evaluation approach. Therefore, before the teacher can integrate the findings of diagnostic teaching with the results of formal assessment, he must be aware of the shortcomings of the latter.

There are several specific limitations of formal testing. The first limitation deals with the sparsity of in-depth information that can be derived from tests. The other limitations are concerned with problems of false positive and false negative diagnoses, which commonly result from formal evaluations. A false positive diagnosis occurs when the results of the evaluation report that the child evidences a particular problem when, in fact, he does not. Conversely, in the false negative cases, the child does, indeed, have a serious problem, which was not detected during the evaluation process.

Lack of Test Information

Standardized tests may be useful for indicating specific areas of deficit; unfortunately, they do not often provide the critical, detailed information upon which an educational strategy can be based for an individual child. For example, low performance on the Wepman test may suggest a sound-discrimination difficulty; however, the results do not specify the particular sounds in need of training. With regard to reading, there is no standardized test that yields the relevant kinds of information provided by the informal reading inventories. The use of these devices provides essential data regarding the child's independent reading level, his instructional level, his frustration level, and his level of listening comprehension. In addition, most inventories distinguish between word-recognition skill and reading comprehension ability, and they measure the child's oral and silent reading speed as well.

Intrasubject Variability

Children, especially children with learning disorders, vary markedly in day-to-day performance. This variability is reflected in their test scores and often results in an apparent inconsistency between testing-room and classroom behavior. A child with a measured IQ of 85 on Monday, can easily have a quotient of 100 or 70 when retested on Tuesday, where the discrepancy is caused by pupil attitude or temperament. What is thought to be an extremely disabling visual-motor deficit, as evidenced in an ITPA profile of one week, has vanished or is hardly detectable two weeks later. To be removed from class, led by the hand down the hall into an examination room, introduced to a stranger who is going to do something that is not quite understood, and then to be left alone, is indeed a strange and threatening experience for the child. If he reacts to the situation rather than to the tests, it is certainly understandable. Diagnostic teaching, over days or weeks, in the familiar classroom, permits the teacher to more fully fathom the learning-disabled child's actual performance level.

Not all of the variability in testing is associated with the subject. Examiners vary daily in their patience, temperament, and skill; and by no means can one assume that an examiner, even a highly trained examiner, is in all cases free from error. This point has recently been demonstrated by C. K. Miller, N. M. Chansky, and G. R. Gredler,[2] who gave a completed WISC protocol to thirty-two psychologists in training, all of whom had completed the course work in the administration and scoring of the WISC. These individuals scored the protocol in a most dissimilar fashion; the resultant Full Scale IQs ranged evenly from 76 to 93.

Overgeneralization of Findings

From time to time, one encounters children who fail, for example, the visual-motor items on a test and become "visual misperception" suspects. Yet, in their school work, little or no disability is noted in that modality; and, the teacher is surprised by the application of the label. This situation can occur when one generalizes the failure on one visual task to probable failure on all tasks in that channel. An example, in the assessment of auding, is the ITPA subtest of Auditory Reception. In this subtest, the child is asked questions that are graded in increasing difficulty, such as "Do dogs fly?" to which he responds "yes" or "no." In terms of the ITPA model, the task is Representational Level, Auditory Channel, and Receptive Process. There exist a score or more of similar but different tasks that are identical to Auditory Reception in level, process, and channel; for example, most tests of listening comprehension, which are frequently included in group measures such as the Metropolitan Readiness Tests (MRT). One cannot predict with confidence a particular child's performance on the MRT Listening subtest from his score in Auditory Reception; and, it is hazardous to diagnose a generalized auditory deficit on the basis of performance on any one test.

With this last point, all psychoeducational examiners would probably agree. Still, lists of remedial suggestions that are based upon low performance on a single test find their way into reports. Only last week, a case came to my attention where a "pronounced visual-motor problem" was diagnosed and a "remedial program geared to these perceptual-motor difficulties" was prescribed; all this on the basis of poor performance on the *Draw-A-Person* and the Bender Gestalt Test. Yet the same evaluation provided ample contradictory findings, which were not mentioned at all. For example, the WISC Verbal IQ was 99; the Performance IQ, which is comprised almost entirely of visuomotor items, was 103. The child actually had scale scores of 14 on Mazes, 10 on Coding,

---

[2] C. K. Miller, N. M. Chansky, and G. R. Gredler, "Rater Agreement on WISC Protocols," *Psychology in the Schools*, VII (1970), 190–193.

and 12 on Block Design. Does the child, in fact, have a visual-motor problem?

Low Test and Subtest Reliabilities

A third reason for false positives and negatives in the formal assessment of children emanates from the comparatively low reliabilities of many standardized tests. For example, Auditory Reception is reported in the ITPA manual, by J. N. Paraskevopoulos and S. A. Kirk (see references), to have a test-retest reliability coefficient of .63 when used with six-year-olds. Six of the twelve ITPA subtests have stability coefficients equal to or below that figure. In the manual of the *Marianne Frostig Developmental Test of Visual Perception,* it is recommended that individual training exercises be initiated on the basis of a child's performance on each of the five subtests. Yet the test-retest reliability coefficients of these subtests range from .33 to .83 at kindergarten and from .40 to .67 at the first-grade level. The statement could be made that most presently available, standardized "diagnostic" batteries lack the necessary reliabilities upon which to base effective educational interventions for *individual* children.

Other Limitations

Occasionally, even when the child's test performance does adequately reflect his ability, difficulties can occur in interpretation. For example, in converting raw scores into intelligence quotients on the *Peabody Picture Vocabulary Test,* a child with a chronological age (CA) of 5–5 who scored 49 has an IQ of 99, while a CA of 5–6 and an identical score of 49 will yield an IQ of 87—an IQ difference of 12 points. The teacher should recall that test scores have standard errors of measurement; subsequently, each score for a child cannot be interpreted as an absolute value. A score is nothing more than an estimate on the child's ability on a particular test. His "true" ability will most likely range above or below that figure. If scores are interpreted absolutely, the discrepancy between a child's performance on two tests may appear greater than it is in fact. This point is demonstrated in the 1961 ITPA manual (p. 102). The Visual and Auditory Decoding scores, if interpreted rigidly, suggest a one-year discrepancy between tests. If the standard errors of measurement are applied to the scores, the similarity between the two is graphically evident.

A final limitation concerning formal testing involves the questioning of the use of tests with groups of children who differ from the standardization population. In manuals, reports of item analyses, validity and reliability coefficients, and administration procedures are meticulously reported. But they are generally based upon the performance of "normal" or "representative" youngsters—the very children with whom we never use the tests. The ITPA normative sample was devoid of both bright and dull children. The Frostig test sample included no lower class or black children. Even where the sample reflects the general population, there is little evidence that the test will hold up when used with children who are called mentally retarded, hyperactive, perceptually handicapped, distractible, learning disabled, etc. Are the test reliabilities and validities affected when the measure is used with these youngsters? Generally, the answer is yes. For example, as the IQ of the sample declines, the validity and reliability coefficients are reduced correspondingly; but no mention of this is made in most test manuals. Subsequently, examiners continue to interpret subtests as if the standardization data reported in the manual were applicable—it often is not. When the WISC was factor analyzed using normal and mentally retarded children, different factor structures emerged.[3] This suggests that procedures for interpretation of subtest results may be different for different samples of children.

If these limitations are kept in mind, coupled with the understanding that diagnostic, informal procedures are the next step in the total evaluation process, the results of formal assessment can contribute to the educational effort. However, where the total evaluation is viewed as testing-room based, as most are in practice, there is little hope that any instructional good will come from the diagnostic effort. The examiner, in such a situation, has no defense against the making of erroneous or irrelevant evaluations and recommendations. Neither will a five- or ten-minute visit with the teacher and a cursory observation of the child in the classroom measurably improve the situation. The formal assessment is only part of the total educational evaluation, which must be considered as incomplete until diagnostic teaching procedures have probed in depth the findings of the formal assessment. It is only after the educational information that resulted from the formal evaluation has been checked out by the diagnostically oriented teacher in the classroom environment, and after feedback is provided to the other members of the diagnostic team, that the total evaluation of a child can be considered complete. Now begins the period of ongoing reevaluation in which the teacher will engage as long as the youngster receives services. Diagnostic teaching

[3] A. A. Baumeister and C. J. Bartlett, "A Comparison of the Factor Structure of Normals and Retardates on the WISC," *American Journal of Mental Deficiency*, LXVI (1962), 641–646; R. T. Osborne and M. H. Tillman, "Normal and Retardate WISC Performances," *American Journal of Mental Deficiency*, LXXII (1967), 257–261.

is one way to minimize the likelihood that the child will be misplaced or miseducated.

THE INFORMAL EVALUATION

The informal evaluation is that part of the total diagnostic process characterized (1) by the use of informal procedures, (2) administered by the educational diagnostician (usually a teacher), (3) in a continuing educational setting and (4) is frequently called "diagnostic teaching." The goals of this part of the total evaluation are to expand, probe, verify, and, if need be, discard the conclusions and recommendations of formal assessment. Optimally, the informal and formal aspects of assessment would occur simultaneously, making possible the continued modification of educational hypotheses about children. Mostly, the informal approach is employed after the formal evaluation is completed. This lessens the likelihood of interaction between the team members. In actual practice, diagnostic teaching, as a systematic ingredient of the total evaluation, is not undertaken at all in most of the schools. And the teachers who engage in such procedures do so for their own classroom benefit, not to improve the evaluation process.

The teacher of learning-disabled children who works in the schools must recognize that in most cases the educational evaluation will be left to him alone. He can learn from the school authorities which types of diagnostic tests or devices he can use without violation of administration policies; but for the most part, he will depend upon informal techniques to obtain the information that is vital for successful teaching. While these techniques can be used to verify the findings of formal assessment; they can also be substituted, if need be, for standardized test results.

It would be impossible to describe all of the possible informal techniques that can be used to assess a child's various abilities. Most of the recent books concerned with the learning disabilities of children provide the reader with a multitude of pertinent activities. Even these, however, will prove insufficient, for the diagnostic teacher will soon be confronted with a unique problem and a need to devise his own procedures.

The following informal procedures do not include every area that can be probed, but the description is detailed enough to provide some insight into the process of informal testing. These particular techniques are borrowed from the book, *Methods for Learning Disorders*.[4]

[4] P. Myers and D. Hammill, *Methods for Learning Disorders* (New York, N.Y.: John Wiley & Sons, Inc., 1969).

AUDITORY FUNCTIONS

The following procedures are primarily auditory in nature; although other functions may be tested simultaneously, they are of lesser importance in the child's performance.

1. Auditory decoding
   a. Recognizes environmental noises.
   b. Understands parts of speech—nouns, verbs, adjectives, prepositions, etc.
   c. Follows one, two, three, or four instructions.
   d. Recognizes names of colors.
   e. Understands a story read to him.
2. Auditory association
   a. Matches noisemakers by sound, e.g., two hours or two whistles.
   b. Speech-sound discrimination—words, nonsense syllables.
3. Auditory closure
   a. Recognizes incomplete words.
   b. Auditory blending of sounds to form words.
   c. Simple analogies.

VISUAL FUNCTIONS

As with the auditory functions, the procedures used to test visual competencies may overlap into other areas of language function, but the tasks are primarily visual in nature.

1. Visual decoding
   a. Recognizes objects and pictures.
   b. Recognizes a picture cut into two, three, or four pieces.
   c. Recognizes colors.
2. Visual association
   a. Matches colors, objects, pictures.
   b. Matches object with picture.
   c. Matches geometric forms—two- or three-dimensional forms or three-dimensional forms with pictures of forms.
3. Visual closure
   a. Recognizes incomplete pictures.
   b. Recognizes incomplete letters, numerals, or words.

TACTILE-KINESTHETIC FUNCTIONS

1. Recognizes by touch alone objects placed in either hand.
2. Matches sandpaper forms by touch.

3. Recognizes simple geometric forms, letters, words, etc., when they are drawn on the back of his hand or on his back.

VOCAL FUNCTIONS

1. Uses words, phrases, or sentences.
2. Uses adequate grammar—proper inflectional endings, tenses, etc.
3. Uses adequate sentence structure—words are not omitted, transposed, substituted.
4. Tells a story in logical sequence.
5. Mean sentence length appropriate for age.

MOTOR FUNCTIONS

1. Imitates examiner's actions.
2. Pantomimes everyday actions—combing hair, brushing teeth, batting a ball.
3. Copies geometric designs.
4. Draws human figures.
5. Writes his name, letters, numerals, words, sentences.

MEMORY FUNCTIONS

1. Repeats series of digits in, or not in, sequence.
2. Recalls a set of objects seen.
3. Recalls a set of pictures, letters, numerals, words.

SEQUENCING FUNCTIONS

1. Recalls a pattern of taps, pitches.
2. Recalls in sequence a series of objects, pictures, forms.
3. Recalls a series of unrelated words, a sentence, a series of related words.

The use of the techniques described above will enable the teacher to assess a child's ability to perform fundamental skills. Informal procedures are just as effective when applied to problems in basic school subjects such as reading, spelling, writing, and arithmetic. The range of information that can be provided by the use of informal reading inventories has already been mentioned; Marjorie Johnson and Roy Kress provide a comprehensive review of these useful instruments in a 1964 publication of The International Reading Association.[5] This work is strongly recommended for those teachers who are unfamiliar with the informal reading approaches.

S. H. Linn's chapter, "Spelling Problems: Diagnosis and Remediation," in *Building Spelling Skills in Dyslexic Children*, includes suggestions for delimiting spelling problems through careful scrutiny of the child's spelling lesson and work habits.[6] Diagnostically significant questions are posed, such as the following: Can the pupil recall the letter and sound symbols quickly, accurately, and produce them on paper correctly? Can he fuse the sound parts of words together into whole words? Can he remember what you have written on the board a few minutes after it is erased? Can he identify sounds?

To assess problems in writing, the book by Doris Johnson and Helmer Myklebust, *Learning Disabilities: Educational Principles and Practices*, is recommended to teachers.[7] Techniques are presented that enable the teacher to distinguish among dysgraphia, deficits in revisualization, and deficiencies in formulation and syntax. As the educational approach will differ with each of these writing problems, proper teacher assessment is fundamental to successful instruction.

An optimal evaluation procedure for use in the public schools has been described in this paper. This process is characterized by its heavy educational orientation, reliance upon informal assessment techniques, and recognition of the teacher as a partner in the diagnostic decision-making phases of the evaluation.

Of course, basic changes will have to be made in present school policies and personnel thinking before this program can be implemented. The school psychologist, who now bears the primary responsibility for the assessment process, will have to share that responsibility with teachers. In the process, he will also have to acquire a considerably better understanding of teachers' needs for, and expectations of, the school evaluation. The teacher, on the other hand, will have to learn the fundamentals of diagnostic teaching and perfect his new skills through experience; he must learn to be specific in expressing what he wants from the other team members when a child is referred for assessment. The school

[5] M. Johnson and R. Kress, "Individual Reading Inventories: Sociological and Psychological Factors in Reading," 21st Annual Reading Institute, Temple University, 1964.

[6] S. H. Linn, "Spelling Problems: Diagnosis and Remediation," *Building Spelling Skills in Dyslexic Children*, ed. John I. Arena (San Rafael, Calif.: Academic Therapy Publications, 1968).

[7] D. Johnson and H. Myklebust, *Learning Disabilities: Educational Principles and Practices* (New York, N.Y.: Grune & Stratton, Inc., 1967).

administration will have to alter existing policies and permit selected teachers to engage actively and openly in evaluative procedures and to establish new programs involving diagnostic classes, transition rooms, itinerant programs, and resource rooms, which lend themselves better to diagnostic education than do self-contained classes. And finally, teacher-education programs must begin to train teachers who can "field" problems as they arise; who feel comfortable in the management of auditory problems, visual deficits, behavioral disturbances, academic deficiencies, motor difficulties, and language inadequacies; and who, most of all, no longer view themselves as the "crippled" teacher, the "emotionally disturbed" teacher, or, the most semantically damaging of all, the "mentally retarded" teacher.

References

Bender, Lauretta. *Visual-Motor Gestalt Test*. Los Angeles, Calif.: Western Psychological Services, 1962.

Benton, A. L. *The Revised Visual Retention Test: Clinical and Experimental Applications*. New York, N.Y.: The Psychological Corp., 1963.

Dunn, L. M. *Peabody Picture Vocabulary Test*. Minneapolis, Minn.: American Guidance Service, 1959.

Durrell, D. D. and H. B. Sullivan. *Durrell-Sullivan Reading Capacity and Achievement Tests*. New York, N.Y.: Harcourt, Brace & World, Inc., 1944.

Frostig, Marianne, *et al. Marianne Frostig Developmental Test of Visual Perception*. Palo Alto, Calif.: Consulting Psychologists Press, Inc., 1964.

Gates, Arthur I. *Gates Reading Readiness Scales*. New York, N.Y.: Bureau of Publications, Teacher's College, Columbia University, 1958.

Graham, Frances K., and Barbara S. Kendall. *Memory for Designs Test*. Missoula, Montana: Psychological Test Specialists, 1946.

Hildreth, Gertrude H., Nellie L. Griffiths, and Mary E. McGauvran. *Metropolitan Readiness Tests*. New York, N.Y.: Harcourt, Brace & World, Inc., 1966.

Jastak, J. F., S. W. Bijou, and S. R. Jastak. *Wide-Range Achievement Test*. Wilmington, Del.: Guidance Associates, 1965.

Kelly, Truman L., *et al. Stanford Achievement Tests*. New York, N.Y.: Harcourt, Brace & World, Inc., 1964.

Kirk, Samuel A., James J. McCarthy, and Winifred Kirk. *Illinois Test of Psycholinguistic Abilities*. Urbana, Ill.: University of Illinois Press, 1968.

Mecham, M. J. *Verbal Language Development Scale*. Minneapolis, Minn.: American Guidance Service, 1959.

Metropolitan Achievement Tests. Tarrytown-on-Hudson, N.Y.: World Book Company, 1959.

Paraskevopoulos, J. N., and S. A. Kirk. *The Development and Psychometric Characteristics of the Illinois Test of Psycholinguistic Abilities.* Urbana, Ill.: University of Illinois Press, 1969.

Slosson, Richard L. *Slosson Intelligence Test for Children and Adults.* East Aurora, N.Y.: Slosson Educational Publications, 1963.

Templin, Mildred D., and F. L. Darley. *The Templin-Darley Tests of Articulation.* Iowa City, Iowa: University of Iowa Bureau of Research and Service, 1960.

Terman, E. Lewis, and Maud A. Merrill. *Stanford-Binet Intelligence Scale.* Boston, Mass.: Houghton Mifflin Company, 1962.

Tiegs, Ernest W., and Willis W. Clark. Monterey, Calif.: California Test Bureau, 1957.

Urban, William H. *Draw-a-Person.* Beverly Hills, Calif.: Western Psychological Services, 1963.

Wechsler, David I. *Wechsler Intelligence Scale for Children* (WISC). New York, N.Y.: Psychological Corporation, 1949.

Wepman, Joseph. *Wepman Auditory Discrimination Test.* Chicago, Ill.: Language Research Associates, 1958.

10. EDUCATIONAL PRINCIPLES FOR CHILDREN WITH LEARNING DISABILITIES

DORIS J. JOHNSON

Educational programing for children with learning disabilities depends on definition of the population and the individual disorders. Since there are many reasons for learning difficulties and school failures, the group must be defined. Because of the variety of symptoms manifested, it is necessary to analyze each child's learning patterns and problems. The homogeneity as well as the heterogeneity of the population must be considered before planning remedial programs. Without a definition and diagnostic study, there is little basis for placing children in special education programs. Moreover, the methods and procedures are apt to be selected randomly without a frame of reference or rationale.

Myklebust[1] has stated that the learning disability group is homogeneous in that it consists of children who are not primarily retarded, emotionally disturbed, sensorially impaired, culturally deprived, or grossly cerebral palsied, yet who are unable to learn and profit from the normal educational experiences. The group is heterogeneous in that the learning problems vary in both type and degree.

SOURCE. Reprinted from *Rehabilitation Literature*, 1967, **28**, 317–322. By permission of the author and publisher.

[1] Myklebust, Helmer R. Learning Disorders: Psychoneurological Disturbances in Childhood. *Rehab. Lit.* Dec., 1964. 25:12, 354–360.

Recognizing the complexity of the human brain as well as the various forms of verbal and nonverbal behavior that a child is expected to learn, it is evident that many types and combinations of problems can result from even a minor disturbance. Whereas some children have difficulty speaking, others have problems in reading, writing, or arithmetic. Others have only nonverbal problems. Some have difficulty with perceptual skills, others with memory. Therefore, none of the typical diagnostic categories such as aphasia, dyslexia, perceptual handicap, or hyperkinesis is sufficiently inclusive to denote the total group. As a result we are compelled to use the broad term *learning disability* but simultaneously to define the individual problems.

DIAGNOSIS AND EVALUATION

The definition and classification of a learning disability evolves from a comprehensive study of the child done by a team of many professional persons, including psychologists, neurologists, pediatricians, electroencephalographers, ophthalmologists, audiologists, specialists in communicative disorders, social workers, and educators. Information regarding sensory integrity, health, neurological integrity, intelligence, language, educational background and achievement, personality, motivation, and other aspects of behavior is basic to the diagnosis.

Such a study can rule out problems of auditory or visual acuity, mental deficiency, primary emotional disturbance, and motivational or other factors that might be a deterrent to learning. Since the psychoeducational dynamics vary according to the cause of an existing problem, every attempt is made to study the nature of the disability. Certain children who have more than one disorder must be considered multiply handicapped, and the educational plan modified accordingly.

In addition to the studies outlined above, an evaluation of the *ways* whereby a particular child learns also is significant. Our concern is with both *capacities* and *processes*. When planning remediation the teacher should be aware of a child's grade or age level in various language and academic skills, but she also must know *how* he deviates. Knowing only that a child performs at a second-grade level in arithmetic is inadequate information for outlining educational goals. Without consideration for processes, the methods tend to be vague or even inappropriate. The psychoeducational study includes a battery of language and achievement tests that yield grade or age levels, but it also includes studies of perception, memory, concept formation, nonverbal functions such as body image, spatial orientation, time orientation, body image, and social perception. Many processes and systems are studied.

In our work at the Institute for Language Disorders, Evanston, Ill., Myklebust has stressed the need for studies of intrasensory, intersensory, and integrative learning. We attempt to determine how a child learns through each sensory modality and how he integrates information he receives from two or more modalities. For instance, we investigate a child's ability to discriminate, interpret, and remember what he hears, sees, or touches. We also study his ability to associate what he hears with what he sees or feels. The purpose is to delineate the sensory channels through which learning is impaired and also investigate the level of the involvement, that is, whether the disability occurs primarily at the level of perception, imagery, symbolization, or conceptualization.

All of the findings are then correlated in order to describe the learning problems as specifically as possible. One cannot study academic achievement without relating the findings to intelligence, motivation, previous educational experiences, and impaired learning processes. Likewise, one cannot study isolated processes such as perception or memory without relating them to areas of underachievement or learning failure.

Evaluation of another aspect of behavior, the modalities for expression or output, should be included. Usually a disorder of perception, memory, or comprehension interferes with output, but certain types of deficits affect only the ability to learn the motor patterns for speaking, writing, or performing certain nonverbal acts, even though there is no paralysis. If the disability affects the oral mechanism, a child may comprehend language but be unable to communicate because he cannot form the motor patterns for speech. If the deficit occurs in visual-motor areas, he may be able to speak, read silently, and think clearly but be unable to copy, write, or carry out nonverbal functions such as tying shoes, brushing teeth, or manipulating utensils.

Although the psychologist is responsible for most of the intensive behavioral study, the teacher has a vital role on the diagnostic team as an observer and one who can gather information about a child's learning patterns. The teacher has unique opportunity and responsibility for observing the child while he is engaged in learning tasks; hence she must be prepared to collect data systematically and categorize, store, utilize, and evaluate the information. The goal is to sift through the data, look for patterns of relationship by noting a child's successes and failures, and then determine which "learning circuits" are intact and which are weak or inoperative.

TASK ANALYSIS

Because teachers need a means for gathering data and also because many are confronted with children who have had inadequate evaluations, we suggest a system of task analysis. By analyzing the nature of a task, considering the expected mode of response and the processes necessary to complete it, and then noting a child's performance, a teacher can learn a great deal about the learning disability and areas to be remedied. Furthermore, an emphasis on task analysis will shift the teacher's orientation from subject matter in the curriculum to processes.

As an example, note the information that can be obtained by inspecting spelling assignments and student performance. Most average children show little variation in spelling ability irrespective of the presentation. Those with learning disabilities, however, may show wide discrepancies in performance, depending upon the nature of the assignment and their particular disorder. An eight-year-old dyslexic boy with severe visual memory deficits made only three errors on an oral spelling test but missed more than half of the words when they were dictated because he could not revisualize letters. The boy was able to associate the spoken letters *j-a-m* with the sweet substance he put on bread but could not associate the printed word with the object.

A high school sophomore girl had a different type of spelling disability. On a multiple choice spelling test she received a B but made only a D on a dictated test. Examine the nature of the task. The first was purely visual and required recognition of the correct spelling. The second called for the conversion of an auditory stimulus to a visual-motor pattern. Because this student was unable to transduce information from the auditory to the visual modality, she could not write words from dictation. In contrast, some can write but are unable to spell orally because they cannot reauditorize letter names. Throughout the diagnostic study and daily teaching, this type of task analysis is invaluable. A sample guideline for tasks is given below.

First, a task is examined to note whether it is primarily *intrasensory* or *intersensory*. For example, on auditory discrimination exercises, is the child asked to close his eyes, listen to two sounds, and tell whether they are the same (intrasensory) or is he asked to point to a picture or letter that goes with the sound (intersensory)? Similarly with tactile discrimination, is he asked to feel objects and select one that is different (intrasensory) or to feel an object and match it with a picture (intersensory)?

Next, tasks are studied with regard to the *sensory modalities* that are involved. Since most learning is done auditorially and visually, these avenues are explored to the greatest extent, but taction is not ignored, particularly if it is to be used as a supplementary teaching modality. Task analysis at these two levels assists the teacher in discovering which channels are intact and in deciding whether the child can tolerate multisensory stimulation or whether stimulation needs to be reduced to a single modality.

A third type of analysis is suggested. This pertains to whether the task is primarily *verbal* or *nonverbal*. Although many children have difficulty with both types of learning, some have problems only with verbal and others only with nonverbal. For instance, certain children with auditory disabilities cannot associate the bark of the dog with the animal, nor can they understand the verbal symbol *dog*. Others, however, have no difficulty interpreting nonverbal sounds but cannot comprehend spoken words. In the area of visual learning, some can read (interpret visual verbal symbols) but cannot grasp the significance of nonverbal events. Therefore, the teacher examines each assignment and notes the successes and failures. In a science experiment she considers whether the student must read and comprehend or whether he must look at a series of pictures to draw conclusions. In geometry she considers whether the problems are presented orally, in writing, or in the form of diagrams and other nonverbal figures. This aspect of our analysis is particularly crucial for determining the *ways* in which new material is to be presented.

A fourth part of the study relates to the *level* of the task. Often learning disabilities are viewed only in terms of a perceptual or symbolic disturbance, whereas they must be studied at many levels. Specifically we try to see the involvement primarily at the level of perception, memory, symbolization, or conceptualization.

A fifth type of analysis pertains to the *expected mode of response*. The teacher should ask, "How am I expecting him to answer?" Most responses fall into one of three major categories. The first is pointing, marking, gesturing, or manipulation of objects; the second is speaking; and the third is writing. An analysis of response patterns is beneficial for planning specific remediation and also for suggesting modifications of assignments in the classroom. All too often children are penalized because they cannot respond in the expected manner, and frequently the teacher feels they do not know the answer or have not acquired the information.

For purposes of remediation it is necessary to know if the problem is one of reception or expression. If it is in output, the learning disabilities teacher tries to work through the problem, but, in the meantime, the classroom teacher should try to present assignments so the student can demonstrate his ability. For instance, in exploring a pupil's knowledge of numbers in sequence one considers the available modes of response. Depending upon the particular disorder, the instructor might ask the child to say numbers from one to 10, write them, or arrange cutout numbers.

Similarly in language, a nontalking child can demonstrate his ability to understand if he is presented questions that do not demand an oral response. One who is unable to write spelling words because of a visual-motor disturbance might be permitted to spell orally, type, or arrange anagrams in order. As indicated previously, the learning disabilities teacher will work on the specific deficit but the classroom instructor should become aware of alternative ways of wording questions or modifying tasks so the student can remain in the group and respond successfully.

Another means of gathering data about learning problems is analysis of a pupil's oral and written expression. Extended periods of lessons are recorded and transcribed so his spoken language can be examined for productivity, vocabulary, syntax, articulation, and other factors. A study also is made of each child's response in relation to the input, *i.e.*, the teacher's questions. Often the intuitive teacher is unaware of the ways in which he modified statements so the pupil could respond. By seeing the transcribed material, one can observe the types of questions each child failed and note any discrepancies between input and output.

Analyses of written language are made in a similar manner, often in a discussion with the child himself. Themes, reports, and stories are examined to note errors of formation of letters, spacing, alignment, spelling, ideation, word usage, punctuation, and other dimensions of written language. A systematic monitoring of errors is a major part of remediation.

RELATIONSHIP OF LEARNING FUNCTIONS

Critical to educational planning is an understanding of the interrelationships of language and learning processes. Consideration must be given to the relative impact of a disability on various forms of learning and behavior. For example, disorders of input impede output; a receptive language disorder interferes with expression. Reading disabilities affect written language. Problems of visual memory often affect reading and spelling but most likely will interfere with revisualization of numbers and other symbols.

Moreover, a learning disability generally affects far more than academic achievement; it interferes with total social maturity. Those with reading disabilities cannot read warning signs, fill out application forms for employment, or use telephone books for emergencies. Those with oral language problems cannot give and take messages or relate experiences. Those who are hyperactive or unable to learn motor skills cannot participate in activities with their peers or perhaps even perform simple routine responsibilities without help or supervision. As a result, over-all social competence is reduced. Even though some disorders appear to be relatively specific, one should be aware of the interrelationship of functions both in diagnosis and remediation.

Without an understanding of the reciprocity of functions, there are certain hazards in teaching. If the problem is defined solely as a reading disorder, the specifics and implications for education are overlooked. Procedures may become too general or the program too narrow. On the other hand, if only symptoms such as a visual-perceptual impairment or an auditory memory problem are delineated, there is a tendency to teach "dead-end" skills without relating them to basic areas of language, communication, and learning.

For example, innumerable writing disorders occur and each must be treated according to the nature of the deficit. Note the illustrations in Fig. 1.

Child A could not write because he could not read. Although he could copy letters, words meant nothing to him. His oral language was excellent; he could participate in class discussions and pass oral examinations. His primary disability was dyslexia based on a visual memory problem. The emphasis of training was on reading, that is, input before output. A phonics approach was used in teaching but supplemental training for visual memory and sequencing was provided. After about three years in the program the boy remarked, "I can finally see words in my mind." Prior to that time, he had attacked each word as though he had never seen it before.

Child B had no difficulty reading but could not remember the sequence of letters within words or the visual image of certain letters. Hence he could not spell. He could remember for purposes of recognition but did not have full recall. Revisualization of letters improved with training in taction, and emphasis was given to simultaneous association of the auditory and visual sequences of letters within words.

Child C had no difficulty in oral language or reading, but he could not formulate ideas properly in writing.

Child D, on the other hand, had difficulties in both oral and written formulation. He wrote as he spoke. The emphasis in training initially was on the improvement of oral language, which was then translated into written form.

Child E could not write because he could not form the motor patterns for letters. Oral language and reading were superior. Similarly, written formulation and spelling were good, but because of a visual-motor disturbance his writing was more like that of a 6-year-old than a 10-year-old.

Similar illustrations could be given with regard to arithmetic. Whereas some children cannot grasp ideas of quantity, others cannot associate

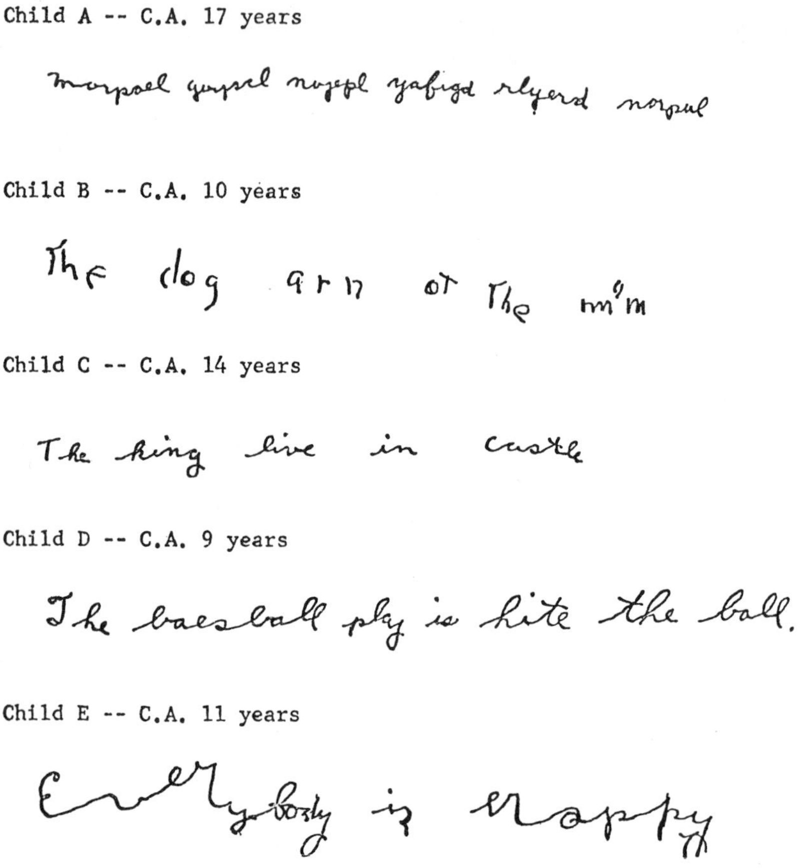

Child A -- C.A. 17 years

morpael gupsel nojepl yabigd rlyerd norpul

Child B -- C.A. 10 years

The dog q r η or The m'm

Child C -- C.A. 14 years

The king live in castle

Child D -- C.A. 9 years

The baesball ply is hite the ball.

Child E -- C.A. 11 years

Everybody is happy

FIG. 1. *Illustrations of writing disabilities.*

ideas of quantity with auditory symbols, others with visual symbols. Some can calculate when the problems are given auditorially but they cannot revisualize numbers. Repeatedly we see the need for specific descriptions of each disability.

PLANNING THE REMEDIATION PROGRAM

The primary purpose of a comprehensive study is to outline a program of remediation. The goal is to help the child learn more effectively. Learning sometimes has been defined broadly as a modification of behavior. In order to help a child modify his behavior, teaching procedures frequently must be modified. We have suggested that children with learning disabilities do not profit from the normal educational or environmental experiences; therefore, teaching technics will vary. An alteration of procedures, however, is not synonymous with over-all reduction of goals but rather suggests that material may need to be more structured, presented at a slower rate, or in a different manner. It is the route to the goal, not the goal itself, which varies.

If one examines any area of learning such as reading or language, the complexity of the processes and need for varied methodology become obvious. The child who is unable to read because of an auditory-perceptual or memory problem is not taught in the same way as one who has visual problems. Similarly, the child who cannot remember words receives different remediation than does the one who cannot understand.

In our clinical teaching approach, intact modalities are utilized to facilitate learning in deficit areas. The educational objective is not merely to raise self-confidence by working on assets, since this can lead to overcompensation with little or no improvement in weaker areas. A receptive aphasic who is taught only to read and write may never talk if auditory capacities are not developed. On the other hand, a program that emphasizes training to the deficits may be equally ineffective.

To cite a specific example, an eighth-grade boy with visual perceptual and memory disorders had failed a test in his graphic arts course twice. The test involved the memorizing of a complex plate of letters and numbers in a specific arrangement. Parents and teachers had worked with him for several weeks trying to help him memorize the visual pattern but with little success. Finally, the father brought the test to the learning disabilities teacher for suggestions. After a 20-minute period with the therapist, the boy learned the pattern and, on the following day, he passed the test. The therapist had utilized an intact modality, which in this case was audition, outlined structured auditory units, and simultaneously presented them with the visual pattern. Modification of the task meant success rather than failure for him.

It is evident from this example that educational planning requires knowledge of intact areas of function as well as knowledge of the deficit areas. We need to know the most effective avenues for learning. It is possible that a child different from this boy would learn more readily from taction and kinesthesis than audition. Therefore, the presentation would not be the same. Often a period of diagnostic teaching is necessary to establish the most effective combinations for learning.

Multisensory stimulation is not necessarily the solution. Although it is sometimes assumed that bombardment from all sensory avenues will be beneficial, in certain instances it actually impedes learning since the child may not be able to tolerate the excessive stimulation or integrate the information. Therefore, we attempt to find and utilize the most effective combination of modalities for learning.

Not all procedures are new. Whereas some new technics will be devised, many existing educational practices can be utilized if they are applied appropriately.

EDUCATIONAL PROGRAM AND GOALS

A major point to be emphasized is that the child must be *taught*. New concepts, new materials, and new experiences should be introduced. The mere presentation of an interesting worksheet or exercises is not necessarily teaching. Moreover, keeping children quiet or busy is not sufficient for education and learning. New experiences must be provided that are in keeping with the child's level. Each of these should be carefully timed and paced, since many children become very frustrated and overwhelmed with the introduction of new material. Nevertheless some frustration is essential in all learning. A program that is understimulating is as ineffective as one that is overstimulating. The goal is to foster, not inhibit, intellectual growth.

The nature of the educational program depends upon the severity of the disorder and the multiplicity of involvements. Most communities need at least two types of programs. Special classrooms are needed for those whose learning and adjustment problems are so great that they cannot profit from any regular classroom instruction. Others, however, do not need to be removed from the group all day and can profit from many classroom activities. The teacher, trained in learning disabilities, sees a child each day for an hour or more, depending upon his needs. These programs should be differentiated from tutoring, in which a teacher provides only supplemental help in academic subject matter. Emphasis should be given to the improvement of the disability so the student can acquire information for himself or from normal classroom experiences.

Careful planning of an integrated educational program is essential. Decisions regarding the type and number of activities a child can handle are based on discussions with many members of the school staff. One literally "walks" through the child's curriculum to determine in which areas he deviates. It should not be assumed that integration in the normal class begins with art, music, gym, or other nonacademic periods, for these may be the most difficult or overstimulating. Integration into regular classroom activities depends upon the nature of the deficit, the child's level of functioning, and the specific skills or subject matter to be learned. Frequently suggestions must be given to classroom teachers regarding educational management. A slight change in a seating arrangement, or in the rate of dictation of spelling words, or in the daily sequence of activities could mean the difference between success and failure for many boys and girls.

Progress must be evaluated periodically and goals may need to be adjusted. In some cases progress is rapid; in others it is slow, but improvement can be demonstrated. Prognosis is dependent upon many factors, including over-all level of intelligence, motivation, parental cooperation, age at identification, appropriate remediation, and level of aspiration.

Part of the population will go to college; others will terminate their education at the end of high school. Guidance throughout the entire academic career is needed. Selection of courses, academic load, and sequence of courses are critical factors in educational planning. One very bright dyslexic boy decided to go through high school in five years and take a lighter load rather than fail with a full load. As a result of this decision his grade record changed from failing to passing and he is currently enrolled in a small liberal arts college. Pupils ending their education with high school need special vocational planning. There residual disabilities may interfere with certain occupations and must, therefore, be taken into consideration. Guidance for those whose expectations are beyond their capabilities also is necessary. Throughout all of the planning, the student should be involved in decisions. He perhaps knows his abilities and limitations better than anyone and should be encouraged to verbalize the things that are difficult for him. Often he provides valuable insight into the learning problems and process.

Educational programs for children who have learning disabilities are not only justified; they are mandatory if we are to meet the needs of a rather large segment of the population. Although not all of these need special class placement, school administrators should be aware of the needs. It is not enough to send these children through school and give them diplomas; they need to be educated in order to utilize their potential. Without appropriate habilitation, they may well be on school dropout lists, in juvenile courts, in mental hospitals, or on relief rolls. If their needs are met, they may become independent self-supporting citizens who feel a sense of personal worth and can contribute to society.

11. TESTING AS A BASIS FOR EDUCATIONAL THERAPY

MARIANNE FROSTIG

Theories and practices in special education must be constantly modified as new research findings accumulate in various branches of education, psychology, sociology, and other pertinent basic and applied sciences.

Many educators today still believe that the general educational rules and procedures derived from psychological theories are all that need to be considered in teaching children with learning difficulties. Such rules are, for instance, to begin at the level of the child's ability, to proceed in step-by-step sequence, to inform the child immediately of the correctness of his response, and so on. Proponents of this point of view emphasize the analysis of subject matter and believe that an analysis of the learner can be neglected. In their view, adjustment to individual needs is sufficiently provided by a program that allows each learner to proceed at a speed commensurate with his ability. The adjustment to individual needs is thus seen as *quantitative*—being accomplished through a modification of the amount of material taught or the pace at which teaching and learning proceed.

Other research workers believe that *qualitative* differences in curricula,

SOURCE. Reprinted from *The Journal of Special Education*, 1967, 2, 15–34. By permission of the publisher.

teaching methods, and even programmed instruction are necessary when special types of children are to be taught.

Special adaptations of curricula for children with learning difficulties along such lines have been developed by the pioneers in the field— Strauss and Lehtinen (1947), Cruickshank (Cruickshank, Bice & Wallen, 1957, Cruickshank, Bentzen, Ratzeburg & Tannhauser, 1961, 1967), and others. Their programs attempt to help children in overcoming the difficulties believed to be most frequent, if not universal, in the groups to which they have been assigned on diagnostic grounds. These programs are most valuable, and techniques such as those developed by Cruickshank, for example, are a great contribution to the field of special education.

The point of view advanced in this paper, however, is that, in addition to programming for children on the basis of group differences, it is of advantage to take into account their individual differences as well. For although grouping children according to various administrative, symptomatic, or etiological classification schemes may suggest uniformity in the group, in reality groups of children classified on any basis are usually very heterogeneous, with differing personality characteristics, abilities, and deficits in their members, and educational methods effective with one pupil in a group may well be ineffective with another.

The general rules of teaching based on educational and psychological theories hold for all children, but they do not guide the educator in adjusting to individual differences. Two fields of investigation which have contributed to this aspect of special education are those of *child development* and *individual differences*. *Child development* has contributed to our understanding of the multitudinal needs of the child with learning disabilities in longitudinal as well as cross-sectional studies which reveal a great variety of individual patterns that modify general developmental trends (e.g., Meyers, 1966). These can help us to determine the most effective sequencing for various curricula as well as their modifications to meet the needs of the individual child.

The study of *individual differences* through tests and measurements helps bring developmental patterns and specific abilities and disabilities into clear relief and provides us with guidelines to teaching and training children. Tests are being designed increasingly for diagnostic purposes, with the evaluation of various abilities replacing or complementing general intelligence testing. With every use of these instruments, the knowledge of specific disabilities that inhibit the learning process increases.

The present paper is concerned with testing as a basis of assessing individual differences for the purpose of designing special educational methods which may improve the learning process in children. I will now discuss some of the principles of evaluation that are pertinent to this approach.

THE CLINICAL APPROACH TO EDUCATION

The total evaluation of a child and programming on this basis constitute a clinical approach to education that has been termed variously *educational therapy, psychoeducation, therapeutic education, diagnostic education.* Such evaluation includes the identification of abilities and disabilities important in the learning process.

The importance of identifying and assessing specific abilities can be considered in light of the following quotation by Bandura (1967). It was made in reference to behavioral therapy but it certainly applies to education as well. Bandura writes:

"The developments . . . in some respects parallel those in medicine, where all-purpose therapies of limited efficacy were eventually replaced by powerful specific procedures designed to treat particular physical disorders. The treatment process is not piecemeal, since favorable changes in one area of behavior tend to produce beneficial modifications in other areas (p. 86)."

"Powerful specific procedures" in education, too, must be based upon appropriate diagnostic findings. New evaluative techniques had and will have to be developed before all abilities which play roles in learning can be identified and measured for the purposes of optimum training.

It is of special interest for the educator that the great educators of the past have intuitively developed educational practices that recognize the existence of basic underlying abilities and disabilities in the educational adjustment of children. Montessori (1955), Froebel (1900), Itard (1932), and Seguin (1907) introduced methods in which one sense modality was substituted for another, and helped the child to associate and coordinate the input of several sense modalities. They prescribed a broad range of training activities for such purposes, suggested definite systematic educational sequencing, applying educational principles which could not be fully conceptualized at the time of their writing but which their intuition had propelled them to understand far in advance of the science of their time.

Present-day educators continue to develop new teaching techniques along such lines that still await scientific verification.

Modern programs directed towards training specific abilities found by testing to improve learning date back as early as 1940, when Kirk described certain procedures for training reading aptitudes. This pioneer work, however, threw into relief the deficiencies at that time in evaluative instruments designed to provide a basis for the remediation of specific disabilities. Kirk and his associates accordingly developed a test of language skills which tapped many of the abilities pertinent to school achievement. This was the Illinois Test of Psycholinguistic Abilities (ITPA).

The same difficulty in finding a test instrument to expose the underlying causes of learning disabilities was encountered by my staff and myself. In the 1950's I worked with many brain-damaged children in whom perceptual difficulties were apparent but seemed to vary in kind from child to child. Some of my previous research, and research conducted by Thurstone (1944), Wedell (1960a, b), Cruickshank (1957), and others, had established, or at least strongly suggested, that a number of perceptual abilities are involved in the solution of most perceptual tasks. A measuring instrument was developed by my associates and myself to measure these perceptual abilities, the Marianne Frostig Developmental Test of Visual Perception.

In seeking other techniques to help provide the best possible basis for remedial education, it was difficult to determine appropriate instruments for evaluation. A number of guidelines were used for this purpose.

First, my contact with the University of Southern California has led me to the use of Guilford's (1959) model of the structure of the intellect as a guide to the selection of the tests now used by the Marianne Frostig Center of Educational Therapy and as a check on their completeness and appropriateness. While I realize that many psychologists are doubtful about the necessity for recognizing more than 100 different abilities, as Guilford has done, the model has been helpful to us in our testing of children because it has indicated that our test selection covers the factors found at the young child's level of development, with the exception of physical abilities.

Also contributing to the selection of tests at the Frostig Center are the contributions of developmental psychology discussed earlier: it is generally accepted that the specific abilities which are necessary for school learning and for any other dealings with the environment emerge in a developmental sequence. This sequence appears to encompass the sensory-motor functions, which develop maximally during the first year-and-a-half or two years of life; language and perceptual abilities, which develop maximally during the preschool and initial school years; and the higher cognitive functions (or as Piaget [1952] has called them, the concrete and formal operations), which develop later on. The selection of our test battery was based on the need to evaluate these abilities.

THE FOUR BASIC TESTS

The test battery used at our center includes what we call our four basic tests: the Frostig Test for evaluation of visual perception, the Wepman Test for the evaluation of auditory perception of speech sounds; the ITPA, which focuses on language functions; and the Wechsler Intelligence Scale for Children for the appraisal of what is called general intelligence and, more specifically, for the evaluation of thought processes. A survey of the child's motor abilities (not discussed in this paper) is also used. We are aware that these tests overlap in what they measure. Yet we do not know enough about them to simplify the battery.

The four basic tests are so called because their results constitute the basis for planning the child's curriculum and, with the exception of physical education, for selecting the teaching methods of the remedial program.

Excluding motor functions, the ITPA and the Frostig Test seem to suffice as instruments of measurement at the 6-year-old level. For older children it is necessary to add the WISC. The Wepman Test is included for the discrimination of speech sounds as an additional help for the evaluation of auditory perception; the motor survey forms the basis of our physical education program. Other ability and achievement tests are sometimes used to implement this battery in order to fully understand a child's basic skills and problems.

The tests we use have been criticized. I agree with much of the criticism. But criticism is also warranted in the case of many other diagnostic and treatment measures frequently used in psychotherapy, education, and even in general medicine. Many instruments and methods are full of flaws, but we still have to use them until something better becomes available. I believe it is better to make mistakes than to do nothing when ground has to be broken.

It is important to be aware of the flaws of the new tests with which we measure abilities, but it is equally important to be aware of the need for measuring specific learning abilities even though the tests have not yet been perfected. By being aware of the deficiencies of the tests, we may add additional measures to make up for these deficiencies. For instance, auditory-motor association and visual-vocal association are not represented in the ITPA, although they have implications for reading and writing, and so when using the ITPA we may need to test additional perceptual functions or associational abilities. The scores of Subtest IV (*position in space*) of the Frostig Test may be influenced by guessing, and sequential abilities are insufficiently measured by Subtest V (*spatial relations*). Therefore, the visual-motor sequencing subtest of the ITPA should be used also to assess sequential abilities in the visual modality.

One of the greatest advantages of the present tests of specific learning abilities is that they provide the psychologist and teacher with a rationale for exploring a child's problems further.

A warning should be raised to the effect that a child's characteristics cannot be fully appraised through single test scores alone. The understanding of relationships between the various scores is equally important. The child's "characteristics" (i.e., his interests, attitudes, temperament, energy level, abilities and disabilities, formal education, social environment—everything which may contribute to his manner of learning—and their inter-relationships) are further of major significance.

It is of course also essential to recognize that a child's adjustment to his environment and the environment itself interact at every stage of the development. This must be carefully taken into account before any adequate judgment can be made about the child's present functioning and his prognosis. At our center observations, interviews, case studies, and projective tests are invariably used to evaluate social and emotional adjustment of children with learning problems.

It should be understood, in any case, that the choice of educational procedures based upon test results should never be regarded as final. Follow-up in the classroom is also necessary. The teacher's observations may indicate that some of the subtest scores have been erroneous. A child may have performed poorly on the subtest for visual-motor coordination not because he had sensory-motor difficulties, but because he was anxious, for example, or misunderstood the directions. (Test results should always be taken with a tablespoon of salt.)

I will now attempt to discuss the significance of our four basic tests and their subtests. I will start by illustrating first with the Frostig Test how subtest scores may indicate to the teacher the choice of curriculum and teaching methods.

The Frostig Test

The first subtest of the Frostig is the *visual-motor subtest*. In general, poor performance on this subtest will indicate that writing may be difficult for the child and that kinaesthetic methods, which are widely used in remedial reading (e.g., Fernald, 1943), may in his particular case have only limited success.

The second subtest assesses *figure-ground perception*. The child who has difficulties in figure-ground perception probably has difficulties in sustaining and shifting attention. He may show not only difficulties in perceptual decentration (Elkind, 1965) but also rigidity in thought processes. Such a child may therefore need training both in figure-ground perception and in structuring his learning tasks until he is able to structure the tasks by himself. These children need Cruickshank methods.

The third subtest is for *form constancy*. Difficulties on this subtest indicate the probable need for exercises in the form discrimination of plane figures and for special methods of teaching the recognition of letter forms. For example, before the child can grasp the forms of individual letters, the teacher may have to show him how individual letters can be built up from smaller parts. The letter *e*, for instance, may be taught as *c* with a horizontal line added; *d* as a circle with a long stick; *a* as a circle with a short stick; and so on. A variety of different kinds of print may also have to be used even during the first attempts to read to help the child transfer his reading skills from one context or size of print to another.

The fourth subtest is for *perception of position in space*. A child who has difficulties in this area will need careful help in gaining awareness of the right and left sides of his body. He may also need intensive training in the discrimination of position in space in a two-dimensional plane if he is to learn to discriminate between letters with the same form but different direction, such as *b* and *d*. When the child writes, the teacher may have to provide him with paper on which spatial cues are marked so that he can avoid reversals. Figure 1 shows an example of the grid we use for this purpose.

The fifth and final subtest requires the recognition of *spatial relationships*. If a child has a disability in this area, his ability to learn to read and spell will be affected. It will be difficult for him to construct words from letters and syllables and to recognize the sequence of letters in a word. Such a child may improve if he is given practice in constructing words, either by writing them or arranging printed letters in the correct order. The use of color cues is also helpful (cf. Frostig, 1965).

The Wepman Test

The child who has difficulties in auditory discrimination, as evidenced by the Wepman Test of Auditory Discrimination, requires careful training in the perception of sounds and especially of speech sounds. While his phonic skills are still being carefully developed, it may be necessary to teach him beginning reading using kinaesthetic and visual methods. Evaluation of his mistakes will indicate whether he has general difficulties in the perception of speech sounds or whether his problems are only with certain sounds.

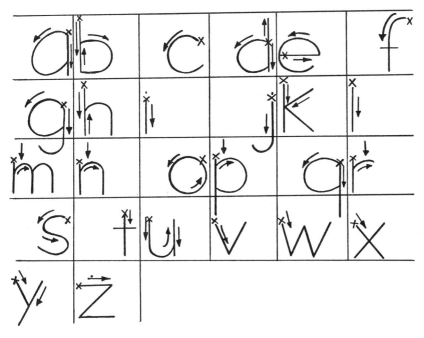

FIG. 1. *TEACHER'S GUIDE SHEET* (*for teaching manuscript letter formation*). *This sheet shows the use of starting points and directional cues. Individual letters are presented to child on a grid with these cues to help prevent reversals.*

The Wechsler Intelligence Test for Children

We do not use the WISC as the basis for the choice of curriculum and teaching methods in the same way as we use the other three tests. There are several reasons for this. First (as has been discussed by Silverstein, 1964), there is much communality among the subtests. Secondly, the WISC was designed as a predictive test, and its scores can be used in retesting to provide a basis for judging the general efficacy of the training instituted on the basis of the other evaluations. This would not be possible if the WISC subtests were used as a model for training.

Nevertheless, the WISC scores can give important indications for the curriculum. For example, the scores for *information* and *comprehension* can provide insight into the influence of difficulties in auditory and visual perception on the conceptual processes involved in these subtests; and the scores for *object assembly* and *block design* can suggest the child's ability to analyze and synthesize patterns. The test also provides the teacher with useful information of a more general kind. It is helpful to know a child's general standing in comparison with his age-mates, or how well-informed he is, or how well he comprehends.

In the performance scale, we have found the *coding* subtest to be of special significance. Moya Tyson (1961) has explored this question in depth. My interpretation is as follows: It often happens that children with severe learning difficulties score high in comprehension, have at least average information scores, show no difficulties on the similarities subtest, and are able to master abstract concepts. All of these abilities may be acquired through their understanding of *spoken language.* The same children may perform poorly in reading, writing, spelling, and computation because they have difficulty with *visual symbols.* This disability is often indicated by a low score in the subtest for coding. The child's score will be affected by his ability to shift attention, direct eye movements, remember for short periods, handle symbols, perceive position in space and spatial relationships, write with facility, and react speedily—all of which influence the acquisition of academic skills. No other subtest seems to test the integration of these abilities as efficiently as this one. The information gained from this subtest therefore needs to be carefully considered in the development of remedial reading programs. Children who score low in coding should be given many forms of practice in translating symbols from one system to another (for instance, by learning the Morse code, studying algebra, and solving puzzles).

The Illinois Test of Psycholinguistic Abilities

The Illinois Test of Psycholinguistic Abilities, designed to detect specific abilities and disabilities in communication, can provide a basis for the institution of effective remedial education programs. Its nine subtests involve not only language functions in the usual sense, but perceptual-motor tasks, memory, higher thought processes, and other abilities as well. The test is based on a theoretical linguistic model developed by Osgood (1957). I will discuss in some detail its nine subtests as they relate to learning problems that we have encountered in our center.

The first group of subtests are the decoding subtests. *Auditory decoding* explores the child's understanding of the spoken word, *visual decoding* his comprehension of visual stimuli.

In our sample of children with learning difficulties, the decoding functions are the least often disturbed. In visual decoding, only 28% of the children had low scores; in auditory decoding, only 19%.

The second group of subtests are the encoding subtests. The subtest for *motor encoding* requires visual motor planning and imagery. The subtest for *vocal encoding* explores the ability to express ideas through spoken words. In the encoding subtests, the percentage of children who did poorly was much higher than with the decoding subtests; 37% showed deficits in motor encoding and 48% in vocal encoding.

The next group of subtests involve associations. The *auditory-vocal association* subtest assesses a child's ability to relate words on a meaningful basis through the completion of analogies. The *visual-motor association* subtest, on the other hand, is a concept-formation test which requires motor rather than verbal responses to visual stimuli (pictures).

As Kass (1966), Bateman (1963), and others have shown, associative abilities are very frequently disturbed in children with learning difficulties. Of the children in our own sample, 46% had difficulties in the analogies subtest (*auditory-vocal association*) and 59% in *visual-motor association*.

I should like to add, with regard to the associational subtests, that I regret that no auditory-motor association subtest and no visual-vocal association subtest is included, because such tests would be most important for the diagnosis and prognosis of reading difficulties. (This opinion is shared by Kass [1966] and also by McCarthy and Olson [1964].) I regret also that although associations between input and output are included in the test, there is no subtest for integration of sensory input. Integration of sensory input is necessary for all learning; indeed, for any accurate perception of the environment. The ability to associate auditory and visual stimuli is essential for reading, for example, and the ability to associate kinaesthetic and tactile stimuli is most important for learning writing by tactile methods and even for the haptic perception of an object.

The last three subtests of the ITPA concern automatic and short-term memory functions. The first is the *auditory vocal automatic* subtest, which assesses a child's ability to speak grammatically. McCarthy and Olson (1964) have stated that the *auditory vocal automatic* subtest does not assess what the authors originally intended it to, since neither linguistic ability nor linguistic sophistication are explored. My own experience indicates that the test assesses what it explores directly, namely, the ability to use simple grammatical forms—such as plurals and the past, present, and future tenses—in everyday language. Therefore, in my opinion this subtest is valuable. Forty-one percent of the children in the sample I am discussing had difficulties with it.

The two final subtests are both sequencing subtests which assess memory functions. *Auditory vocal sequencing* requires the repetition of sequences of digits. *Visual motor sequencing* involves memory for visual stimuli. The child is shown pictures or geometric forms in a certain order; then he has to pick out these pictures from a group and arrange them in the original sequence.

The *visual-motor sequencing* subtest is of special significance. At least 74% of the children in our sample failed in this subtest—the highest proportion of failure for any of the subtests in our battery. Yet to the best of my knowledge, no test except the ITPA has attempted to assess this ability, which is necessary for learning to spell and to a lesser degree for learning to write. Since none of the subtests correlates significantly with the *visual-motor sequencing subtest*, I believe that even in cases in which it is impossible to give the ITPA, the ability to remember a visual sequence and to reproduce it motorically should at least be tested.

Taking all four tests into account, what are the most frequent disabilities? We have already mentioned that the *visual-motor sequencing* test of the ITPA showed the greatest percentage of failure—74%. The next most frequent failure occurred in the *figure-ground perception* subtest of the Frostig, in which 72% of the children in our sample scored in the lowest quartile.

The subtests showed low correlations with each other. But the test patterns of children without learning difficulties show a rather even development, with little inter- and intra-test scatter. In contrast, the subtest results of children with learning difficulties show little consistency (Frostig et al, 1961). These findings give weight to Gallagher's (1966) suggestion that the underlying difficulties of children with learning disabilities can be understood profitably as being the reflection of a developmental imbalance.

CONCLUSION

It is most important that teachers understand that any of a great range of underlying abilities may be lagging or lacking in a child, and that any such deficit may cause learning difficulties. Four tests that analyze underlying abilities and pinpoint deficits have been discussed. They are the Marianne Frostig Developmental Test of Visual Perception, the Wepman Test of Auditory Discrimination, the Illinois Test of Psycholinguistic Abilities, and the Wechsler Intelligence Scale for Children. These tests analyze children's abilities in perception, language, and thought processes, and the test scores may be used in choosing the most effective methods of teaching for a given child. Please note that sensory-motor functioning is also invariably assessed with a special motor survey, and a selection of additional tests is used according to the child's needs.

No one kind of teaching materials, methods, or curricula is the best approach for all the children in a classroom. The ways in which children learn vary greatly, and teaching techniques must take individual differences into account. The use of groups of unselected children in attempting to prove the superiority of certain teaching methods is of doubtful value—for example, assessing the effectiveness of the Initial Teaching Alphabet (Downing, 1965) as opposed to color cueing (Bannatyne, 1965), or comparing linguistic methods (Fries, 1962) with the use of basal readers. In each classroom there will be children with reading difficulties. A single method cannot be best for all these children. To use a somewhat coarse analogy, a comparable practice in medicine would be to compare two diets, one with low protein content and the other with low carbohydrate content, each of which has been given to an unselected population of patients containing both cases of kidney disease and cases of diabetes.

With the exception of the WISC, the tests that I have discussed are comparatively new, still in an experimental stage, and far from flawless; moreover, they are not often accessible to the teacher. If, however, the teacher is familiar with the tests and understands the rationale underlying their use, she will be aware of the full range of possible disabilities and may be in a position to identify those disabilities by using informal testing and by personal observation when formal testing is not available. Her choice of methods will at least be based on an educated guess about a given child's specific difficulties, instead of a total reliance upon trial and error or on the indiscriminate use of a single remedial procedure.

References

Bandura, A. Behavioral psychotherapy. *Scientific American*, 1967, 216, 78–86.

Bannatyne, A. D. The colour phonics system. In J. Money and G. Schiffman (Eds.), *The disabled reader: education of the dyslexic child*. Baltimore: Johns Hopkins, 1965.

Bateman, B. D. Reading and psycholinguistic processes of partially seeing children. *CEC Research Monographs*, Series A, #5, 1963.

Cruickshank, W. M./Bice, H. V./Wallen, N. E. *Perception and cerebral palsy*. Syracuse: Syracuse University Press, 1957.

Cruickshank, W. M. *Brain-injured child in home, school, and community*. Syracuse: Syracuse University Press, 1961.

Cruickshank, W. M./Bentzen, F. A./Ratzeburg, F. H./Tannhauser, M. T. *A teaching method for brain-injured and hyperactive children: a demonstration pilot study*. Syracuse: Syracuse University Press, 1961, 1967.

Downing, J. The prevention of communication disorders by the use of a simplified alphabet. *Developmental Medicine and Child Neurology*, 1946, 6, 113–124.

Elkind, D./Larson, M./Van Doornick, W. Perceptual decentration learning and performance in slow and average readers. *Journal of Educational Psychology*, 1965, 56, I 50–56.

Fernald, G. M. *Remedial techniques in basic school subjects*. New York: McGraw Hill, 1943.

Fries, C. C. *Linguistics and reading*. New York: Holt, Rinehart, & Winston, 1962.

Froebel, F. *The education of man*. New York: D. Appleton, 1900.

Frostig, M./Lefever, D. W./Whittlesey, J. R. B. Developmental test of visual perception for evaluating normal and neurologically handicapped children. *Perceptual and Motor Skills*, 1961, 12, 383–394.

Frostig, M./Lefever, D. W./Whittlesey, J. R. B. *Marianne Frostig developmental test of visual perception*. Palo Alto, Calif.: Consulting Psychologists Press, 1964.

Frostig, M. Corrective reading in the classroom. *The Reading Teacher*, 1965, 18, 573–580.

Gallagher, J. J. Children with developmental imbalances: A psycho-educational definition. In W. M. Cruickshank (Ed.), *The teacher of brain-injured children: a discussion of the basis for competency*. Syracuse: Syracuse University Press, 1966. Pp. 21–34.

Guilford, J. P. Three faces of intellect. *American Psychologist*, 1959, 14, 469–479.

Itard, J. M. G. *The wild boy of Aveyron*. (Translation; G. and M. Humphrey.) New York: Century, 1932.

Kass, C. E. Psycholinguistic disabilities of children with reading problems. *Exceptional Children*, 1966, 32, 533–539.

Kephart, N. C. *The slow learner in the classroom*. Columbus, Ohio: Charles F. Merrill, 1960.

Kirk, S. A. *Teaching reading to slow reading children*. Boston: Houghton Mifflin, 1940.

Maslow, P./Frostig, M./Lefever, D. W./Whittlesey, J. R. B. The Marianne Frostig developmental test of visual perception: 1963 standardization. *Perceptual and Motor Skills*, Monograph Supplement 2–VI9, 1964.

McCarthy, J. J., & Olson, J. L. *Validity studies on the Illinois test of psycholinguistic abilities*. Milwaukee: University of Wisconsin, 1964.

Meyers, C. E. New trends in child study. In *Child Study*, Bulletin of the Institute of Child Study, University of Toronto, 1966, 28, 3, 110.

Montessori, M. *Dr. Montessori's own handbook*. New York: Shocken, 1965.

Orpet, R. E., & Meyers, C. E. A study of eight structure-of-intellect hypotheses in six-year-old children. Draft report, NIMH Grant #MH 08666–01, June 9, 1965.

Osgood, C. E. A behaviorist analysis of perception and language as cognitive phenomena. In J. Bruner (Ed.), *Contemporary approaches to cognition.* Cambridge: Harvard University Press, 1957.

Piaget, J. *The child's conception of numbers.* New York: Humanities Press, 1952.

Seguin, E. *Idiocy: its treatment by physiological method.* Albany, N.Y.: Brandow, 1907.

Silverstein, A. B. Variance components in the developmental test of visual perception. *Perceptual & Motor Skills,* 1965, 20, 973–976.

Strauss, A. A., & Lehtinen, L. E. *Psychopathology and education of the brain-injured child.* Vol. 1. New York: Grune & Stratton, 1947.

Suppes, P. The uses of computers in education. *Scientific American,* 1966, 215, 207–220.

Thurstone, L. L. A factorial study of perception. *Psychometric Monograph,* No. 4. Chicago: University of Chicago Press, 1944.

Thurstone, L. L. Primary mental abilities, *Psychometrika Monographs,* 1938. Pp. 1–121.

Tyson, M. A comparison of the abilities of normal and subnormal children to match and discriminate figures. Unpublished doctoral thesis. University of London, 1961.

Wechsler, D. *Wechsler intelligence scale for children.* New York: Psychological Corporation, 1949.

Wedell, K. Variations in perceptual ability among types of cerebral palsy. *Cerebral Palsy Bulletin,* 1960, 2, 3, 149–157. (a)

Wedell, K. The visual perception of cerebral palsied children. *Journal of Child Psychology and Psychiatry,* 1960, 1, 215–227. (b)

Wepman, J. M. *Wepman test of auditory discrimination.* Chicago: Language Research Associates, 1958.

12. FROM DIAGNOSIS TO REMEDIATION

HAROLD J. McGRADY

The characteristic knowledge of our century is psychological. We are living in an age in which many persons are studying behavior so that they may devise methods by which to modify it. In fact, the future of our world has been depicted by George Orwell in his now famous *1984*,[1] by B. F. Skinner in his Utopian novel, *Walden II*,[2] and by others at a time when essentially all behavior will be manipulated or controlled. These predictions suggest the fulfillment of the fondest hopes of John B. Watson, the famed behaviorist, who stated: "Give me a dozen healthy infants, well-formed, and my own special world to bring them up in, and I'll guarantee to take any one at random and train him to become any type of specialist I might select—doctor, lawyer . . . (etc.) regardless of his talents, penchants, tendencies, abilities, or vocations and race of his ancestors."[3]

SOURCE. Reprinted from *Selected papers on learning disabilities. Management of the child with learning disabilities: An interdisciplinary challenge.* Fourth annual conference of the Association for Children with Learning Disabilities, New York, March 1967, 37–41.
By permission of the author and publisher.

[1] George Orwell, *1984* (New York: Harcourt, Brace, 1949).

[2] B. F. Skinner, *Walden II* (New York: The Macmillan Co., 1948).

[3] John B. Watson, *Behaviorism* (Chicago: The University of Chicago Press, 1958), p. 104.

Psychologists interested in learning processes have tried for years to define "laws of learning." They have had little applicable success. Ernest Hilgard has, in fact, stated that "there are no laws of learning that can be taught with confidence."[4] Even more depressing is a statement by one psychologist who said "the sad truth is that, after fifty years of careful, honest, and occasionally brilliant research on the nature of learning, the only people who can be proved to have received any practical benefits from learning theory are the learning theorists themselves."[5] The application of learning principles to the modification of behavior has often met with failure.

B. R. Bugelski states: "Perhaps the whole effort to bring science to education is misguided."[6] Notwithstanding the success of teaching machines, not only is it difficult to develop techniques based on learning theory, but educators and psychologists are not even sure that the practice of teaching can be taught. We do not prefer to be so pessimistic. Progress is being made in the delineation of principles for teaching. In fact, we feel that the work with learning disabilities children is of great help in this dilemma. As more effective techniques are developed in our field they assist us in our understanding of the learning processes for all children. For this reason the work with learning disabled children has important implications for the practice of education in this country.

Despite these recent advances in clinical teaching and the significant progress that has been made in identifying and evaluating such children, there seems to be a gulf between these two processes. There seems to be a tremendous gap between our ability to analyze behavior and our ability to use this information to change behavior.

Thus, in our work with learning disabilities, there often is a noticeable gap between the diagnostic process (the analysis) and the prescription of procedures for remediation (the modification process). We might call this a "diagnosis-remediation gap." It represents a serious problem in dealing with children who have learning disabilities. Thousands of children each year are taught with little regard for intensive evaluations that have been completed, reported, filed, and forgotten. The severity of the gap depends on circumstances. In a university program such as ours where the diagnosis and remediation are done consecutively by persons

[4] Ernest R. Hilgard, *Theories of Learning*, 2d ed. (New York: Appleton-Century-Crofts, Inc., 1956), p. 457.

[5] Donald Snygg, "Learning: An Aspect of Personality Development," in *Learning Theory, Personality Theory, and Clinical Research: The Kentucky Symposium* (New York: John Wiley and Sons, 1954), p. 130.

[6] *The Psychology of Learning Applied to Teaching* (New York: Bobbs-Merrill Co., Inc., 1964), p. 31.

with essentially the same background and training, and where communication between examiner and teacher continues, the diagnosis-remediation gap will be small.

In other circumstances where children are evaluated and then referred to other agencies for the remedial process, the degree of communication will vary. This is a situation common to any diagnostic referral clinic. The type of training or the professional disciplines of the involved individuals will determine the size of the diagnosis-remediation gap. In some instances the gap seems insurmountable—as some of you have wrestled with diagnostic reports in an attempt to arrive at a remediation plan will attest.

Our comments today will be concerned with diagnosis and how it can contribute to better management of the child with learning disabilities. As we discuss this we shall try to keep as a guideline the notion that the purpose of diagnosis is to clarify—not to mystify.

What is diagnosis? It is, of course, the process through which information relative to a problem is gathered and analyzed. But if we define it only as such we have merely "evaluated" not diagnosed. If we truly diagnose we must determine two further characteristics, namely etiology and prognosis of the problem. As Robert I. Watson has stated "the diagnostic phase of the clinical method culminates in the formulation of a theory or hypothesis of causation. Once causation has been established, emphasis shifts to questions of what can be done and what corrective steps can be instituted."[7]

Diagnosis implies treatment or remediation. Otherwise it would be of no practical value. It is for this reason that some degree of ascertaining etiology (or cause) is necessary. The same basic presenting problem may be due to a number of causes. For example a child who does not read (the presenting problem) may be mentally retarded, deaf, blind, partially sighted, emotionally disturbed, aphasic, otherwise neurologically impaired, culturally deprived, just plain unmotivated, or the victim of poor teaching. The objective of diagnosis should be to determine which of these conditions is responsible for his disability. Merely to say that he does not read or reads at such and such a grade level, which is below his grade level, is not enough. If we assumed that all children with reading disorders were to receive the same training, then a diagnosis would not be necessary. We would need only to evaluate the child, that is, to determine the level of reading at which he is performing and proceed from there. The collective example of this would be called "descriptive diagnosis." In such an instance we would merely say that the child has

---

[7] *The Clinical Method in Psychology* (New York: Harper & Brothers, 1951), p. 25.

this symptom plus that symptom, and another. Diagnosis which is only a cataloging of symptoms cannot be justified as diagnosis. Such a procedure represents only a complex evaluation resulting in a description of the problem.

The degree of specificity of the etiology is another matter. We feel that the initial diagnostician's role should be that of indicating the broad etiological category in which the child belongs. We operate under the general principle that learning can be disrupted for several basic reasons. A review of these factors may be pertinent at this time.

• Sensory deprivation consists of those conditions which are due to pathology of the peripheral nervous system. Deafness and blindness are the primary disorders.

• Disorders of emotional organization represent factors of individual psychodynamics which have interfered with learning. This might include a variety of psychoses and neuroses.

• Experience deprivation will also disrupt learning. This represents lack of opportunity to learn and includes a range of conditions such as "cultural deprivation" or lack of schooling and might be extended to include such circumstances as poor teaching. These represent social variables which have deprived the individual of normal experiences prerequisite to adequate learning.

• Neurological dysfunction represents a prominent etiological factor for consideration. There is perhaps a wider scope of subtypes of disorder and a higher incidence in the population than for any of the other etiological categories. Under this category we include mental retardation and lesser degrees of generalized intellectual incapacity. If other causating possibilities can be ruled out, the assumption is made that the central nervous system is implicated. Specific learning disabilities include perceptual disorders, language disorders, memory disorders, disorders of cognition, abstraction or thinking, and motor disorders.

A child who fails to learn, despite adequate sensory integrity, emotional stability, opportunity to learn and mental capacity, is classified as a child with a specific learning disability. The assumption is that such disorders have neurogenic bases.

The individual who initially evaluates a child should determine which of these primary causative factors is responsible for the problem. It may not be necessary at this stage to be more specific about cause. For example, he need not determine whether the mental retardation is endogenous or exogenous to refer the child to a remedial program. (This information will be of benefit, however, in determining other problems to look for in the specifics of remediation.) The broad causative factor, however, should be sufficient for the initial post-diagnostic stage. Establishing such etiologies, however, implies a bringing together of information from a variety of disciplines in medicine, psychology, and education. Subsequent evaluations would be aimed at delineating the specifics of the child's learning problem by a professional from the area of special education which represents the established cause, whether it be deafness, emotional disturbance, or specific learning disabilities.

The learning disorders specialist will further delineate the behavioral disorders by means of sampling a variety of pertinent areas. We screen for vision and hearing defects and evaluate the child's perceptual abilities; we check his memory, his motor abilities, and his social maturity. These are in addition to the establishment of guidelines for levels of intelligence, language, and emotional behavior. In doing this we are looking for several contrasts:

1. between verbal and nonverbal abilities,
2. between learning as it occurs through various sensory channels, particularly visual and auditory,
3. between receptive comprehension and expressive functions, and
4. among types of cognitive functions, such as perception, memory, language, and conceptualization.

We attempt to evaluate the individual against himself—to establish that he has legitimate learning disabilities, that he is not mentally retarded, deaf, emotionally disturbed, etc. This kind of diagnosis and evaluation lead the teacher to a more thorough knowledge of the child's problem so that she may work with it.

Our concept of diagnosis is that it should be thorough; it is concerned with causes; it is concerned with prognosis; it is concerned with comprehensive behavioral assessment that allows the teacher to "know the problem" as the basis for her remediation. The resultant remediation is then an individualized matter for each child-therapist combination. It is based on a consideration of the child's assets against his deficits.

One question to be resolved is: "Who is responsible for diagnosis?" In many instances the diagnosis-remediation gap is large because of the psychologist-teacher gap, or the psychologist-physician gap, or other interdisciplinary combinations. In our communities and colleges we need to define the role of the psychologist (clinical or school), the classroom teacher, the remedial reading teacher, the social worker, the principal, the family doctor, the speech therapist, etc., in diagnosis and remediation. As one man asked at a conference some months ago: "How many people will it take to deal with one reading problem?" This is a question which we must all resolve.

It means to a certain degree that all teachers must be diagnosticians, that all school and medical personnel must be knowledgeable concerning learning disabilities, and that we must learn to cooperate and coordinate rather than to proliferate.

What is the solution to the diagnosis-remediation gap? My feeling is that it involves some degree of rethinking and restructuring of our training programs in education: for the regular classroom teacher, for special education teachers, and for other specialists such as school psychologists. Three suggestions are offered:

Regular teachers must receive some orientation to learning disabilities. One of our problems may be that the typically trained regular teacher in the classroom does not really have the background necessary even to recognize, let alone to deal with learning disabilities children whom she sees. The classroom teacher needs to be sensitized to learning disabilities. She should be given more exposure to the theory and practice of utilizing learning processes as they apply specifically to learning disabilities children. In this way she would not only enhance her own general teaching by being able to deal more efficiently with individual differences in the classroom, but she would be able to work effectively with some types of learning disabilities children. This would include children who can succeed adequately with a minimum of structuring, slight changes in seating, use of special materials, etc.

There are a significant number of students in our classrooms today who could be prevented from developing into full-blown learning disabilities children if every classroom teacher had enough knowledge to identify such children and to deal with the more common and less severe problems in the classroom. Particularly she should know when to refer a child with possible learning problems.

We do not feel that the amount of training necessary to accomplish this would overburden the curriculum. It could, in fact, replace some of the stale repetitions, or outdated requirements we are all familiar with in teacher training. We feel that inclusion of this type of information in their programs is a must. It should make them better teachers for all children; and if we can believe the statistics regarding incidence of learning disabilities, every teacher who has twenty children in her classroom has one of these children to deal with. If this suggestion would be accepted, the diagnosis-remediation gap would be decreased because identification and remediation would begin in the classroom.

· A second suggestion for closing the diagnosis-remediation gap is that the school psychologist's training must allow him to provide remediation suggestions or hypotheses after completing his evaluations. He needs to be able to translate psychological findings into educational prescriptions. A school psychologist who is only a psychometrician—not a psychologist—needs someone else to integrate the test information. In Britain all school psychologists (i.e. educational psychologists) work with remediation. They must have at least three years teaching experience, as I understand it, and must continue to work with remediation while working as psychologists. This, I believe, is a superior system to ours where, although many school psychologists do fit the above qualifications, it is not universal. The school psychologists' primary function will continue to be that of ruling out mental retardation or primary emotional disorders.

· A third way of reducing the diagnosis-remediation gap would be to insure that every special teacher of children with learning disabilities has the proficiency to perform screening level evaluations of such children. This person would be provided with training in psychoeducational testing. The learning disabilities teacher should be thoroughly trained to give achievement tests, group intelligence tests, and pertinent special abilities tests. We are assuming, of course, that she is also a thoroughly trained teacher. We are also assuming that a complete program for training such a person cannot be accomplished in a regular undergraduate program alone; it will require some amount of graduate-level education. We feel that the teacher of children with learning disabilities is the one who can best serve to close the diagnosis-remediation gap. She will be a kind of unicorn who will be part psychologist—part teacher.

Thus, if this system were to work, the following would occur:

(a) The regular classroom teacher would suggest or tentatively identify the child suspected of being learning disabled. The better her training and clinical acumen, the less false leads she would provide.

(b) After tentative affirmation by the teacher of children with learning disabilities, the school psychologist would evaluate the child thoroughly to determine causation. That is, he would attempt to classify the child into the appropriate special education category, utilizing his own testing together with that of other professionals in psychology, medicine, and education. If the child still classifies as learning disabilitied, then

(c) the third step would be to have the learning disabilities teacher devise a remediation plan and begin.

A system such as this must be fluid and the various personnel must function cooperatively as a team. We feel that interdisciplinary effort is necessary. As more professionals learn to accept this and diminish the effect of territorial instincts, the diagnosis-remediation gap will be closed.

13. ASSESSMENT OF CHILDREN WITH LEARNING DISABILITIES

THOMAS C. LOVITT

A review of the literature on learning disabilities strongly suggests that there is no need for another psychological or medical definition of that population whose achievement does not coincide with its assumed potential. Already there has been as much time expended in attempts to delineate this learning disabilities population as has been spent in its actual diagnosis and treatment. Rather, then, a review of this literature suggests the need for a rationale and a method of evaluation based on a thorough behavioral assessment of individual performance.

Recent concern with learning disorders has prompted not only the publication of books devoted specifically to the diagnosis and remediation of such problems (Hellmuth, 1965; Frierson and Barbe, 1967), but also has stimulated an allocation of government funds for the training of professionals in this field. Further, a number of diagnostic centers has been established for the evaluation of children with minimal brain injury or learning disorders.

Characteristically, a diagnosis at these centers involves the formal administration of standardized educational and psychological test batteries, usually including the Illinois Test of Psycholinguistic Abilities

SOURCE. Reprinted from *Exceptional Children*, 1967, 34, 233–239. By permission of the author and publisher.

(ITPA), the Parsons Language Sample, the Detroit Tests of Learning Aptitude, the Wepman Auditory Discrimination Test, and reading measures such as the Syracuse Informal Reading Inventory, the Gates, or the Durrell Diagnostic Tests. Following the administration of these tests, portions of which may correlate with the reason for referral, a summary report is presented to the teacher. The tacit assumption behind this diagnostic procedure is that the classroom teacher will be able to translate these evaluations and recommendations into effective programing.

The teacher or referring agent receives (a) such statements as those based upon the ITPA, which reveal the child's auditory decoding and vocal encoding abilities; (b) such data as that obtained from the Parsons Language Sample, which are relevant to his manding, tacting, and intraverbal behaviors; and (c) further comments as to his auditory discrimination, oral reading, comprehension, and phonic abilities. However, these statements are at least one step removed from the direct programing tasks of the referring agent.

For example, there is the teacher who refers a child with an observed deficiency in describing specific objects within the classroom. This teacher will be unable to design a remediation program from a diagnostic report which merely states that, in comparison with someone of his age, the referred child scores poorly on a vocal encoding subtest. This subtest would only be helpful to the teacher were the child referred because of a vocal encoding deficit. Further confusion can result when a teacher actually misuses the indirect information. A teacher, for example, might seek diagnostic solace as a means of rationalizing her own programing inadequacies. Such a teacher, when finding a child who does not adapt to her program or choice of curricular materials, could have her programing decisions greatly reinforced by a diagnostician who solves her dilemma with a report that the child is dyslexic or aphasic. As a result, when the child does not adequately perform, the teacher need only draw out her file and read the diagnosis to reassure herself that the student's poor performance is unalterably determined by some medical or psychological malady. Then, no teaching obligation follows for altering the stimulus or consequence conditions of the program, nor is there any necessity for an assessment of possible errors within the teacher's management techniques.

These difficulties suggest the need for a four point diagnostic procedure based on a methodological assessment rather than an assessment superimposing a set of population characteristics on an individual child. This four point procedure is outlined as follows: (a) baseline assessment, (b) assessment of behavioral components, (c) assessment based on referral, and (d) generalization of assessment. In this manner, it is judged, more children displaying discrepant behaviors will be served, for when diagnosis and treatment are based on direct observations and not on the supposition that one deviant behavior presupposes the presence of a syndrome of related events, time is spent in treatment of explicit behaviors rather than in what is frequently a fruitless search for correlate but often unrevealed behaviors.

BASELINE ASSESSMENT

The proposed diagnostic procedure is initiated by continuously assessing behavior over a period of time, until a specified level of stability has been obtained. This continuous diagnosis is certainly more reliable than traditional diagnostic procedures that represent a single evaluation of behavior or, at most, two samplings of behavior in the pre-posttest paradigm.

In the case where only one or two measures of the behavior are obtained, not only is minimal data acquired, but the total range of variability remains undetected. This minimal evaluative information is often misleading when the objective of a diagnosis is to make a probability statement in regard to the child's future performance. In instances during evaluation when the individual's behavior is under weak or undetected stimulus control, his performance may be extremely variable. The subject, for example, may perform at a very slow rate one day and quite rapidly on another. If only before and after treatment impressions of performance are obtained, the diagnostician cannot be certain if the behavioral change is due to treatment modification or if it is merely fluctuation due to variability.

The diagnostician is concerned not only with the reliability of baseline performance, but also with the validity of his evaluation. In behavioral diagnoses, a valid measure of performance is provided through objective observations of behavior (for example, direct analysis of reading or attention span) rather than subjective inferences of behavior (indirect assessment through the use of standardized tests). Validity, then, obtained from direct measurements that can exactly match recorded observations to those the evaluator will subsequently modify, is assuredly greater than that derived from the indirect sampling of standardized tests that only infer future performance.

ASSESSMENT OF BEHAVIORAL COMPONENTS

The second aspect of the proposed evaluation process is the assessment of those behavioral components that maintain and modify behavior, such as stimulus or antecedent events, behavioral movements or responses, the contingency system or arrangement of events, and the consequences provided contingent upon a specified behavior (Lindsley, 1964).

Antecedent or Stimulus Events. Until recently, most educational researchers have focused on the antecedents of behavior—the stimulus materials presented to children. Their experimental efforts can be seen in the vast amount of research that contrasts the efficiency of one curricular method with another. Although such research provides data meaningful for large groups of children, it does not meaningfully measure the effects of various curricular procedures on individuals. It is suggested that the current high level of concern over individual differences should also extend to an assessment of the effects of the programing of materials on individual performance.

It is quite possible that stimulus or curricular research, with regard to children with learning disabilities, will need to evaluate more discrete aspects of the stimulus process than a mere assessment of various texts, workbooks, slides, or filmstrips. For example, to accelerate or maintain the response behaviors of some children, it may be necessary to analyze experimentally individual preferences for several stimulus dimensions. Many of these preferences can be obtained in a free operant situation: for example, the child selects his preferred rate of visual or aural narration, the intensity or brightness of the aural or visual theme, and/or the configuration or size of the visual stimulus.

Stimulus preferences relevant to the preferred rate of listening are already the object of some research consideration (Lovitt, 1966). By continuously listening to a story, at five varying word per minute (wpm) rates, retarded and normal subjects were able to select their preferred speed of speech. The results of this investigation revealed that, for most boys, a rather discrete preference for a particular narrative rate did exist. Most normal boys operated to acquire, and verbalized a preference for, speech at normal rates, while all of the retarded subjects in the study rejected the normal 180 wpm rate. Furthermore, they verbalized preferences that were often inconsistent with their operant selections.

A second investigation (Lovitt, 1967a) to assess stimulus preference for the type of person reading a story has recently been completed. Seven preteenage boys from regular and special classes were assessed as to preference for a male or female reader by allowing each boy to listen simultaneously to two recorded versions of a story, one read by a female and the other by a male. In both conditions the story was the same and the wpm rate of speech was nearly identical. Both stories were available throughout the experimental conditions and the boys were provided with a manual device that allowed them to select continuously one reader over the other and to sample portions of both recorded tapes. The results of this study revealed that five of the boys preferred the male reader and one preferred the female reader. One boy's performance indicated that, for him, the reinforcing effects of both readers were nearly the same.

Thus, a programer, supplied with such individually relevant data as preferred rate of narration or preferred type of reader, could design programs based on these or other stimulus dimensions, such as preference of rate and size of visual presentation or timbre and intensity of auditory delivery.

Movement or Response Behaviors. The response behavior of the child with learning disabilities is a second behavioral component that should be assessed. His responses need to be evaluated in regard to both topography (the counting or quantification of responses) and function (the effect of these responses on the environment).

Literature in learning disabilities is abundant in regard to such topographic parameters of language as mean sentence length, type-token ratios, psycholinguistic processes, and manding and tacting behaviors (Spradlin, 1963). Other dimensions that could be assessed include speaking rate, timbre of speech, and intensity of speech.

However, as Ferster (1967) has pointed out, topographic analysis is a static measure, while a functional analysis is dynamic. Although a topographic record may be as objective and as easily reproduced as any other datum, it lacks the functional or dynamic relation of the behavior to its controlling environment.

In order to obtain this functional analysis of verbal behavior, it is necessary to assess the many verbal situations in which the deviate or disabled child functions and to determine how often, how long, and by what type of speech the child maintains interpersonal communicative acts. It is necessary also to observe how often he emits vocalizations classified as demands or commands, and the frequency with which these mands are consequated or reinforced.

If modification procedures are based only on such topographic measure as mean sentence length or speech rate, an individual's effect (function) on his environment could remain unchanged. However, by observing behavior within a specific setting and by altering certain topographic elements coincident with this analysis, functional changes may occur. For example, in a situational analysis of language it may be determined that when an individual speaks faster and uses longer sentences he is able to maintain a communicative act longer than when he speaks more slowly and uses shorter phrases. In this instance, if the goal requires longer communicative interactions, procedures would be arranged to modify the person's rate and duration of speech. Only by altering the individual's responses according to such a two dimensional evaluation, which contains sentence length and duration of interpersonal communicative contact, may a functional change be achieved.

Arrangement or Contingency System. The third behavioral component that should be evaluated and assessed is the temporal arrangement of the consequences of behavior. It is necessary to determine how often or how many consequences are necessary to affect performance. Many normal children seem to function with few spuriously dispensed consequences. Most children fulfill teacher expectations even though the consequences of child behaviors are delivered at irregular and extended intervals. However, these same lean and unsystematic contingencies that maintain acceptable response rates in normal children may be either too subtle or too infrequent to evoke similar behaviors in some exceptional children. Thus, the child described as having an attention span deviation may functionally have a contingency deficit.

Kunzelmann, Aronin, Hulten, and Nolen (1967), at the Experimental Education Unit of the University of Washington, have designed an observation system that should provide data relevant to the contingency requirements of children. By recording the rate of teacher interactions with individual children and by simultaneously plotting pupil performance rate, data should be obtained relevant to pupil performance as a function of teacher interaction. Data from such a system would enable a classroom teacher to arrange the rate of her interactions to promote optimal pupil response rate. The maintenance of high rates of performance for some children may require few systematically spaced interactions. However, for pupils with contingency deficits, high response rates may be produced only by a high rate of teacher interaction.

Subsequent or Consequent Events. The final behavioral component for measurement and evaluation is the assessment of environmental consequences that maintain behavior. It is necessary to identify an individual's hierarchy of consequences, those events that either increase or decrease his rate of performance. These consequences should be selected so that they coincide with those available in the individual's home or school, and, whenever possible, they should take the form of the complex social consequences that will eventually control the child's behavior in most settings.

Generally there has been more success in determining what these high payoff activities are by observing the child or by asking the child's teacher or his parent, rather than asking the child himself. Parents and teachers are in immediate and close contact with the child many hours each day. They are aware of the child's free time preferences—whether he watches television, builds models, rides his bike, colors in a book, or reads science fiction. These frequently occurring self initiated activities could be used later by the diagnostician or programer as initial consequences when remediation programs are inaugurated.

The reliability of observation and interview techniques in determining potential reinforcers for children has recently been experimentally analyzed. Haughton (1967) asked teachers, peers, and the children themselves which events or commodities they believed would affect pupil performance. Children were also observed in free time situations in order to obtain data relevant to potential reinforcers. The suggested and observed events were then used as consequences in an academic setting to determine their relative function on pupil performance. Haughton reported that although some teachers were accurate in predicting which events could be used to increase academic response rate of children, the most reliable information was that data obtained by actually observing the child.

Many instances, however, will arise that require the use of consequences not ordinarily available in a classroom setting, such as tokens, marks, or the classic use of candy, M&M's (Haring and Lovitt, 1967). With some children it may even be necessary to explore the use of continuous narration (such as stories or music) as a potential controlling consequence. It could be that such continuously available narration will generate higher rates of response from those individuals than will bursts or episodes of reinforcement, such as tokens, marks, or social contacts.

Another approach is the method of conjugate assessment, which requires that a child be placed in an enclosed room and told that he will be listening to or looking at something and that he can press the provided hand switch if he so desires. Without further instructions, the child usually realizes that by pressing or not pressing the switch he can continuously select the narration of his choice. Since many children with learning disabilities possess limited verbal repertoires, this free operant technique, which requires minimal verbalization from the examiner and none from the child, obtains a more reliable assessment than those requiring a verbal report from the child.

The conjugate tactic has been used to compare the continuous reinforcing strengths of five types of narration (Lovitt, 1967b) and to compare the relative reinforcing strengths of two stories (Lovitt, 1967c). In the first investigation, when a story, a poem, words and sentences in reverse order, and a journal article were serially presented, it was observed that young children responded at stable rates to acquire the story, but they demonstrated great response variability when the other narrations were programed. Some exceptional children, however, responded at more stable rates to acquire words or sentences in reverse order than they did for the story, a narrative form that was conceivably understood or meaningful.

In the second investigation (Lovitt, 1967c) of the comparative strengths of consequences, two stories were offered simultaneously rather than serially. The data from this study not only revealed each subject's quantitative preference for a story, but also provided a continuous, moment to moment analysis of the holding power of each story.

ASSESSMENT BASED ON REFERRAL

The third factor which must be considered in this recommended evaluation process is the referring agent—the teacher or parent—as well as the referred child. The possibility always exists that the managerial and programing skills of the adult may be as incompetent as the compliance skills of the child. In other words, there are those educators and psychologists who, given an option as to program types, would select the program for adults with programing disabilities, rather than one for children with learning disabilities. In some cases, it is expedient for the diagnostician to deal directly with the programing disability of the adult rather than with the performing disability of the child.

Involving a parent or teacher in the evaluation process enables the referring agent to collaborate with the diagnostician on the determination of target behaviors specified for subsequent treatment. It would not be uncommon to find a child referred and diagnosed because of poor performance in oral and silent reading, inadequate mathematics computation, and other discrepant activities such as tantrums or social isolate behavior. In this case the deviant behaviors need to be ranked by priority—a rank order not necessarily in accord with the diagnostician's treatment sequence. Such a decision should be mutually agreed upon by the diagnostician and referring agent.

Although the diagnostician sometimes runs the risk of reinforcing the referring agent's poor judgment and analysis by allowing her to play a role in deciding the future course of educational treatment and modification, there are indications that a breakdown in programing results from the failure to take the referring agent's goals into account. On some occasions, when a disagreement in terminal goals results in dual programing, either the child becomes adept at discerning inconsistent environment expectations or his behavior collapses completely. On other occasions, a parent may verbalize agreement but fail to carry out any modification procedures as outlined by the diagnostician. For the optimal programing sequence, then, a coincidence of goals held by the adults must be actively pursued.

GENERALIZATION OF ASSESSMENT

The fourth aspect of the proposed method of assessment is to emphasize the generalization of diagnostic information. The end product of an evaluation should be to present to the referring agent information that can be immediately transmitted into programing procedures. The teacher, when provided with diagnostic information from the clinician, should be in a position to provide a stable learning environment for the referred child.

One reason for the fact that diagnostic information has not been translated into academic programs has been discussed earlier, namely that teachers have not always been able to design functional teaching programs and procedures from the data derived from standardized tests and the accompanying clinical jargon. A second reason that clinical evaluations fail to result in functional academic programs may be that the environmental conditions that prevailed during evaluation were not specified to the teacher. It is as important to report the process that was in operation during an evaluation as it is to report the product of an assessment. An evaluation report that simply states the child's rate of response on certain materials would be a topographic analysis. However, an assessment report that not only describes the child's performance rate, but details the environmental contingencies that were in effect during assessment, would be a functional analysis. The probability of successfully generalizing a remediation program is far greater when functional data are provided than when only topographic information is reported.

Attempts are being made at the Experimental Education Unit and Division of Child Health of the University of Washington to report diagnostic data to teachers in a functional manner (Lovitt and Kidder, in press). Data are reported which are relevant to each of the following: the antecedent prompts or instructions given during the evaluation, the exact material that was given the performer, the subsequent events that followed the child's responses, and the child's responses to the various programs. The assessment of explicit academic behaviors and the reporting of prevailing environmental conditions have facilitated diagnostic generalization. Thus, diagnostic generalization can be obtained when data are reported relevant to process and product rather than product alone.

CONCLUSION

The concern throughout this paper has been directed toward assessment. Although treatment or remediation was not the emphasis at this

time, this detailed method of objective specification and direct observation of behavior which has actually been established by the teacher or
diagnostician represents the first step toward successful modification.

The utilization of direct behavioral assessment as an initial step toward future teaching plans carries with it both optimism and a high
degree of responsibility. Optimism is implied in that the discovery within
a detailed behavioral analysis of those conditions that alter or maintain
behavior may lead to the alteration of many deviant behaviors. There is
no need to seek a validation of the referred behavior from some indirect
or irrelevant standardized test. Furthermore, there is no need to probe for
hidden behaviors that are often suspiciously believed to be correlated
with the referred behavior. Responsibility is implied in that now the
remediational obligation rests with the programer. For when remediation procedures are initiated and accordingly measured in a direct manner but resulting pupil responses are unacceptable, it is indicated that
the variables in a teaching situation have not been appropriately arranged. Therefore, the ultimate successes and failures of the proposed
assessment and modification method are always subject to immediate
and accurate observation. By direct assessment of such behaviors as rates
of reading, computation, or listening and speaking, and by the application of modification procedures functionally related to these skills, pupil
and/or programer progress is discerned immediately and empirically.

References

Ferster, C. B. Classification of behavioral pathology. In L. Krasner and
L. Ullmann (Editors), *Research in behavior modification.* New York:
Holt, Rinehart and Winston, 1967. Pp. 6–26.

Frierson, E. C., and Barbe, W. B. (Editors) *Educating children with learning
disabilities: selected readings.* New York: Appleton-Century-Crofts,
1967.

Haring, N. G., and Lovitt, T. C. Operant methodology and educational
technology in special education. In N. G. Haring and R. L. Schiefelbush
(Editors), *Methods in special education.* New York: McGraw-Hill,
1967. Pp. 12–48.

Haughton, E. A practical way of individually tailoring classroom consequences.
Unpublished doctoral dissertation, University of Kansas, 1967.

Hellmuth, J. (Editor) *Learning disorders.* Vol. 1. Seattle, Washington:
Special Child Publications, 1965.

Kunzelmann, H., Aronin, M., Hulten, W., and Nolen, P.

Simultaneous cumulative observation record for interaction analysis. Unpublished manuscript, University of Washington, 1967.

Lindsley, O. R. Direct measurement and prosthesis of retarded behavior. *Journal of Education,* 1964, **147**, 62–81.

Lovitt, T. C. Narrative rate preference of normal and retarded males as assessed by conjugate reinforcement. Unpublished doctoral dissertation, University of Kansas, 1966.

Lovitt, T. C. Reader preference: a free-operant assessment. Unpublished manuscript, University of Washington, 1967. (a)

Lovitt, T. C. Use of conjugate reinforcement to evaluate the relative reinforcing effects of various narrative forms. *Journal of Experimental Child Psychology,* 1967, **5**, 164–171. (b)

Lovitt, T. C. Free-operant preference for one of two stories: a methodological note. *Journal of Educational Psychology,* 1967, **58**, 84–87. (c)

Lovitt, T. C., and Kidder, J. D. Experimental analysis of children with learning disabilities. In R. C. Jones (Editor), *Prospectives in contemporary education.* New York: Allyn and Bacon, in press.

Spradlin, J. E. Language and communication of mental defectives. In N. R. Ellis (Editor), *Handbook of mental deficiency.* New York: McGraw-Hill, 1963. Pp. 512–555.

14. COLLECTING DIAGNOSTIC DATA IN THE CLASSROOM

ROBERT M. SMITH

This is the second of two articles on the educational diagnosis of exceptional children. The first article dealt with the different ways children vary and how this effects designing an instructional program. An effective instructional program can occur only after the teacher has gained a clear understanding of the nature of the individual differences that characterize each child. Perfunctory acknowledgement that individual differences exist within a class of children, whether they be located in a regular or special education classroom, is too imprecise and in no way will lead to informed judgments concerning the use of proper methodology, curricula, and instructional media. Furthermore, the use of general achievement scores as the sole criterion for deciding on the nature of educational programing is open to question. Several students of identical age and intelligence in the same classroom could be achieving poorly for entirely different reasons. A proper response to the educational problems of each child can occur only after a systematic observation has been made of each student and his environment. On the basis of these data, then, a teacher can properly identify and structure all of the components of instruction.

SOURCE. Reprinted from *Teaching Exceptional Children,* 1969, 1, 128–133. By permission of the author and publisher.

Most teachers believe to some extent that these notions are valid; however, many are unclear as to the form that the data collection should take and where to start the process. Also, there is a general tendency to rely totally on the school psychologist or some other well trained specialist for specific direction in testing, assessing, and recommending remedial steps for problem children. The position which will be expressed here is that the teacher can, should, and must actively participate along with others in the diagnostic-remedial process. This paper will present and discuss a means by which diagnostic information can be collected by the teacher and interpreted into programs of instruction. Particular emphasis will be placed on informal techniques for observing behavior.

DIAGNOSTIC AND REMEDIAL STEPS

The procedure which will be recommended as a model for identifying the nature of educational disorders in children involves five levels of diagnostic-remedial activity. If the information which is collected at each of these levels is reliable and the observations are valid, proper educational programing for an individual child can be made.

Level One. The child should be screened by the teacher and others, including the parents, for relatively obvious gross disorders which could subsequently influence functioning in areas such as social, emotional, cognitive, language, or speech. The problems might include "the lazy-eye-syndrome," serious delays in language development, unintelligible speech, constant hearing problems, developmental lags in various physical systems, constant lethargy, perpetual anger or hostility, self-destructive behavior, and malnutrition. It is difficult to be specific about what constitutes a significant disorder in any of these areas; however, if a child shows any of these types of problems for a large portion of the day, he should be referred to an appropriate specialist. The important point to consider at this first level is to do everything possible to refer the youngster to a proper specialist at as early an age as possible. At this level of diagnosis it is better to err on the side of over-referral than to allow a significant problem to prevail, since as it gets more serious, it will begin to generate a whole galaxy of related problems which will only further complicate the child's educational future.

Level Two. Assuming that all problems which were identified at Level 1 received proper attention, at Level 2 a determination is made of the existence of possible problems in learning. This determination is most commonly based on each child's achievement test scores. It is not a difficult procedure at all to profile each child's scores in a number of educational areas and identify those in which a youngster seems to be having trouble and those in which he has particular strength. A more thorough discussion of this profiling procedure appears in Kirk (1962).

Level Three. The teacher will need to more thoroughly investigate the nature or peculiar characteristics of the learning problems in those areas of particular weakness. A more penetrating analysis could involve the administration of specific formal diagnostic tests which have been designed to probe into precise skill areas, e.g., Diagnostic Chart for Fundamental Processes in Arithmetic, Diagnostic Tests and Self-Helps in Arithmetic, Spache Diagnostic Reading Scales, or Gray Oral Reading Tests. At the same time, the more informal observations of the teacher and the child's parents will be of great help as data sources as the child's weaknesses are analyzed.

The teacher might want to survey the child's reading performance in certain broad areas, such as silent reading, oral reading, word recognition, and comprehension. The child's production in each of these areas can be profiled to determine if weaknesses seem to exist in one or more of the areas. Closely related to the child's performance in these areas is the process which he uses in reading or in any other subject area. Two important questions to be asked are "How does he go about attacking words?" and "What process is used to obtain a certain level of production?" At this level, then, the teacher should look both at the performance, or products, of the child in the various areas of a subject as well as the process, or techniques, which he employs in dealing with the task.

From the diagnostic clues obtained from this type of observation, the teacher can decide in which direction to move for purposes of obtaining more information. For example, the teacher might be suspicious about and test for auditory or visual memory problems or difficulties in discrimination, visual-auditory integration, sound blending, left to right progression, and/or reversals. Problems in any of these specific areas could influence the child's performance in the more general aspects of reading which were mentioned earlier.

Level Four. An attempt should be made to identify the possible causes for the educational disorder. In the preceding three levels some attempt has been made to identify characteristics of the difficulty. Observation of a child's behavior could reveal that his educational difficulties could be caused by problems such as, (a) exposure to an instructional program which was inconsistent or ambiguous, (b) association with an improperly sequenced course of study, (c) an inability to work under conditions of speed, (d) too much pressure to achieve from the parents, (e) difficulty in following directions, or (f) the rewarding of unpleasant behavior. Factors such as these might be considered as possible causes of educational problems. If the teacher or a parent has some notion as to the possible cause of a problem, data should be systematically collected in an attempt to verify the hypothesis.

The suggestions which are made in this section are presented with some degree of trepidation. Be careful not to get trapped into a situation where unwarranted associations are made between some historical event in the child's life and his classroom performance, as if some cause and effect is operating. Don't engage in mystic psychologizing with yourself or with others. Consider the conclusions you reach, as a result of the historical data you collect at each level thus far, as hypotheses. View your conclusions as educated guesses and not necessarily fact. The proof of the validity of these tentative conclusions will occur after you have tried and evaluated the child's program of remediation, which is based on the hypotheses of disorder which you have formulated from the information which has been gathered.

Level Five. From these data, then, core areas of difficulty can be delineated and hypotheses generated concerning possible specific causes for a youngster doing poorly in certain subject areas. These hypotheses can be used to plan an appropriate program of placement and remediation which is based on evidence and not on impulsive or random selection of any instructional technique from all of those which might be available to the teacher.

For example, let's assume that a teacher's observation of a child leads to the conclusion that he seems to be having problems with general use of the auditory channel but does not manifest unusual difficulty in using and processing visual stimuli. The teacher may find that the youngster is weak in one or more auditorally related skills, such as oral reading, phonic analysis, remembering what he hears, relating a sound to its appropriate visual stimuli, singing, understanding directions, and sound blending. After studying the child's record of performance, the teacher might decide that since all of these areas require some degree of skill in auditory discrimination and auditory memory, a program of evaluation should be initiated to determine if either or both of these skill areas represent a common core of difficulty. Prior to that, of course, the teacher would want to have the child's hearing acuity checked by an audiologist.

If after all necessary testing has been accomplished the teacher is able to identify what might be viewed as significant weaknesses in discrimination and memory of auditory stimuli, a program of remediation in those areas should be started before the child is engaged in more complex activities, such as phonic analyses or sound blending, which require a certain level of skill in the more specific areas of auditory discrimination and memory. To engage a child in phonic analysis activities before he can discriminate among sounds will only result in failure and frustration. The problem that the teacher has, then, is not only to identify the core areas of difficulty but to provide remediation according to proper sequence. Again, placing a child in phonic analysis activities before he has developed auditory discrimination skills is like "putting the cart before the horse."

TYPES OF DATA USED TO DETERMINE THE NATURE OF A CHILD'S EDUCATIONAL DISABILITY

Use of Formal Test Data. The teacher can use information from formal instruments to determine the nature of each youngster's educational difficulty. For this reason the school psychologist should report relevant information from psychological reports in understandable language. In most instances the entire protocol, including specific test scores, should be provided to the special education teacher, so that subtest performances can be analyzed and a determination made regarding the child's relatively strong or weak areas. These profiles, then, will help the teacher to formulate a plan for instruction.

Use of Informally Collected Data. The teacher will find great advantage in making use of informal diagnostic strategies which might be used on a day by day and week by week basis within the classroom. There are numerous advantages in the teacher using information which has been collected in an informal way as a basis for devising an appropriate instructional environment. The teacher is in the best position to assess educational problems of a child because the rapport between him and the student is typically stronger than between the child and other adults. Second, the teacher has more opportunity to sample characteristic behavior of each child as opposed to biased, somewhat extreme behavior. Third, the classroom environment allows for observing the child's performance in a variety of situations.

Criteria for Selecting Activities for Informal Diagnostic Observation of Behavior. Smith (1969) has suggested that the following criteria be used by the teacher in selecting activities for the informal diagnostic observation of the behavior of children.

1. Every activity used for the purpose of evaluating a skill should be part of the ongoing program and should not be used in a contrived setting. Try to incorporate informal diagnostic activities into the daily classroom routine. A child may not respond with his usual behavior if he is engaged in diagnostic activities during periods which are set aside for only that type of activity.

2. Activities should be interesting so that attitudinal or motivational dif-

ficulties don't cloud the real performance. Select the content of each diagnostic activity so that it is compatible with the ongoing instructional sequences and inherently interesting to the youngster. In a sense, then, a necessary prelude to evaluation is to determine what type of activity interests each child.

3. Activities for diagnosis should be selected to measure specific educational dimensions. For example, if you wish to evaluate the auditory memory performance of a youngster, the child should be asked to repeat digits or remember other types of stimuli which have been presented via the auditory channel.

4. Activities should be presented so that each child's performance can be measured directly in specific skill areas. Don't select tasks which require the diagnostician to make inordinate assumptions, extrapolations, or generalizations beyond the data. For example, because a child does poorly on arithmetic computations, do not assume that he will show a faulty arithmetic reasoning performance. Determination on this issue can properly be ascertained only by engaging him in activities which are designed to check on arithmetic reasoning variables.

5. Every diagnostic activity should be selected for objectivity, and attempts should be made to control possible sources of bias in the collection, interpretation, and translation of the data. Report what you observe; don't succumb to the temptation of overclassifying behavior. For example, if you observe that a child plays unusually roughly, throws things at other children, gets into an inordinate number of fights, and breaks many pencil points, describe these behaviors and don't engage in mystic psychologizing by suggesting that the youngster is angry and anxious because his father and mother are divorced, etc.

6. Activities should be varied enough so that each child does not become too familiar with the tasks. For example, if you wish to informally check on how well a child is able to borrow in subtraction, you would need to have a substantial repertoire of activities that require these skills, so that they can be used on different occasions.

7. Each child should be tested on more than one occasion in order to gain a reliable evaluation of his performance. Observations and other assessment devices are unreliable to some extent. If decisions regarding a child's future are going to be made from such data, make sure that ample opportunities have been given for sampling relevant behaviors. This implies that evaluation should be conducted frequently, unobtrusively, and at various times during the day. You would feel that it was unfair to be placed, irreversibly in many instances, into a special remedial program on the sole basis of your behavior having

been observed at an inopportune moment when your performance was "off" for any of a variety of possible reasons. This very same point is pertinent when we consider the value in initiating or withholding any technique, device, or curriculum for exceptional children.

CONCLUSION

This paper has developed a rationale for teachers developing increasingly higher level skills in educational diagnosis. This justification was based on a review of the various dimensions of variability. It was emphasized that if teachers are going to "do things to children" by manipulating their environment, documentation is needed in order to determine the manner in which intervention should occur. This documentation should be based on systematic observation of student behavior.

References

Kirk, S. A. *Teaching exceptional children*. Boston: Houghton-Mifflin, 1962.

Smith, R. M. *Teacher diagnosis of educational difficulties*. Columbus, Ohio: Charles E. Merrill, 1969.

15. INDIVIDUAL READING INVENTORIES

MARJORIE SEDDON JOHNSON and
ROY A. KRESS

WHAT IS AN INFORMAL READING INVENTORY?

Basic Concepts

The term informal reading inventory is one in our language which with three words expresses three fundamental concepts. Consider first the basic noun in the title. This technique of evaluating a child's performance is an inventory in the sense that it is a detailed study of his whole performance in the reading area and those language and thinking functions related to reading. The second major concept is that of reading itself. In the label informal reading inventory, the function reading is widely conceived. The interest is not in mere pronunciation of words, but also in the manipulation of ideas which are represented by these words. Finally, the technique is an informal one in that specific methods are not standardized, and no norms have been established for performance compared with what other students can do. Instead evaluations are made in terms of absolute standards. A child's performance is judged

SOURCE. Reprinted from *Sociological and psychological factors in reading*, 21st Annual Reading Institute, Temple University, 1964, 48–60. By permission of the authors and publisher.

against virtual perfection rather than by comparing it with what the majority of children might do given the same job.

An informal reading inventory therefore offers the opportunity of evaluating a child's actual reading performance as he deals with materials varying in difficulty. While an appraisal is being made of these specific reading abilities, opportunities are also present to make informal evaluations of his expressive and receptive abilities in the oral language area.

Specific Purposes

A number of very specific kinds of information can be obtained from careful administration of an informal reading inventory. Accomplishing of these purposes is inherent in the administration of the informal reading inventory provided a competent examiner makes the evaluation. Because the information to be gotten is dependent on accurate observation of the individual's performance in the testing situation, and interpretation based on these observations, only a competent examiner can accomplish the purposes.

The informal reading inventory can serve as a means of appraising achievement levels in reading. To be more exact in this statement, careful administration of such an inventory can determine the level at which the child is ready to function independently, that point at which he can now profit from instruction, the level where he reaches complete frustration with the material, and his hearing comprehension level. Three of these levels have special every day significance for the teacher. It is imperative that he know the level of material the child can handle adequately when he is working on his own. A great deal of the child's school work and certainly that reading which will make of him a mature and avid reader are done on an independent basis. Unless materials at the proper level are provided, the child can hardly be expected to do an adequate job in independent work and thereby establish for himself high standards for performance. In the same fashion all instructional work must be provided at a level where the child meets sufficient challenge to learn and yet has adequate readiness for learning. This means that he must achieve well enough to be able to absorb the instruction which is being given. However, to give instruction in materials which the child could handle virtually independently would be foolhardy. Finally, for oral activities, it is important to know the child's hearing comprehension level. Too often the false assumption is made that if material is read to the child, he will be able to understand it regardless of the level of complexity it represents. For profitable listening activities, one must know the hearing comprehension level.

A second purpose to be served by the informal reading inventory is the determination of the child's specific strengths and weaknesses. Only in terms of such analysis of specific skills and his adequacy of achievement in these skills can a suitable instructional program be planned. Teaching at the right level is not enough. The teaching must be directed toward the overcoming of any specific weaknesses which exist. It must also be given in areas where the child has adequate readiness for learning.

A third purpose of the inventory is to help the learner himself become aware of his levels of achievement and his specific strengths and weaknesses. As he works with materials of increasing difficulty, he should be able, with the aid of the examiner, to detect those points at which he functions well and those at which he demonstrates a need for assistance. In the same fashion, he should be able to develop an awareness of the kinds of thinking and word recognition which he is capable of handling and those in which he needs to improve himself. Without adequate learner literacy the task of instruction becomes an exceedingly difficult if not an impossible one.

A final area of purposes to be accomplished by an inventory is that of evaluation of progress. Repeated inventories at periodic intervals should make it possible to determine changes in levels and in the handling of individual skills and abilities. In this way a true measure of the child's growth can be obtained.

Criteria for Levels

One of the problems in the determination of independent, instructional and hearing comprehension levels is the variability which exists in the criteria used for judgment. It would seem safe to say that all too often the criteria are quite low. Consequently the level at which a child's performance is judged adequate for independent work often turns out to be one at which he is meeting many problems. Instead of doing a virtually perfect job with the material, he is perhaps operating at something close to the old seventy-percent-passing level. In the same fashion children are often considered ready for instruction when they have a great many deficiencies in their operating patterns at a particular level. Experience has shown that when there is too much to be accomplished through instruction, the child does not perform adequately in terms of profiting from instruction and retaining those things which are taught. In order to overcome these weaknesses, high standards must be used for judging the achievement levels. In the following paragraphs each of the levels previously noted is discussed in terms of the specific criteria to be applied.

Independent Level. This is the level at which a child can function on his own and do a virtually perfect job with the handling of the material.

His reading should be free from observable symptoms of difficulty such as figure pointing, vocalization, lip movement, and other evidences of general tension in the reading situation. Oral reading should be done in a rhythmical fashion and a conversational tone. Materials, in order to be considered to be at an independent level, should be read with ninety-nine percent accuracy in terms of word recognition. This does not mean merely final recognition of the words in the selection. Rather this means that even in a situation of oral reading at sight the child should be able to handle the material accurately, making not more than one error of even a minor nature in one hundred running words. In terms of comprehension the score should be no lower than ninety percent. Whether the reading has been done silently or orally at sight, the child should be able to respond with this degree of accuracy to questions which will test factual recall, ability to interpret and infer, and to handle any other comprehension ability which happens to be required for full understanding of the material. He should be able to respond adequately to humor, for instance, or to follow any sequence of events involved in the material. In addition the child should be able to make adequate applications of information and ideas to other situations.

Attention to the independent level can be a key point in the determination of progress in reading. The child, his teacher, his parents, and the librarian should all be concerned with this level. All are involved in the process of selection of materials for his independent reading. Books bought for his own reading, his personal library, should be ones he can read well. References suggested to him by the librarian, as she helps him get resources for carrying out a project, must be ones he can use successfully. Homework assignments should be ones he can read without the need for someone to help him. It is through wide reading at the independent level that the child has opportunities to apply the abilities he has acquired, to learn through his own efforts, to increase the rate and flexibility of his reading—in short, to bring his reading ability to the point that it provides him with real satisfaction. Only through his independent reading will an individual become a "spontaneous reader," one who reads as a natural part of his living.

Instructional Level. This is the level at which the child should be and can profitably be instructed. Here again the child should be free from externally observable symptoms of difficulty. Again as at the independent level, he should be able to read rhythmically and in a conversational tone. However, one would expect that certain difficulties might arise in the course of oral reading at sight. When he has a chance to read the material silently, most of these difficulties should be overcome. Consequently, oral rereading should be definitely improved over oral reading at sight. In order to be able to profit from instruction, the child should encounter no more difficulty than can reasonably be expected to be overcome through good instruction. In terms of specific criteria in word recognition, this means that he should be able to perceive accurately at least ninety-five percent of the words in the selection. In terms of comprehension, he should have the ability to attain a seventy-five percent level of understanding of the material without instructional aid. When this is true, he in all probability will be able to reach, with teacher help, the same high levels of performance as were indicated as criteria for the independent level. In general, one should strive in instruction to have the child handling the material independently by the time the lesson is completed. If he begins the lesson with less adequacy than indicated in these criteria, there is very little likelihood that he will overcome all of his problems.

Certain other evidences of ability to profit from instruction can be observed at this level. The child should know, for instance, when he is running into difficulty. He should be able to profit from minimal clues offered by the examiner to help him overcome his difficulties. He should also know when he needs to ask for direct help because he does not have the skills necessary to solve his problem. Here, as at the independent level, the child should be able to set continuing purposes for reading once he has been helped to develop an initial readiness.

It is in his guided work at the instructional level that the child will have the opportunity to build new reading and thinking abilities. Building on the foundation of his previously acquired skill, he can profit from teaching and thus extend his concepts, his word analysis skills, and his specific comprehension abilities. Their extension, through both increased range of abilities and greater depth in their applicability, is the purpose of instruction. If it is to be accomplished, knowledge of the child's instructional level is essential to the teacher.

Frustration Level. The point at which the child becomes completely unable to handle reading materials is of more clinical than classroom importance. For the classroom teacher, however, knowing this level may serve two purposes. Information on the frustration level may give the teacher some guidance about the kinds of material to avoid for this child's work. It may also give him some indication of the rate at which the child might be able to progress when he is taught at his proper instructional level. If a child is ready for instruction at one level and completely frustrated at the next, there is clear cut evidence that he has many problems to be overcome through the instruction at the appropriate level.

The likelihood is not that this instruction will progress rapidly because of the complexity of problems to be met. On the other hand, if there is a considerable spread between the instructional and the frustration levels, there is a better chance for fairly rapid progress. There is evidence that he can continue to use his reading abilities with fair effectiveness when he meets more difficult material than that truly appropriate for instruction. This fact would seem to indicate that the needs to be met at the instructional level and somewhat above are not terribly serious or complex ones. Consequently, he might be expected to solve his problem relatively rapidly with good teaching to help him. Specific criteria for the frustration level are these: comprehension of fifty percent or less and word recognition of ninety percent or less. Failure to meet the other criteria already described for independent or instructional levels would also be indicative of frustration.

Hearing Comprehension Level. This is the highest level at which the child can satisfactorily understand materials when they are read to him by the examiner. The hearing comprehension level can serve as an index to the child's current capacity for reading achievement. It indicates, in other words, the kinds of materials that he would be able to understand if his reading levels were at this moment brought to a maximum point. Criteria for judgment of adequacy of hearing comprehension are parallel to those for the establishment of the instructional level. The child should be able to understand at least seventy-five percent of the material when it is read to him. A second measure and a very important one is the index given by his own speaking vocabulary and language structure. He should, in responding to the material, show an oral language level which is comparable to the language level of the material which has been read to him. The necessity for the examiner to translate questions down in language level or for the child to answer in a lower level of language would indicate that he is not comprehending fully at this point.

All instructional activities involving listening should take into account each child's hearing comprehension level. Whether materials are being read to the class or spoken, there can be no real profit to an individual if they are beyond his hearing comprehension level. He may simply tune out when he finds himself failing to understand. Knowing the appropriate levels for oral language activities can lead, then, to better classroom attention and thus to greater learning.

The hearing comprehension level has one other kind of significance for the teacher. It gives him an indication of the level at which the child *should be reading*. The criteria in terms of comprehension are the same for the instructional reading level and the listening level. One should not feel completely satisfied until the child can do as well with the material when he reads it himself as when it is read to him. Therefore, a goal to aim for is equivalence of the reading instructional and the hearing comprehension levels.

MATERIALS

The types of materials to be used in an informal reading inventory are dictated by the purposes of the inventory itself. Because the establishment of levels is one of the expected outcomes of the administration, it is obviously necessary that the materials represent a variety of levels. In a clinical instrument, for instance, it is usual to have the difficulty level of the material progress from preprimer level to the highest point that one is likely to need. These materials may sample a variety of subject areas and types of writing. However, if one were interested primarily in the achievement levels of the child in the science area, then materials relevant to this content field should be used for the inventory. Because an evaluation of competency in handling specific skills and abilities is the desired outcome, the materials of the inventory must present the opportunity for evaluating this competence. Obviously, not every ability which is a part of reading comprehension could be tapped in the course of each inventory; however, an adequate sampling should certainly be made.

The length of materials must be controlled sufficiently to allow the inventory to be administered without undue fatigue on the part of the child. In general, selections of increasing length can be handled as the difficulty level of the material increases. Specific materials and arrangement of them for the inventory depend, to some degree, on whether the evaluation is to be in an individual or group situation. For an individual inventory, most frequently used on a clinical basis, two selections, preferably connected, should be chosen for each level, from preprimer to the highest level to be tested. One of these is used for oral reading at sight and the other for silent reading. Oral rereading ability is evaluated by having the child reread aloud a portion of the material designed for silent reading.

Ideally, the materials chosen for the inventory should parallel as closely as possible those materials which will be used for instruction. However, they should not be materials which the child has actually encountered in his instructional program. The inadequacies of material which had been used for instruction seem obvious. There would certainly be the real possibility that the child would respond in terms of what had gone on in the classroom rather than in terms of what he was reading at the moment.

PROCEDURES FOR ADMINISTRATION

The total process of an individual informal inventory of reading ability may be divided for convenience into four major sections. These might be labeled pupil and examiner readiness, the word recognition test, the reading inventory, and the listening inventory. All four must be included if a thorough and competent job is to be accomplished.

Pupil-Examiner Readiness

Two major purposes are to be accomplished during this period. There is, of course, a need to enlist the cooperation of the person being examined if the inventory is to give valid and reliable results. Consequently, this period must be one during which rapport is established, both with the examiner and with the examining technique to be used. It is important that the pupil have at least a minimum degree of literacy about the method which is to be used to evaluate his accomplishments and needs in the reading area.

During this period, the examiner has an opportunity to appraise the child's oral language facility in many different ways. As they engage in informal conversation, he can pick up any actual defects in speech, appraise the degree of spontaneity in informal situations, determine the child's ability to respond to specific questions, and get some measure of the maturity level of the child's vocabulary, sentence structure and pronunciation. Likewise, there will be some reflection of the child's ability to concentrate on oral language activities and to respond appropriately. While all of this is going on, a great deal can also be learned about the child's attitude toward himself and the reading process. All of this material is significant in the total evaluation of his strengths and weaknesses in the reading area.

With the information gained in the course of this period and any previous data on the child, the examiner should also be able to estimate the possible level at which to begin with the word recognition test. The materials which the child is currently using for instruction, for instance, may give some clue. His own evaluation of the problems that he faces in reading may be indicative of the kinds of needs which will be uncovered, and may well dictate that testing should be begun at a very low level.

One guiding theme in the course of this period should be the attempt to get the child as serious and yet relaxed as possible about the job which faces him. He should understand that he is going to face tasks of increasing difficulty, so that he may go as far as his abilities will allow him to reach at this particular time. He should become aware of the fact that, if it is at all possible, the examiner will begin with materials which are quite easy for him, so that he will be able to demonstrate those things which he has accomplished in the reading area.

Word Recognition Test

To appraise the child's immediate recognition vocabulary and use of word analysis skills, words are presented in isolation. Lists of words from pre-primer at least through sixth should be available for this testing. In a clinical word recognition test, these lists should be samplings of common vocabulary at the various levels. For classroom use, however, the sampling is more often from the specific instructional materials. Twenty to twenty-five words appear to constitute an adequate sampling at each of the reader levels.

For actual test material, these lists of words should be typed clearly, at least double-spaced, so that they can be flashed with a manual tachistoscopic technique for immediate recognition purposes. Clear, readable type should be provided so that there is no possibility of difficulty which results from the vagueness of the visual stimulus rather than from the child's inability to handle the particular word recognition task required. From each list of words two scores will be derived, one representing the child's immediate recognition of the words (flash presentation), and the second, his performance in working words out in an untimed situation. In each case, the percentage of words correct is the score. On the flash test, only those correct responses which are given immediately are counted in the basic score. If corrections are made spontaneously, without a re-exposure of the word, credit is given for independent correction, but the basic score does not change. Thus if a child, on a list of 20 words, pronounced 19 correctly and one wrong, his basic score would be 95%; if he made an immediate correction of the twentieth word without seeing it again, a plus one would be added to the record of the scoring. The 95% + 1 would indicate, then, that he had corrected his one error without examiner aid.

The manual technique for flashing the words to the child is a relatively simple one, but requires practice so that it can be executed smoothly. Two cards (3 × 5 index cards suggested) comprise the materials needed. To flash a word to the child, the two cards are held together immediately above the word form. The lower card is moved down to expose the word; the upper card is then moved down to close the opening between them. This complete series of motions is carried out quickly so that the child gets only a flash presentation of the word. However, it is important that the word be exposed completely and clearly. A tendency in inexperienced examiners is to follow the lower card with the upper one, thus never really giving a clear exposure of the word. If a child responds correctly on the flash presentation, the examiner goes on to repeat the performance with the next word. If, however, an incorrect response is given, the word is re-exposed by pushing up the upper card so that the word can again be seen. No clues are given to its recognition, but the child has the opportunity to re-examine the word and to apply whatever word analysis skills he has at his command.

Immediate responses are recorded in a flash response column. The responses for re-exposures of the word appear in the untimed column. The untimed score is the basic sight vocabulary plus all corrections made without examiner help. It is important that responses be recorded immediately, so that there is complete accuracy in the record of the performance. Delay in writing down the child's response for even a few seconds may lead to confusion and incorrect reporting on the part of the examiner.

The word recognition test is continued, moving from level to level until the point at which the child is no longer able to function adequately at any given level. Unless the situation is extremely frustrating to the child, it is advisable to continue the test until the child is able to recognize only a very few of the words in the list at the level then being administered.

Figure 1 shows two levels of one boy's word recognition test as his responses were recorded. A check indicates a correct response; zero, no response; d.k., a statement that he did not know the word; separated letters, a naming of the letters. Single letters or phonetic symbols represent attempts to reproduce the indicated speech sound. Where an incorrect response was recorded and followed by a check, Robert made a spontaneous connection. A zero preceding a word or a check mark indicates an unusual delay before responding

The seventy-five percent score, plus one, at preprimer level, for example, indicates that Robert had fifteen words of the twenty correct initially, during the flash presentation, and made one spontaneous correction without seeing the word again. His eighty percent untimed score represents credit only for sixteen words which were gotten at flash because Robert made no additional corrections during the untimed presentation. At primer level, however, he worked out three in the untimed exposure. Here, his untimed score represents forty percent finally gotten correct during the flash presentation plus an additional twelve points for those three corrected when he had unlimited time to consider the word.

The Reading Clinic, Department of Psychology
Temple University, Philadelphia, Pennsylvania

Individual Word Recognition Test C

Name *Robert* _____ Age ___ 9 ___ Date ___ 1/2/64 ___

(The following is a random sampling of words taken from the
Daniels' READING VOCABULARY STUDY)

— — — — — — Pre-Primer Level — — — — — —   — — — — — — Primer Level — — — — — —

Stimulus	Flash	Untimed
1. little	✓	
2. you	✓	
3. can	✓	
	✓	
5. said	o	*something* (circled)
6. Want	o	o
7. come	✓	
8. it	✓	
9. comes	*came* (circled)	o
10. Come	✓	
11. for	✓	
12. see	✓	
13. play	✓	
14. It	✓	
15. I	✓	
16. to	✓	
17. in	m ✓	
18. Big	✓	
19. not	*down* (circled)	o
20. big	✓	
	75+1	80%

*"only four wrong!
I did good.
I'm reading"* (circled)

Stimulus	Flash	
1. Good	*o-o-dog?* (circled)	*what story was it in* (circled)
2. Run	✓	
3. are	*can* (circled)	o-o *and*
4. like	*little* (circled)	o
5. one	✓	
6. Away	*never say that word* (circled)	o
7. All	o	*Ik* (circled)
8. duck	o	*b-b-b*/o (circled)
9. yes	*y-e s* (circled)	✓
10. get	o	o
11. She	*her*	✓
12. make	o	m-m/o
13. my	✓	
14. No	o-o ✓	
15. This	o	*they*
16. am	*it-at*	o
17. red	✓	
18. run	✓	
19. Do	✓	
20. he	*I remember*	o
21. yellow	✓	
22. will	*what*	✓
23. home	✓	
24. went	o	o
25. they	o	*came* ✓
	36+1	52%

FIG. 1

The Reading Inventory

A wise procedure for starting the reading inventory is to begin at least one level lower than that at which the child first encountered difficulty in the word recognition test. The one situation in which this might not be suitable would be that in which the child has definitely revealed in his conversation or in his past history severe difficulties with comprehension. In this case, it would be best to begin at the very lowest level in order to present as few comprehension problems as possible on the initial selection.

Once the starting level has been determined, the procedure at each level is the same. Before any reading is done a definite readiness for the particular selection should be established. In the course of this readiness, a purpose for reading should be brought out. The examiner must be careful not to reveal so much in the way of vocabulary used in the selection or ideas contained that he gets no opportunity to measure the child's actual reading performance. Instead, some orientation should be given which will give the child a reason for reading, and a set in the right direction. As soon as this is accomplished, the selection designed for oral reading at sight is read aloud by the child in order for him to accomplish the established purpose. The examiner keeps a careful record of the exact way in which the selection was read. Each hesitation or error is recorded for example. If there is need for examiner help with pronunciation of words, this is given, but the amount is very carefully checked. As soon as the reading has been completed, the comprehension check is administered. The examiner must keep in mind that his purpose here is to evaluate the child's comprehension, and not to teach him. If a question is answered incorrectly, this does not mean that the examiner should help the child arrive at the right answer. Instead, he should go on to the next question. Responses to the comprehension questions should be recorded verbatim wherever this is possible. If such recording is not done, the immediate reaction to the adequacy of the response is oftentimes in question.

When the check on the reading of the first selection is completed, readiness for reading the second selection should be established immediately. Again, a purpose must be set for the reading. This time, the child reads the second selection at the same level silently. While this reading is being done, the examiner should observe carefully, keeping track of the time required for the reading as well as any signs of difficulty or specific reactions to the material. The comprehension check on the silent reading should be administered in the same fashion as was that for the oral reading at sight. When this has been completed, a new purpose should be established for re-reading a portion of the selection orally. Here, the performance should be recorded exactly as was done during the oral reading at sight.

This same procedure is followed at each level until a frustration point has been reached. When this occurs, the reading inventory itself is discontinued.

Figure 2 shows one child's performance on oral reading at sight at primer level. The notations indicate that he hesitated twice during the reading, apparently to give some thought to the words. Two actual errors were made. He read *cows* for *cow* and repeated to correct the error. He read *so* for *too* and apparently never noticed his error. Generally, he showed good fluency with the rest of the selection.

On the comprehension check, he responded freely, and showed ability to handle various types of questions. He forgot one bit of necessary information for the inference about the boy's name—the father's name. However, he made it clear that, had he remembered this, he would have been able to make the inference. His other error seemed to be one of failing to realize that the boy showed no signs of expecting to help until he was told he could and then went to bring the cow to his father rather than milk her himself.

All in all, indications are that the performance certainly meets the criteria for an instructional level. This is not to say that he might not also meet these criteria at a higher level or demonstrate similar needs at a lower level.

The Listening Inventory

The process of determining the highest level at which the child can understand materials read to him is usually begun at the next level following the one at which frustration was reached. In this process, the examiner again develops a readiness for the handling of the selection, and sees that a purpose is established just as it was for the reading of the materials by the child himself. In this case, however, the actual reading is done by the examiner. When this has been completed, listening comprehension is evaluated in a manner similar to that used for measuring the child's reading comprehension. This process is continued at successively higher levels until the child fails to maintain a level of 75% accuracy in comprehension.

When difficulties with understanding are at the root of the reading problem, the child may be able to do no better in the hearing comprehension test than when he was doing the reading himself. In such cases, it may be necessary to use alternate selections at lower levels to establish a hearing comprehension level.

Primer
Oral at sight   AT THE BARN
56 words

Bob and his father came out of the house.

They went to the big red barn.

They were going to get some milk.

"You can help me," said Mr. Black.

"I will get the cow!" called bob as

he ran on into the barn.

"Don't go too fast," called Mr. Black.

"You will make her jump."

(handwritten margin calculations:)

$$\begin{array}{r} 120 \text{ WPM} \\ sec.\ 28\overline{)3360} \\ 28 \\ \overline{56} \end{array}$$

$$\begin{array}{r} .0357\% \text{ error} \\ 56\overline{)2.00} \\ 158 \\ \overline{320} \\ 280 \\ \overline{40} \end{array}$$

(handwritten note, circled:) good rhythm Expressive WR-96%

(over "cow":) ✓ s
(over "too":) 50

✓ How do you know Bob and his father had not been outside? *came out of the house*

✓ Where had Bob and his father been? ✓

✓ Where were they going? *to the barn*

✓ What did they want to get? *milk*

(circled note:) 80% comp. Quick, natural response

✓ In what were they going to put the milk? (picture clue)

0 What was Bob's last name? *I forget—it told his father's name but I forget.*

✓ Did Bob expect to milk the cow? How do you know? *yes* *He went right to the barn ( ) to milk the cow.*

✓ How did Bob feel about being allowed to help? How do you know? *I guess he liked it. Most boys would.*

✓ What warning did Mr. Black give Bob? *(Q)He ran right away (0) when his father told him he would help.*

✓ How do you know Mr. Black was afraid Bob might scare the cow? *He yelled at him to) show up or she'd jump.*

(circled note:) Ques. not really to push for thinking what did he do? When?

Recapitulation

WR ___96___   ___80___   ORR: Time _____

Oral WRM _120_   Silent Comp._____   Correct?_____

Silent WPM _____   Avg. Comp. _____   Rythm _____

FIG. 2

INSTRUCTIONS FOR SCORING

The effectiveness of the evaluation made by informal inventory techniques depends on the adequacy of the observations which are made. Considered judgments based on these observations are required. It is essential, therefore, that the examiner have an accurate record of the examinee's total performance. Only with complete information available can he really analyze the child's performance, comparing what happened in one situation with what happened in another, and arrive at reliable conclusions. For this kind of evaluation, no examiner can depend on his memory. Too many things happen too quickly for him to recall them. Therefore, complete recording must be achieved and accurate scoring and interpretation done on the basis of this record.

Recording

Teachers using informal reading inventories will find it helpful to develop a "short-hand" for use in recording all significant elements of the behavior noted during the administration. Unlike the word recognition test, where ample time for recording can be taken whenever needed, in the inventory proper the child's reading of a selection is never interrupted for recording purposes. At the independent and instructional levels, where symptoms of difficulty are at a minimum, the examiner usually experiences few problems in recording behavior. However, as the selections become more difficult for the examinee these symptoms multiply and it becomes an increasingly complex task for the examiner to keep pace with the reader and still note all of the errors made.

In addition to the above, all other pertinent behavioral symptoms and comments should be noted. The following example (Fig. 3) will serve to indicate one clinician's method of recording the oral reading.

In this case the examiner, following the establishing of a purpose for reading, asked the child to locate the story "about a farm" in the book—the resultant method employed is noted. The actual reading began with a substitution of *Bill* for *Bob*, a slight pause and then an initial consonant attack on *father*, followed by correct pronunciation of the word. Next came two substitutions which were corrected by repetition after a two second pause. No pause occurred at the end of the first sentence. Both finger pointing and head movement were evidenced during the reading. In the second sentence, in addition to inappropriate pauses and a substitution, *see* was inserted and, after an extended pause, the word *barn* was given by the examiner. By the third line the child's rhythm had deteriorated to a word by word performance. He further substituted *meat* for *milk*, but in a questioning tone, and the examiner told him the word.

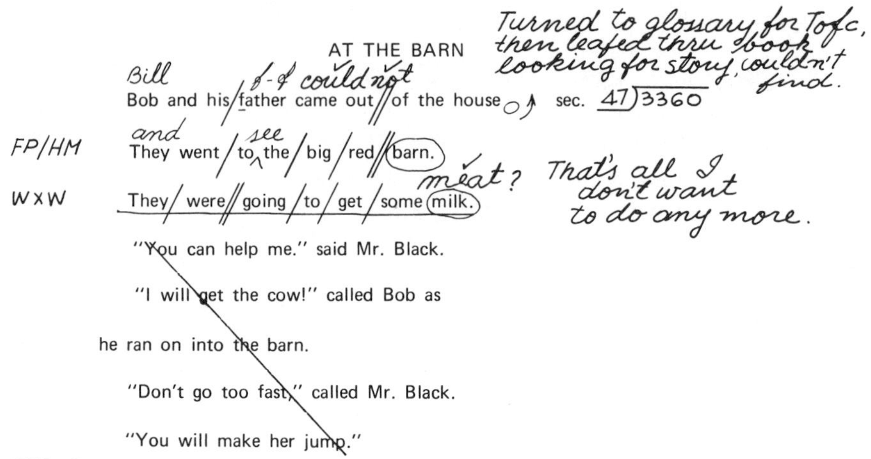

Turned to glossary for 'ofc,' then leafed thru book looking for story, couldn't find.

AT THE BARN

Bill   *d-d couldn't*

Bob and his/father came out//of the house ○↗ sec. 47)3360

FP/HM

and / *see*

They went / to the / big / red / barn.   *meat?*   *That's all I don't want to do any more.*

W x W

They/ were// going /to/ get /some milk.

"You can help me." said Mr. Black.

"I will get the cow!" called Bob as

he ran on into the barn.

"Don't go too fast," called Mr. Black.

"You will make her jump."

FIG. 3

The entire line was then repeated with the final word correctly recognized in this reading. This was followed by the refusal to continue indicated in the margin of the illustration. The entire performance, from the initial substitution to the final repetition, consumed forty-seven seconds.

Scoring

The objective criteria suggested for identifying the various levels of a child's reading performance are based upon measurement of word recognition and comprehension abilities. The former is computed, in the individual inventory, for the oral reading at sight, while the latter is found for both selections used at each level of material. Although nearly all the behavioral symptoms suggested as indications of difficulty with a selection are positively related to word perception skills, only four of these are usually counted in computing the word recognition score—substitutions, insertions, omissions and requests for examiner aid. The clinician should count the number of such errors and compute a percent score by dividing this number by the total number of words in the selection (see Fig. 2). When the resultant quotient is subtracted from 100, a percent correct score for the selection is obtained. This should be recorded in the recapitulation table at the bottom of the page for each oral reading selection employed in the administration.

Similarly, the comprehension score for *each* selection at every level of materials used may be computed by dividing the number of questions answered correctly by the total number of questions asked.* When ques-

---

* Assuming that each question rates the same numerical value in the inventory being employed.

tions are included which require multiple responses, partial credit is usually given and included on a fractional basis in this total. These scores should be recorded in the spaces provided in the recapitulation box and averaged for a total comprehension score at each level of material.

The computation of words-per-minute scores for both oral and silent reading is facilitated when advanced provision has been made for this in the preparation of an inventory. In the sample shown, an appropriate dividend for division by the elapsed time in seconds taken for the reading has been included. This dividend represents the product of the number of running words in the selection and sixty (seconds). Thus, the quotient obtained when the division has been completed is a words-per-minute score. The score for both the oral and silent selections should also be recorded in the recapitulation table.

Evaluating Oral Rereading (ORR)

The oral rereading mission in an informal reading inventory serves three specific purposes: It provides (1) a gauge of the child's ability to skim for the re-location of specific information; (2) another measure of his ability to read for a specific purpose and stop when that purpose has been satisfied; and (3) an index of his ability to profit from his previous visual contact with the material and thus improve, essentially in accuracy and rhythm, his oral reading performance here over his oral reading at sight. Improvement in rhythm is to be expected, if it was not originally good, in all selections ranging between a child's independent and his frustration level. When this is not the case, such non-improvement is often interpreted as a sign of the need for the use of multi-sensory materials for word learning. The level recapitulation box provides a place for recording the ORR performance appropriate to these three purposes.

Recapitulating the Results

The Recapitulation Record shown in Fig. 4 is suggested as a means of summarizing the objective data obtained in the administration of an informal reading inventory. In Part I the percent scores in word recognition from both the *Individual Word Recognition Test* and the oral reading at sight (context) are recorded for each level tested. Similarly, comprehension scores for reading and listening activities are summarized. Successful or non-successful completion of the oral rereading task and some indication of the improvement or non-improvement of rhythm should be noted at each level given. Finally, the words-per-minute scores for both oral and silent reading should be recorded.

From examination of the summarized data and inspection of the recorded performance at each of the levels tested, the examiner will be able to assign a reader level for each of the "Estimated Levels" in Part

Informal Reading Inventory

Recapitulation Record

Name _____   Date _____ Grade _____

Case No. _____ C.A. ____   Examiner _____

I. Test Data

| Level | Word Recognition | | | Comprehension | | | | ORR | WPM oral / silent |
| | Isolation | | | | | | | | |
	Flash	Untimed	Context	Hearing	Oral	Silent	Average		oral / silent
PP	100%	100%	99%		100%	90%	95%	✓	123/157
P	95 +1	100	99		95	85	90	✓	129/149
1	75	95	96		80	75	78	✓I	114/138
2	60 +1	80	93		65	70	68	✓I	90/110
3	20	50	89		60	45	58	✓HI	67/72
4				90%					
5				78					
6				62					
7									
8									
9									

II. Estimated Levels

Independent _____ P _____

Instructional _____ 1 _____

Frustration _____ 2 _____

Hear. Comp. _____ 5 _____

III. Recommendations

Modified experience appr.
Utilize interest in animals
Parents read content mater,
   to him for a while
Discontinue formal spells
Have nurse check vision
   & refer if necessary

IV. Summary of Specific Needs

Retarded three years in rdg.
   achv't.
Phonics needs:
   bl, str, long vowels final e,
   vowel digraphs, diphtongs
Syllabication:
   compound words, prefixes
   suffixes, varient endings
Uses content clues well,
   especially pictures
      (over dependence)
Broaden interest experience
   from animals to other areas.

FIG. 4

II. The criteria suggested for each of these levels must be kept constantly in mind when one is drawing conclusions on the basis of the data obtained.

Parts III and IV provide space for a summary of specific needs in word recognition, comprehension, conceptual development, etc. and for brief statements of pedagogical techniques to be tried or materials to be used. Any observations made which indicated the need for further testing or referral to specialists in related disciplines should also be reflected in appropriate recommendations here.

CONCLUSION

The individual informal reading inventory is a clinical device. It is designed to reveal extensive information about a child's reading strengths and needs as well as to establish the levels at which he can function independently and with instruction. The results obtained from administration of such an inventory are as good as the examiner, no better. Specific criteria for the establishment of levels have been indicated. However, the powers of observation and the standards of judgment of the examiner are the final determinants of the adequacy of the information gained.

16. PREDICTING READING FAILURE: BEYOND THE READINESS MODEL

HOWARD S. ADELMAN and SEYMOUR FESHBACH

There has been a considerable amount of research effort directed toward the problem of predicting school failure, especially reading failure (Austin & Morrison, 1963; Barrett, 1965; Chall, Roswell, Alshan, & Bloomfield, 1965; Cohen, 1963; de Hirsch, Jansky, & Langford, 1966; Haring & Ridgway, 1967; Harrington & Durrell, 1955; Henig, 1949; Kermoian, 1962; Koppitz, 1964; Martin, 1955; Monroe, 1935; Weiner & Feldman, 1963). While some of these studies have yielded significant correlations between predictors and criterion variables, the relationships have been weak, particularly when subjected to crossvalidation procedures. A principal thesis of this article is that this relative lack of success is in large part a consequence of the fact that these efforts have been based upon what is essentially a reading readiness model, i.e., a model which traditionally has emphasized the assessment of a youngster's deficits with reference to a delimited set of reading correlates such as perceptual-motor and linguistic skills. At the very least, it is evident that most of these investigations have been restricted to procedures which do not assess the impact of many key variables which interact in shaping school success and failure.

The work of de Hirsch and her colleagues (1966), while of consider-

---

SOURCE. Reprinted from *Exceptional Children*, 1971, 37, No. 5, 349–354, with permission of the author and publisher.

able interest and importance, nevertheless provides a recent example of such a restricted approach. They focus almost exclusively on readiness variables although they are aware of the dynamic process by which reading skill is acquired. As the investigators themselves point out:

"We recognize that a variety of social, environmental, and psychological factors are significant in the acquisition of reading skills,· and we concur with Abraham Fabian (1951), who maintains that learning to read requires the developmental timing and integration of both neurophysiological and psychological aspects of readiness. Nevertheless, we limited ourselves to the preschool child's perceptumotor and linguistic functioning because in this area we had found considerable deviation from the norm among children who subsequently failed in reading and spelling. We therefore put together a battery of tests which we hoped would reflect the children's perceptumotor and linguistic status at kindergarten level [de Hirsch, et. al., 1966, p. 5]."

Thus, despite recognition of the importance of socio-emotional and environmental factors, the decision was made to ignore such variables. This decision is reflected not only by the limiting of assessment to perceptual-motor and linguistic functioning but also by the choice of a "battery of tests" which are administered to each youngster individually. Such assessment procedures obviously entail markedly different performance conditions than are to be found in the classroom. For example, the adult tester provides undivided attention in contrast to a classroom teacher whose attention is almost always divided when she is teaching. In addition, such relevant factors as distractions, peer group pressures, and other classroom situational variables are removed. In using such procedures, one attempts to predict later classroom performance, based on admittedly limited information, derived under conditions which are dissimilar from those in the classroom. (This dissimilarity alone could account for many of the "false negatives" in the de Hirsch study and certainly would result in a great number of undetected potential failures in a large scale predictive program.)

A discussion of all the theoretical and practical limitations of such restricted approaches to the problem of predicting school failure is beyond the scope of this article. (For further critical discussion see de Hirsch, et al., 1966; Rozeboom, 1966; Zieky & Ellis, 1968.)

BEYOND THE READINESS MODEL

The purpose of this article is to go beyond the readiness model and suggest a viable alternative—an approach which provides a closer approximation between predictor and criterion. As implied above, a youngster's success or failure in school is most fruitfully seen as a function of the interaction between his strengths, weaknesses, and limitations and the specific classroom situational factors he encounters—including individual differences among teachers and differing approaches to instruction. This interactional model infers that success in the first grade depends not only on the youngster's having the necessary skills and behaviors for learning what is being taught, but also on the characteristics of the classroom situation to which he is assigned. Thus, it is hypothesized that the greater the congruity between a youngster's skills and behaviors (as manifested under representative classroom conditions) and those required of him in a specific first grade classroom, the greater the likelihood of success; conversely, the greater the discrepancy between the child's skills and behaviors and those required in his classroom, the greater the likelihood of failure. (For purposes of this discussion, failure is viewed as reading performance which results in a child receiving a D or F reading grade.)

A major implication of this hypothesis is that one effective strategy for predicting reading failure is to assess the degree to which the kindergarten youngster can successfully cope under classroom conditions with tasks which are as similar as possible to those which he will encounter in the first grade reading program. Such an assessment can be accomplished by (a) evaluating, in situ, deficits in or absence of reading-relevant skills and behaviors, as well as evaluating the presence of interfering behaviors in each kindergarten child, (b) evaluating each first grade program to determine the pattern and degree of skills and behaviors which assigned youngsters will find critical in coping with the reading-relevant tasks, and (c) analyzing the discrepancy between a youngster's skills and behaviors and what is being required for success in that classroom.

The following brief description of how these steps will be implemented in an experimental program should help to clarify this approach to predicting reading failure.

EVALUATION OF KINDERGARTEN CHILDREN

In developing a specific assessment procedure to aid in predicting which children will fail in the first grade reading program, the emphasis has been on those behaviors and skills which first grade teachers generally require and those behaviors which they will not tolerate during reading-related activities. The specific instrument currently being developed is a rating scale consisting of items which reflect a recent analysis of such requirements. This analysis is based on observation of numerous first grade and kindergarten classrooms, a survey of available readiness inventories and curriculum manuals, a review of various writers (Bruner, Olver, Greenfield, Hornsby, Kenney, Maccoby, Modian, Mosher, Olson, Potter, Reich, & Sonstroem, 1966; Fernald, 1943; Havighurst, 1952; Hebb, 1949; Hewett, 1966; Hunt, 1961; Piaget, 1950), and relevant personal experiences in the field of learning disabilities over the past 10 years. To date, this analysis has yielded the following list of abilities.

Abilities

With regard to physical and motor development and general health, the important areas and functioning levels are viewed as:

1. Adequate sensory capacity i.e., Johnson and Myklebust (1967) indicate that hearing loss greater than 30 to 35 dB (computed as an average for the speech range of the better ear) might result in a detriment to learning. Lawson (1967) indicates a visual impairment of 20/40 or greater (when glasses are worn) should be considered consequential for learning. In addition to visual acuity, color blindness may contribute to learning difficulties, especially in the early grades. (Impairment of other senses has not been demonstrated to be a serious problem in learning academic skills.)
2. Adequate eye-hand coordination i.e., the youngster performs such skills as using a pencil appropriately and with enough control to keep close to the outline of large figures.
3. General health which is good enough so that the youngster maintains regular attendance at school.

With regard to language skills, the important abilities are viewed as:

1. Expressive i.e., the youngster speaks clearly and plainly enough to be understood in class and manifests a working vocabulary.
2. Receptive i.e., the youngster understands what is said in class.
3. Use i.e., using at least simple sentences, the youngster expresses ideas, thoughts, feelings; the youngster also has an awareness of the relationship between spoken and written language.

With regard to perceptual abilities, the important abilities are viewed as:

1. Visual discrimination i.e., the youngster discriminates differences and similarities in letters, words, numbers, and colors, and sees the relationship of a part to the whole.
2. Auditory discrimination i.e., the youngster discriminates differences and similarities in sounds of letters.

With regard to other general school behaviors and skills, items are being developed to allow for evaluation of the degree to which a youngster manifests interest in pursuing reading-relevant activities and the degree to which he manifests the ability to:

1. Follow simple directions.
2. Maintain seatwork attention for sufficient periods of time to accomplish a simple classroom task.
3. Observe and remember.
4. Answer questions about a simple story.
5. Tell a story from a picture (associate symbols with pictures, objects and facts).
6. Direct attention toward print or pictures displayed to the class by the teacher.
7. Solve simple problems.
8. Tolerate failure sufficiently to persist on a task.
9. Make transitions from one activity to another.
10. Carry on with a task over several days.
11. Accept adult direction without objection or resentment.
12. Work without constant supervision or reminders.
13. Respond to normal classroom routines.
14. Suppress tendencies to interrupt others.

In addition to these skills and behaviors, it is obvious that if a child manifests certain other negative behaviors, he may well have serious difficulties in school. These include problems in terms of teacher and/or peer relationships, and of being able to care for himself, control himself, and so forth. Therefore, an assessment of such factors is also viewed as necessary in screening for potential reading failure.

In general, then, the child evaluation instrument being developed covers all the areas listed above and is designed for use in the kindergarten classroom by the kindergarten teacher. Three examples of scale items are presented below:

"When the task requires it, how often do you find he can and does speak clearly enough so that you can understand him?"

"When the task requires it, how often can and does he discriminate the differences and similarities in letters and words when he is looking at them?"

"When the task requires it, how often can and does he answer questions about a simple story?"

Such items are rated on a 5 point scale with 1 being the lowest point and indicating that in situations requiring the specific behavior or skill the youngster's response never or hardly ever is adequate or appropriate. ("Never or hardly ever" is defined as 0-10 percent of the time and the frame of reference established for "adequate or appropriate" responding is performance which the teacher would grade C or better. The highest point on the scale, 5, indicates that in situations requiring the specific behavior or skill the child's response is adequate or appropriate always or almost always, 90–100 percent of the time).

The proposed procedures for using this instrument involve training the kindergarten teacher to observe his students with specific reference to the rating scale items over the last 2–3 months of the kindergarten year. At the end of the school year, he rates the child on the items, thereby evaluating the pattern and degree of skills and positive and negative behaviors which the youngster has manifested. (If the kindergarten teaching program does not include activities which require some of the skills and behaviors which are included on the rating scale, then a series of "lessons" will be initiated by the teacher so that he will be able to rate all items. In addition, it is assumed that general medical screening of visual and auditory acuity will be accomplished by competent physicians, especially in those instances when a youngster is evaluated as being a potential failure.)

It may be noted that these procedures have several major advantages over procedures that typically have been used in the prediction of reading failure. For example, since the assessment is made over an extended period of time, it involves a broader sample of behavior than can be obtained during a single test session; in addition, specially trained testers are not necessary and this is both more economical and can also facilitate the use of the findings as an educational aid.

EVALUATION OF FIRST GRADE PROGRAMS

For evaluating the critical demands of a specific first grade classroom situation and teacher, a separate but parallel rating scale is currently being developed. For example, the following three sample items parallel the kindergarten items presented above.

"How often does the teacher require clarity of speech in order for a student to be able to perform adequately and appropriately on a reading-relevant task?"

"How often does the teacher require the ability to discriminate visually between the differences and similarities in letters and words in order for a student to be able to perform adequately and appropriately on a reading-relevant task?"

"How often does the teacher require at least the ability to answer questions about a simple story in order for a student to be able to perform adequately and appropriately on a reading-relevant task?"

Again, such scale items are rated on a 5 point scale with 1 being the lowest point. In this case, 1 indicates that the teacher never or hardly ever (0–10 percent of the time) appears to require the particular behavior or skill in order to consider performance adequate and appropriate. (Performance which the teacher would not consider adequate or appropriate is defined as behavior which he assigns a grade of D or F.) With minimum training, the school counselor or some other member of a particular school's staff can use such a first grade evaluation scale to rate the level of skill and behavioral performance required of a pupil for success during the reading period. In making such ratings, a rater observes a first grade teacher during the reading instruction period, particularly in the pattern-setting initial weeks of the program. Primary focus is on the teacher's interactions with those students who are doing poorly in reading-relevant activities. The final ratings on the scale, which will probably require a number of weeks, are made at the conclusion of the entire period of observation. Every first grade teacher in a given school is to be rated in this manner, thereby empirically determining not only which student skills and behaviors are required but which ones are critical i.e., the degree to which the teacher requires certain levels of performance and the degree to which he tolerates and/or compensates for particular deviations.

DISCREPANCY ANALYSIS

The above procedures, then, can yield (a) an indication of which skills and behaviors are critical for succeeding in the first grade program in a particular classroom, school, and district, and (b) the level of performance of a particular kindergarten child with regard to these critical skills and behaviors. These data permit an analysis of the discrepancy between a specific youngster's skills and behaviors and the requirements for successful first grade performance. For research purposes, all three levels of discrepancy analyses can be carried out i.e., a separate discrepancy score may be derived from the differences between the ratings given a youngster on each item and the normative rating for the district, the normative rating for a particular school, and the idiosyncratic rating given to the first grade teacher to whom the youngster is assigned. A comparison of these sources provides an empirical means for determining the significance of variations in requirements in different first grade classes as compared to the normative skills demanded of each child during reading instruction.

DISCUSSION

The procedures that have been proposed and described here are in their initial stages of development. Nevertheless, it is hoped that the description of these efforts convey the differences between a predictive approach which attempts only to assess a youngster's strengths, weaknesses, and/or limitations under standardized conditions and one which attempts to assess such factors and their relative importance with particular reference to the conditions under which they are to be manifested. It is these differences which are viewed as critical in effectively predicting which children are most likely to fail in the area of reading.

In addition to improving predictive accuracy, two other benefits may accrue from such an approach. First, since the kindergarten evaluation procedures assess aspects of socio-emotional functioning, such a screening program for potential reading failures also provides the opportunity (with several additional rating items) for the rapid, first level screening of disturbed preschool and school age children (see Bower, 1960, 1963; Kohn & Silverman, 1966a, 1966b; Lambert, 1963; Rubin, Simson, & Betwee, 1966). Further, the first grade evaluations allow for an assessment of the actual demands of the reading programs in these classrooms, as well as the determination of how closely these demands resemble the first grade curriculum established by the school district. Thus, as the efforts expand to assess the problems of the child and the teaching process, educators are in a better position to alleviate the weaknesses in the system as well as in the child. Stated more generally, as less restrictive models are employed in efforts to predict reading failure, it is likely that more comprehensive remedial and preventive measures will evolve.

The views presented above may be summarized as suggesting that the readiness model applied to the prediction of reading failure has proven to be too restrictive, that there is a viable alternative to this model, and that the implications derived from research based on the alternative model may lead to more comprehensive efforts to remedy and prevent reading failure. It seems reasonable to suggest that exploration based on a less restrictive model should aid in further identifying the key variables which are involved in this crucial problem area.

References

Austin, M. C., & Morrison, C. *The first R: The Harvard report on reading in elementary schools.* New York: Macmillan, 1963.

Barrett, T. C. Visual discrimination tasks as predictors of first grade reading achievement. *Reading Teacher*, 1965, 18, 276–282.

Bower, E. M. *Early identification of emotionally handicapped children in school.* Springfield, Ill.: Charles C. Thomas, 1960.

Bower, E. M. Primary prevention of mental and emotional disorders. *American Journal of Orthopsychiatry,* 1963, 33, 832–848.

Bruner, J. S., Olver, R. R., Greenfield, P. M., Hornsby, J. R., Kenney, H. J., Maccoby, M., Modian, N., Mosher, F. A., Olson, D. R., Potter, M. C., Reich, L. C., & Sonstroem, A. M. *Studies in cognitive growth.* New York: John Wiley & Sons, 1966.

Chall, J., & Roswell, F. Language, visual, auditory and visual-motor factors in beginning reading: A preliminary analysis. Paper presented at meeting of the American Educational Research Association, Chicago, February, 1965.

Cohen, T. B. Diagnostic and predictive methods with young children. *American Journal of Orthopsychiatry,* 1963, 33, 330–331.

de Hirsch, K., Jansky, J. J., & Langford, W. S. *Predicting reading failure.* New York: Harper & Row, 1966.

Fabian, A. A. Clinical and experimental studies of school children who are retarded in reading. *Quarterly Journal of Child Behavior,* 1951, 3, 15–37.

Fernald, G. M. *Remedial techniques in basic school subjects.* New York: McGraw-Hill, 1943.

Haring, M. G., & Ridgway, R. W. Early identification of children with learning disabilities. *Exceptional Children,* 1967, 33, 387–395.

Harrington, S. M. J., & Durrell, D. Mental maturity vs. perception abilities in primary reading. *Journal of Educational Psychology,* 1955, 46, 375–380.

Havighurst, R. *Developmental tasks and education.* New York: Longmans, 1952.

Hebb, D. O. *The organization of behavior.* New York: John Wiley & Sons, 1949.

Henig, M. A. Predictive value of a reading readiness test and of teacher's forecast. *Elementary School Journal,* 1949, 50, 41–46.

Hewett, F. M. A hierarchy of educational tasks for children with learning disorders. In E. C. Frierson and W. B. Barbe (Eds.), *Educating children with learning disabilities.* New York: Appleton-Century-Crofts, 1966.

Hunt, J. M. *Intelligence and experience.* New York: Ronald Press, 1961.

Johnson, D., & Myklebust, H. *Learning disabilities.* New York: Grune & Stratton, 1967.

Kermoian, S. B. Teacher appraisal of first grade readiness. *Elementary English,* 1962, 39, 196–201.

Kohn, M., & Silverman, H. W. The relationship of competence and symptom factors to each other and to teacher's categorical ratings. Paper presented at meeting of Eastern Psychological Association, New York, April, 1966. (a)

Kohn, M., & Silverman, H. W. A competence scale and a symptom checklist for the preschool child. Paper presented at meeting of Eastern Psychological Association, New York, April, 1966. (b)

Koppitz, E. M. *The Bender Gestalt Test For Young Children.* New York: Grune & Stratton, 1964.

Lambert, N. M. *The development and validation of a process for screening emotionally handicapped children in school.* Sacramento, Cal.: Department of Education, 1963.

Lawson, L. Ophthalmological factors in learning disabilities. In H. Myklebust (Ed.), *Progress in learning disabilities.* New York: Grune & Stratton, 1967.

Martin, C. Developmental interrelationships among language variables in children of first grade. *Elementary English,* 1955, **32**, 167–171.

Monroe, M. Reading aptitude tests for the prediction of success and failure in beginning reading. *Education,* 1935, **56**, 7–14.

Piaget, J. *The psychology of intelligence.* London: Routledge and Kegan Paul, 1950.

Rozeboom, W. W. *Foundations of the theory of prediction.* Homewood, Ill.: Dorsey Press, 1966.

Rubin, E. Z., Simson, C. R., & Betwee, M. C. *Emotionally handicapped children and the elementary school.* Detroit: Wayne State University Press, 1966.

Weiner, M., & Feldman, S. Validation studies of a reading prognosis test for children of lower and middle socio-economic status. *Educational and Psychological Measurement,* 1963, **23**, 807–814.

Zieky, M. J., & Page, E. B. Book review of *Predicting reading failure,* by K. de Hirsch, J. Jansky, & W. Langford. *Harvard Educational Review,* 1968, **38**, 365–366.

17. EARLY IDENTIFICATION OF CHILDREN WITH LEARNING DISABILITIES

NORRIS G. HARING and ROBERT W. RIDGWAY

The child who has difficulty in learning almost without exception faces failure in a conventional school program. Often he experiences months and sometimes years of unsuccessful work before he receives remedial aid. This failure, resulting from the inability to develop potential capacities, can only lead to compounded and more serious problems when the school program demands, through its presentation of academic material, that the child use skills which he has never developed, or tries to build on experience that the child has never had, or requires the utilization of a concept yet unestablished. A situation of this kind arises when a child is expected to copy a square before he can discriminate a square from a triangle, or when the information he receives through his eyes cannot be translated into the movement of his hand, because of insufficient experience with a crayon.

To prevent more serious learning problems from occurring, identification of the child with learning disabilities should be made as early as possible in his school career. When a teacher recognizes a child as having learning disabilities, she can construct an appropriate instructional program for him that will use and develop his skills, experience and poten-

SOURCE. Reprinted from *Exceptional Children*, 1967, 33, 387–395. By permission of the authors and publisher.

tial, while relieving some of the problems that arose from past failure in a conventional school program.

The primary teacher is usually the first person to identify the child with learning disabilities but this identification comes after the child has failed to learn for a considerable period of time. At the kindergarten level, where the child begins his school career, the ability to recognize the child with potential learning disabilities would be invaluable in eliminating possible future problems in academic learning for the child.

The child with a learning disability is characterized by an educationally significant discrepancy between his estimated potential for learning and his day to day level of functioning which is related to basic disorders in the learning process that may or may not be accompanied by demonstrable central nervous system dysfunctioning, and which is not secondary to generalized mental retardation, severe emotional disturbance, extreme environmental or educational deprivation, blindness, or deafness (US Office of Education, 1964). According to this definition, children with normal intelligence, hearing, sight, and emotional development may possess learning disabilities which conventional psychological evaluations could fail to identify.

This study attempted to discover if the child with potential learning disabilities could be identified during his kindergarten year by means of certain tests which are held to be predictors of learning disabilities. Those areas believed to represent the basic processes necessary for the performance of academic tasks were measured by the instruments used in evaluating the child's potential capacities. These areas of child development were assessed in the study: (a) visual perception; (b) eye hand coordination; (c) auditory discrimination; (d) visual attention span; (e) directionality; (f) auditory attention span; (g) large muscle coordination; and (h) general language development.

RELATED LITERATURE

No one to date has reported on research concerned with the identification of children with learning disabilities prior to school years. The rationale of this study centers on the selected variables that are believed to correlate with certain learning disabilities and the exploration of their predictive value when found in kindergarten children.

Auditory Memory. The role of defective auditory memory in learning disabilities was noted more than fifty years ago in the research of Bronner (1917) and Hinshelwood (1917). In more recent years this finding has been consistently verified (Monroe, 1932; Bond, 1935; Robinson, 1953; Kass, 1962; Bateman, 1963). Conversely, the role of good auditory memory in cases of unusually good reading ability has also been reported (Krippner, 1963). Studies showing that groups of retarded readers do poorly on the WISC digit span subtest illustrate the kind of evidence supporting the importance of the role of auditory memory in learning disabilities (Hirst, 1960; Neville, 1961).

Auditory Discrimination. Wepman (1960) found a positive correlation between auditory discrimination and reading level among first graders. Goetzinger, Dirks and Baer (1960) confirmed this and postulated a "primary auditory-cortical dysfunction" in poor readers. Monroe's (1932) study of one hundred disabled readers also showed a definite relationship between auditory word discrimination skills and developmental dyslexia. On the basis of their own and other's past research, Durrell and Murphy (1953) concluded that auditory discrimination is basic to learning language skills.

Visual Memory and Perception. Benton (1962) stated that the type of deficit most frequently associated with dyslexia is impairment of visual perception and that a relationship between visuoperceptive skills and probable retardation in learning to read should be discernible in young school children with disabilities. Extensive experimental evidence on these relationships and further explorations of them can be found in the works of: Fildes (1921); Goins (1958); Cruickshank, Bentzen, Ratzeburg, and Tannhauser (1961); Strauss and Lehtinen (1947); Strauss and Kephart (1955); Frostig, Lefever, and Whittlesey (1961); and Diack (1960). Considerable question still exists concerning the role of visual acuity and eye movements (Robinson, 1946; Eames, 1948; Traxler and Townsend, 1955; and Malmquist, 1958). Fildes (1921), Fendrick (1935), Malmquist (1958), and Bateman (1963), however, have presented definitive evidence that visual memory is related to learning problems.

Laterality, Directionality and Body Image. The case for directional confusion as the basis for many learning disabilities has been clearly stated by Hermann (1959) who sees it as relating to a failure of lateral orientation with reference to the body schema. This failure results in spatial orientation difficulties, which cause problems in operating with symbols, such as letters (Benton, 1962). Recent studies by Harris (1957), Goins (1958), Hermann and Norrie (1958), Benton (1959), Hermann (1959), Silver and Hagin (1960), Cohn (1961), and Rabinovitch (1962) have amply demonstrated defective right-left orientation in children with learning disabilities. Investigations of laterality and orientation in relation to learning disabilities have sometimes rested on controversial theoretical bases (Orton, 1937; Delacato, 1963), but the relationship can be considered established, even if the exact etiology remains unclear.

Motor Coordination. Rabinovitch, Drew, DeJong, Ingram, and Whitby

(1954), Bakwin and Bakwin (1960), Kephart (1960), Cohn (1961), Prechtl (1962), and Delacato (1963) have shown the definite appearance of nonspecific awkwardness and clumsiness in motor functions of children with learning disabilities. Kephart (1960), Cruickshank (1961), and Delacato (1963) have developed programs for sequential development and improvement of motor skills in children with these disabilities.

Overall Language Ability. Language disorders and overall language development are, by definition, closely and integrally related to learning disabilities. The particular approach to the relationship between language ability and disability to be pursued in this study is based on the Illinois Test of Psycholinguistic Abilities (1961). This is a diagnostic test of psycholinguistic patterns, based on theoretical models of Osgood (1957) and Wepman, Jones, Bock, and Pelt (1960), which leads to remedial procedures for deficient language functions.

PROCEDURES

This study selected the 48 kindergarten classes of School District 110 in Johnson County, Kansas, for use in the project. These classes had a total enrollment of over 1,200 children. The class teachers attended a series of instructional meetings designed to acquaint them with the techniques of observing a child's developmental status. Following the same methods of direct, unstructured observation learned in the instructional meetings, the teachers observed the characteristics of each child in their classes.

Initial Screening. The teachers, having learned the characteristics of every child in their classes, were requested to choose one quarter of their children whom they believed to be high risk in the probability of developing learning problems. In this initial screening, the teachers were asked to be particularly aware of problems in the areas of language development, visual perceptual adequacy, and fine and gross motor coordination. Close attention was given to specific behaviors that might indicate slower than normal development.

To those children whom the teachers had identified as probable in developing learning disorders, they administered a screening scale, developed by the project staff. This scale included performance items to help the teachers objectify their observations and assist in collecting information in these areas: (a) personal appearance; (b) psychological characteristics; (c) gross muscle coordination; (d) verbal fluency; (e) speech development; (f) auditory memory; (g) auditory discrimination; (h) visual memory; (i) visual discrimination; (j) visual motor performance; and (k) directionality and laterality. Three ratings—above average, average, and poor—for each of these eleven areas were available to the teachers. If in the judgment of a teacher a child rated poor in any one of the eleven areas, he was referred to the staff psychologists for further study.

Psychological Screening. Those children, identified by their teachers as poor in one of more of the areas covered by the screening scale, were administered intelligence tests by the staff psychologists. The intelligence tests used were the Stanford-Binet and three subtests (block design, coding, and picture arrangement) of the WISC. From the results of these tests and the direct observations made by the psychology staff, the data were assimilated for the final staffing and selection of children for this project.

Staffing. Two hundred twenty children, representing almost one-fifth of the entire kindergarten enrollment in the classes, were carefully studied. A team composed of the project director, a clinical psychologist, a school psychologist, a children's psychiatrist, and a special educator made the selection of children to be incorporated in this study through considerations of the kindergarten screening scale, intelligence tests, and the evaluations of the psychological staff about the developmental status of each child. Final decisions about the children came after thorough discussion of all the available information on each child. Clinical judgment concerning the implications of discrepancies in the performance of each child resulted in 106 children being selected from the 220 children considered in the initial phase of the study.

Experimental Testing. Eight diagnostic instruments were employed in the extensive testing program:

1. Illinois Test of Psycholinguistic Abilities (ITPA). This instrument has subtests designed to measure specific abilities thought to be basic to the processes of learning. The test was used not only to make a diagnosis of learning disability, but also to determine, insofar as possible, what might be restricting learning. The ITPA subtests probe the receptive process (auditory and visual), the associative process, and the expressive process (vocal and motor). The test also involves sequencing ability, memory, and automatic processes.

2. The Detroit Tests of Learning Aptitude. This test, like the ITPA, measures basic elements of the learning process. Four of the nineteen subtests of this instrument were utilized: pictorial opposites, visual attention span for objects, auditory attention span for unrelated words, and auditory attention span for related syllables. Two reasons governed the selection of these subtests: (a) if the auditory and visual

memory tests correlate highly with similar portions of the ITPA, this part of the Detroit test might well supplement the other test (particularly since the ITPA cannot at present be used to test children past the age of eight or nine); and (b) if a low correlation exists between the subtests of the two instruments, it would be important to know which test can be of more use as a predictor in the early identification of children with learning disabilities.

3. PISCI Auditory Discrimination Evaluation. Disorders in auditory discrimination may have a serious effect on the child's ability to process information. This area is of vital importance in the detection of potential learning disabilities and should be thoroughly examined (Seidel, 1963).

4. The Wide Range Achievement Test (WRAT). Because of its extensive use in the field of special education, the WRAT was included in the experimental battery. It is readily administered and samples number concepts, word comprehension, and visual perceptual skills.

5. Beery-Buktenica. The child's developmental status in the areas of visual perception and fine motor coordination is sampled by this instrument. Possibly this test will confirm the results from some of the visual portions of the ITPA, or it may be testing facets of coordination and perception not covered by the other test.

6. Perceptual Motor Survey. The Achievement Center for Children at Purdue University produced this test of development and ability level in the areas of balance, body image, perceptual motor function, and ocular control. If the theories of Kephart (1960) have applicability to the present sample of children, information from these areas of functioning is needed for a thorough study of children with potential learning problems.

7. Test of Left Right Discrimination. This test, developed by Dr. Dan Boone of the Department of Hearing and Speech of the University of Kansas, assessed the child's ability to make discriminations between left and right. Studies of the effect of laterality in relation to language problems give some credence to the idea that information about ability to make discriminations in laterality is important to this project.

8. Physical Measurements. Medical personnel consulted in connection with the project expressed an interest in conducting an extensive series of physical measurements of the children in the project. Variables such as motor strength, muscle tone, range of movement, shape and size of head, tactual and kinesthetic sensory discrimination, postural reflexes, x-ray age of hand and wrist bones, weight, and standing and sitting height were measured and quantified.

DATA ANALYSIS

The University of Kansas Computer Center analyzed the data of this project. Essentially, two analyses were made: a correlation analysis (Cooley and Lohnes, 1962) and a principal components analysis (Harmon, 1960). The correlation analysis provided information on the relations among the 31 predictor measures of the study. The extent of relationships, including all of the subtests, was sought to increase the efficiency in the measurement involved in predicting relationships among performance measures used in the identification of learning disabilities.

The principal components analysis, made possible by modern computer techniques, was chosen because it is an excellent way to obtain the initial factor structure of a correlation matrix. This analysis determined: first, an axis along which the variance is at a maximum; next, a second axis, orthogonal to the first axis, is determined to account for as much of the remaining variance as possible; a third axis, orthogonal to the first two, and as many more axes as needed, until the major portion of the variance is held in account. An attempt was made, through the use of this analysis, to determine whether or not the children identified as having potential learning disabilities made test scores that indicated discernible common characteristics.

Correlation Analysis. Thirty-one variables measured in the project were used in the correlation analysis. With 104 degrees of freedom, an r of .25 was statistically significant at the 1 percent level. Relationships with an r of this magnitude do not provide clear cut evidence from which reliable comments can be made concerning the results. If correlations among the ITPA subtests of a battery are ignored, seven correlations remain that seem worthy of comment. They are:

1. ITPA auditory vocal automatic and the Binet ($r=.49$)
2. ITPA auditory vocal associations and the Binet ($r=.66$)
3. ITPA auditory decoding and the Binet ($r=.54$)
4. ITPA total language age and Binet ($r=.71$)
5. ITPA auditory vocal association and the Detroit auditory related words ($r=.50$)
6. ITPA auditory vocal sequencing and Detroit auditory related words ($r=.52$)
7. Detroit auditory related words and the Binet ($r=.48$)

The testing program used all four subtests of the Detroit to determine the nature and extent of any commonality with the ITPA. The relationships between the visual portions of the Detroit and the visual portions of the ITPA were found to be of questionable significance; the same statement may be made concerning the auditory skill sections of these two tests. It may be inferred, then, that the ITPA and the Detroit are for the most part not measuring common factors in visual and auditory performance areas.

Special educators have used the Detroit and the WRAT to some extent to assess academic learning. From this practice it would be logical to assume a close relationship between the scores on these two instruments. A test of this hypothesis with the present sample of data gives inconclusive results which would make it unwise to assume any predictive efficiency of either test for the other.

A body of literature exists that suggests a relationship between academic learning, and visual motor perception and coordination, directionality and balance. A reasonably high correlation among tests involving these areas of performance and tests involving tasks closely related to academic learning could be hypothesized. The data relevant to these areas did not confirm this hypothesis. In fact, not one of the tests listed below provided results that indicate predictable relationships with any of the other tests:

1. The Beery-Buktenica Visual Motor Test
2. Purdue Perceptual Motor Survey
3. PISCI Auditory Discrimination Evaluation
4. Hand wrist bone age
5. Body ratio
6. Test of left right discrimination
7. Tactual and kinesthetic sensory discrimination
8. Laterality

Present information permits no conclusions concerning the usefulness of these tests in the detection of children with learning disabilities. These tests, however, are not measuring common areas of performance, even on the subtests that propose to measure the common areas of performance, nor even on the subtests that propose to measure the same or similar learning processes.

Principal Components Analysis. The first component, a general language factor, accounted for 20.01 percent of the commonality (see Table I). Statistically, this first component represents the best fitted axis among all the scores with reference to the variance held in common. Composed largely of general language factors, it accounted for 20.01 percent of the total variance. Whether the overall language factor which characterized this population was due to a common pattern of language performance, or the language measurements used in the assessment of the children were overpowering, presents a question unanswerable with

TABLE I

Table of Principal Components Accounting for 54.06 Percent of the Trace of r from Thirty-one Measures on 106 Subjects

	First Component	Second Component	Third Component	Fourth Component	Fifth Component	Sixth Component	Seventh Component
Latent root	6.2037	2.3299	1.9077	1.7556	1.6369	1.5116	1.4133
Percent of trace	20.01	7.52	6.15	5.66	5.28	4.88	4.56
Cumulative Percent of trace	20.01	27.53	33.68	39.34	44.62	49.50	54.06

Variable	Factor Loadings						
1.	.2632	.3123	.3194	−.1544	.5897	−.4204	.0921
2.	.8222	−.0194	.0263	.0680	−.1782	−.1338	−.0656
3.	.3119	.3353	.0012	−.1879	.4520	.1955	−.0450
4.	.3779	.4221	.1980	−.1901	−.1160	.1554	−.0833
5.	.1129	.4178	−.4676	−.1561	.2974	.0619	−.1158
6.	.5702	−.2958	−.1119	.2304	−.0862	−.1715	−.3746
7.	.4745	.2256	.0897	.2065	.2013	.0676	.0850
8.	.4499	−.1621	.1309	.2252	.0961	.0196	−.0433
9.	.6935	−.0800	.0385	.1149	−.1484	−.0505	.0955
10.	−.0725	.5637	−.2758	.2845	−.2123	.0213	−.0192
11.	.4190	−.2540	.1342	−.0116	−.1813	−.0231	−.2703
12.	.6077	−.1310	−.3623	.1732	−.0014	.3335	.1228
13.	.3824	.0760	−.2362	−.2056	.0653	.0792	.4270
14.	.6253	−.0278	−.1358	.0327	.1185	−.0974	.0458
15.	.9070	−.0886	−.1925	.2227	−.1104	−.0169	.0217
16.	.0338	.0434	−.0050	.1427	−.1300	−.4128	.4545
17.	.4259	.0418	−.0484	−.4145	.0618	−.1548	.2191
18.	.4764	−.3443	−.1135	−.2977	−.0025	.4027	−.0222
19.	.5044	−.0842	−.0316	−.4040	−.1138	.0700	.2516
20.	.7112	−.1537	−.1183	−.1710	−.1586	.1140	.0867
21.	.2121	.0902	.3677	−.2942	−.1080	−.3024	−.0170
22.	.4114	.3160	.1047	−.1839	−.0505	−.0921	−.2803
23.	.0988	.5634	.3490	−.3107	.0552	.0058	−.1343
24.	.5545	.3816	.1969	−.1284	−.3417	−.1753	−.2532
25.	.0238	.4520	−.1729	.2319	.0940	−.0173	.0501
26.	.3876	.0585	.5807	.2625	.4886	.3369	.1205
27.	.1329	.0336	.6444	.4533	−.2848	.2552	.2575
28.	.3852	.0845	−.2131	.4021	.4759	−.2591	−.2005
29.	.0024	−.1287	.0503	.0059	.0319	.3113	−.5317
30.	−.1528	−.1095	.0405	−.1721	.0527	.4712	.0587
31.	−.1426	−.4619	.0486	−.2038	−.2622	.1243	−.2225

the present data. But a concerted effort was made to insure a balance across the performance areas in the selection of measuring instruments.

The second component accounted for 7.5 percent of the total variance. There is insufficient commonality of variance here to discuss any common factor. Individually, the remaining components did not adequately account for a large enough percentage of the variance to suggest that the 106 subjects as a group were characterized by common discernible factors.

RESULTS

The following inferences can be made from the data obtained in this study:

1. When provided with a structured guide to observation, kindergarten teachers can select children who have developmental retardation by specific areas of performance. Eye hand coordination, auditory memory, language, and visual memory are some of the areas of performance upon which selection is based.
2. The kindergarten children identified as possessing potential learning disabilities by teacher observation and confirmed through psychological testing revealed few common identifiable learning patterns.
3. When the results of the performance of these children on this battery of assessment instruments were considered as a group, no significant distinctions from those results of a typical population of children were revealed. Differences in rate and accuracy of performance noted by the teacher through individual observations were masked when performance scores were treated as group scores.
4. Relationships that current and past literature suggest exist between areas of physical and intellectual performance have little if any predictive value in identifying children with learning disabilities.
5. Of the 31 variables measured, the most significant were the language related variables that accounted for 20.01 percent of the commonality in the principal components analysis.

CONCLUSION

For the educator, the data from this study have certain implications for many of our present practices. On the one hand, it confirms the teacher's key role in the early identification of children with learning disabilities. It suggests that a valid basis for the selection of children developmentally retarded is an analysis of individual performance behaviors. Where the skills of eye hand coordination, language, and visual and auditory memory are practiced in the school setting, is where an assessment of these areas of performance is functional.

On the other hand, few common learning patterns emerged from the results of the performance of these children on the battery of assessment instruments; this suggests that a sampling of performance behavior on such tests does not allow a predictive generality commensurate with teacher observations of the individual child. In the treatment of scores of children on a variety of tests as an aggregate, the individual learning abilities of the specific child may be masked. Where both individual abilities and disabilities are concealed, no adequate basis for teaching decisions, remedial or preventive, exists. Individual assessment, individual programing, and individual teaching decisions for the modification of individual behaviors are implied by these findings.

Further, the data has called into question that set of relationships heretofore considered significant between areas of physical and intellectual performance. Where little if any predictive value is to be expected from such relationships as far as the identification of children with learning disabilities is concerned, it follows that individual teaching prescriptions on the basis of such inferential predictions are not functional.

While it is premature to discuss the accuracy of identification of children with learning disabilities since this information will be revealed at the conclusion of the project, it appears that the individual behavior analysis done by teachers may prove to be a more effective procedure than group testing in identification. It must also be remembered that learning deficits may be as much a function of the learning environment as they are a function of the organism. Possibly in many instances of learning disabilities, the crux of this may involve ongoing relationships between the two. Should this become more evident, teaching may require a continuous functional analysis of behavior on the part of the teacher to insure appropriate behavior management. It suggests that an adequate basis for preventive and/or remedial teaching decisions is provided by an ongoing analysis of classroom behavior, with emphasis on the skill performance and language related variables as they involve classroom learning tasks. Following the indications of this and similar studies, investigations in the identification and modification of maladaptive learning behaviors as continuous functional analyses are the bases of several current research projects (Haring and Kunzelmann, 1966).

References

Bakwin, H., and Bakwin, R. N. *Clinical management of behavior disorders in children.* (Second edition) Philadelphia: W. B. Saunders Company, 1960.

Bateman, Barbara. *Reading and psycholinguistic processes of partially seeing children.* Washington, D. C.: The Council for Exceptional Children, 1963.

Benton, A. L. *Right-left discrimination and finger localization: development and pathology.* New York: Hoeber-Harper, 1959.

Benton, A. L. Dyslexia in relation to form perception and directional sense. In J. Money (Editor), *Reading disability: progress and research needs in dyslexia.* Baltimore: The Johns Hopkins Press, 1962. Pp. 81–102.

Bond, G. *The auditory and speech characteristics of poor readers.* New York: Teachers College, Columbia University, 1935.

Bronner, A. F. *The psychology of special abilities and disabilities.* Boston: Little, Brown and Company, 1917.

Cohn, R. Delayed acquisition of reading and writing abilities in children: a neurological study. *Archives of Neurology,* 1961, 4, 153–164.

Cooley, W. W., and Lohnes, P. R. *Multivariate procedures for the behavioral sciences.* New York: John Wiley and Sons, 1962.

Cruickshank, W. M., Bentzen, Frances A., Ratzeburg, F. H., and Tannhauser, Mirian. *A teaching method for brain-injured and hyperactive children.* New York: Syracuse University Press, 1961.

Delacato, C. H. *The diagnosis and treatment of speech and reading problems.* Springfield, Illinois: Charles C Thomas, 1964.

Diack, H. *Reading and the psychology of perception.* New York: Philosophical Library, 1960.

Durrell, D. C., and Murphy, H. The auditory discrimination factor in reading readiness and reading disability. *Education,* 1953, 73, 556–560.

Eames, T. H. Comparison of eye conditions among 1000 reading failures, 500 ophthalmic patients, and 150 unselected children. *American Journal of Ophthalmology,* 1948, 31, 713-717.

Fendrick, P. *Visual characteristics of poor readers.* New York: Teachers College, Columbia University, 1935.

Fildes, L. G. A psychological inquiry into the nature of the condition known as congenital word-blindness. *Brain,* 1921, 44, 286–407.

Frostig, M., Lefever, D. W., and Whittlesey, J. R. B. A developmental test of visual perception. *Perceptual and Motor Skills,* 1961, 12, 383–394.

Goetzinger, C. P., Dirks, D. D., and Baer, C. J. Auditory discrimination and visual perception in good and poor readers. *Annals of Otology, Rhinology and Laryngology,* 1960, 69, 121–136.

Goins, J. T. *Visual perceptual abilities and early reading progress.* Chicago: University of Chicago Press, 1958.

Haring, N. G., and Kunzelmann, H. P. The finer focus on therapeutic behavioral management. *Educational Therapy,* Volume 1. Seattle, Washington: Bernie Straub, 1966.

Harmon, H. H. *Modern factor analysis*. Chicago: University of Chicago Press, 1960.

Harris, A. J. Lateral dominance, directional confusion and reading disability. *Journal of Psychology*, 1957, **44**, 283–294.

Hermann, K. *Reading disability: a medical study of word-blindness and related handicaps*. Springfield, Illinois: Charles C Thomas, 1959.

Hermann, K., and Norrie, E. Is congenital word-blindness a hereditary type of Gerstmann's syndrome? *Monatscchrift fur Psychiatrie und Neurologie*, 1958, **136**, 59–73.

Hinshelwood, J. *Congenital word-blindness*. London: H. K. Lewis, 1917.

Hirst, L. S. The usefulness of a two-way analysis of WISC subtests in the diagnosis of remedial reading problems. *Journal of Experimental Education*, 1960, **29**, 153–160.

Kass, Corrine. Some psychological correlates of severe reading disability (dyslexia). Unpublished doctoral dissertation, University of Illinois, 1962.

Kephart, N. *The slow-learner in the classroom*. Columbus, Ohio: Charles E. Merrill Books, Inc., 1960.

Kirk, S. A., and McCarthy, J. J. *The Illinois Test of Psycholinguistic Abilities: experimental edition*. Urbana: University of Illinois, 1961.

Krippner, B. The boy who read at 18 months. *Exceptional Children*, 1963, **30**, 105–109.

Malmquist, E. *Factors related to reading disabilities in the first grade of the elementary school*. Stockholm: Almquist and Wiksell, 1958.

Monroe, M. *Children who cannot read*. Chicago: University of Chicago Press, 1932.

Neville, D. A comparison of the WISC patterns of male retarded and non-retarded readers. *Journal of Educational Research*, 1960–1961, **54**, 195–197.

Orton, S. T. *Reading, writing and speech problems in children*. New York: W. W. Norton and Company, 1937.

Osgood, C. *Contemporary approaches to cognition*. Cambridge, Massachusetts: Harvard University Press, 1957.

Prechtl, H. Reading difficulties as a neurological problem in childhood. In J. Money (Editor), *Reading disability: progress and research needs in dyslexia*, Baltimore: The Johns Hopkins Press, 1962. Pp. 187–193.

Rabinovitch, R. D., Drew, A. L., DeJong, R. N., Ingram, W., and Whitbey, L. Research approach to reading retardation. *Neurology and Psychiatry in Childhood*, 1954, **34**, 363–396.

Rabinovitch, R. D., and Ingram, W. Neuropsychiatric considerations in reading retardation. *Reading Teacher*, 1962, **15**, 433–438.

Robinson, H. *Diagnosis and treatment of poor readers with visual problems:*

clinical studies in reading 2. Chicago: University of Chicago Press, 1953.

Robinson, H. *Why pupils fail in reading.* Chicago: University of Chicago Press, 1957.

Seidel, Susan. PISCI auditory discrimination evaluation. Unpublished master's thesis, University of Illinois, 1963.

Silver, A. A., and Hagin, R. Specific reading disability: delineation of the syndrome and relationship to cerebral dominance. *Comprehensive Psychiatry,* 1960, 1, 126–134.

Strauss, A. A., and Kephart, N. C. *Psycho-pathology and education of the brain-injured child: volume 2.* New York: Grune and Stratton, 1955.

Strauss, A. A., and Lehtinen, L. E. *Psycho-pathology and education of the brain-injured child.* New York: Grune and Stratton, 1947.

Traxler, A., and Townsend, A. *Eight more years of research in reading: summary and bibliography.* New York: Educational Records Bureau, 1955.

US Office of Education. Proceedings of Conference on Learning Disorders, University of Kansas Medical Center, Kansas City, November 23–25, 1964. (Unpublished manuscript)

Wepman, J. M. Auditory discrimination, speech and reading. *Elementary School Journal,* 1960, 60, 325–333.

Wepman, J. M., Jones, L. V., Bock, R. D., and Pelt, D. V. Studies in aphasia: background and theoretical formulations. *Journal of Speech and Hearing Disorders,* 1960, 25, 323–332.

Part IV

Organization of School Services for Children With Learning Disabilities

For years, the administrative panacea for exceptional children has been the special class or the special school. However, educators and legislators have recently been seriously questioning the efficacy of these traditional forms of special education. The cold, comfortless fact emerging from a host of studies is that the child labeled "mentally retarded" or "emotionally disturbed" does less well, or at best, only as well as, his counterpart left in the regular classes. If failure to learn in the regular grades mandates some other placement for exceptional children, doesn't failure to learn in special classes mandate serious consideration of other educational alternatives? Can expensive special-education arrangements be justified if special educators can't show that they really work? Can **227** we, in good conscience, continue to stigmatize children with negatively viewed placements (it's no compliment to be put in a special class) without demonstrating that sound educational benefits offset these negative aspects?

These disquieting questions are being raised within the profession at the very time as, and perhaps partly because of, the emergence of learning disabilities as a new force in the field. The learning-disabilities concept implies that individual differences are of such paramount significance that no one administrative grouping—no matter how ingenious —can possibly accommodate these children properly. Rather, they must be programmed for according to individual learning styles and disabilities, in a variety of settings.

This approach to the education of children with special learning needs mitigates against the establishment and proliferation of numbers of traditional-type special classes adapted for children with learning disabilities—although, doubtlessly, the need will continue to exist for the maintenance of some self-contained classes for those few learning-disabled youngsters who, because of severe hyperactivity or profound language disorders, cannot be integrated into the regular class. But even this placement should be viewed as temporary. There are, however, a few traditionalists who maintain that special classes and special schools are the only way to deal with exceptional children. In any event, unique forms of educational programming are being devised for children with learning disabilities, and older ideas are being adapted for the special needs of these children.

Dunn's article, with which this section begins, has become a classic in special education. He argues that the special-class concept is unsatisfactory for a variety of reasons and suggests an alternative model for dispensing special educational services. Although Dunn is primarily interested in improving the education of the mildly retarded, his model is directly applicable and particularly appropriate for children with learning disabilities. Christoplos and Renz are opposed on philosophic grounds to the segregation of exceptional children into self-contained classrooms or schools, especially since the literature they review strongly suggests that such placement may well not be in the child's best interest.

The problems raised by special-class placement are further elucidated in the article by Towne and Joiner. They suggest that the most debilitating aspects of this type of placement are social in nature, and issue a warning to those specialists who would use the special-class treatment as the only viable option for learning-disabled children.

In the next article, Valett describes an interesting arrangement for broadening the scope of special services. A unique aspect of the program he describes is parent education and parental involvement in educational therapy. The learning-resource-center concept is particularly appropriate for educators who feel that special education must be defined more broadly—that is, to include not only direct services to children, but also upgrading of professional personnel through inservice training, projects for parents, and counseling services to both pupils and parents.

McCarthy's article is more concerned with the mechanics of actually implementing a program for learning-disabled children. Besides delineating the sequence of procedures that can be followed, she raises significant issues regarding the format that such services are to take—for example, shall a resource-room or an itinerant program be implemented?

18. SPECIAL EDUCATION FOR THE MILDLY RETARDED—IS MUCH OF IT JUSTIFIABLE?

LLOYD M. DUNN

A better education than special class placement is needed for socio-culturally deprived children with mild learning problems who have been labeled educable mentally retarded. Over the years, the status of these pupils who come from poverty, broken and inadequate homes, and low status ethnic groups has been a checkered one. In the early days, these children were simply excluded from school. Then, as Hollingsworth (1923) pointed out, with the advent of compulsory attendance laws, the schools and these children "were forced into a reluctant mutual recognition of each other." This resulted in the establishment of self contained special schools and classes as a method of transferring these "misfits" out of the regular grades. This practice continues to this day and, unless counterforces are set in motion now, it will probably become even more prevalent in the immediate future due in large measure to increased racial integration and militant teacher organizations. For example, a local affiliate of the National Education Association demanded of a local school board recently that more special classes be provided for disruptive and slow learning children (Nashville *Tennessean,* December 18, 1967).

SOURCE. Reprinted from *Exceptional Children,* 1968, **35,** 5–22.
By permission of the author and publisher.

The number of special day classes for the retarded has been increasing by leaps and bounds. The most recent 1967–1968 statistics compiled by the US Office of Education now indicate that there are approximately 32,000 teachers of the retarded employed by local school systems—over one-third of all special educators in the nation. In my best judgment, about 60 to 80 percent of the pupils taught by these teachers are children from low status backgrounds—including Afro-Americans, American Indians, Mexicans, and Puerto Rican Americans; those from nonstandard English speaking, broken, disorganized, and inadequate homes; and children from other nonmiddle class environments. This expensive proliferation of self contained special schools and classes raises serious educational and civil rights issues which must be squarely faced. It is my thesis that we must stop labeling these deprived children as mentally retarded. Furthermore we must stop segregating them by placing them into our allegedly special programs.

The purpose of this article is twofold: first, to provide reasons for taking the position that a large proportion of this so called special education in its present form is obsolete and unjustifiable from the point of view of the pupils so placed; and second, to outline a blueprint for changing this major segment of education for exceptional children to make it more acceptable. We are not arguing that we do away with our special education programs for the moderately and severely retarded, for other types of more handicapped children, or for the multiply handicapped. The emphasis is on doing something better for slow learning children who live in slum conditions, although much of what is said should also have relevance for those children we are labeling emotionally disturbed, perceptually impaired, brain injured, and learning disordered. Furthermore, the emphasis of the article is on children, in that no attempt is made to suggest an adequate high school environment for adolescents still functioning as slow learners.

REASONS FOR CHANGE

Regular teachers and administrators have sincerely felt they were doing these pupils a favor by removing them from the pressures of an unrealistic and inappropriate program of studies. Special educators have also fully believed that the children involved would make greater progress in special schools and classes. However, the overwhelming evidence is that our present and past practices have their major justification in removing pressures on regular teachers and pupils, at the expense of the socioculturally deprived slow learning pupils themselves. Some major arguments for this position are outlined below.

Homogeneous Grouping

Homogeneous groupings tend to work to the disadvantage of the slow learners and underprivileged. Apparently such pupils learn much from being in the same class with children from white middle class homes. Also, teachers seem to concentrate on the slower children to bring them up to standard. This principle was dramatically applied in the Judge J. Skelly Wright decision in the District of Columbia concerning the track system. Judge Wright ordered that tracks be abolished, contending they discriminated against the racially and/or economically disadvantaged and therefore were in violation of the Fifth Amendment of the Constitution of the United States. One may object to the Judge's making educational decisions based on legal considerations. However, Passow (1967), upon the completion of a study of the same school system, reached the same conclusion concerning tracking. The recent national study by Coleman, et al. (1966), provides supporting evidence in finding that academically disadvantaged Negro children in racially segregated schools made less progress than those of comparable ability in integrated schools. Furthermore, racial integration appeared to deter school progress very little for Caucasian and more academically able students.

What are the implications of Judge Wright's rulings for special education? Clearly special schools and classes are a form of homogeneous grouping and tracking. This fact was demonstrated in September, 1967, when the District of Columbia (as a result of the Wright decision) abolished Track 5, into which had been routed the slowest learning pupils in the District of Columbia schools. These pupils and their teachers were returned to the regular classrooms. Complaints followed from the regular teachers that these children were taking an inordinate amount of their time. A few parents observed that their slow learning children were frustrated by the more academic program and were rejected by the other students. Thus, there are efforts afoot to develop a special education program in D.C. which cannot be labeled a track. Self contained special classes will probably not be tolerated under the present court ruling but perhaps itinerant and resource room programs would be. What if the Supreme Court ruled against tracks, and all self contained special classes across the nation which serve primarily ethnically and/or economically disadvantaged children were forced to close down? Make no mistake— this could happen! If I were a Negro from the slums or a disadvantaged parent who had heard of the Judge Wright decision and knew what I know now about special classes for the educable mentally retarded, other things being equal, I would then go to court before allowing the schools to label my child as "mentally retarded" and place him in a "self contained special school or class." Thus there is the real possibility that additional court actions will be forthcoming.*

Efficacy Studies

The findings of studies on the efficacy of special classes for the educable mentally retarded constitute another argument for change. These results are well known (Kirk, 1964) and suggest consistently that retarded pupils make as much or more progress in the regular grades as they do in special education. Recent studies such as those by Hoelke (1966) and Smith and Kennedy (1967) continue to provide similar evidence. Johnson (1962) has summarized the situation well:

"It is indeed paradoxical that mentally handicapped children having teachers especially trained, having more money (per capita) spent on their education, and being designed to provide for their unique needs, should be accomplishing the objectives of their education at the same or at a lower level than similar mentally handicapped children who have not had these advantages and have been forced to remain in the regular grades [p. 66]."

Efficacy studies on special day classes for other mildly handicapped children, including the emotionally handicapped, reveal the same results. For example, Rubin, Senison, and Betwee (1966) found that disturbed children did as well in the regular grades as in special classes, concluding that there is little or no evidence that special class programing is generally beneficial to emotionally disturbed children as a specific method of intervention and correction. Evidence such as this is another reason to find better ways of serving children with mild learning disorders than placing them in self contained special schools and classes.

Labeling Processes

Our past and present diagnostic procedures comprise another reason for change. These procedures have probably been doing more harm than

---

* Litigation has now occurred. According to an item in a June 8, 1968, issue of the *Los Angeles Times* received after this article was sent to the printer, the attorneys in the national office for the rights of the indigent filed a suit in behalf of the Mexican-American parents of the Santa Ana Unified School District asking for an injunction against the District's classes for the educable mentally retarded because the psychological examinations required prior to placement are unconstitutional since they have failed to use adequate evaluation techniques for children from different language and cultural backgrounds, and because parents have been denied the right of hearing to refute evidence for placement. Furthermore, the suit seeks to force the district to grant hearings on all children currently in such special classes to allow for the chance to remove the stigma of the label "mentally retarded" from school records of such pupils.

good in that they have resulted in disability labels and in that they have grouped children homogeneously in school on the basis of these labels. Generally, these diagnostic practices have been conducted by one or two procedures. In rare cases, the workup has been provided by a multidisciplinary team, usually consisting of physicians, social workers, psychologists, speech and hearing specialists, and occasionally educators. The avowed goal of this approach has been to look at the complete child, but the outcome has been merely to label him mentally retarded, perceptually impaired, emotionally disturbed, minimally brain injured, or some other such term depending on the predispositions, idiosyncracies, and backgrounds of the team members. Too, the team usually has looked for causation, and diagnosis tends to stop when something has been found wrong with the child, when the why has either been found or conjectured, and when some justification has been found for recommending placement in a special education class.

In the second and more common case, the assessment of educational potential has been left to the school psychologist who generally administers—in an hour or so—a psychometric battery, at best consisting of individual tests of intelligence, achievement, and social and personal adjustment. Again the purpose has been to find out what is wrong with the child in order to label him and thus make him eligible for special education services. In large measure this has resulted in digging the educational graves of many racially and/or economically disadvantaged children by using a WISC or Binet IQ score to justify the label "mentally retarded." This term then becomes a destructive, self fulfilling prophecy.

What is the evidence against the continued use of these diagnostic practices and disability labels?

First, we must examine the effects of these disability labels on the attitudes and expectancies of teachers. Here we can extrapolate from studies by Rosenthal and Jacobson (1966) who set out to determine whether or not the expectancies of teachers influenced pupil progress. Working with elementary school teachers across the first six grades, they obtained pretest measures on pupils by using intelligence and achievement tests. A sample of pupils was randomly drawn and labeled "rapid learners" with hidden potential. Teachers were told that these children would show unusual intellectual gains and school progress during the year. All pupils were retested late in the school year. Not all differences were statistically significant, but the gains of the children who had been arbitrarily labeled rapid learners were generally significantly greater than those of the other pupils, with especially dramatic changes in the first and second grades. To extrapolate from this study, we must expect that labeling a child "handicapped" reduces the teacher's expectancy for him to succeed.

Second, we must examine the effects of these disability labels on the pupils themselves. Certainly none of these labels are badges of distinction. Separating a child from other children in his neighborhood—or removing him from the regular classroom for therapy or special class placement—probably has a serious debilitating effect upon his self image. Here again our research is limited but supportive of this contention. Goffman (1961) has described the stripping and mortification process that takes place when an individual is placed in a residential facility. Meyerowitz (1965) demonstrated that a group of educable mentally retarded pupils increased in feelings of self derogation after one year in special classes. More recent results indicate that special class placement, instead of helping such a pupil adjust to his neighborhood peers, actually hinders him (Meyerowitz, 1967). While much more research is needed, we cannot ignore the evidence that removing a handicapped child from the regular grades for special education probably contributes significantly to his feelings of inferiority and problems of acceptance.

Improvements in General Education

Another reason self contained special classes are less justifiable today than in the past is that regular school programs are now better able to deal with individual differences in pupils. No longer is the choice just between a self contained special class and a self contained regular elementary classroom. Although the impact of the American Revolution in Education is just beginning to be felt and is still more an ideal than a reality, special education should begin moving now to fit into a changing general education program and to assist in achieving the program's goals. Because of increased support at the local, state, and federal levels, four powerful forces are at work:

Changes in School Organization. In place of self contained regular classrooms, there is increasingly more team teaching, ungraded primary departments, and flexible groupings. Radical departures in school organization are projected—educational parks in place of neighborhood schools, metropolitan school districts cutting across our inner cities and wealthy suburbs, and, perhaps most revolutionary of all, competing public school systems. Furthermore, and of great significance to those of us who have focused our careers on slow learning children, public kindergartens and nurseries are becoming more available for children of the poor.

Curricular Changes. Instead of the standard diet of Look and Say readers, many new and exciting options for teaching reading are evolving. Contemporary mathematics programs teach in the primary grades concepts formerly reserved for high school. More programed textbooks and other materials are finding their way into the classroom. Ingenious procedures, such as those by Bereiter and Engelmann (1966), are being developed to teach oral language and reasoning to preschool disadvantaged children.

Changes in Professional Public School Personnel. More ancillary personnel are now employed by the schools—i.e., psychologists, guidance workers, physical educators, remedial educators, teacher aides, and technicians. Furthermore, some teachers are functioning in different ways, serving as teacher coordinators, or cluster teachers who provide released time for other teachers to prepare lessons, etc. Too, regular classroom teachers are increasingly better trained to deal with individual differences—although much still remains to be done.

Hardware Changes. Computerized teaching, teaching machines, feedback typewriters, ETV, videotapes, and other materials are making auto-instruction possible, as never before.

We must ask what the implications of this American Revolution in Education are for special educators. Mackie (1967), formerly of the US Office of Education, addressed herself to the question: "Is the modern school changing sufficiently to provide [adequate services in general education] for large numbers of pupils who have functional mental retardation due to environmental factors [p. 5]?" In her view, hundreds—perhaps even thousands—of so called retarded pupils may make satisfactory progress in schools with diversified programs of instruction and thus will never need placement in self contained special classes. With earlier, better, and more flexible regular school programs many of the children should not need to be relegated to the type of special education we have so often provided.

In my view, the above four reasons for change are cogent ones. Much of special education for the mildly retarded is becoming obsolete. Never in our history has there been a greater urgency to take stock and to search out new roles for a large number of today's special educators.

A BLUEPRINT FOR CHANGE

Two major suggestions which constitute my attempt at a blueprint for change are developed below. First, a fairly radical departure from conventional methods will be proposed in procedures for diagnosing, placing, and teaching children with mild learning difficulties. Second, a proposal for curriculum revision will be sketched out. These are intended as proposals which should be examined, studied, and tested. What is needed are programs based on scientific evidence of worth and not more of those founded on philosophy, tradition, and expediency.

A THOUGHT

> *There is an important difference between regular educators talking us into trying to remediate or live with the learning difficulties of pupils with which they haven't been able to deal; versus striving to evolve a special education program that is either developmental in nature, wherein we assume responsibility for the total education of more severely handicapped children from an early age, or is supportive in nature, wherein general education would continue to have central responsibility for the vast majority of the children with mild learning disabilities—with us serving as resource teachers in devising effective prescriptions and in tutoring such pupils.*

A Clinical Approach

Existing diagnostic procedures should be replaced by expecting special educators, in large measure, to be responsible for their own diagnostic teaching and their clinical teaching. In this regard, it is suggested that we do away with many existing disability labels and the present practice of grouping children homogeneously by these labels into special classes. Instead, we should try keeping slow learning children more in the mainstream of education, with special educators serving as diagnostic, clinical, remedial, resource room, itinerant and/or team teachers, consultants, and developers of instructional materials and prescriptions for effective teaching.

The accomplishment of the above *modus operandi* will require a revolution in much of special education. A moratorium needs to be placed on the proliferation (if not continuance) of self contained special classes which enroll primarily the ethnically and/or economically disadvantaged children we have been labeling educable mentally retarded. Such pupils should be left in (or returned to) the regular elementary grades until we are "tooled up" to do something better for them.

Prescriptive Teaching. In diagnosis one needs to know how much a child can learn, under what circumstances, and with what materials. To accomplish this, there are three administrative procedures possible. One would be for each large school system—or two or more small districts—to establish a "Special Education Diagnostic and Prescription Generating Center." Pupils with school learning problems would be enrolled in this center on a day and/or boarding school basis for a period of time —probably up to a month and hopefully until a successful prescription for effective teaching had been evolved. The core of the staff would be a variety of master teachers with different specialties—such as in motor development, perceptual training, language development, social and personality development, remedial education, and so forth. Noneducators such as physicians, psychologists, and social workers would be retained in a consultative role, or pupils would be referred out to such paraeducational professionals, as needed. A second procedure, in lieu of such centers with their cadres of educational specialists, would be for one generalist in diagnostic teaching to perform the diagnostic and prescription devising functions on her own. A third and even less desirable procedure would be for one person to combine the roles of prescriptive and clinical teacher which will be presented next. It is suggested that 15 to 20 percent of the most insightful special educators be prepared for and/or assigned to prescriptive teaching. One clear virtue of the center is that a skilled director could coordinate an inservice training program and the staff could learn through, and be stimulated by, one another. In fact, many special educators could rotate through this program.

Under any of these procedures, educators would be responsible for the administration and interpretation of individual and group psychoeducational tests on cognitive development (such as the WISC and Binet), on language development (such as the ITPA), and on social maturity (such as the Vineland Social Maturity Scale). However, these instruments—with the exception of the ITPA which yields a profile of abilities and disabilities—will be of little use except in providing baseline data on the level at which a child is functioning. In place of these psychometric tests which usually yield only global scores, diagnostic educators would need to rely heavily on a combination of the various tools of behavior shapers and clinical teachers. The first step would be to make a study of the child to find what behaviors he has acquired along the dimension being considered. Next, samples of a sequential program would be designed to move him forward from that point. In presenting the program, the utility of different reinforcers, administered under various conditions, would be investigated. Also, the method by which he can best be taught the material should be determined. Different modalities for reaching the child would also be tried. Thus, since the instructional program itself becomes the diagnostic device, this procedure can be called diagnostic teaching. Failures are program and instructor failures, not pupil failures. In large measure, we would be guided by Bruner's dictum (1967) that almost any child can be taught almost anything if it is programed correctly.*

---

* By ignoring genetic influences, on the behavioral characteristics of children with learning difficulties, we place responsibility on an inadequate society, inadequate parents, unmotivated pupils, and/or in this case inadequate teachers. Taking this extreme environmental approach could result in placing too much

This diagnostic procedure is viewed as the best available since it enables us to assess continuously the problem points of the instructional program against the assets of the child. After a successful and appropriate prescription has been devised, it would be communicated to the teachers in the pupil's home school and they would continue the procedure as long as it is necessary and brings results. From time to time, the child may need to return to the center for reappraisal and redirection.

Clearly the above approach to special education diagnosis and treatment is highly clinical and intuitive. In fact, it is analogous to the rural doctor of the past who depended on his insights and a few diagnostic and treatment devices carried in his small, black bag. It may remain with us for some time to come. However, it will be improved upon by more standardized procedures. Perhaps the two most outstanding, pioneering efforts in this regard are now being made by Feuerstein (1968) in Israel, and by Kirk (1966) in the United States. Feuerstein has devised a *Learning Potential Assessment Device* for determining the degree of modifiability of the behavior of an individual pupil, the level at which he is functioning, the strategies by which he can best learn, and the areas in which he needs to be taught. Also, he is developing a variety of exercises for teaching children with specific learning difficulties. Kirk and his associates have not only given us the ITPA which yields a profile of abilities and disabilities in the psycholinguistic area, but they have also devised exercises for remediating specific psycholinguistic disabilities reflected by particular types of profiles (Kirk, 1966). Both of these scientists are structuring the assessment and remediation procedures to reduce clinical judgment, although it would be undesirable to formalize to too great a degree. Like the country doctor versus modern medicine, special education in the next fifty years will move from clinical intuition to a more precise science of clinical instruction based on diagnostic instruments which yield a profile of abilities and disabilities about a specific facet of behavior and which have incorporated within them measures of a child's ability to learn samples or units of materials at each of the points on the profile. If psychoeducational tests had these two characteristics, they would accomplish essentially the same thing as

blame for failure on the teacher and too much pressure on the child. While we could set our level of aspiration too high, this has hardly been the direction of our error to date in special education of the handicapped. Perhaps the sustained push proposed in this paper may not succeed, but we will not know until we try it. Insightful teachers should be able to determine when the pressures on the pupil and system are too great.

does the diagnostic approach described above—only under more standardized conditions.

Itinerant and Resource Room Teaching. It is proposed that a second echelon of special educators be itinerant or resource teachers. One or more resource teachers might be available to each sizable school, while an itinerant teacher would serve two or more smaller schools. General educators would refer their children with learning difficulties to these teachers. If possible, the clinical teacher would evolve an effective prescription for remediating the problem. If this is not possible, she would refer the child to the Special Education Diagnostic and Prescription Generating Center or to the more specialized prescriptive teacher who would study the child and work out an appropriate regimen of instruction for him. In either event, the key role of the resource room and itinerant clinical educators would be to develop instructional materials and lessons for implementing the prescription found effective for the child, and to consult and work with the other educators who serve the child. Thus, the job of special educators would be to work as members of the schools' instructional teams and to focus on children with mild to moderate school learning problems. Special educators would be available to all children in trouble (except the severely handicapped) regardless of whether they had, in the past, been labeled educable mentally retarded, minimally brain injured, educationally handicapped, or emotionally disturbed. Children would be regrouped continually throughout the school day. For specific help these children who had a learning problem might need to work with the itinerant or resource room special educator. But, for the remainder of the day, the special educator would probably be more effective in developing specific exercises which could be taught by others in consultation with her. Thus, the special educator would begin to function as a part of, and not apart from, general education. Clearly this proposed approach recognizes that all children have assets and deficits, not all of which are permanent. When a child was having trouble in one or more areas of learning, special educators would be available to devise a successful teaching approach for him and to tutor him when necessary. Perhaps as many as 20 to 35 percent of our present special educators are or could be prepared for this vital role.

Two Other Observations. First, it is recognized that some of today's special educators—especially of the educable mentally retarded—are not prepared to serve the functions discussed. These teachers would need to either withdraw from special education or develop the needed competencies. Assuming an open door policy and playing the role of the expert educational diagnostician and the prescriptive and clinical educator would place us in the limelight. Only the best will succeed. But surely this is a responsibility we will not shirk. Our avowed *raison d'etre* has been to provide special education for children unable to make adequate progress in the regular grades. More would be lost than gained by assigning less than master teachers from self contained classes to the diagnostic and clinical educator roles. Ainsworth (1959) has already compared the relative effectiveness of the special class versus itinerant special educators of the retarded and found that neither group accomplished much in pupil progress. A virtue of these new roles for special education is that they are high status positions which should appeal to the best and therefore enhance the recruitment of master regular teachers who should be outstanding in these positions after having obtained specialized graduate training in behavior shaping, psychoeducational diagnostics, remedial education, and so forth.

Second, if one accepts these procedures for special education, the need for disability labels is reduced. In their stead we may need to substitute labels which describe the educational intervention needed. We would thus talk of pupils who need special instruction in language or cognitive development, in sensory training, in personality development, in vocational training, and other areas. However, some labels may be needed for administrative reasons. If so, we need to find broad generic terms such as "school learning disorders."

New Curricular Approaches

Master teachers are at the heart of an effective school program for children with mild to moderate learning difficulties—master teachers skilled at educational diagnosis and creative in designing and carrying out interventions to remediate the problems that exist. But what should they teach? In my view, there has been too great an emphasis in special classes on practical arts and practical academics, to the conclusion of other ingredients. Let us be honest with ourselves. Our courses of study have tended to be watered down regular curriculum. If we are to move from the clinical stage to a science of instruction, we will need a rich array of validated prescriptive programs of instruction at our disposal. To assemble these programs will take time, talent, and money; teams of specialists including creative teachers, curriculum specialists, programers, and theoreticians will be needed to do the job.

What is proposed is a chain of Special Education Curriculum Development Centers across the nation. Perhaps these could best be affiliated with colleges and universities, but could also be attached to state and local school systems. For these centers to be successful, creative educators must be found. Only a few teachers are remarkably able to develop new materials. An analogy is that some people can play music adequately, if not brilliantly, but only a few people can compose it. Therefore, to move special education forward, some 15 to 20 percent of our most creative special educators need to be identified, freed from routine classroom instruction, and placed in a stimulating setting where they can be maximally productive in curriculum development. These creative teachers and their associates would concentrate on developing, field testing, and modifying programs of systematic sequences of exercises for developing specific facets of human endeavor. As never before, funds are now available from the US Office of Education under Titles III and VI of PL 89–10 to embark upon at least one such venture in each state. In fact, Title III was designed to support innovations in education and 15 percent of the funds were earmarked for special education. Furthermore, most of the money is now to be administered through state departments of education which could build these curriculum centers into their state plans.

The first step in establishing specialized programs of study would be to evolve conceptual models upon which to build our treatments. In this regard the creative teachers would need to join with the theoreticians, curriculum specialists, and other behavioral scientists. Even the identification of the broad areas will take time, effort, and thought. Each would require many subdivisions and extensive internal model building. A beginning taxonomy might include the following eight broad areas: (a) environmental modifications, (b) motor development, (c) sensory and perceptual training, (d) cognitive and language development including academic instruction, (e) speech and communication training, (f) connative (or personality) development, (g) social interaction training, and (h) vocational training. (Of course, under cognitive development alone we might evolve a model of intellect with some ninety plus facets such as that of Guilford [1967], and as many training programs.)

In the area of motor development we might, for example, involve creative special and physical educators, occupational and physical therapists, and experts in recreation and physical medicine, while in the area of language development a team of speech and hearing specialists, special educators, psychologists, linguists, and others would need to come together to evolve a conceptual model, to identify the parameters, and to develop the specialized programs of exercises. No attempt is made in this article to do more than provide an overview of the problem and the approach. Conceptualizing the specific working models would be the responsibility of cadres of experts in the various specialties.

Environmental Modifications. It would seem futile and rather unrealistic to believe we will be able to remediate the learning difficulties of children from ethnically and/or economically disadvantaged backgrounds when the schools are operating in a vacuum even though top flight special education instructional programs are used. Perhaps, if intensive around the clock and full calendar year instruction were provided beginning at the nursery school level, we might be able to counter appreciably the physiological weaknesses and inadequate home and community conditions of the child. However, the field of education would be enhanced in its chances of success if it became a part of a total ecological approach to improve the environments of these children. Thus special educators need to collaborate with others—social workers, public health officials, and other community specialists. Interventions in this category might include (a) foster home placement, (b) improved community conditions and out of school activities, (c) parent education, (d) public education, and (e) improved cultural exposures. For optimal pupil development, we should see that children are placed in a setting that is both supportive and stimulating. Therefore, we must participate in environmental manipulations and test their efficacy. We have made a slight beginning in measuring the effects of foster home placement and there is evidence that working with parents of the disadvantaged has paid off. The model cities programs would also seem to have promise. But much more human and financial effort must be invested in this area.

Motor Development. Initial work has been done with psychomotor training programs by a number of persons including Delacato (1966), Oliver (1958), Cratty (1967), Lillie (1967), and others. But we still need sets of sequential daily activities built around an inclusive model. Under this category, we need to move from the early stages of psychomotor development to the development of fine and large movements required as vocational skills. Programs to develop improved motor skills are important for a variety of children with learning problems. In fact, one could argue that adequate psychomotor skills constitute the first link in the chain of learning.

Sensory and Perceptual Training. Much of our early efforts in special education consisted of sensory and perceptual training applied to severe handicapping conditions such as blindness, deafness, and mental deficiency. Consequently, we have made a good beginning in outlining programs of instruction in the areas of auditory, visual, and tactual training. Now we must apply our emerging technology to work out the step by step sequence of activities needed for children with mild to moderate learning difficulties. In this regard, visual perceptual training has received growing emphasis, pioneered by Frostig (1964), but auditory perceptual training has been neglected. The latter is more important for school instruction than the visual channel. Much attention needs to be given to this second link in the chain of learning. Children with learning problems need to be systematically taught the perceptual processes: they need to be able to organize and convert bits of input from the various sense modalities into units of awareness which have meaning.

Cognitive and Language Development Including Academic Instruction. This is the heart of special education for slow learning children. Our business is to facilitate their thinking processes. We should help them not only to acquire and store knowledge, but also to generate and evaluate it. Language development could largely be included under this caption—especially the integrative components—since there is much overlap between the development of oral language and verbal intelligence. However, much of receptive language training might be considered under sensory and perceptual training, while expressive language will be considered in the next topic.

A major fault of our present courses of study is failure to focus on the third link in the chain of learning—that of teaching our children systematically in the areas of cognitive development and concept formation. A major goal of our school program should be to increase the intellectual functioning of children we are now classifying as socioculturally retarded. For such children, perhaps as much as 25 percent of the school day in the early years should be devoted to this topic. Yet the author has not seen one curriculum guide for these children with a major emphasis on cognitive development—which is a sad state of affairs indeed!

Basic psychological research by Guilford (1959) has provided us with a useful model of intellect. However, little is yet known about the trainability of the various cognitive processes. Actually, Thurstone (1948) has contributed the one established set of materials for training primary mental abilities. Thus, much work lies ahead in developing programs of instruction for the training of intellect.

We are seeing more and more sets of programed materials in the academic areas, most of which have been designed for average children. The most exciting examples today are in the computer assisted instruction studies. Our major problem is to determine how these programed exercises need to be modified to be maximally effective for children with specific learning problems. Work will be especially needed in the classical areas of instruction including written language and mathematics. Hopefully, however, regular teachers will handle much of the instruction in science and social studies, while specialists would instruct in such areas as music and the fine arts. This will free special educators to focus on better ways of teaching the basic 3 R's, especially written language.

Speech and Communication Training. This area has received much attention, particularly from speech correctionists and teachers of the deaf.

Corrective techniques for specific speech problems are probably more advanced than for any other area, yet essentially no carefully controlled research has been done on the efficacy of these programs. Speech correctionists have tended to be clinicians, not applied behavioral scientists. They often create the details of their corrective exercises while working with their clients in a one to one relationship. Thus, the programs have often been intuitive. Furthermore, public school speech therapists have been spread very thin, usually working with 75 to 100 children. Many have been convinced that only *they* could be effective in this work. But remarkable changes have recently occurred in the thinking of speech therapists; they are recognizing that total programs of oral language development go far beyond correcting articulation defects. Furthermore, some speech therapists believe they could be more productive in working with only the more severe speech handicaps and devoting much attention to the development and field testing of systematic exercises to stimulate overall language and to improve articulation, pitch, loudness, quality, duration, and other speech disorders of a mild to moderate nature. These exercises need to be programed to the point at which teachers, technicians, and perhaps teacher aides can use them. Goldman (1968) is now developing such a program of exercises to correct articulation defects. This seems to be a pioneering and heartening first step.

Connative (or Personality) Development. This emerging area requires careful attention. We must accept the position that much of a person's behavior is shaped by his environment. This applies to all aspects of human thought, including attitudes, beliefs, and mores. Research oriented clinical psychologists are providing useful information on motivation and personality development and before long we will see reports of research in shaping insights into self, the effects of others on self, and one's effects on others. It is not too early for teams of clinical psychologists, psychiatric social workers, creative special educators (especially for the so called emotionally disturbed), and others to begin developing programs of instruction in this complex field.

Social Interaction Training. Again we have an emerging area which overlaps considerably with some of those already presented, particularly connative development. Special educators have long recognized that the ability of a handicapped individual to succeed in society depends, in large measure, on his skill to get along with his fellow man. Yet we have done little to develop his social living skills, a complex area of paramount importance. Training programs should be developed to facilitate development in this area of human behavior.

Vocational Training. Closely tied to social interaction training is vocational training. Success on the job for persons that we have labeled educable mentally retarded has depended on good independent work habits, reliability, and social skills, rather than on academic skills. Consequently, early and continuing emphasis on developing these traits is necessary. In fact, it is likely to be even more important in the years ahead with fewer job opportunities and increasing family disintegration providing less shelter and support for the so called retarded. Therefore sophisticated programs of instruction are especially needed in this area. Even with our best efforts in this regard, it is likely that our pupils, upon reaching adolescence, will continue to need a variety of vocational services, including trade and technical schools, work study programs, and vocational training.

Another Observation. It seems to me to be a red herring to predict that special educators will use these hundreds of specialized instructional programs indiscriminately as cookbooks. Perhaps a few of the poor teachers will. But, the clinical teachers proposed in this article would be too sophisticated and competent to do this. They would use them as points of departure, modifying the lessons so that each child would make optimal progress. Therefore, it seems to me that this library of curriculum materials is necessary to move us from a clinical and intuitive approach to a more scientific basis for special education.

AN EPILOGUE

The conscience of special educators needs to rub up against morality. In large measure we have been at the mercy of the general education establishment in that we accept problem pupils who have been referred out of the regular grades. In this way, we contribute to the delinquency of the general educations since we remove the pupils that are problems for them and thus reduce their need to deal with individual differences. The *entente* of mutual delusion between general and special education that special class placement will be advantageous to slow learning children of poor parents can no longer be tolerated. We must face the reality —we are asked to take children others cannot teach, and a large percentage of these are from ethnically and/or economically disadvantaged backgrounds. Thus much of special education will continue to be a sham of dreams unless we immerse ourselves into the total environment of our children from inadequate homes and backgrounds and insist on a comprehensive ecological push—with a quality educational program as part of it. This is hardly compatible with our prevalent practice of expediency in which we employ many untrained and less than master teachers to increase the number of special day classes in response to the pressures of waiting lists. Because of these pressures from the school system, we have been guilty of fostering quantity with little regard for quality of special education instruction. Our first responsibility is to have an abiding commitment to the less fortunate children we aim to serve. Our honor, integrity, and honesty should no longer be subverted and rationalized by what we hope and may believe we are doing for these children —hopes and beliefs which have little basis in reality.

Embarking on an American Revolution in Special Education will require strength of purpose. It is recognized that the structure of most, if not all, school programs becomes self perpetuating. Teachers and state and local directors and supervisors of special education have much at stake in terms of their jobs, their security, and their programs which they have built up over the years. But can we keep our self respect and continue to increase the numbers of these self contained special classes for the educable mentally retarded which are of questionable value for many of the children they are intended to serve? As Ray Graham said in his last article in 1960: [p. 4]:

"We can look at our accomplishments and be proud of the progress we have made; but satisfaction with the past does not assure progress in the future. New developments, ideas, and facts may show us that our past practices have become out-moded. A growing child cannot remain static—he either grows or dies. We cannot become satisfied with a job one-third done. We have a long way to go before we can rest assured that the desires of the parents and the educational needs of handicapped children are being fulfilled [p. 4]."

References

Ainsworth, S. H. *An exploratory study of educational, social and emotional factors in the education of mentally retarded children in Georgia public schools.* US Office of Education Cooperative Research Project Report No. 171(6470). Athens, Ga.: University of Georgia, 1959.

Bereiter, C., & Engelmann, S. *Teaching disadvantaged children in the pre-school.* Englewood Cliffs, N.J.: Prentice-Hall, 1966.

Bruner, J. S., Olver, R. R., & Greenfield, P. M. *Studies in cognitive growth.* New York: Wiley, 1967.

Coleman, J. S., et al. *Equality of educational opportunity.* Washington, D.C.: USGPO, 1966.

Cratty, P. J. *Developmental sequences of perceptual motor tasks.* Freeport, Long Island, N.Y.: Educational Activities, 1967.

Delacato, C. H. (Ed.) *Neurological organization and reading problems.* Springfield, Ill.: Charles C Thomas, 1966.

Feuerstein, R. *The Learning Potential Assessment Device* Jerusalem, Israel: Haddassa Wizo Canada Child Guidance Clinic and Research Unit, 1968.

Frostig, M., & Horne, D. *The Frostig program for the development of visual perception.* Chicago: Follett, 1964.

Graham, R. Special education for the sixties. *Illinois Educational Association Study Unit,* 1960, **23**, 1–4.

Goffman, E. *Asylums: Essays on the social situation of mental patients and other inmates.* Garden City, N.Y.: Anchor, 1961.

Goldman, R. *The phonemic-visual-oral association technique for modifying articulation disorders in young children.* Nashville, Tenn.: Bill Wilkerson Hearing and Speech Center, 1968.

Guilford, J. P. *The nature of human intelligence.* New York: McGraw-Hill, 1967.

Hoelke, G. M. *Effectiveness of special class placement for educable mentally retarded children.* Lincoln, Neb.: University of Nebraska, 1966.

Hollingworth, L. S. *The psychology of subnormal children.* New York: MacMillan, 1923.

Johnson, G. O. Special education for mentally handicapped—a paradox. *Exceptional Children,* 1962, **19**, 62–69.

Kirk, S. A. Research in education. In H. A. Stevens & R. Heber (Eds.), *Mental retardation.* Chicago, Ill.: University of Chicago Press, 1964.

Kirk, S. A. *The diagnosis and remediation of psycholinguistic disabilities.* Urbana, Ill.: University of Illinois Press, 1966.

Lillie, D. L. The development of motor proficiency of educable mentally retarded children. *Education and Training of the Mentally Retarded,* 1967, **2**, 29–32.

Mackie, R. P. *Functional handicaps among school children due to cultural or economic deprivation.* Paper presented at the First Congress of the International Association for the Scientific Study of Mental Deficiency, Montpellier, France, September, 1967.

Meyerowitz, J. H. Family background of educable mentally retarded children. In H. Goldstein, J. W. Moss & L. J. Jordan. *The efficacy of special education training on the development of mentally retarded children.* Urbana, Ill.: University of Illinois Institute for Research on Exceptional Children, 1965. Pp. 152–182.

Meyerowitz, J. H. Peer groups and special classes. *Mental Retardation,* 1967, **5**, 23–26.

Oliver, J. N. The effects of physical conditioning exercises and activities on the mental characteristics of educationally sub-normal boys. *British Journal of Educational Psychology,* 1958, **28**, 155–165.

Passow, A. H. *A summary of findings and recommendations of a study of the Washington, D.C. schools.* New York: Teachers College, Columbia University, 1967.

Rosenthal, R., & Jacobson, L. Teachers' expectancies: Determinants of pupils' IQ gains. *Psychological Reports,* 1966, **19**, 115–118.

Rubin, E. Z., Senison, C. B., & Betwee, M. C. *Emotionally handicapped children in the elementary school.* Detroit: Wayne State University Press, 1966.

Smith, H. W., & Kennedy, W. A. Effects of three educational programs on mentally retarded children. *Perceptual and Motor Skills,* 1967, **24**, 174.

Thurstone, T. G. *Learning to think series.* Chicago, Ill.: Science Research Associates, 1948.

Wright, Judge J. S. *Hobson vs Hansen: U. S. Court of Appeals decision on the District of Columbia's track system. Civil Action No.* 82–66. Washington, D. C.: US Court of Appeals, 1967.

19. A CRITICAL EXAMINATION OF SPECIAL EDUCATION PROGRAMS

FLORENCE CHRISTOPLOS and PAUL RENZ

Special educators have often taken satisfaction and pride in the rapid expansion of special education programs (*American Education,* 1967; Mackie, 1965; NEA, 1967). Recently, however, this pride has been shaken by criticisms emanating from several sources, the most noted among them being Lloyd Dunn (1968), who prefaced an article questioning the justification of special education programs with a plea that special educators "stop being pressured into continuing and expanding a special education program that we know now to be undesirable for many of the children we are dedicated to serve" (p. 5).

Dunn's article was concerned only with special classes for educable and mildly retarded children, and his conclusions were based predominantly on empirical evidence. With the validity of such classes being widely discussed, it seems appropriate to reevaluate the purposes of *all* types of segregated classes for exceptional children on a philosophical as well as an empirical basis. Such is the intent of this paper.

The most commonly stated goal of special education programs is meeting the needs of exceptional children whose needs cannot be adequately met in regular programs (Baker, 1959; Cruickshank & Johnson,

SOURCE. Reprinted from *The Journal of Special Education,* 1969, 3, 371–379. By permission of the publisher.

252   Educational Perspectives in Learning Disabilities

1958; Dunn, 1963; Jordan, 1962; Kirk, 1962). The current proliferation of special education programs, however, cannot be explained on the basis of supporting evidence indicating progress toward such a goal.

Amorphous good intentions have often substituted for lack of more objective accomplishments. Throughout the substantial number of years special education programs have been in operation, research findings have consistently indicated no differences in performance between those placed in special classes and those placed in regular classes. We cannot ignore, therefore, the disquieting possibility that self-perpetuation may be a factor in the continuation and expansion of special education programs.

On the other hand, the complexity of the issues involved in identifying appropriate educational goals cannot be overlooked. Compulsory public school education in a heterogeneous society is a sensitive and emotionally charged assignment, especially when it is extended to include children who deviate widely from the norm. The schizophrenic dilemma of a society trying to reconcile goals of competition and cooperation, quality and equality has been pinpointed by Keppel (1966). Although he believes that quality is necessary for success in a competitive society, he cannot accept the concomitant idea that the teaching of cooperation, which is the foundation of a durable democracy, must suffer in consequence. An avoidance of clearly stated purposes allows educators to verbally support cooperation (and include most children in the educational system) then establish programs appropriate only for a segment of the population; those who are able to manage competition. Indeed, competition is emphasized, and conflicting philosophy and practice are maintained without modification of either. There can be little doubt that a clear establishment of the priority of cooperation, in practice as well as in philosophy, is critical for special education.

"Competition has no place for individuals who, because of injury, illness, or congenital incompetence, are unable to produce. . . . Social cooperation, with value attached to individual pursuits, performance in line with ability, freedom from anxiety, and social as well as economic security for all, are goals which need to be actively sought (Trippe, 1959, p. 175)."

Carlson (1964) further clarified the conflict between philosophy and practice which is so apparent today in education. He categorized organizations in terms of the relationship between the organization and its clients. Public schools are of the organizational type in which there is no control over admission of clients (students), and in which the clients, in turn, have no choice but to accept the service being offered (education) regardless of its quality. There is no problem of the school meeting criterion goals at the risk of being abandoned. Regardless of the quality of the service, students will be available and financing of the schools will be relatively secure. Carlson identified two adaptive responses on the part of the public school to the problem of lack of control over selection of students: segregation and preferential treatment. These adaptations are made not for the purpose of meeting the client's needs, but rather:

"to make the organization-client relationship more tolerable from the point of view of the organization. Through these mechanisms the organization is able to exercise a form of subtle internal selection and sorting of clients as it goes about rendering its service . . . to those students for which the school is geared to supply the most adequate service. Together, these mechanisms facilitate the fulfillment of the goals to which the school commits itself (pp. 272–273)."

The rapidly increasing number of special education classes (*American Education*, 1967; Mackie, 1965; NEA, 1967) indicates that the goals and services of general education are not appropriate for exceptional children. Their segregation into special classes allows educators to attend predominantly to those students for whom the general educational service is beneficial.

Special education programs were not initiated in response to the needs of exceptional children, but rather as an expedient measure to resist a perceived threat to existing goals for "normal" children who were being more or less adequately served by regular school programs. Parent movements pressured public schools to accept hitherto excluded children (Reynolds, 1967b) and hence forced the schools to initiate special education programs so as to avoid disturbing the traditional establishment.

There has been no reliable evidence produced to indicate that differential benefits, either social or academic, accrue to regular students as a result of either the exclusion or inclusion of exceptional students in regular classes. However, even if differential effects were found favoring the former, a democratic philosophy would dictate that the most justifiable course of action in dealing with exceptionality would be the altering of classroom practices whenever possible, rather than the segregation of the deviant individuals. The rapid growth of special classes, in the face of lack of either supporting evidence or acceptable democratic social philosophy, has but limited justification.

Within the logic of the above argument, exceptionality is defined by the nature of society, not by the nature of individuals. Exceptionality in education becomes *the condition of NOT meeting one or more critical general education goals which are of such importance to educators that failure to achieve them on the part of some students is intolerable to the educators and results in total or partial, single or group, segregation of these students.*

A brief review of some of the literature comparing effects of differential placement will serve to clarify the above definition. The problem of special classes may be seen as an extension of the problem of homogeneous versus heterogeneous grouping within regular classes or regular programs. An excellent survey published by the U. S. Office of Education (Franseth & Koury, 1966) found no clear support for either homogeneous or heterogeneous grouping in terms of academic achievement or social/emotional adjustment. The only exceptions to the long line of null results were found when personality variables such as achievement motivation or anxiety formed the basis for grouping (Atkinson & O'Connor, 1963). Sears (1963), Flanders (1964), and Thelan (1967) have also suggested that differential effects may be found when groups are patterned on criteria other than ability *per se*, yet the strongest arguments for grouping the handicapped together have been based on ability.

In spite of the lack of evidence supporting the positive value of ability grouping, a consistent and periodic pressure continues for the establishment of ability grouped classes in the public schools. Teachers and parents prefer ability grouping (Franseth & Koury, 1966, p. 50). Social and personal values appear to be more critical factors than academic realities in explaining the preference for ability grouped classes.

The academic consequences of special class placement on educable mentally handicapped (EMH) children also have been found to be negligible (Bacher, 1965; Baldwin, 1958; Blatt, 1958; Carroll, 1967; Cassidy & Stanton, 1959; Diggs, 1964; Goldstein, Moss & Jordan, 1965; Kern & Pfaeffle, 1962; Mayer, 1966; Meyerowitz, 1962, 1967b; Porter & Milazzo, 1958; Stanton & Cassidy, 1964; Thurstone, 1959). At times, a slight advantage from regular class placement for academic skills and a slight advantage from special class placement for social/emotional adjustment has been found. However, varying definitions of academic skills and social/emotional adjustment make questionable even these slight differences. In addition, the selective factors involved in determining placement of EMH children in special classes or their retention in regular classes are critical (Robinson & Robinson, 1965, p. 465).

One of the most impressive investigations of the comparative effects of special and regular classes, in which the student selection bias was carefully controlled, was conducted by Goldstein, Moss & Jordan (1965). Blackman (1967) succinctly summarized this study and concluded:

"Goldstein, Moss, and Jordan (1965) controlled for methodological inadequacies which had characterized previous investigations and conducted what was perhaps the most definitive study to date of the efficacy of special class training for the educable mentally retarded with respect to intellectual development, academic achievement, and social and personal development. . . . What emerges is the sobering generality that this methodologically sophisticated study of the efficacy of special classes for mentally retarded children blends into the long line of negative findings that have characterized this area of research for the past 30 years (p. 8).

The possibility of attitudinal effects on parents whose children have been given special class placement should not be minimized. Meyerowitz (1967a) examined the attitudes and awareness of *parents* of EMH children in special classes and in regular classes. He found that parents of EMH children in special classes generally showed greater awareness of their child's retardation but tended to derogate and devalue their child to a greater degree than did parents of EMH children in regular classes. Meyerowitz cautioned that special classes may lead, in the long run, to increased maladaptive behavior.

It is difficult moreover, to find research on the effects *on the regular students* of the inclusion in regular classes of various kinds of exceptionalities. If, as the present argument suggests, such effects are the major concern of educators, such research is critically needed. Deliberate inclusion of exceptionalities so as to determine the academic and social effects on regular students demands the researcher's attention.

The research on special class placement for gifted children has produced results similar to those obtained for the handicapped (Balow & Curtin, 1965).

Since gifted children are usually smart enough to know how to avoid interfering with the school's unwritten social mores, there is little school pressure to isolate them. Efforts to make special provisions for gifted children usually emanate from pressure applied on school personnel by industrial and other non-school people, who wish to utilize the gifted upon completion of their schooling. These efforts are generally concerned with refining the quality or accelerating the rate of doling out the educational fare (Pressey, 1963) or with early school admission (Reynolds, 1967a).

Special programs for brain-injured children (with recognition of the proverbial teapot tempest over nomenclature) and emotionally disturbed children are clearly established for reasons of intolerable social behavior. But so-called special methods recommended for these children are likely to be equally beneficial (or equally ineffective) for normal children in regular classrooms.

Placing orthopedic, blind, deaf, or even trainable children in regular classrooms is not usually considered feasible. Yet their isolation has frequently been cited as producing adverse effects. Cutsforth (1962) has found that vocation adjustment for the blind is handicapped by institutionalization with its "parental type supervision" and "lack of opportunity to develop aggressive social attitudes" (p. 183). A similar criticism of all special classes in public schools would not be remiss. Pintner (1942) found that the more able students tended to leave special classes for the visually handicapped, while the less able remained. This may also imply that regular classes contribute to making the more able child *even more* able, whereas the special class has the reverse effect. Meyerson (1963) found similar results with children who had impaired hearing. He concluded that "present evidence indicates that a child may be well adjusted regardless of the method by which he is taught, the way in which he communicates, or his place of residence" (p. 138).

Another case in point is a study done in Scotland by T. T. S. Ingram (1965) with 200 cerebral palsied patients from the cities of Dundee and Edinburgh, and from surrounding rural areas. School placement of these children had been determined by the type of school locally available, rather than through "optimum placement." Ingram compared the vocational and social adjustments of the rural patients, who were generally in a "sink or swim" situation, with those of the urban pupils, who had "specialized" programs.

"The rural patients managed to hold a place in normal schools or they did not receive education. They either remained in touch with normal people or they became homebound. There were no clubs for the handicapped and no special buses to take them for picnics. *It can be seen that there were more children in open and niche employment in the small towns than in Dundee and Edinburgh* (italics added). It seems possible that this may have been because patients in the small towns were kept in touch with their families and with normal people throughout their childhood. Segregation was avoided (p. 11)."

Ingram's argument is that special educators must consider the value for out-of-school life adjustment of what they are teaching exceptional children. Not only the purposelessness of much of the special class curriculum, but also the deleterious effects of the pressure to learn is at issue here. If clearly beneficial objectives, unique for a particular exceptionality, cannot be identified, then the exceptional group in question should not be segregated from normal society, to suffer the additional hardship of categorization in a demeaned minority group.

Even if children with obvious and severe physical exceptionalities are assumed to require highly specialized teaching, unique for each exceptionality (and this assumption is questionable), isolation in special classes is not thereby the only action feasible. Special helping teachers (itinerant or school-based), resource rooms, and other well-known educational manipulations are possible alternatives. *Anticipated interference with social intercourse resulting from regular class placement of exceptional children is an indefensible explanation for their placement in special classes.*

Considering the overall picture of research evidence, what guidelines can be proposed in planning for the exceptional child? First, it should be recognized that the adjustment of the exceptional child to the normal world is unlikely to occur unless he has frequent and familiar interaction with it. The risk that such interaction may contribute to a greater *maladjustment* of the exceptional child is undeniable, yet adequate adjustment is dependent on taking such risks. Care must be taken lest the discomfort and anxiety of the normal population at the possibility of having daily and close interaction with deviant individuals become the cause of restriction of such interaction. That segregation is for the good of the exceptional, rather than for the comfort of the normal population, may be a deluding rationalization.

Secondly, lack of intimate knowledge about, and experience with, deviants denies the *normal* individual opportunities for social learning which may have the broadest implications for the understanding of human differences (Doll, 1966). An example is Billings' (1963) study which highlights the problem of segregation as it affects *normal* children. She examined attitudes of non-crippled children toward crippled ones and found that after third grade the attitudes of the non-crippled toward the crippled became more unfavorable and that *students judged to be high in social and emotional adjustment had the most unfavorable attitudes toward crippled children!* Surely it is appropriate to ask, "What price social adjustment in our public schools?" The positive effects of familiar intercourse with exceptionalities is exemplified by Bateman's (1962) study whereby sighted children who knew blind children were found to be more positive in their appraisals of blind children's abilities than were those who did not know any blind children.

The possibility that special education is a solution to the "problem" of educators in achieving their own goal of social homogeneity, instead of educational goals for children, should not be ignored. Specifically identified educational goals for children can insure that such improper solutions do not occur. Amorphous goals allow for surreptitious manipulation of a variety of behaviors far removed from those ethically in the realm of educational concern. This problem is common to the education of *all* children, but is more blatant with handicapped children, whose greater dependency and vulnerability may facilitate a wider use of unjustifiable manipulations. Before an exceptional child is segregated from the regular classroom, those behaviors which he must master for re-entry into it need to be identified and, if possible, programmed into his education. Such an identification can elicit a more frequent and healthy analysis of *why* certain specified behaviors are desirable or mandatory and whether all those students not segregated exhibit the desirable (or omit the undesirable) behavior. Considering handicapped children in terms of behaviors rather than in terms of classified exceptionalities would inhibit the establishment of segregated classes for any minority based on anything other than specifically-delineated educational goals.

The Exceptional as a Minority Group

The 1954 Supreme Court decision on segregation in public schools (Warren, 1954) assumes great significance when applied to exceptional children as well as to racial minorities. Consider the following excerpts in which the underlined words have been changed to make the text apply to exceptional children:

"Segregation of *regular* and *exceptional* children in public schools has a detrimental effect on the *exceptional* children. The impact is greater when it has the sanction of the law; for the policy of separating the *students* is usually interpreted as denoting the inferiority of the *exceptional* group. A sense of inferiority affects the motivation of a child to learn. Segregation with the sanction of the law, therefore, has a tendency to retard the educational and mental development of *exceptional* children and to deprive them of some of the benefits they would receive in a *totally* integrated system. . . . We conclude that in the field of public education the doctrine of "separate but equal" has no place. Separate educational facilities are inherently unequal (pp. 10–11)."

Considering educationally exceptional persons as a minority group is not new (Barker, 1948; Tenny, 1953; Wright, 1960). However, as in Jordan's discussion (1963), attempts have been made to differentiate between the benevolent attitudes shown toward some minorities (e.g., the handicapped) and the malicious attitudes shown toward others (e.g., Negroes). This is begging the question. As long as any type of individual is segregated, the majority group avoids familiar interaction with it, thus avoiding having to make changes in its own values. The previously-identified distinction between benevolence and maliciousness on the part of the majority appears to parallel the difference between high and low potential for independence and power on the part of the minorities. It is not difficult to feel more benevolent toward handicapped minorities, who are more vulnerable to majority manipulations, than toward a struggling and militant racial minority. But it appears equally difficult for a majority group member to associate with either minority!

Another social analogy to educational exceptionality is that of delinquent youth. Empey (1967) wrote about delinquency in ways which special educators may find disquietingly pertinent to their own problems. He noted that only within special programs are delinquents' attitudes being changed:

"But somehow these changes are not translated to the community where the offender's adjustment is submitted to the ultimate test. . . . Delinquency and crime, and reactions to them, are social products and are socially defined. Society, not individuals, defines rules, labels those who break rules, and prescribes ways for reacting to the labeled person. The labeling process is often a means of isolating offenders from, rather than integrating them in, effective participation in such major societal institutions as schools, businesses, unions, churches, and political organizations (pp. 4–5)."

Empey also believes that the basis of programming decisions for the delinquent should be clear with specific identification of goals:

"When there is no consensus on objectives, there is no logical means for choosing one approach over another, one kind of staff over another, one program component over another. It would not make sense to initiate an experimental effort unless objectives were made explicit and a set of priorities chosen (p. 81)."

A final aspect of special education programs to be considered is the possibility that once segregation becomes institutionalized, it is most difficult to eliminate. Any initial steps toward educational segregation should therefore be cautious, judicious, and adequately supported by research *before* wide implementation or dissemination is initiated. The difficulty is magnified if current special education programs are administratively well-entrenched and continue to multiply, giving rise to the very real danger that the primary goal of special education may become self-perpetuation. There are indications that this has already occurred to some degree.

In conclusion, we ought to point out that attitudes of fear and rejection are concomitants of unfamiliarity. Familiarization with deviation, via inclusion of deviates in regular classrooms, should minimize undesirable attitudes on the part of the "normal" population. So, too, should familiarization with the "normal" world have beneficial effects on the deviants. Evidence of difficult interactions between deviant and normal individuals in an integrated situation should lead to remedial manipulations of the environment before segregation is considered as an alternative. This approach would be consistent with the establishment of a general pattern of positive reaction to, and inclusion of, the strange or different. Such positive valuing of differences is consistent with Francis Keppel's (1966) urgent message that we must not lose sight of the cooperative basis that must underlie our competitive society. The implications go beyond special education and general education to our national goals of world-wide understanding, peace, and cooperation.

References

Atkinson, J. W. & O'Connor, Patricia. *Effects of ability grouping in schools related to individual differences in achievement related motivation.* Cooperative Research Project 1283. Washington, D.C.: Dept. HEW, Office Education, 1963.

Bacher, J. H. The effect of special class placement on the self-concept, social adjustment, and reading growth of slow learners. *Diss. Abstr.*, 1965, 25, 7071.

Baker, H. J. *Introduction to exceptional children.* New York: Macmillan, 1959.

Baldwin, W. The social position of the educable mentally retarded child in the regular grades in the public school. *Except. Child.*, 1958, 25, 106–8, 112.

Balow, B. & Curtin, J. Ability grouping of bright pupils. *Elem. sch. J.*, 1965, 321–6.

Barker, R. G. The social psychology of physical disability. *J. soc. Issues*, 1948, 4, 28–38.

Bateman, Barbara. Sighted children's perceptions of blind children's abilities. *Except. Child.*, 1962, 29, 42–6.

Billings, Helen K. An exploratory study of the attitudes of noncrippled children toward crippled children in three selected elementary schools. *J. exp. Educ.*, 1963, 31, 381–7.

Blackman, L. S. The dimensions of a science of special education. *Ment. Retard.*, 1967, 5, (4) 7–11.

Blatt, B. The physical, personality, and academic status of children who are mentally retarded attending special classes as compared with children who are mentally retarded attending regular classes. *Amer. J. ment. Defic.*, 1958, 62, 810–18.

Carlson, R. O. Environmental constraints and organizational consequences: The public school and its clients. In D. E. Griffiths (Ed.), *Behavioral Science and Educational Administration*. (63rd Yearbook of the NSSE). Chicago Univ. Chicago Press, 1964, 262–76.

Carroll, Ann W. The effects of segregated and partially integrated school programs on self-concept and academic achievement of educable mentally retarded. *Except. Child.*, 1967, 34, 93–6.

Cassidy, V. M. & Stanton, J. E. *An investigation of factors involved in the educational placement of mentally retarded children: A study of differences between children in special and regular classes in Ohio.* Cooperative Research Project 043. Washington, D.C.: Dept. HEW, Office Education, 1959.

Cruickshank, W. & Johnson, G. O. *Education of exceptional children and youth*. Englewood Cliffs, N.J.: Prentice-Hall, 1958.

Cutsforth, T. D. Personality and social adjustment among the blind. In P. A. Zahl (Ed.) *Blindness*. New York: Hafner, 1962. Pp. 174–90.

Diggs, E. A. A study of change in the social status of rejected mentally retarded children in regular classrooms. *Diss. Abstr.*, 1964, 25, 220–1.

Doll, E. A. Retrospect and prospect. *Educ. Train. ment. Retard.*, 1966, 1, 3–7.

Dunn, L. M. *Exceptional children in the schools*. New York: Holt, Rinehart & Winston, 1963.

Dunn, L. M. Special education for the mildly retarded—is much of it justifiable? *Except. Child.*, 1968, 35, 5–24.

Dunn, L. M. Education of the handicapped. *Amer. Educ.*, July–Aug. 1967, 3, 30–1.

Empey, LaM. T. *Alternatives to incarceration*. Washington, D.C.: Dept. HEW, Office Juvenile Delinquency and Youth Development, 1967.

Flanders, N. A. Teacher and classroom influences on individual learning. In A. H. Passow (Ed.), *Nurturing Individual Potential*. Washington, D.C.: Assoc. Super. Curr. Dev., 1964. Pp. 57–65.

Franseth, Jane & Koury, Rose. *Survey of research on grouping as related to pupil learning*. Washington, D.C.: U.S. Printing Office, Dept. HEW, Office Educ., CE 20089, 1966.

Gallagher, J. J. *Analysis of research on the education of gifted children*. State of Illinois, Office Superintendent Public Instruction, Special Study Project for Gifted Children, 1960.

Goldstein, H., Moss, J. W. & Jordan, L. J. *The efficacy of special class training on the development of mentally retarded children*. Cooperative Research Project 619. Washington, D.C.: Dept. HEW, Office Education, 1965.

Ingram, T. T. S. Education—for what purpose? In J. Loring (Ed.), *Teaching the Cerebral Palsied Child*. Lavenham, Suffolk, England: Lavenham Press, Ltd., 1965. Pp. 1–13.

Jordan, S. The disadvantaged group: a concept applicable to the handicapped. *J. Psychol.*, 1963, 55, 313–22.

Jordan, T. E. *The exceptional child.* Columbus, Ohio: Charles E. Merrill, 1962.

Keppel, F. *The necessary revolution in American education.* New York: Harper & Row, 1966.

Kern, W. H. & Plaffle, H. A comparison of social adjustment of mentally retarded children in various educational settings. *Amer. J. ment. Defic.*, 1962, 67, 407–13.

Kirk, S. A. *Educating exceptional children.* Boston: Houghton-Mifflin, 1962.

Mackie, R. P. Spotlighting advances in special education. *Except. Child.*, 1965, 32, 77–81.

Mayer, L. The relationship of early special class placement and the self-concepts of mentally handicapped children. *Except. Child.*, 1966, 33, 77–80.

Meyerowitz, J. H. Self-derogations in young retardates and special class placement. *Child. Dev.*, 1962, 33, 443–51.

Meyerowitz, J. H. Parental awareness of retardation. *Amer. J. ment. Defic.*, 1967, 71, 637–43. (a)

Meyerowitz, J. H. Peer groups and special classes. *Ment. Retard.*, 1967, 5, (5) 23–6. (b)

Meyerson, L. A psychology of impaired hearing. In W. M. Cruickshank (Ed.) *Psychology of Exceptional Children and Youth.* Englewood Cliffs, N.J.: Prentice-Hall, 1963, Pp. 118–91.

NEA. *Programs for handicapped children.* Washington, D.C.: NEA Research Div., 1967, 115–7.

Pintner, R. Intelligence testing of partially sighted children. *J. educ. Psychol.*, 1942, 33, 265–72.

Porter, R. B. & Milazzo, T. C. A comparison of mentally retarded adults who attended a special class with those who attended regular school classes. *Except. Child.*, 1958, 24, 410–2, 420.

Pressey, S. L. *Acceleration and the gifted.* Columbus: Ohio State Dept. Educ., 1963.

Reynolds, M. C. (Ed.) *Early school admission for mentally advanced children.* Washington, D.C.: NEA, 1967. (a)

Reynolds, M. C. The surge in special education. *Nat. educ. Assn. J.*, 1967, 56, (8). (b)

Robinson, H. B. & Robinson, Nancy M. *The mentally retarded child.* New York: McGraw-Hill, 1965.

Sears, Pauline S. *The effects of classroom conditions on the strength of achievement motive and work output of elementary school children.* Cooperative Research Project 873. Washington, D.C.: Dept. HEW, Office Education, 1963.

Stanton, Jeannette E. & Cassidy, Viola M. Effectiveness of special classes for educable mentally retarded. *Ment. Retard.*, 1964, 2, 8–13.

Tenny, J. W. The minority status of the handicapped. *Except. Child.*, 1953, 18, 260–4.

Thelan, H. A. *Classroom grouping for teachability.* New York: John Wiley, 1967.

Thurstone, Thelma G. *An evaluation of educating mentally handicapped children in special classes and in regular classes.* Cooperative Research Project OE-SAE 6452. Washington, D.C.: Dept. HEW, Office Education, 1959.

Trippe, M. J. The social psychology of exceptional children: Part II. *Except. Child.*, 1959, 26, 171–5, 188.

Warren, E. *Brown* vs. *Board of Education.* Washington, D.C.: U.S. Supreme Court, 1954.

Wright, B. A. *Physical disability: A psychological approach.* New York: Harper & Row, 1960.

20. SOME NEGATIVE IMPLICATIONS OF SPECIAL PLACEMENT FOR CHILDREN WITH LEARNING DISABILITIES

RICHARD C. TOWNE and LEE M. JOINER

Learning disabilities[1] is a new, rapidly developing field; one has only to read Barbara Bateman's recent AERA review (1966) to gain a feeling for the groping, unresolved nature of current efforts for knowledge about the many conditions crowded beneath the disabilities umbrella.

Bateman's review also makes it clear that, to date, psychologists, educators, and medical specialists are doing all the work, with efforts being focused primarily upon refining diagnostic tools and devising remediation procedures. Consequently, little energy is being devoted to studying the social aspects of special programs for the learning disabled. This is understandable in light of the strengths of the professions involved. But if part of the remedial educational plan for a child involves placing him in a special class, then it should be recognized that a social act is taking place that bears upon the success of the program. Erickson made a similar point some time ago regarding treatment for the mentally ill:

". . . the clinician's understanding of the therapeutic environment he creates for his patient may be sharpened by the concepts of the

SOURCE. Reprinted from *The Journal of Special Education*, 1968, 2, 217–222. By permission of the publisher.

[1] A child with a learning disability is any child so labeled for whatever reason. See Becker (1964) for a discussion of the implications of such a definition.

social sciences, particularly where these concepts help to view both patient and psychiatry as participants in the cultural context of social life. The sociologist must point out that whenever a psychiatrist makes the clinical diagnosis of an existing need for treatment, society makes the social diagnosis of a changed status of one of its members. And while the clinician must insist that the treatment which follows and the setting provided for it have to be geared to the inner-dynamic realities of the patient's illness, the sociologist proposes that recovery may also depend upon gearing the ongoing treatment to the social realities of the patient's changed status (Erickson, 1957, pp. 273–274)."

Similarly, in the belief that the things a child learns in the social situations associated with going to school are as important as what he learns in the formal curriculum, a sociological perspective has been adopted here so that we can examine some little noted consequences of special classes for children with learning disabilities. The discussion draws heavily on Parson's analysis of the sick role in our culture (1951) and Erickson's application of that position to the mentally ill (1957). Even more basic is Merton's (1957) elaboration of *latent functions*.

Hopefully, special educators will be stimulated by this discussion to take a second look at their special classes, and social scientists—particularly sociologists and social psychologists—will be challenged to contribute their skills to an interdisciplinary approach to planning for children with learning disabilities.[2] And even if ideal planning doesn't occur, perhaps a few social problems will be anticipated and steps taken to ameliorate their effects.

LATENT FUNCTIONS

Initially, it may be helpful to outline Merton's idea of *latent functions* and relate it to planning for children with learning disabilities. To avoid confusion between conscious motivations for social behavior and the objective consequence of that behavior, Merton (1957) distinguished between *manifest functions* and *latent functions*. He defined *manifest functions* as ". . . those objective consequences contributing to the adjustment or adaptation of the system which are intended and recognized by participants in the system" (p. 51), and *latent functions* as ". . . un-

---

[2] While they are not directly concerned with learning disabled children, see the Erickson (1957) article mentioned above, Rosengren's (1961) research with the emotionally disturbed. Mercer's (1965) research with the mentally retarded, and Goffman's *Stigma* (1963) for examples of the dimensions which a social orientation can contribute to educational planning.

intended and unrecognized consequences of the same order" (p. 63). He pointed out that behavior may perform a function quite remote from its avowed purpose, either in place of the anticipated consequences or in addition to them. Consequently, the concept of *latent function*, by directing attention beyond intended consequences, sensitizes investigators to a range of social variables that might otherwise be overlooked. For instance, the acquisition of an automobile may be studied not only as it satisfies a need for a particular means of transportation, its *manifest function*, but also as a symbol of social status, a *latent function*.

Grouping children with learning disabilities may be studied in a like manner. On the level of *manifest function*, for example, special grouping might be studied from the viewpoint of enhanced learning for both the children with learning disorders and the normal children with whom they were once housed. Another *manifest function* of special classes may be the reduction of anxiety in regular classroom teachers, and this could also be studied. Or special placement could be studied in terms of *latent functions*, the central concern of this paper.

BEING CLASSIFIED

An unintended function of special placement for children is reflected in the often heard dictum: "Remember, he is a child with a disability, not a disabled child." Essentially, this statement acknowledges a formalized deviant status which threatens to replace the old status, *child*. And once deviance is formalized, and the child successfully labeled deviant, action is taken toward him on the basis of his new deviant status.

While all societies develop techniques for suppressing deviant behavior, they all create as well particular statuses where deviant behavior is both expected and legitimate. Actually, means are devised for absorbing certain kinds of deviant individuals into society's structure (Erickson, 1957). For the public schools of our society this is an important undertaking since they are committed to an open door policy yet are held responsible for maintaining academic standards. So while nearly all children are permitted to enter our public schools, a substantial number of them inadequately perform the required academic tasks—that is, they engage in deviant behavior. Of late, more and more of these students, the ones who do not measure up (Bateman's [1966] "leftover child") are being diagnosed as "learning disabilities" and placed in special classes.

A brief description of the process by which students become members of special classes would begin with children entering school expecting to do whatever will be required of them. Even though some, because of previous experiences with their parents and with other children, may doubt their chances of doing well, it is within the classroom itself that children first hear the click of the sorting and singling out mechanism. If the child performs academic tasks very slowly and ineptly, or if he becomes a management problem, he is singled out by the teacher and referred for a "psychological." Then, depending in part upon the school's diagnostic sophistication and its special services structure as well as upon the test profiles, the student will be diagnosed as mentally retarded, emotionally disturbed, or learning disabled. Finally, a committee will meet to discuss other concerns like openings available, parental reaction, and teacher behavior. If after everything is considered it is decided to formally classify the child as either mentally retarded, emotionally disturbed, or learning disabled, the decision is made public by placement in a separate classroom where the student will be with others who are supposed to have similar learning problems. In effect he is declared deviant and is given over to the school's mechanism for handling its deviant members.[3]

THE SOCIAL IMPLICATIONS OF BEING LABELED

Since being labeled and placed in a special class changes the student's position in the social structure, it may be expected that this will influence his behavior (Gross, Mason, & McEachern, 1958). Others will act toward him in terms of their understanding of the new status. "Misplaced concreteness" (Guttchen, 1963) may be attributed to the abstract, formal diagnostic category. The meaning of the label "learning disabled" (or of "cerebral dysfunction," "neurological handicap," "brain injury," or whatever other terms may be applied) will expand beyond the set of diagnostic behaviors that define the category so that the child is now thought of as being generally personally defective rather than as a child deficient in specific learning skills.

Thus, whatever the label means to others, regardless of its accuracy or connection with the child's immediate behavior, each person's expectations and interpretations of the child's behavior will be affected by his definition of what this kind of person is supposed to be like. Vague feelings and observations about the child's behavior become anchored to the label. A social object is created by developing a cognitive category which connects many disparate characteristics. And the social object is "authenticated" since the observed behaviors are defined as causal condi-

---

[3] This function of the special class—creating a place where deviant behavior is legitimate and expected—may be an important reason for the continued expansion of special classes for the educable mentally retarded even though "efficacy" research continues to disappoint special educators.

tions in explaining the behavior. Thus, the student's inept performance of an important task will be explained by defining him as a member of a subset who is supposed to behave that way by definition.

There are benefits to the child, of course, in his new status. To the extent that the new status replaces descriptions like "naughty," "ill-mannered," or "bad-tempered" with descriptions related to illness or sickness, rejection and exasperation should be replaced by shelter and understanding. Also, insofar as others perceive the label "learning disability" as casting the student in a sick role, the child's problems in performing expected roles will be reduced. As Parsons (1964) argues, two features of the sick role are: (a) the sick person cannot be held responsible for being sick; and (b) he is exempted from performing certain normal role and task obligations.

These benefits, however, are bought at a price. Parsons (1964) points out two additional characteristics of the sick role: (a) that the sick person is obligated both to try to get well and to seek competent help; and (b) that he is to cooperate in the attempts to help him get well. Thus, illness is stigmatized as undesirable in a culture stressing accomplishment or productivity, and considerable pains are taken to prevent the healthy from being tempted to become sick (Parsons, 1964). It might be expected, for example, that the more flexible, less academically demanding curricula of special classes for the learning disabled would appeal to certain students were it not for the price they must pay for membership in such classes. Theoretically, if there were no stigma—let us say that efforts to reduce whatever stigma is attached to special classes were to be completely successful—there would be no motivation to avoid deviant behavior (Parsons, 1964) and numbers would be an even bigger problem than they are at present.

THE SPECIAL CLASS AS A SOCIAL SETTING FOR SELF REDEFINITION

Most of the literature regarding what goes on in special classes for children with learning disabilities discusses specific remedial techniques without acknowledging that these techniques are applied in social settings and that their effectiveness is influenced by social processes.

To highlight these influences Brookover's (1959) social psychological theory of learning is sketched here and related to classroom practices with the learning disabled. Four hypotheses form the substance of Brookover's conception of school learning:

"1. Persons learn to behave in ways that each considers appropriate to himself. . . .

"2. Appropriateness of behavior is defined by each person through the internalization of the expectation of significant others. . . .
"3. The functional limits of one's ability to learn are determined by his self conception or self-image as acquired in social interaction. . . .
"4. The individual learns what he believes significant others expect him to learn in the classroom and other situations. (Brookover, 1959)."

This model for learning should not be interpreted to mean that biological differences—for example, those resulting from a neurological impairment—play no part in academic performance. Genetic, organic limits do provide a framework in determining what is learned. But within that framework, a child's perceptions of what is appropriate, desirable, and possible for him to learn set the functional limits of his learning (Brookover & Gottlieb, 1964).

SOME IMPLICATIONS FOR SPECIAL EDUCATION

For teachers of learning disabled students the above theory has several implications. For example:

1. Since many prescriptive teaching techniques give the child tasks that differ considerably from typical academic tasks, the student may perceive these tasks as inappropriate, as "kid stuff" or "for dummies," thus limiting the planned remedial outcomes. Attention should therefore be given to determining what behaviors and tasks students consider appropriate or inappropriate to their new social status. And if certain perceptions conflict with program objectives, efforts should be directed toward manipulating those perceptions along positive lines.

2. Research has shown that when there is consensus among parents, peers, and teachers regarding what behavior is appropriate, and when these expectations are coupled with high surveillance and given high importance, a situation of high social obligation develops in the participants (Brookover, Erickson, & Joiner, 1967). Efforts should therefore be directed toward developing such conditions—for example, parents should be enlisted to communicate repeatedly to their children definitions of appropriate and inappropriate behavior.

3. Students can so learn that they can't learn that even the most sophisticated remedial programs are jeopardized. There is a good deal of evidence that if a student defines himself as unable to learn certain forms of academic behavior, he will not attempt to learn them. But we also know that his definitions of himself as a student are emergents, i.e., subject to the changing stances toward him adopted by others important to him. And when others who are important to the student purposefully

set out to develop in him a self-conception of ability rather than inability, positive changes and improved academic performance have been found to occur. So we can be optimistic about purposefully changing negative self-conceptions that would otherwise threaten remedial efforts.

SUMMARY AND CONCLUSION

Special classes for the learning disabled have been discussed from a perspective that emphasizes their social nature. The concept of *latent function* was introduced to direct attention beyond the intended functions of placement of children in special classes. The process of being labeled has been sketched, and implications have been drawn regarding the assumption of a sick role. Finally, a social psychological concept of learning has been briefly related to remedial practices. Admittedly this has been a speculative venture; we have only suggested some types of variables that somehow must be taken into account. But if such concerns are introduced early enough, when the rest of the field is still in a state of flux, they too may mature under study, and understanding can advance on a broad enough plane to result finally in programs that will really do something for the children we are trying to help.

References

Bateman, B. Learning disorders. *Review of Educational Research*, 1966, 36, 93–119.

Becker, H. S. Introduction. In H. S. Becker (Ed.), *The other side: perspectives on deviance*. Glencoe, Ill.: The Free Press, 1964.

Brookover, W. B. A social psychological conception of classroom learning. *School and Society*, 1959, 87, 84–87.

Brookover, W. B./Erickson, E. L./Joiner, L. M. *Self concept of ability and school achievement, III*. Cooperative Research Project, #2831, U. S. Office of Education, East Lansing, Mich.: Educational Publication Services, College of Education, Michigan State University, 1967.

Brookover, W. B. & Gottlieb, D. *A sociology of education*. (2nd ed.) New York: American Book Company, 1964.

Erickson, K. T. Patient role and social uncertainty—a dilemma of the mentally ill. *Psychiatry*, 1957, 20, 263–274.

Goffman, E. *Stigma*. Englewood Cliffs, N. J.: Prentice-Hall, 1963.

Gross, N./Mason, W. S./McEachern, A. W. Explorations in role analysis. New York: Wiley, 1958.

Guttchen, R. A. On the classification of human beings. *Indian Journal of Social Research*, 1963, 4, 42–48.

Mercer, J. R. Social system perspective and clinical perspective frames of reference for understanding career patterns of persons labelled as mentally retarded. *Social Problems*, 1965, 13, 18–34.

Merton, R. K. *Social theory and social structure.* New York: Free Press, 1957.

Parsons, T. *The social system.* Glencoe, Ill.: The Free Press, 1951.

Parsons, T. *Social structure and personality.* New York: The Free Press of Glencoe, 1964.

Rosengren, W. R. The self in the emotionally disturbed. *American Journal of Sociology*, 1961, 67, 454–462.

21. THE LEARNING RESOURCE CENTER FOR EXCEPTIONAL CHILDREN

ROBERT E. VALETT

Although a variety of special education classes have been made available in most school districts, these have usually been limited and have not been sufficient to meet the needs of the pupils. For instance, special educators have recognized the importance of providing individualized instruction, proper programing, consultant help in curriculum development, and continued inservice training. The need to provide for multiply handicapped pupils and those requiring special educational therapy or counseling has also been recognized, but seldom met. Similarly, parent participation, counseling, and education have been identified as a necessary part of the educational process although such programs have been seldom been given much priority.

THE LEARNING RESOURCE CENTER

In the spring of 1968 the Sacramento City Unified School District was awarded funds under Title VI of the Elementary and Secondary Education Act to establish a Learning Resource Center for Exceptional Children

---

SOURCE. Reprinted from *Exceptional Children*, 1970, 36, 527–530. By permission of the author and publisher.

with the primary objective of stimulating the development of prescriptive teaching approaches by providing supplemental services to the regular special education program. No attempt was made to provide additional classes for exceptional children. Emphasis was placed on the development of resource services in the areas of psychoeducational evaluation and programing, educational therapy, pupil and parent counseling, in-service training, and parent education. Priority was given to multiply handicapped pupils with significant learning disabilities for whom the existing educational program was inadequate.

STAFF AND FACILITIES

The staff of the Learning Resource Center consists of four professionals and two secretaries. A psychoeducational specialist is the director and consulting psychologist for the staff, parents, and teachers involved. An educational therapist provides direct therapy for a number of children who come to the center on an appointment basis. The educational psychologist assists teachers in educational programing and planning classroom pilot projects, conducts special evaluations, and works with parent groups. A demonstration teacher helps teachers develop exemplary programs and works with selected children upon assignment. All four members of the team work directly with pupils in some continuing capacity. In addition to the center staff, seven school psychologists and three program coordinators (for the physically handicapped, educationally handicapped, and mentally retarded) serve special education teachers and are involved in consultation and the screening of referrals.

The Learning Resource Center is located in the wing of a regular elementary school. One room, equipped with an observation window and a sound recording system, is the psychoeducational clinic for task analysis of motor and perceptual skills and related learning disabilities. The adjacent room is used for educational therapy and is equipped with educational materials and programing aids. The third room is the resource training room and houses conference tables for inservice training, parent education, and educational materials classified by specific learning disabilities.

PSYCHOLOGICAL EVALUATION AND PROGRAMING

The goal of the Learning Resource Center staff is to provide specific consulting services to teachers, coordinators, and psychologists. When the center receives a request for help in developing an effective special education program for an individual pupil and his parents, the center personnel may meet with the requesting school's staff to review the problem and cooperatively plan a number of positive interventions. These interventions usually include the individualization of the program with special materials, flexible scheduling, behavior modification, parent involvement, and the planning of classroom strategies.

The center also has consulting sessions where teachers and psychologists come to the center to discuss selected cases, to request help in designing special projects, or to confer on educational problems. An example of this approach would be a staff meeting, including the parents, to devise a cooperative home and school behavior modification program for a disturbed boy.

In most cases in which children are referred to the center considerable psychological and related information is already available. The usual initial procedure is to make some developmental task analysis of functional performance in gross motor, sensory motor, perceptual, language, conceptual, and social skill areas (Valett, 1967) in order to select appropriate tasks and thus create an effective program allowing the child to function in some school setting. For example, a six year old, deaf, blind, and mildly retarded child was successfully, but gradually, programed into special education following task analysis and prescriptive programing.

EDUCATIONAL THERAPY

The educational therapy program began with several severely handicapped pupils who had been exempted from school attendance. Following task analysis and evaluation of each child's basic learning abilities with specially developed instruments (Valett, 1966, 1968), individualized therapy programs were developed. Special emphasis was placed on programing specific motor, perceptual, language, and cognitive abilities with parental involvement. Parents first viewed their children through the observation window; gradually, they participated directly in the therapy room and were expected to follow up on home assignments with special prescriptions for learning (Valett, 1970) as specified by the assigned therapist. During the year, 21 children, their parents, and all the staff members worked on this basis.

Educational therapy is supplemental to regular special education placement. However, due to the extent of their disability, eight children continued in intensive therapy three to five sessions per week without school placement. The major problem continues to be effective liaison with special class teachers so that the pupil can continue in the class, or return to it as soon as possible, while receiving the essential supporting help.

The center operates a small activity group for teaching children basic socialization skills prior to integration into special classes. The group is conducted twice a week under the leadership of the demonstration teacher, with parents participating on a regularly assigned basis.

PARENT AND PUPIL COUNSELING

A number of parents of exceptional children have requested counseling or consulting services for themselves or their children. As a result of a brochure sent to parents describing the services of the center, many requests for special help were received. Of these requests, 28 were given to consulting school psychologists and program coordinators who then worked with the pupils and parents concerned.

An additional 17 parents were seen at the center for special counseling and programing. In most cases several sessions were held with each parent to help each one define and cope with the problems of his exceptional child. Typical cases consisted of helping parents select and modify specific child behaviors, such as aggression, which were upsetting both at home and in school; many other sessions focused on parental concerns in dealing with enuresis and self help skills.

Although most pupil counseling is conducted by the special education teachers and school counselors or psychologists, occasional help is requested from the center. Cases, such as working with a boy with suicidal inclinations or with a child who has repeatedly run away from home, involve close liaison with the referring teacher or psychologist. During the year, seven pupils were seen for this kind of supportive counseling.

PARENT EDUCATION

One of the most exciting and successful programs offered by the center has been parent education. At the beginning of the school year, announcements were sent out that interested parents could register for 10 week courses on understanding and managing children's behavior problems. Both morning and evening sessions were offered under the leadership of the educational psychologist and the psychoeducational specialist. Semiprogramed lessons (Patterson & Gullion, 1968; Valett, 1969a) and other materials which were used covered such subjects as establishing objectives, teaching desirable behavior, using reinforcement, and managing special problems.

Throughout the year four classes and three followup discussion groups were held with 93 parents participating. Classes usually began with the instructor's introducing the topic. Then lesson materials for parents to work on in the class were distributed, and the subsequent discussion centered around selected problems or concerns relevant to the topic. "Homework" consisted of projects requiring systematic observation of children, selection and modification of target behaviors, and the development of reward and recording systems. Parents then brought their projects to class for a discussion of their approaches to a problem. Approximately 75 percent of the parents who began the classes finished and reported positive results in modifying their children's behavior.

Seventy-nine percent of the parents reported that the classes were of "very much" or "much" help in teaching them how to understand and manage their children's behavior; other responses were "average" (12 percent), "little help" (7 percent), and "very little help" (2 percent). Some other significant responses were the following: 94 percent felt the course material and topics to be "very good" or "good" while 93 percent found the class discussions "very helpful" or "helpful." Numerous statements were also received of which the following are typical:

"It taught us how to observe and where to start in trying to modify our boy's behavior. The specific directions were most helpful.

"It helped me to find a more positive and effective way of dealing with my child, and in that way to really enjoy him more. It showed me that parents first must change their attitude before they can help their children overcome behavior problems.

"It gave me a completely new approach to controlling our kids."

Suggestions from parents for improving the course included longer class periods, more audiovisual materials, specialized classes for parents of teenagers, more followup classes, and more provision for individual counseling of parents.

INSERVICE TRAINING

A major function of the Learning Resource Center has been to provide resources and training programs for special education personnel. The resource training room and the demonstration teacher have served as the focal points of this program, although all staff members have been involved. Many different inservice training programs and services were made available including the following:

1. A preschool workshop on prescriptive teaching for 14 selected teachers and special educators was held.

2. A preschool workshop on prescriptive planning in special education for 23 administrators, psychologists, and program coordinators was held.
3. Special group meetings were conducted with 162 special education teachers introducing them to program materials available through the center.
4. New materials (over 790 items) were checked out for use by special education teachers.
5. More than 300 teachers, college students, and out of district persons visited the resource training room for help in program development.
6. Demonstration teacher services were provided upon request to 30 special education teachers.
7. A 17 week two unit salary credit course on behavior modification and task analysis in special education for 19 teachers interested in developing prescriptive teaching programs with their own classrooms was offered.

Future plans include extending inservice credit courses to cover specialized courses for secondary teachers and additional prescriptive teaching courses for new elementary special educators. Demonstration teacher services will be extended to permit large blocks of time (up to a month or more) to be spent assisting interested teachers in developing model classrooms.

IMPLICATIONS

On the basis of experience to date, several major program implications warrant careful consideration.

Parent education should receive priority and should be rapidly extended. Emphasis should be placed on the early involvement of parents in parent education and participation programs. Programs should be available to all parents of referred children with learning or behavioral problems.

More attention should be given to early consultation with teachers concerned with learning problems by encouraging teachers to request consultation on exceptional children and their programs early in the school year. A more intensive followup service, which may require the psychologist or other specialist to spend a number of consecutive days in a classroom to work through a given problem, should be provided.

Educational therapy is an additional resource program and does not replace the ongoing special education class. All exceptional children should have some group or class placement. Since it is difficult to bridge the gap between individual educational therapy and the more usual special education program, a number of varied level activity groups for multiply handicapped children could be used as a stepping stone to the usual special program. Since educational therapy should be viewed as a temporary resource, it should be provided on a contract basis to the children of parents who agree to become directly involved in home training and parent education. Educational therapy needs to be continued in the summer if these handicapped children are to retain the gains made during the school year.

Learning Resource Center counseling services should continue to emphasize behavior modification and short term involvement. Conjoint family counseling and group counseling should be developed. Parent and adolescent groups should be continuous to allow group placement of exceptional children and/or their parents when necessary. With the participation of district counselors and psychologists in specialized counseling groups such a situation would be feasible.

The inservice training program has been particularly effective in stimulating innovative practices, since teachers have participated voluntarily in special classes. Summer workshops should also be developed as an extended part of inservice training with priority given to new teachers. Demonstration teacher effectiveness can be enhanced through longer assignments to teachers interested in working on classroom planning and organization problems.

References

Patterson, G., & Gullion, M. E. *Living with children.* Champaign, Ill.: Research Press, 1968.

Valett, R. *The Valett development survey of basic learning abilities.* Palo Alto: Consulting Psychologists Press, 1966.

Valett, R. *The remediation of learning disabilities.* Palo Alto: Fearon, 1967.

Valett, R. *The psychoeducational inventory.* Palo Alto: Fearon, 1968.

Valett, R. *Modifying children's behavior.* Palo Alto: Fearon, 1969.

Valett, R. *Prescriptions for learning.* Palo Alto: Fearon, 1970.

22. PROVIDING SERVICES IN THE PUBLIC SCHOOLS FOR CHILDREN WITH LEARNING DISABILITIES

JEANNE McRAE McCARTHY

This talk is directed to those of you who are in a position in your school system to do something in the way of program modification for the children in your schools who would be diagnosed as having severe learning disabilities.

I would like to describe one such program and then present the steps necessary in The Natural History of the Development of a Program for Children with Learning Disabilities, which I have distilled from my experience in Schaumburg Consolidated District 54, Hoffman Estates, Illinois. My purpose in describing to you the program for children with special learning disabilities in Schaumburg District 54 is to present a realistic model which may bear some resemblance to your own situation, and which you can modify to fit your own set of circumstances.

Perhaps you are in the same situation as we were not too long ago. I am sure the facts of our state of development could be generalized to thousands of similar districts throughout the United States.

Schaumburg Township is located thirty miles northwest of Chicago.

SOURCE. Reprinted from *Selected papers on learning disabilities. International approach to learning disabilities of children and youth.* Fifth annual conference of the Association of Children with Learning Disabilities, Boston, Massachusetts, February 1968, 43–52. By permission of the author and publisher.

279

Twelve years ago, the area was primarily agricultural, broken into large farms of 200–300 acres. Because of the strategic location in close proximity to O'Hare International Airport and toll roads leading to Chicago, large real estate developers laid out planned communities within the township and built hundreds of homes per year.

Ten years ago District 54 consisted of one white frame school house, with seventy-seven students. In September 1968, we opened the doors of fourteen buildings to eleven thousand students. Next year, we will have sixteen buildings, four additions, and thirteen thousand students.

Over this ten-year period, the average increase in student population has been 32 percent per year. The average assessed valuation per enrolled student has ranged between ten and eleven thousand dollars. Schaumburg School District 54 is not a wealthy district. The brick and mortar problems involved in building fifteen new schools in the last ten years are duplicated in many suburban communities adjacent to large cities throughout the country.

The problems of curriculum, personnel, and program development are probably also typical. The solutions which have evolved in District 54 may not be quite so typical. In spite of limited funds, and prior to the passage of mandatory legislation in Illinois, District 54 united with nine other school districts to form the Northwest Suburban Special Education Organization, in an effort to meet the educational need of all children who deviated sufficiently from the norm that they could not be served adequately in the regular classroom.

Through this joint agreement, District 54 was able to place in special classes those children whose disability occurred with such low incidence that we could not have enough children in our district to provide a sequential educational program. Four social workers provide service for maladjusted children; six hundred children receive speech therapy from seven speech correctionists each month. The needs of these children with observable disabilities are being met adequately within School District 54.

As these programs have been developed, and the most obviously handicapped children provided for, another group of handicapped children has emerged for whom no service was available. This is the group of children with severe learning disabilities. The child with normal intelligence, adequate sensory processes, and reasonably adequate emotional adjustment who is not learning in school, despite the finest teaching we have been able to provide, presents the greatest unsolved problem in the public schools of our district, as it does in most of your districts.

We have attempted to meet the needs of the most severely disabled children with two resource rooms for perceptually handicapped children, one primary and one secondary. Under the Illinois Plan for Maladjusted Children, Type B, a public school district may be reimbursed by the state $4,000 per professional worker, for special-education programs for children with "extreme discrepancies between ability and achievement associated with minimal cerebral dysfunction, psycholinguistic disabilities, or perceptual impairments." The resource room program required that a child be transferred from the school he would normally attend to Hillcrest School, that he be placed in a regular grade—first, second, third, etc.—and that he receive individual tutoring for one period a day. The numbers of children were, of course, limited to the number of periods in the teacher's day; and could not exceed ten children per resource room teacher. This program was reasonably successful for the children fortunate enough to be placed in the class. At most, this kind of program served twenty children, out of a total school population that year of seven thousand five hundred—or two-tenths of 1 percent! In order to serve a realistic proportion of the school population with learning disabilities with our resource-room program, we would have had to open fifty-eight more resource rooms, and hire fifty-eight more specially trained teachers.

In addition to the problems of sheer numbers, we found that for every teacher who was relieved and happy that a child with whom she was concerned was placed, there were some two hundred teachers unhappy because they were unable to receive service for a child in their room who was just as bad as, or worse than, the children in the resource-room program.

At about the time that awareness of the magnitude of the problem was most keen in the minds of our teachers, our principals, and our administrative office personnel, our superintendent rather casually asked what I thought we should do with two teachers. Since it was my first year in the district, I had never heard of them, and very brightly asked, "Who are they?" "They" turned out to be two master teachers, who were on sabbatical leave finishing their master's degrees at the Reading Clinic at Northern Illinois University. I threw it back to him, and said "What have you got in mind?" His response was, "I don't know, a classroom, I guess." As this question was mulled over and over, it seemed a great waste to put two teachers with advanced training in the clinical diagnosis of reading problems back into a regular classroom. This dilemma was the single most important force which resulted in our federal proposal to establish a Psycho-Educational Diagnostic Center for Children with Special Learning Disabilities within our district.

The Diagnostic Center was seen as a possible solution to four problems which were then, and still are, facing educators:

• If the incidence of such severe learning disabilities is as high as other research studies indicate, the problem cannot be solved with special class placement whether it be a self-contained classroom or a resource-room program. The solution must involve the only professional group available in sufficient numbers to public schools, i.e., regular classroom teachers.

• The trainability of certain psycholinguistic functions frequently found to be associated with severe learning disability had been demonstrated by other researchers (Samuel Kirk, Corrine Kass) but only in a university-clinic setting involving an intensive individualized program of remediation. The feasibility of incorporating these remediation techniques into a public-school setting, utilizing classroom teachers who will carry out carefully programed remediation activities, needed to be demonstrated.

• Current research emphasis on etiology of learning disability, with a resultant lack of agreement, had not led to an educationally sound program which can be implemented in the public schools. The classroom teacher is still left with the problem of teaching these children every day, regardless of how much knowledge she may receive on why he is not able to learn by ordinary teaching methods. Programing based upon intensive diagnosis of the behavioral symptoms of learning disability was seen as a possible answer to this problem.

• Adequate diagnosis of severe learning disabilities was largely confined to agencies outside the public schools, i.e., university reading clinics, the Institute of Language Disorders, the Institute for Research on Exceptional Children, private or university-connected child guidance clinics, clinics connected with medical schools, etc. Lack of knowledge of public-school personnel, methods, problems, and services frequently causes a gap in communication which results in nothing being done in school to implement the recommendations of the clinic team, no matter how excellent they may seem to the diagnosticians. Diagnosis within the framework of the public schools, by persons familiar with the school system, who will carry the burden of remediation, may help to bridge this gap so that some change in teaching method or in materials can be seen in the classroom. This concept of the intermediate person—christened the psychoeducational diagnostician—to bridge the gap between the psychologist who has never taught and the teacher who does not understand psychological jargon, is the crux of our plan.

These four problem areas: numbers, trainability of psycholinguistic function, behavioral diagnosis of symptoms, and clinical diagnosis within the public schools, were designated for primary emphasis in our proposal.

It was not planned that this program of the psychoeducational diagnosticians, involving *intensive diagnosis, clinical teaching, and consultation to the classroom teacher* would meet the needs of all children with severe learning disabilities. It was accepted that, among the approximately 5 percent of the children with special learning disabilities, some could not possibly function outside of a self-contained classroom. Others might need the more intensive program involved in a resource room. However, it was hypothesized that a large majority of these children with a "disorder or delay in the use of symbolic language" could function in a regular classroom if they, and their teachers, were given special assistance in overcoming their handicap.

With the encouragement of the superintendent and the interest and enthusiasm of the teachers, I began the arduous task of thinking through the practical details of a proposal. This problem of proposal writing may seem insurmountable to some of you, but can be solved now most simply by consultant help.

The first stumbling block was, of course, money. Our board of education has a very strong commitment to special services, but our assessed valuation per student is only $10,953, putting us fourth from the bottom among districts of over one thousand in the state of Illinois. Our board is also quite conservative and was unwilling to accept federal monies. Last year, less than one-half of 1 percent of our total income came from federal sources, whereas the average for districts across the country is four and one-half percent. So it looked like everyone was for the proposal, the need was there and recognized, but local school funds were not available and the door to federal funds closed. This situation, fortunately, has changed considerably, with the advent of Title I, Title III, Title VI EPDA, etc.

In the meantime, I contacted the United States Office of Education to check into the possibilities of a federal grant for such a proposal in a district like ours. At that time, Spring 1965, the Elementary and Secondary Education Act (P.L. 89–10) had not been passed. The numbers of low-income families in our district was so low that little help could be anticipated from this source.

Dr. James Chalfant and Dr. James Moss of the United States Office of Education provided very practical consultant help and much encouragement during the early planning stages. The biggest problem seemed to center around the fact that we were not planning on seeking a university affiliation. P.L. 88–164, an amended version of P.L. 85–926, seemed the most suitable source of federal support at that time. Few grants had been made to public schools under P.L. 88–164 because of the difficulties involved in doing research in the public schools without research oriented personnel available.

For that reason, it was decided to move into the program without federal funds, on a pilot project basis. Two new positions were created and approved by the board. These were the positions of "psychoeducational diagnostician," a word which our superintendent said he could not even pronounce.

We also received board approval to employ an intern psychologist (in Illinois, a psychologist must have one year's experience as an intern in the schools, before he can be approved as a school psychologist). Interns are much less expensive than school psychologists, since it is recommended that they be employed on the teacher's salary schedule, and the district can be reimbursed $3,500 of their salary.

So, the first year, utilizing existing personnel (myself, two psychoeducational diagnosticians, plus one new person, our psychologist-intern) we created a psychoeducational diagnostic center with a director, two psychologists, and two psychoeducational diagnosticians, supplemented by the existing staff of nurses, social workers, speech correctionists, and resource-room teachers. Total cost to the district, after state reimbursement, was $17,250, and all but one would have been employed anyway.

As the program gained momentum, it became apparent that the success of the project made it necessary to increase staff, services, and scope. At that time, the climate in Washington had changed just enough so "university-affiliation" was not necessary. The magic word in the 1965–1966 school year was "public schools."

In order to condense a series of very exciting events, I shall just outline them and not try to fill in the vitally interesting blank spaces:

1. The proposal was finally written, and submitted to the board of education for approval. Although our board of education is rather conservative and disinclined to request federal funds, no one would go on record as voting against children with learning disabilities. For this reason the board approved the request for federal funds to provide a program for children with learning disabilities.
2. The proposal was mailed to Washington in early December, naively asking for a February 1st starting date.
3. Then followed an almost interminable wait, with little feedback from Washington. At this point it becomes quite necessary for those involved with the project to devise a series of defenses and rationalizations which can be called into use in case the proposal is turned down.
4. In late May came the fateful phone call, with the information that the proposal "probably will be approved." There was a need to make some

changes, largely in the area of reducing the demonstration aspects and increasing the research aspects. As an aside, the phone call was a little difficult to hear, because the extension in each of the administrator's offices was in use, with our superintendent, our assistant superintendent, our administrative assistant, and even the secretaries listening to the news.

5. Final approval came, with specific budget changes required. These were largely in the area of indirect costs which are generally not allowed unless the school system has a very sophisticated kind of bookkeeping and can provide the details required by the budget bureau.

6. It should be noted that the timing of the approval did not coincide with the timing of activities in the public schools. In other words, contracts all had to be sent in early April, without knowing whether or not the proposal would be approved. Specialized personnel had to be recruited, again before approval had been given.

7. At the beginning of the second year of the project, which was the first year of the funded project, four diagnosticians were employed to serve twelve schools. An additional psychologist was also hired.

During the second year of the project, it was necessary to tighten up the research aspects of the program somewhat and to be somewhat less flexible than we had been the first year.

In addition, the role of the school social worker needed clarification and expansion. It was decided to attempt to get a measure of behavioral change in those children included in the program. After much sorting and sifting, and consultation with Dr. Herbert Quay, Dr. Marjorie McQueen, and correspondence with Dr. William Morse, it was decided to use Quay's Behavioral Problem Checklist, and a 'Q' Sort of Behavior Adjustment used by Buff Oldridge at the University of British Columbia. These are done by the classroom teacher and the mother in September and in June (before and after treatment), under the direction of the school social worker.

Some of the speech correctionists have begun to work actively in programs in language development, an area they had not previously had the opportunity to explore. Since many of the children with learning disabilities in the auditory-vocal area are also being seen by the speech correctionists, their role and involvement in the learning disabilities project has also been expanded. During the third year of the project two more psychoeducational diagnosticians were added, and another psychologist.

This current year involves, so far as federal funds are concerned, only one half-time position in order to write up the results of the project.

To summarize, I would like to outline some of the elements of our program which may be most fruitful in working through your solution to your problems.

• We have utilized to a large degree, existing personnel and resources within our own district. In every school district there are teachers who, because of personal qualifications and previous training, could with a minimum of additional training implement a program for children with severe learning disabilities.

• We have involved regular teachers in the program of remediation: This requires a change in their expectations of the special service. We are not there to solve their problems but to create more by deeply involving them in special teaching programs for the one-and-one-half children in each of their classes.

• We have involved all the ancillary services available in the schools. The nurses are deeply involved, the speech correctionists frequently function as remediators of auditory-vocal disabilities or language developers, the physical-education teachers have become involved in sensory-motor training or remedial gym.

• We have accepted the fact that there is a communication barrier which exists too frequently between psychologists and teachers. We have plugged this gap by creating the role of the psychoeducational diagnostician.

• We have established a materials resources center as part of the consultant role. The regular classroom teacher can be supplied with specialized teaching materials without going through the usual process of requisitions, interminable delays, etc. The diagnosticians scout up new methods, learn how to apply them, and translate them to the teachers.

• The 5 percent incidence figure will give you some idea of the numbers of children needing service. If you start out by serving one-half of one percent, do not be surprised if you hear many complaints from parents and teachers who are not being served.

Let me also summarize our findings as the result of our experience of planning and implementing a program:

Funding

If a program is sound it will not collapse with the withdrawal of federal monies. The learning disabilities program in Schaumburg is continuing to grow and flourish—with the total budget of over $260,000 being assumed by the district.

Early Identification

The earlier you can find these children, the greater the probability of getting them going academically. These children can be found in kindergarten and placed in special first grades—developmental first grade—rather than being ground up in the regular academic curriculum.

Perhaps the most significant deficit in "nonready" children is their encoding disability. They seem to be "bottled-up kids" who need and do respond to a program which frees them to express themselves verbally and motorically.

Itinerant Program vs. Resource Room

The farther you move these children from the school they "belong in," the less effective is their program. We have compared two matched groups of children—those in the resource-room program and those in the itinerant program—and find that the children in the itinerant program do as well as, or better than, the resource-room children on all measures. Keep them where they "belong" but provide the necessary services for them to learn.

The resource-room program seems to have less value than the itinerant program, except perhaps in the initial stages of the program. The only plus we can see involves the availability of the teacher in a crisis situation. We are now converting our resource-room teachers to itinerant teachers, except at the junior high.

Labels

It is an inexcusable waste of professional time to argue about whether a child is brain-damaged, emotionally disturbed, or learning disabled. For some borderline children, the same is true of mental retardation versus learning disability. We have found it quite useful to use a statement of Lauretta Bender in order to resolve the brain-damage problem: "Everyone who has managed to survive the birth process is brain damaged—so then we can get on to the important business of how to teach him. We also assume that anyone with a specific learning disability is probably emotionally disturbed—and if he isn't, that is pathological in itself—because he ought to be."

Essentials

Ideally, it seems to me that a learning-disability program in a district like ours should include:

• An early identification program, where problems can be prevented rather than remediated.

• A self-contained primary class for severe learning disability, especially for those whose social behavior is not tenable in a regular first or second grade.

• An itinerant teacher to serve all grades on a daily basis, two or three buildings at most, performing the three-fold functions of diagnosis, clinical teaching, and consultation. The goal is to design a program which can be implemented by the classroom teacher.

• A resource room at the junior high school to give support and specialized help in all content areas. This seems necessary at the junior high because of the larger departmentalized program and the need to articulate the special learning needs of these children to secondary-trained teachers who are more concerned with content than with kids.

With this background, it is easy to see that the battle is far from won, but it is a little easier this year than ever before, largely because several of the initial steps in what I call "The Natural History of the Development of a Program for Children with Learning Disabilities" have been expedited for you.

I would like to describe the sequence of steps which seem to be necessary before you can hope to develop a program for these children. (By a program I do not mean badgering your superintendent into hiring a teacher, or changing your title to Learning Disability Teacher and setting aside a room for ten children. A teacher and her class will soon die of malnutrition unless some of the back-up services are available to her, and unless a program is begun with the full commitment of everyone in your schools.)

What are the steps that are involved in the "Natural History of the Development of a Program for Children with Special Learning Disabilities?" I shall go through step by step, as I see them, because it is absolutely imperative that you touch all bases rather than attempt to jump from step one to step eighteen. The time sequence will necessarily vary from one school district to another. The time interval between steps will also differ greatly. It may be necessary to spend a year on step one in order to check off rapidly three or four of the following steps.

Do not lose patience if you again find it necessary to spend an inordinate amount of time at another step, because jumping in the sequence may cause you to be tackling a "Mission Impossible"—with a program designed to self-destruct five minutes after you turn your back on it.

1. The first step must involve a commitment on the part of your state legislature, local administrators, and your school board to provide a suitable education for all children.

2. The second step involves the state of sophistication of your state or your district in serving all handicapped children. It is unreasonable to assume that your superintendent will provide services for a subtle, often

invisible, handicap like a learning disability if he does not yet see the need for teaching Braille to a blind child.

This necessary step suggests the need for your organization to promote and encourage interest and support for programs for all handicapped children, not just for the child with a special learning disability.

3. Your local administrator, or your state legislature, whichever end of the continuum you happen to be tackling, needs next to become aware of the existence of the problem.

4. There must exist a state of readiness to look for possible solutions. If your superintendent is so pressed financially that he is concerned about the very basics of education—books, space, and teachers' salaries—he probably is not in a state of readiness to think about our children. Help him solve some of his financial problems by working to help pass a bond referendum, or an increase in the educational tax rate, and then tackle him on a program for our children.

5. The next step involves the delineation of the problem:

a. Commitment to serve all children.

b. A degree of maturity of the program to serve the more obviously handicapped children in the school.

c. An awareness of the existence of the learning-disabilities problem.

d. A state of readiness to look for a possible solution—someone has the time, the energy, and the commitment to care enough to want to do something.

e. Now you are ready to get serious—you have cleared away much of the underbrush.

6. What children are you proposing to serve in the learning-disabilities program? Are you going to include only those children with a medical etiology or a medical diagnosis of brain damage? What about the emotionally disturbed? The mentally retarded? The environmentally disadvantaged? Those children who have not been exposed to good instruction?

This sixth step in the sequence is probably one of the most critical, since your decision on definition will lead directly to prevalence rates, to selection criteria, to teacher selection, and to the development of an appropriate curriculum.

There are many good definitions of learning disability now available. These have been produced by knowledgeable experts in the field as well as by committees of knowledgeable experts with divergent points of view who have labored hours in an attempt to come up with an educational definition which will facilitate the development of good programs. All of these definitions seem to have two concepts in common:

a. The intact clause.

b. The deviation or discrepancy clause.

One of the most current and most workable definitions which you need to be aware of is the definition proposed by the National Advisory Committee to the Bureau for the Handicapped, which is currently being used as the basis for federal legislation and federal funding:

"Children with special learning disabilities exhibit a disorder in one or more of the basic psychological processes involved in understanding or in using spoken languages. These may be manifested in disorders of listening, thinking, talking, reading, writing, spelling, or arithmetic. They include conditions which have been referred to as perceptual handicaps, brain injury, minimal brain dysfunction, dyslexia, developmental aphasia, etc. They do not include learning problems which are due primarily to visual, hearing, or motor handicaps, to mental retardation, emotional disturbance, or to environmental disadvantage."

Using this definition, the United States Office of Education has suggested a prevalence figure of one to three percent of the school population as having learning disabilities so severe as to need special educational provisions if they are to profit from formal education. Please don't be confused by the variation in prevalence figures which you may hear. We do not yet know how many children have special learning disabilities. The best guesstimates run from 1 to 20 percent. I have heard guesses running as high as 40 percent of the total school population. Prevalence figures are a direct derivative of the definition used, and the age of the group being measured.

7. The seventh step involves a decision on where to begin to provide services. It is a foregone conclusion that no one can begin to serve all eligible children at one time:

a. Intermediate—where pressure is.

b. Primary—where greatest successes are made most rapidly.

c. Most severely disabled—no turn-ons.

8. The eighth step involves a decision on the kinds of service which will be provided: resource rooms, itinerant, self-contained. A choice must be made of what other specialists will be involved—psychoeducational diagnosticians, speech correctionists, social workers, psychologists, counselors, occupational therapists, remedial reading specialists, etc.

9. The ninth step is a decision on selection criteria. Among the most difficult are those involving ten cut-off points, decisions on differences be-

tween emotionally disturbed and learning disabled, and decisions on the problem of organicity.

10. The tenth step includes methods and procedures for screening the total school population. It is important to keep in mind that screening differs from diagnosis and must be feasible for large groups.

11. The eleventh step relates to procedures to be included in the diagnostic process. The establishment of the most efficient diagnostic procedure is worth the planning time which is required. It is imperative that diagnosis be tied directly to the remedial possibilities available.

12. The most critical step in the whole process concerns the selection and training of the teacher. Caution needs to be exercised to select a teacher whose philosophy and training match the definition which you have selected. By careful preplanning, the role and function of the teacher can be designed in such a way that her potential can be realized.

13. Selection of the space in which the teacher will teach is the next step in the process. Of critical importance in this decision is the philosophy of the principal in whose building the class will be taught.

14. Once you have the teacher and the classroom, you need to turn your attention to curriculum modification. If the teacher is not teaching a different curriculum in a special way, you have not provided a program for children with learning disabilities.

Part V

Emerging Directions in Learning Disabilities

The field of learning disabilities is coming of age at a time when special education is undergoing both a reexamination of perspective and a reformulation of approaches. In part, learning disabilities has contributed to these changes; in part, changes affecting the entire special education area have brought about concomitant changes in the learning-disabilities field. An example of the former would be the new emphasis on assessing individual differences and diagnostic teaching based on such differences. On the other hand, the behavioral approach especially applied to the classroom appears to have been borrowed from the field of psychology as a result of its demonstrated effectiveness in teaching the mentally retarded.

It is our belief that special education in general and learning disabilities in particular have reached an uncommonly creative and significant stage of development. As perhaps never before, discerning spokesmen are transcending the superficial, the irrelevant, and the non-consequential, and are beginning to probe issues from which future directions may evolve. With this in mind, the following articles have been selected as particularly significant.

The issues raised by these writers are crucial in determining how the learning-disabled child is defined, how his deficits are conceptualized, and on what basis his remediation is predicated. Since the issues have by no means been resolved, articles maintaining a variety of points of view are presented to stimulate thinking on the subject.

Bateman raises fundamental questions inherent in the learning-disabilities approach, as she seeks to apply the orientation to the field of mental retardation. Although Bateman addresses herself to problems in teaching the mentally retarded, the issues she raises are significant in their implications for learning-disabled children. Can specific cognitive factors in children's learning be isolated in such a way that they can be assessed and provide a basis for curriculum planning? Should teachers teach to the strengths or to the weaknesses of children? Should an attempt be made to directly develop the processes of thinking rather than the products of someone else's thinking.

Kirk deals with similar questions. His article makes clear that the tremendous diversity of children presently known as brain-injured, aphasic, cerebral dysfunctioning, and the like, precludes the routine applicability of any one educational technique. What is effective for one child may not be for another. "What we really want is not labels, but analyses of behavior," and Kirk proceeds to present case studies to illustrate his point. Using profiles obtained from administrations of the Illinois Test of Psycholinguistic Abilities, he shows how the functioning of children in the various areas of ability and disability can be improved with careful training geared to their specific strengths and weaknesses.

Mann and Phillips take issue with this type of approach, which they call "fractional." In their thoughtful and stimulating article, they raise significant and disturbing issues related to the assessment and remediation of "specific areas and subareas of functioning and malfunctioning in perception, intellective performance, communication, etc. . . ." Mann and Phillips are concerned with the widespread, uncritical acceptance of such devices as the Illinois Test of Psycholinguistic Abilities (presumably based on Osgood's model of language functioning—a model that is controversial at best) or the largely nonvalidated Frostig battery. Do the posited abilities really exist and, if so, are they amenable to training? How does this approach differ from the school of faculty psychology popular in the late 1800s? In a response to Mann and Phillips by Reynolds, the question is reformulated in such a way that a general approach is not seen as competitive with a "fractional" approach, but rather that the former is seen as more useful for predictive purposes, and the latter for making instructional decisions.

Quay's article presents a conceptual model for viewing exceptional children in terms of various aspects of the learning process relevant to educational exceptionality—stimulus, response, and reinforcement. Exceptional children are seen as possessing deficits in one or more of these three functions in one or more modality. The utility of the model resides in its cutting across disability areas, in its avoidance of hypothetical mentalistic and neurological constructs, and in its direct implications for assessment and educational programming. Its emphasis on specific areas of disability represents a natural outgrowth of the learning-disabilities approach.

An interesting counterpoint to Quay's approach, which defines exceptionality in terms of characteristics of the child, is the article by Lilly. Lilly raises the question of whether any definition that describes traits or behaviors of children leads to inconsistencies in policy and treatment decision. As an alternative, Lilly proposes that exceptionality be defined in terms of the situations in which it occurs.

Hewett, in an important article, describes a hierarchy of task levels at which learning-disabled children may be found. The article delineates a sequence of priorities that must be recognized if the teacher is to be effective in the assessment and programming of learning tasks. Hewett notes that a basic condition for an effective educational program is the "establishment of a point of meaningful contact between the teacher and the child."

Adelman takes the position that any child's success in school depends on an interaction between his own characteristics and the specific classroom situational factors he encounters. "Learning-disabled" children, then, are those who have experienced a breakdown in either a personal attribute (such as a perceptual or linguistic problem), or in the school environment (such as the degree to which the classroom is "personalized" or motivating), or in some combination of both. Adelman moves on from this reformulation to a delineation of the treatment implications of his approach. His article should be of considerable use to personnel responsible for educational programming for learning-disabled children.

The article by Brown delineates a unique teacher-pupil interaction that is especially appropriate for exceptional children. She proposes that the teacher conceive of himself as a "guide" rather than a "guru" and that he actively engage the pupil in the formulation of instructional goals, the implementation of procedures, and the recording of results.

The remaining two articles in this section deal with general strategies to be employed by the classroom teacher in working with learning-disabled children. The first of these, by Ensminger, proposes a model by means of which instructional materials can be selected on a rational basis. The article by Clarizio and Yelon moves from Ensminger's focus on curriculum to management aspects. These authors describe, in succinct form, the major techniques that can be adopted from learning theory and implemented in classrooms.

23. IMPLICATIONS OF A LEARNING DISABILITY APPROACH FOR TEACHING EDUCABLE RETARDATES[1]

BARBARA BATEMAN

The purpose of this paper is to suggest some possible implications from learning disabilities research for application to the education of educable mentally handicapped (EMH) children. The work from which these suggestions are derived is for the most part currently in progress and therefore some of what follows is only speculative at this point. Our purpose here is not to provide answers, but to suggest paths for further exploration. Some of them may be fruitful avenues; some are undoubtedly dead-end streets.

The distinction between learning disability research and other research relevant to teaching mentally handicapped is very obscure, if in fact it exists at all. Recent surveys of research literature on how the mentally retarded learn reveal that our state of knowledge is really much more primitive than sheer numbers of studies could indicate. We know that retarded do learn, that much learning is related to MA and/or IQ, and that normals learn "better" than retardates do. However, direct

SOURCE. Reprinted from *Mental Retardation*, 1967, **5**, 23–25.
By permission of the publisher.

[1] This article was adapted from a paper presented at the 43rd Annual Convention of the Council for Exceptional Children in Portland, Oregon, April, 1965.

evidence of how the classroom teacher of EMH can facilitate initial learning and retention is conspicuous by its absence.

One contribution of the learning disabilities approach has been in the matter of question-asking. When we in learning disabilities are faced with a child of above average intelligence, from a "good" home, who's been in school four years and can't yet read, we have to first ask some questions. If we're to help him, the questions must be the right ones. We don't always ask the right ones immediately, but perhaps we're learning. We might ask, "Is he brain-injured?" Often the neurologist will tell us, "Perhaps he has minimal, diffuse brain injury," but then perhaps so does his teacher! Or we might be told, "Yes, he definitely shows an abnormal EEG." Have we gained anything? Do we know any more about how to teach him than we did before?

Suppose we asked, "Is there undue sibling rivalry at home?" "Has he properly identified with his father?" And again imagine we get a definite opinion to the effect that the oedipal situation has not been resolved. Do we yet know how to teach him to read?

In short, while the organic condition of his brain and the condition of his libido or psyche or id or ego are undoubtedly very pertinent to some aspects of his functioning, we do not yet know enough to know how they relate to our job of classroom teaching. Now we are learning to ask a new set of questions—questions which have more educational significance. We ask whether he can sound blend? Can he form the necessary association or bond between the visual symbol we call a letter and the vocal response we call its sound? How is his auditory memory? Does he respond better to massed or distributed practice? Does he learn new rules readily but forget them even more readily? Does he comprehend slowly, but retain well? Can he apply a rule once it is learned? The answers to these kinds of questions do begin to provide us with clues about how to teach him.

These types of questions point directly toward a second possible contribution of the learning disability approach to teaching EMH children, *i.e.*, a rejuvenation of interest in actual learning processes and factors which help or hinder classroom learning. Attention is being given to the effects of the teacher's verbal behavior on certain types of thought processes in children (Gallagher, 1963). We have long been aware that the way a question is asked influences the type of answer offered, but this is now being systematically studied in such a way that we can apply this knowledge to the direct teaching of certain kinds of thinking. Similarly, more systematic attention is being focused on the effects of other environmental factors such as the amount and intensity of relevant and irrelevant cues present in the learning situation. Revived interest in and re-evaluation and application of principles of learning such as repetition, simultaneous multi-sensory approaches, retroactive and associative inhibition, distributed and massed practice, incidental learning, readiness, and feedback is also in evidence (Bryant, 1965).

Just one example of this kind of research which has particular implication to teaching EMH is Vergason's (1964) study in which he trained retarded and normal subjects on a paired associates learning task. Some pairs of words were barely learned and others were overlearned. When retention was checked after 30 days, the retarded remembered significantly fewer of the barely learned words, but remembered as many of the overlearned words as did the normal subjects. This study clearly suggests the importance of overlearning if we wish to increase the EMH child's retention of the material to which he has been exposed.

In a further, unpublished study, Vergason compared retardates' ability to learn sight vocabulary words by traditional teaching methods and by an automated teaching machine. They learned the words equally well by either method, as measured by their recall the next day. But when they were retested at intervals up to four months, the words taught by the machine were clearly remembered better. Why? Perhaps again, it was due to more systematic overlearning.

COGNITIVE ABILITIES

An area of learning disability research which may contribute substantially to teaching the retarded is that on patterns of cognitive abilities. The field of learning disabilities is, of necessity, exploring the different ways by which children learn. If a youngster does not readily learn by the usual procedure, as children with learning disabilities do not, then the study of how they can and do learn becomes crucial. For this reason, the concept of individual diagnoses and program planning based on patterns of cognitive functioning is central to the field of learning disabilities. We know that it is not only likely but highly possible that two EMH children can have the same MA and IQ and yet have radically different cognitive strengths and weaknesses as revealed in testing. These kinds of differences in patterns of abilities and disabilities are also clearly revealed by the Illinois Test of Psycholinguistic Abilities (ITPA). A recent study by Jeanne McCarthy (1965) found 24 unique combinations of high-low ITPA subtest combinations among 30 severely retarded children. We must find ways to teach differentially as a necessary consequent of the fact that children learn differently. Not only do they learn new material differently, but they come to us with differing kinds and amounts of stored knowledge.

Many of the differences in the way children learn and have learned can be broadly categorized as being evidence of either an auditory-vocal or visual-motor preference. The ITPA tester speaks of children who are low on the A-V channel or on the V-M channel; the clinical psychologist might speak of the aphasoid or the Strauss-syndrome child; the experimental psychologist might use the terms "audile" or "visile"; the teacher might describe him as a phonics user or a whole-word reader, and the parents would perhaps say, "He doesn't understand what we say to him but he can do it if we show him."

As teachers of EMH children, we must learn from all of this that a label alone—in this case "EMH"—does not insure that there is a way to teach these children. There are many ways and the crucial task is to efficiently match instructional techniques to each child. We would be surprised if a physician had only one antibiotic drug which he administered to all his patients who needed antibiotics, even though some of them were allergic to it. Let us keep more than one reading pill on our shelves and more than one arithmetic pill in the drawer.

TEACHING TO STRENGTHS OR WEAKNESSES?

A question that has frequently been asked in learning disability circles is, "After patterns of cognitive, language, or intellectual strengths and weaknesses have been identified in a given youngster, should we then use those instructional methods which are geared to his strengths or those geared to his weaknesses?" Preliminary analysis of unpublished data on this topic suggests that once again we've been asking the wrong question. (In the field of mental retardation, we have hopefully just finished a long session of asking another wrong question: "Are special classes better than regular grade placement for EMH children?" Now that the fallacies in this question have been shown, perhaps we can begin to explore a more appropriate question: "For which EMH child is what type of program best under which circumstances?")

In place of the question, "Should we plan remedial teaching to strengthen the child's deficits or to utilize his assets?" it now appears we must ask "For which child, at what age of learning, should we teach to the strengths and for which child should we teach to the deficits?" Further preliminary data analyses from this study suggested that normal first grade children who preferred the auditory channel did better with instruction geared to their strengths, while those who preferred the visual channel did better when taught to their weakness!

Perhaps the most important single finding for our purposes from learning disability research has been the observation that children who have reading difficulty (and several other types of learning problems) share with the mentally retarded a disproportionate deficiency in the ability to deal with the mechanical, automatic or rote aspects of language. Specifically, retarded children have significant deficits in short-term memory, in incidental verbal conditioning (grammar) and in structured association (analogies).

The general finding that retarded are relatively stronger in dealing with the meaningful (semantic or conceptual) aspects of language than they are with the nonmeaningful (rote, automatic, perceptual) has far ranging implications for educational practice.

If a child has strong legs and weak arms and we plan a therapeutic program to build up his already strong legs we are doing something quite parallel to insisting that in the education of the retarded we must "make all material meaningful to the child." Is it possible that in our eagerness to put all content on the level of the child's understanding, we have failed miserably to extend his ability to deal with new unfamiliar material?

HOW TO LEARN

Since today's world is full of so many things that we cannot realistically retain exposure to the "content" of this world as a reasonable educational goal, perhaps we can now focus more cogently on another possible goal of schooling, namely, teaching children how to learn.

If we view language behavior as a three-fold process of receiving or perceiving bits of information from the environment, processing those bits of information (organizing, storing, recalling) and then expressing the results of the processing or expressing the need for more bits of information, we find we have a useful model for curriculum development.

We know from studies of transfer of training that what actually can or does transfer is not specific bits of information, but rather general principles, which in turn are equal to rules or programs for processing information. Thus, what we should be teaching, especially to retarded children who do not learn how to organize, store, and recall what has been received automatically or without direct teaching, is just this model —the understanding of what is seen, heard, felt, smelled, and tested; rules or procedures for generalizing, deducing and relating; and the expression of ideas both vocally and motorically.

If a pesky little observer were to pop into every classroom in the country several times a day and demand of the teacher, "Why is this child doing that exercise right now?" there might be times when the teacher would have to pause. But if each child had posted on the front of his desk a profile view of his present level of development in areas such as understanding what he hears, categorizing ability, visual memory, etc., with the normal development sequence of ability in each area clearly spelled out, she could see at a glance (a) where the child is, (b) what step comes next and (c) types of classroom activities suitable to move him a bit higher up the ladder.

To come full cycle to our starting point, the learning disabilities approach to teaching educable mentally retarded children suggests above all else that we need to ask a new series of questions at every level. We must take a hard look at the very basic question of why are we teaching. What are we trying to do? If we can get away from the global generalities such as "facilitate effective communication," "foster good citizenship," "teach further awareness of the world around us," which permeate our curriculum guides and teacher training courses, we can get down to the real business of teaching children to behave more intelligently by direct training in understanding visual and auditory cues, concept formation, recall, vocal expression of ideas, etc. Then on the level of minute-by-minute classroom teaching we must ask such questions as how can this task, which Johnny did not master, be taught to him? Must I change the task, i.e., present it to his ears instead of his eyes, break it into smaller parts, and decrease the difficulty level, or must I first change Johnny, i.e., increase his visual memory span, or his auditory discrimination?

In summary, the learning disability approach to teaching EMH redirects our attention to question-asking as the foundation of teaching and curriculum planning, to specific factors affecting and determining learning processes, to individual appraisal of patterns of cognitive abilities, to a re-examination of a philosophy of teaching through strengths or to weaknesses, and to the need for direct teaching of the processes of thinking rather than the products of someone else's thinking.

A paradox now presents itself. One who believes in the learning disabilities approach to teaching quickly finds that it applies to all children everywhere. Thus we have not really been talking about mentally retarded children, but about a scientific pedagogy for all children.

References

Bryant, N. D. Some Principles of Remedial Instruction for Dyslexia. *The Reading Teacher*, 1965, *18*, April, 567–572.

Gallagher, J. J. & Aschner, M. J. A Preliminary Report on Analyses of Classroom Interaction. *Merrill-Palmer Quarterly of Behavior and Development*, 1963, 9, 3, 183–194.

McCarthy, J. M. Patterns of Psycholinguistic Development of Mongoloid and Non-Mongoloid Severely Retarded Children. Unpublished doctoral dissertation, University of Illinois, 1965.

Vergason, G. A. Retention in Retarded and Normal Subjects as a Function of Amount of Original Learning. *American Journal of Mental Deficiency,* 1964, *68,* 5, 623–629.

24. FROM LABELS TO ACTION

SAMUEL A. KIRK

In the United States we have given a great deal of lip service to the education of "all the children of all the people." We have, as a result of this American ideal, established by law, under compulsory education, schools for all the children. To accommodate the volume of children who enrolled in the schools we attempted mass education—the education of all children by the same methods and materials. We of course differentiated the children into classes, with six-year-old children in the first grade, seven-year-old children in the second grade and so forth. For the majority of children this procedure has been successful, since the majority progressed in school because of, *or* in spite of, our mass education procedures.

But all the children of all of the people did not learn in the same way or at the same rate. Before we had compulsory education, these failures, for one reason or another, dropped out of school, often working on farms in rural America. It soon dawned upon authorities that children of the same age differed markedly in many respects. Some were slow learners,

SOURCE. Reprinted from *Selected papers on learning disabilities: International approaches to learning disabilities of children and adults.* Third annual conference of American Association for Children with Learning Disabilities, Tulsa, Oklahoma, March 1966, 36–44. By permission of the author and publisher.

others very fast learners; some could not hear, and were either deaf or markedly hard of hearing; some were blind or very defective in vision; some were crippled; some were defective in speech; and some were emotionally disturbed . . .

The totally deaf, the totally blind, and the severely crippled have always been recognized as different and treated accordingly. These children did not require differential diagnosis since their condition was obvious, and schools for the deaf and for the blind were organized in the early days. Public school classes for the education of exceptional children (the deaf, blind, mentally retarded, crippled, emotionally disturbed, and the gifted) were initiated at the beginning of this century, and have gradually grown to substantial numbers in all areas of the United States.

But there is one group of children who were not deaf but could not hear, or who were not blind but could not see, or who had difficulty in learning but were not mentally retarded. It was obvious that these children had difficulties—but their difficulties were hard to label as they were not deaf, or blind, or mentally retarded. As a matter of fact some of these children differed from each other so markedly that they could not be categorized. This situation became very frustrating to doctors, psychologists, social workers, teachers, and parents. We had no name that would encompass them all. But soon names were invented in order to decrease the frustration of professionals and parents. "Johnny is brain injured—that is why he does not learn." But how do you know he is brain injured?" "Because he does not learn although he is not deaf, blind or mentally retarded." Few such children could be diagnosed neurologically as brain damaged; but nevertheless it was a satisfying label. People believed that the word "brain-injured," even though not neurologically verified, actually explained the functional deficit. Also—because of the remnants of concern with family inheritance—it was better to tell a parent that he had a brain-injured child than that he had a mentally retarded child.

But attaching the term "brain-injury" did not solve the problem. Some children so labeled were hopelessly mentally retarded. Some with a label of brain-injury (cerebral palsy) were able to obtain M.D. or Ph.D. degrees. Thus the term "brain-injury" came to have little meaning since it applied to children with very different abilities. So we used other labels —brain-injury, brain crippled, minimal brain damage, minimal cerebral dysfunction, cerebral palsy, just plain cerebral dysfunction, organic driveness, organic behavior disorders, psychoneurological disorders, and a host of others. Actually, all in this group of terms, regardless of which ones were used, attempted to establish an etiological basis for the behavior deviation of the child. It was a label that implied a biological cause.

Another group of labels dealt not with etiology but with behavior. I shall enumerate a few of them:

Perceptual disorder, meaning that the child can hear and see, but does not see and hear like others. His perceptual processes, presumably due to a brain dysfunction, do not serve him effectively.

Hyperkinetic behavior which describes the child who is always in motion.

Conceptual disorder, a disturbance of thinking, reasoning, generalizing, memory or other cognitive functions.

Catastrophic behavior.

Impulsive behavior.

Disinhibited behavior.

Another group of labels deals primarily with communication disorders. And here we have evolved an extensive vocabulary of labels—aphasia, apraxia, agnosia, dyslexia, agraphia, acalculia, and many other terms. These are primarily neurological terms. Dyslexia could mean that the child has a problem in learning to read, but the term implies that the difficulty in learning to read is related to some brain dysfunction. I should like to read to you a hypothetical conversation between a psychologist and a sophisticated ten-year-old child who was having difficulty in learning to read.

PSYCHOLOGIST: You took a great number of tests yesterday. Did you like them?

BOY: No, because I couldn't read them so good.

PSYCHOLOGIST: Yes, that is why we have the tests—to find out why you haven't learned to read.

BOY: What did you find? What is wrong with me?

PSYCHOLOGIST: We have found that you have a severe problem in learning to read.

BOY: Yes, that's what my teacher said. But why?

PSYCHOLOGIST: You have dyslexia.

BOY: Where did I pick that up?

PSYCHOLOGIST: You didn't pick it up. You've probably had it all along.

BOY: Is it catching?

PSYCHOLOGIST: No, it's not contagious.

BOY: Is it a bad diseases?

PSYCHOLOGIST: No, it's not a disease—it's a condition—a condition in the brain.

BOY:	A condition in the brain? Am I nuts?
PSYCHOLOGIST:	No. You're not sick.
BOY:	Will it get worse? Will I die?
PSYCHOLOGIST:	No. It's just a condition that makes it hard for you to learn to read.
BOY:	Oh, I see! That's what my teacher said—I can't read so good, huh?

The point I am trying to make is that labelling or classification of children into separate categories may be satisfying to us but not very helpful to the child. The Binet and Wechsler tests have been used primarily to determine whether a child is mentally retarded, dull, average, or superior, and have been used to place him into one or another program. Many psychologists have been concerned with the limited use of these instruments. They have become critical of an indiscriminate use of the IQ or MA and have sought a more differential diagnosis. Many have consequently fallen into the trap of differentiating some types of children and labelling them as brain damaged even when there is no neurological evidence supporting the diagnosis—and even though the term includes children with widely different problems. In a small proportion of these cases, the diagnosis may lead to medication, but unless it does the diagnosis is of little value. From an etiological point of view it does not disclose any cause which can be removed; and from the point of view of treatment or management or training it gives no direction or purpose. Treatment advisable for one may be contraindicated for the next.

What we really want is not labels, but analysis of behavior. Such steps may be found to re-educate or re-orient or supply needed experiences on which improved functioning may be developed. At this meeting you will hear, or have heard, of the different approaches to diagnosing and treating learning disabilities. Most of the speakers are interested in diagnosis for treatment purposes, not for testing for classification.

Fortunately many are now becoming interested in organizing programs for those children—programs based on a behavioral and psychological assessment. These methods take many forms and deal with different problems. Diagnosis and treatment can work hand in hand to utilize our knowledge, understanding, and creative approaches in utilizing what we do know in order to alleviate conditions and remedy behavior.

One five-year-old child, for example, spent a great deal of time with her thumb in her mouth. We could label the child as neurotic, or we could say the child has a tic, or we could call the child by many other names. We could tell the mother she is rejecting the child, or the child did not have the right suckling experiences, or she is brain damaged. But a more effective approach was found by observing the behavior and applying well-known psychological principles. It was noticed that when the child was playing she did not suck her thumb. But when she was watching her favorite shows on the television her thumb was always in her mouth. The question here was what to do about it. One method was to remove the television, but this would not stop thumb sucking, since it would occur in other situations. A simple procedure was devised whereby the mother pressed a button to turn off the television when the child's thumb went into her mouth, and then pressed the button to turn on the television when the thumb was out of the mouth. It did not take the child long to learn that if she wanted the television on, this would occur only when she was not sucking her thumb. This simple device was enough to break the habit of thumb sucking. This is what I mean by moving on from labels to action.

I think the best way to illustrate the variety of individuals who have different kinds of disabilities is to cite several case studies.

Some years ago a high school graduate applied for admission to a college in which I was serving as selection officer. I refused admission because his grades in English in high school were very low and his tests on a reading intelligence test were below the lowest 25 percent of high school graduates. He then took courses in a junior college, repeated his English I three times before passing it with a grade of D, but obtained fairly good grades in mathematics and in drafting. After two years at the junior college he again applied to the college in which I was the selection officer, and again I rejected his application because of low scores on intelligence tests and his poor showing in rhetoric. But this time he was persistent. He appealed to the president for admission. At this point I was required to give adequate reasons for rejection, or at least look into his case further. Upon analysis of this individual based on a number of tests, I found that he was quite superior in spacial ability and in quantitative ability, but very inferior in verbal fluency. I admitted him into the College with the recommendation to the English department that he be given special tutoring in diction and in English.

Four years later this individual had not only completed his bachelor's degree in art, but also his master's degree. He was now art director in a very large city. He still had difficulty in English and diction but the supervision of art programs in schools did not require great verbal fluency. Here was an individual who had a learning disability in one area, who could have been denied an education had we not been forced to look into his situation a little more closely. His case made me wonder how many others were denied further education because of a learning disability in one area.

Some years ago a boy of ten years was brought to me by a school principal because of the child's inability to learn to read. On an individual intelligence test his IQ was 140. He was now in the 5th grade but was practically a non-reader. I found that he had two disabilities, one in auditorizing and one in visualizing. I recommended to the father that he have his eyes checked and that he obtain a good remedial teacher. I did not see this boy until he was 22. He had graduated from high school, and had served in the Army for two years. He was also enrolled in a junior college. But his basic problem remained. On tests he now scored fifth and sixth grade in reading and spelling. He had completed high school work because his mother read his lessons to him. He was admitted to a junior college and again succeeded partially with the aid of his mother. He now requested admission to a large university but was not accepted. After six months of special tutoring by a special tutor on his disability areas he now scored 9th and 10th grade. We asked that he be admitted into the university as an experimental case. Tutoring for one year in the university resulted in passing grades. Five years later this individual had passed all of the examinations and courses in animal science but had still failed his rhetoric exam because of a disability in spelling. It was necessary to waive the rhetoric examination which he had failed twice in order to award him a bachelor's degree in animal science.

Another interesting child was one who was committed to an institution for mental defectives at the age of two and one-half years because of convulsions and severe mental retardation. At the age of four and one-half he was given a series of examinations and scored around 50 and 60 IQ, but at that time he did not have any further convulsions. An EEG at this time, however, showed an abnormality. Here, according to our knowledge was a child who was and could be labeled "feeble-minded." He was thus certified and labeled as such by physicians and psychologists. At this time we initiated an experiment on early training of mental defectives in the institution. Fifteen children, ages four to five, were taken out of the wards daily and offered intensive preschool education, while another group remained in the wards. This boy was a member of the 15 experimental children. At this time his IQ was 50 to 60. His convulsions did not continue, although he still had an abnormal EEG. He made rapid progress in mental and social development in the preschool and was paroled from the institution to a foster home in the community. He was later adopted by a highly educated family. An EEG was repeated at the age of seven, and again it showed an abnormality. Much tutoring and care was given this boy in school, by his mother, and others. Today, at the age of 19 he is a freshman in college, with an average grade of B. Where would this boy be today had he remained in the wards? How many more of these children have we labeled, without taking the time to do what should be done with children with problems?

I should like to present a slide (Fig. 1) of a child who was diagnosed a number of times as mentally retarded, but who was probably a severe case of learning disabilities.

Here is a child who at the age of four and one-half tested below 50 IQ except for tests that required no language, and on these she was low average. On certain tests she showed that she was able to understand and receive visual and auditory meanings, and was able to discriminate forms visually at an average age. She was, however, very defective in all other areas.

Intensive training with this child over a period of four years showed the following development:

She progressed mentally a year per year under remediation on psychological tests, whether they were performance or verbal intelligence tests. Although she was mentally about two years at the age of four, she now, at the age of eight is mentally six. She is still two years retarded but since the beginning of remediation she has progressed one year per year. The profile shows a more even development. In addition to this psychological profile, the child is doing second grade reading and arithmetic and is only slightly retarded in academic work.

The next child (Fig. 2) is one who is eight or nine years of age and who appears to be average in intelligence, and average in all abilities except the ability to express himself. It will be noticed from this chart that this is a child who cannot express himself vocally, or gesturally. Speech correction and counselling seemed not to help him. The treatment for this boy was by the use of programmed instruction in which the child filled in what he did not know on a typewriter and a tape recorder. It will be noticed from this profile that the boy made rapid progress in seven months of remedial instruction.

The reports of various type of disability at this conference show a major change in the approach to children with learning disabilities. Instead of classifying children into categories, and instead of worrying about the etiological classifications, names, labels, and categories, the concentration of most workers at this conference—Kephart, Myklebust, Frostig, and many others—is an attempt to analyze the child's ability in such a way that remediation and training can follow. The philosophy of

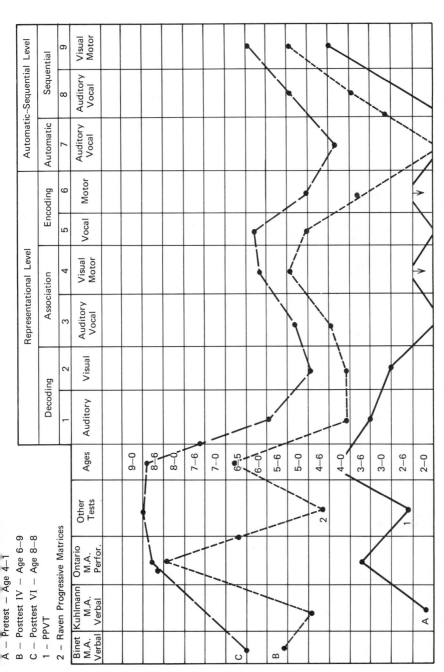

FIG. 1. *Results of remediation. A = pretest—age 4-1; B = posttest IV—age 6-9; C = posttest VI—age 8-8; 1 = PPVT; and 2 = Raven Progressive Matrices.*

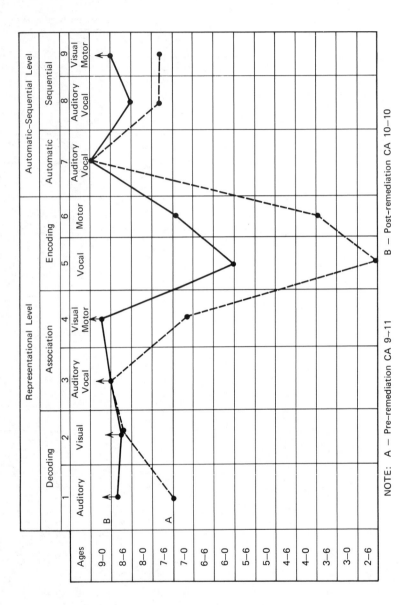

FIG. 2. *Comparison of pre- and post-remediation language age profiles. A = pre-remediation CA 9–11; B = post-remediation CA 10–10.*

312

remediation does not deny a basic cerebral dysfunction. It implies, however, that in the growing stages children withdraw from areas that are uncomfortable, or are unsuccessful, and exaggerate the areas of response on which they are successful. If a biological defect causes a child to be unsuccessful in one area, that child will tend to avoid those areas and function in fields in which he is successful. At a later age when we test the child and find a marked behavior deficit, that deficit may be only partly the result of the biological defect, and partly the result of lack of development due to avoidance experience. An analogy can be made between the use of hands. If a cerebral dysfunction in the motor area makes the child's left hand uncoordinated, the child will avoid using the left hand, and over-use the right hand. As a result the growth of the use of the right hand is average or above, while the left hand grows in coordination more slowly. Remediation in this case would be special exercise of the left hand. Thus the philosophy of remediation of deficits asserts that the deficits are totally or partially environmentally caused, generally through avoidance of essential experience. Remediation then tends to reinstate this experience, even at a later date.

25. FRACTIONAL PRACTICES IN SPECIAL EDUCATION: A CRITIQUE

LESTER MANN and WILLIAM A. PHILLIPS

Recent interest and effort in special education have been directed towards the development of techniques designed to fractionate global or molar areas of behavior and functioning for evaluation and educational purposes (Bateman, 1964). A number of new assessment and testing procedures have been recommended for or developed to delineate specific areas and subareas of functioning and malfunctioning in perception, intellective performance, communication, etc. (Frostig, Lefever, and Whittlesey, 1961; McCarthy and Kirk, 1961; Ayres, 1962; Money, 1962; Silver and Hagin, 1964; Beck, Rubin, Llorens, Beall, and Mottley, 1965). Special approaches have been programed to develop potentialities and remediate inadequacies therein (Frostig and Horne, 1964; Llorens, Rubin, Braun, Beck, Mottley, and Beall, 1964; Silver and Hagin, 1965).

Such fractional approaches are indeed laudable in their attempts to provide greater structure and specificity to the sprawling field of special education practice. They hold, however, some disturbing portents for special education: in their often facile extrapolation of unsettled and

SOURCE. Reprinted from *Exceptional Children*, 1967, 33, 311–317. By permission of the author and publisher.

controversial experimental and theoretical issues into educational and clinical dicta and practice; in their establishment of techniques of uncertain and, at best, limited validity, as prime diagnostic and treatment instruments; in their seeming disregard of the handicapped child as a unitary, though complex, organism; in their approach to him as a collection of discrete and isolated functions.

The writers hope that an overview of this new wave in special education, and a critical assessment of it, may be useful as a corrective to the enthusiastic endorsements which are presently appearing in many quarters (Bateman, 1964; Gallagher, 1964; Stevens, 1965).

OVERVIEW

In attempting to obtain historical perspective of the present fractional trend in special education, one is impressed firstly by the fact that attempts to fractionate behavior, whether under the rubric of soul, or psyche, or other hypothetical constructs, appear to characterize man's efforts to understand man, from the four element theory of Empedocles and Anaxagoras through Guilford's (1956b) multidimensional conceptualization of intelligence.

Special education has its unique history of fractional practices. Indeed, much of what has been termed its clinical approach and what the writers less euphemistically assess as fractional appear as revivals and occasionally as transmogrifications of very old techniques, indeed. The work of such pioneers as Itard, Seguin, and Decroly, whose training approaches emphasized sensory and motor training, appears in many instances to have been directly, if not literally, translated into modern day special education practice.

In attempting to understand the current appeal of fractional approaches to special education, it becomes apparent that they are very much an expression of the present day scientific zeitgeist, with its emphasis upon discrimination and manipulation of precisely delineated variables. They represent an extension of modern behavioral and educational sciences which have been increasingly emphatic in recent years in their attempts to dissect behavior, stimulated by sophisticated multivariate approaches, by new developments in experimental manipulanda, and by computer accommodation. They are a reflection of the labors of the test makers of our day who increasingly work toward differential evaluation of abilities and achievement in testing programs. They express, additionally, the growing interest and participation of the physician in special education with his tradition of differential diagnosis, and of the clinical psychologist with his orientation towards test analysis.

Finally, the very real, cogent, and compelling realities of helping the handicapped child appear to have directed special education's present orientation to fractional practices. It has become increasingly clear that classification of handicapped children according to diagnosis provides insufficient and inadequate guidelines for educational and remedial practices. It has become additionally clear that there are vast areas of communality and similarity in the needs, problems, and dysfunctioning of handicapped children with diverse diagnoses (Bryant, 1964; Gallagher, 1964). As a consequence, attention has quite necessarily been directed to the "dysfunctions" themselves and to the diagnostic and educational techniques that might be used in their remediation. The new fractional approaches appear to offer manifest answers in these respects. It is for this reason, lest special education overcommit itself, that a critical examination of fractional diagnosis and training is needed.

The present criticisms of the fractional approaches are promulgated on both epistemological and empirical grounds. They are not intended to be fully exhaustive but rather to highlight certain significant issues. A number of these are inextricably entwined and must be considered as but different facets of the same problem. However, they will be categorized under different headings for convenience of exposition.

ASSESSMENT OF SPECIFIC ABILITIES

The basic assumption underlying the development and utilization of fractional approaches is that human behavior may be successfully separated, as it were, into specific entities, units, or functions, these being essentially independent and capable of being individually evaluated and/or exercised. Advocates of fractional approaches appear to be proceeding as if this assumption were a fully demonstrated and effective operational viability (Bateman, 1964; Lindsley, 1965).

The evidence to date hardly justifies their position. The writers do not question the possibilities of effective delineation through conceptual and experimental operations, or statistical manipulation of certain behavioral specificities. We may accept on conceptual and heuristic grounds the separation of hue from intensity, pitch from loudness, pain from heat, sweet from sour—these representing fractional separations of the more molar behaviors of sight, hearing, touch, and taste. Within limitations, such fractional behaviors may be precisely and operationally anchored in objective realities. They are associated, in reasonably veridical fashion, with concrete environmental events. Their variations can be validated through the latter.

However, the picture is not as sanguine when we turn to the higher or more complex functions such as are subsumed under perception, intelligence, language—behaviors with which the special education fractionator is specifically concerned. While certain gross and general ability areas can be differentiated and assessed effectively (McNemar, 1942; Cropley, 1964; McNemar, 1964), one finds but little convincing empirical substantiation for the claimed specificities of such widely heralded tests as the ITPA or Frostig approaches.

It is important to note that the failure of special educators to clearly and effectively establish useful specificities through their assessment techniques is by no means unique to them. It is a continuing and pervasive problem for psychological and educational measurement (Guilford, 1956a). This is dramatically apparent when we examine the areas of intelligence and achievement assessments, ones with long histories of assiduous endeavor in respect to fractionation practices. It is in these areas, where voluminous research has been carried out, that we might most likely expect to find breakthroughs. The practical consequences of such endeavors, however, have been surprisingly limited. Despite repeated efforts to establish "primary mental abilities" and subareas of achievement functioning, measures of intelligence tapping g rather than s still remain the most meaningful assessors and predictors of performance.

In respect to school achievement, for example, a survey of efforts with the DAT, a possessor of 4096 validity coefficients, leads to the conclusion that "better predictions are possible via old fashioned general intelligence tests than through multi-test batteries" (McNemar, 1964, p. 875). And in this context, it is worth remembering that initial attempts at intellectual and performance mensuration through fractional methods, such as those of Cattell, Jastrow, and Galton, were without useful consequence (Terman, 1916). It remained for Binet, with his global appreciation of man's functioning capacities, to shotgun a test approach that, with all its failings, remains the "standard" of intellectual assessment.

If the above is the case for sophisticated measurement approaches in areas which provide reasonably clearcut opportunities to establish criteria and carry out normative, validation, and predictive studies, it behooves the special educator, who is proceeding on far more uncertain ground, to tread lightly in his assumptions of specificity. While human behavior appears complex indeed, recognition of that complexity does not represent a solution to its measurement. The day when abilities may be precisely articulated is still not with us. Certainly not in special education. For the latter, the concept of general ability may well be a myth (Lindsley, 1965), but it has proven to be a most serviceable one. In assessing and predicting behavior, the small g stands for goodness.

RELATION OF FRACTIONAL TESTS TO RESPONSE VARIABLES

The special education fractionator appears to presume that the behaviors he assesses through his tests and other procedures are related directly to basic events, processes, variables in the individuals being assessed; that in fact their tests and measures tap and mensurate these processes, and that the results obtained can be used to effectively order individuals ipsatively or normatively in accordance to the quality, effectiveness, or amount possessed of the latter. Thus, one child is tested and found to be better in establishing object constancy than another; another individual is better in auding than he is in encoding; one child has more firmly established laterality.

How does the special education fractionator know what his tests are measuring, assuming for the time being that the latter are capable of the fractional analyses he claims for them. Unless he wishes to resort to an outmoded and sterile operationism, he will have to take the arduous route of construct validity (Cronbach and Meehl, 1955; Campbell and Fiske, 1959) to legitimately presume that auditory decoding, spatial ability, figure ground perception, or what have you, are properly being assessed by his techniques. This the special education fractionator does not appear to have effectively done. Retitling standard types of intelligence test items as has been done in the ITPA does not constitute construct validation, nor does Frostig's quasiscientific utilization of constructs from areas of experimental psychology or the extrapolation of labels assigned to the factor analyst's products as we find in Ayres' tests.

Many fractionators appear to have made the stimulus error, in their proceedings, of directly identifying test responses and the processes they putatively represent with the names of the tests which elicit and supposedly measure them—an exercise in tautology, not scientific procedure. They have proceeded still further along the path of error by implicitly reifying the response variables associated with their tests into separate abilities and functions in ways unfortunately reminiscent of faculty psychology. The consequences of reification are all too blatantly on view in such concretizations as the IQ to encourage their multiplication in fractional test practices.

TRAINING OF SPECIFIC FUNCTIONS

Special education, being a training oriented discipline, is concerned first and foremost with programs of teaching and management. It is because of this that the fractional practices have been so well received in special education. Rather than diffuse, ill defined programs of general teaching, the fractionators offer techniques to specifically train and remediate areas of weakness and impairment (Bateman, 1964).

Unfortunately, the overwhelming bulk of evidence from investigations in learning and transfer of training does not support the effectiveness of training procedures directed towards the formal training of abilities in the ways intended by many of the fractional approaches. Specific skills may certainly be trained and are, continually, in a vast variety of educational endeavors. It would be entirely inappropriate to equate success of this variety with the ancient and once discredited faculty psychology that appears to be renascent in many of the recent fractional approaches. Shape constancy, for example, is a multiple problem (Epstein and Park, 1963), not a specific mental process to be exercised as Frostig might suggest.

Much of the research in child development contraindicates the value of the vertical, incremental building block type of training recommended by fractionators. Behavior apparently develops from diffuse states to those of articulation and delineation (Gibson, 1963). Its development may also be discontinuous (Piaget and Inhelder, 1956). It is certainly hierarchical from many standpoints (Haynes and Sells, 1963) and a dynamic interactional process (Klapper, 1965). Most fractional training approaches appear far too simple in conception and execution to do justice to its complexity.

EVIDENCE FOR FRACTIONAL APPROACHES

It would be unfair and inaccurate to give the impression that proponents of the fractional approaches have not marshaled evidence to support their positions. Considerable effort has been devoted to substantiating and validating such techniques. Can it be sustained upon critical examination?

Factor Analysis. Factor analysis appears to have been one of the major impetuses to fractional practices, and a bulwark of support (Guilford, 1961). However, it would be incorrect to presume that factor analysis of and by itself can prove anything (McNemar, 1964), or that its methods and implications and values have been firmly established and agreed upon by behavioral scientists (Horst, 1950; Riegel and Riegel, 1962; Thompson, 1962; Coan, 1964; Overall, 1964; Smedslund, 1964; Vernon, 1965). Factors are statistical artifacts which may or may not manifest relevant relationships to significant behavioral variables. Such relationships have not been satisfactorily demonstrated in special education for such procedures as the Ayres Space Test.

Validity Studies. Proponents of fractional measurement can point out legitimately that their techniques have been demonstrated to differentiate different types of handicaps one from the other and in comparison with normal groups (Sievers, McCarthy, Olson, Bateman, and Kass, 1963). However, their validation efforts are typically of the concurrent validity variety, the limitations of which are well discussed by Yates (1966). They appear to have disregarded the problem of base rates (Meehl and Rosen, 1955). And in any case it must be questioned whether their techniques improve in the diagnoses of such groups over and above the results of many other tests of such conditions (Safrin, 1964; Holroyd and Wright, 1965); this they have not demonstrated.

However, the special education fractionator also professes to differentially assess functions and dysfunctions. Our critique has already found their efforts insufficient and unconvincing. Several additional points can be made in respect to this particular and most important issue. Firstly, it would be in error to assume that differential patterns revealed through the fractional tests can be regarded as veridically representative of variations in organismic functioning. It has been demonstrated (Haynes and Sells, 1963) that the properties of the tests, rather than the properties of the individual, may be responsible for such patterns. It would be equally in error to assume that the latter are, in any case, more significant than a variety of others that could be established if testing of a different sort were carried out (Graham and Berman, 1961; Safrin, 1964). If the aphasic child, for example, is found lacking in one or several areas of the ITPA, ipsatively opposed to other areas or normatively compared to a normal child's performance, further study may show that this malfunctioning extends into many areas other than those assessed by the ITPA (Jenkins and Schuell, 1964). The brain injured child generally manifests problems in gait, gripping of pencil, visual scanning, etc., as well as in the specific areas assessed by perceptual tests (Holroyd and Wright, 1965). In short, handicapped individuals show problems in a great number of ways and through a variety of assessment approaches. And it is quite possible to conceptualize their varied problems in terms of general molar abilities and disabilities differentially reflected in varied types of test situations. It behooves the special education fractionator to demonstrate otherwise, and, if able to do so, why the areas he has chosen to assess are more important than others he might choose from, either diagnostically or therapeutically.

Finally, let us consider the claims for therapeutic efficacy of fractional instruments. The most immediate and glaring error is seen in attempts to demonstrate their value through tests that have a close facsimilitude to the training devices themselves. The Frostig tests, for one, and the

Frostig training techniques appear quite similar, and it seems to these writers entirely inappropriate to assess the efficacy of one through the other. We would appear to be merely assessing a sustained practice effect by so doing.

It is unfortunate, additionally, that the efficacy of an instrument cannot be simply assessed on the basis of success with it. The entire problem of Hawthorne and placebo effects is at issue here, which inevitably affect all attempts to remedially or therapeutically influence people (Rosenthal and Frank, 1956). In medical efforts placebo effects are reported to account for from one-fourth to two-thirds of therapeutic successes. Recent investigations into drug effects, wherein such effects may be more efficaciously controlled than in education, have revealed surprising complications and interactions between patient expectancies and drug action (Kurland, 1960; Ross and Cole, 1960; Conners, Eisenberg, and Sharp, 1964). The situation in education, where double blind procedures and other precautions are not possible, is considerably more involved. Much of any improvement that we see in special education may be due to novelty effects, enthusiasm, teacher expectancies (Rosenthal and Jacobson, 1966), and a vast variety of other motivational variables. The well known therapeutic fallacy of medicine applies with a vengeance in special education.

At a time when special education has not been found to be special in its successes (Johnson, 1962), and when specific programs have been demonstrated in the past to be less successful than general ones (Sparks and Blackman, 1965), claims of therapeutic success through fractional approaches should be accepted with caution.

CONCLUSIONS

Special education, like nature, abhors a vacuum. Faced with a multitude of perplexing problems, and a rather impoverished armamentarium to utilize in helping the handicapped child, the special educator finds the charisma of the new fractional approaches dazzling indeed. With them he is now able to program remedial approaches to a variety of problems. There is, additionally, an air of space age sophistication and novelty accompanying these new approaches. Like others in the field, the writers are fascinated by their brave new world. However, they are also disturbed by the hard sell accompanying a number of them that appears to have precipitated programs of evaluation and training on the basis of unsubstantial evidence.

The writers' exposition, by this time, may well appear to the reader to be a calculated exercise in critical nihilism. But they have attempted, rather, to place the fractional approaches in better perspective. This with the hope that the latter will continue to be welcomed as new and challenging approaches to the problems of the handicapped, but only tentatively and cautiously until they have appropriately proven their worth. Till then, the special educator might well consider continuing with perhaps dull and unromantic but reasonably productive techniques of assessment via traditional psychometric approaches, and the education of handicapped children with modified curricular approaches.

Pavlov, the great pioneer in modern day fractional methodology was nevertheless, reports Razran, a steadfast votary of interdependent and holistic interaction. He once explained that "of course a behavior is not just a sum of reflexes, a sort of sack filled pell-mell with potatoes, apples, cucumbers . . ." (Razran, 1965). It is to the child and his behavior as a total organism, rather than the "potatoes, apples, cucumbers" of fractional practices that the special educator, at least for the present, can most effectively direct his efforts.

References

Ayres, A. J. *The Ayres space test*. Los Angeles: Western Psychological Services, 1962.

Bateman, Barbara. Learning disabilities—yesterday, today, and tomorrow. *Exceptional Children*, 1964, **31**, 167–177.

Beck, G. R., Rubin, Jean B., Llorens, Lela A., Beall, C. D., and Mottley, N. Educational aspects of cognitive-perceptual-motor deficits in emotionally disturbed children. *Psychology in Schools*, 1965, **2**, 233–238.

Bryant, N. D. Characteristics of dyslexia and their remedial implication. *Exceptional Children*, 1964, **31**, 195–199.

Campbell, D. T., and Fiske, D. W. Convergent and discriminant validation by the multitrait-multimethod matrix. *Psychological Bulletin*, 1959, **56**, 81–105.

Coan, R. W. Facts, factors, and artifacts: the quest for psychological meaning. *Psychological Review*, 1964, **71**, 123–140.

Conners, C. K., Eisenberg, L., and Sharp, L. Effects of Methylphenidate (Ritalin) on paired-associate learning and Porteus Maze performance in emotionally disturbed children. *Journal of Consulting Psychology*, 1964, **28**, 14–22.

Cronbach, L. J., and Meehl, P. E. Construct validity in psychological tests. *Psychological Bulletin*, 1955, **52**, 281–302.

Cropley, A. J. Differentiation of abilities, socio-economic status, and the WISC. *Journal of Consulting Psychology*, 1964, **28**, 512–517.

Epstein, W., and Park, J. N. Shape constancy: functional relationships and theoretical formulations. *Psychological Bulletin*, 1963, 60, 265–288.

Frostig, Marianne, and Horne, D. The Frostig program for the development of visual perception. Chicago: Follett Publishing Company, 1964.

Frostig, Marianne, Lefever, D. W., and Whittlesey, J. R. B. A developmental test of visual perception evaluating normal and neurologically handicapped children. *Perceptual Motor Skills*, 1961, 12, 383–394.

Gallagher, J. J. Learning disabilities: an introduction to selected papers. *Exceptional Children*, 1964, 31, 165–166.

Gibson, Eleanor J. Perceptual development. In H. W. Stevenson, J. Kagan, and C. Spiker (Editors), *Child psychology, part I.* Chicago: University of Chicago Press, 1963. Pp. 144–195.

Graham, F. K., and Berman, P. W. Current status of behavior tests for brain damage in infants and preschool children. *American Journal of Orthopsychiatry*, 1961, 31, 713–728.

Guilford, J. P. *Fundamental statistics in psychology and education.* (Third edition) New York: McGraw-Hill, 1956. (a)

Guilford, J. P. The structure of intellect. *Psychological Bulletin*, 1956, 53, 257–293. (b)

Guilford, J. P. Factorial angles to psychology. *Psychological Review*, 1961, 68, 1–19.

Haynes, J. R., and Sells, S. B. Assessment of organic brain damage by psychological tests. *Psychological Bulletin*, 1963, 60, 316–325.

Holroyd, Jean, and Wright, F. Neurological implications of WISC verbal performance discrepancies in a psychiatric setting. *Journal of Consulting Psychology*, 1965, 29, 206–212.

Horst, P. Uses and limitations of factor analysis in psychological research. In *Proceedings, 1949 invitational conference on testing problems.* Princeton, New Jersey: Educational Testing Service, 1950. Pp. 50–56.

Jenkins, J. J., and Schuell, H. Further work on language deficit in aphasia. *Psychological Review*, 1964, 71, 87–93.

Johnson, G. Special education for the mentally handicapped—a paradox. *Exceptional Children*, 1962, 29, 62–69.

Klapper, Zelda. Perception and cerebral palsy. *Rehabilitation Literature*, 1965, 26, 370–372.

Kurland, A. A. Placebo effect. In L. Uhr and J. G. Miller (Editors), *Drugs and behavior.* New York: Wiley, 1960. Pp. 156–165.

Lindsley, O. R. Can deficiency produce specific superiority—the challenge of the idiot savant. *Exceptional Children*, 1965, 31, 225–232.

Llorens, Lela A., Rubin, E. Z., Braun, Jean, Beck, Gayle R., Mottley, N., and Beall, D. Training in cognitive-perceptual-motor functions: a preliminary report. *American Journal of Occupational Therapy*, 1964, 17, 5.

McCarthy, J. J., and Kirk, S. A. *Illinois Test of Psycholinguistic Abilities: experimental edition.* Urbana: University of Illinois, 1961.

McNemar, Q. *The revision of the Stanford-Binet scale.* Boston: Houghton Mifflin, 1942.

McNemar, Q. Lost: our intelligence? why? *American Psychologist,* 1964, **19**, 871–882.

Meehl, P. E., and Rosen, A. Antecedent probability and the efficiency of psychometric signs, patterns, or cutting scores. *Psychological Bulletin,* 1955, **52**, 194–216.

Money, J. (Editor). *Reading disability: progress in research needs in dyslexia.* Baltimore: Johns Hopkins Press, 1962.

Overall, J. E. Note on the scientific status of factors. *Psychological Bulletin,* 1964, **61**, 270–276.

Piaget, J., and Inhelder, B. *The child's conception of space.* London: Routledge, 1956.

Razran, G. Russian physiologists' psychology and American experimental psychology: a historical and a systematic collation and a look into the future. *Psychological Bulletin,* 1965, **63**, 42–64.

Riegel, Ruth M., and Riegel, K. F. A. A comparative reinterpretation of factor structures of the W-B, the WAIS, and the HAWIE on aged persons. *Journal of Consulting Psychology,* 1962, **26**, 31–37.

Rosenthal, D., and Frank, J. D. Psychotherapy and the placebo effect. *Psychological Bulletin,* 1956, **53**, 294–302.

Rosenthal, R., and Jacobson, Lenore. Teachers' expectancies: determinants of pupils' IQ gains. *Psychological Reports,* 1966, **19**, 115–118.

Ross, S., and Cole, J. O. Psychopharmacology. *Annual Review of Psychology,* 1960, **11**, 415–438.

Safrin, R. K. Differences in visual perception and in visual-motor functioning between psychotic and nonpsychotic children. *Journal of Consulting Psychology,* 1964, **28**, 41–45.

Sievers, Dorothy J., McCarthy, J. J., Olson, J. L., Bateman, Barbara, and Kass, Corrine E. *Selected studies on the Illinois Test of Psycholinguistic Abilities.* Madison, Wisconsin: Photo Press, Inc., 1963.

Silver, A., and Hagin, Rosa A. Specific reading disability: follow-up studies. *American Journal of Orthopsychiatry,* 1964, **34**, 95–102.

Silver, A. A., and Hagin, Rosa A. Specific reading disability: teaching through stimulation of deficit perceptual areas. *American Journal of Orthopsychiatry,* 1965, **65**, 350–351.

Smedslund, J. Educational psychology. In P. Farnsworth, Olga McNemar, and Q. McNemar (Editors), *Annual review of psychology.* Palo Alto, California: Annual Reviews, Inc., 1964. Pp. 251–276.

Sparks, H. L., and Blackman, L. S. What is special about special education revisited: the mentally retarded. *Exceptional Children,* 1965, **31**, 242–249.

Stevens, H. A. ". . . The field is rich . . . and ready for harvest. . . ." *American Journal of Mental Deficiency*, 1965, **70**, 4–15.

Terman, L. M. *The measurement of intelligence.* Boston: Houghton Mifflin, 1916.

Thompson, J. W. Meaningful and unmeaningful rotation of factors. *Psychological Bulletin*, 1962, **59**, 221–223.

Vernon, P. E. Ability factors and environmental influence. *American Psychologist*, 1965, **20**, 723–733.

Yates, A. J. Psychological deficit. In P. R. Farnsworth, Olga McNemar, and Q. McNemar (Editors), *Annual review of psychology.* Palo Alto, California: Annual Reviews, Inc., 1966. Pp. 111–144.

26. A REACTION

MAYNARD C. REYNOLDS

I have been asked to react to the paper by Mann and Phillips and am glad to do so because I believe they deal thoughtfully with some important and timely issues. Although these brief comments may appear to be negative in tone, let me record here that I read the paper with much interest and profit.

In one fundamental way Mann and Phillips mislead us, I believe, and to that extent fail in their mission to "place fractional approaches in better perspective." It appears that they think of tests mainly as devices for quantifying attributes (assessment) and making predictions. Furthermore, if several tests of presumably independent attributes can be shown to collapse into a single dimension (in a Guttman type analysis, for example) or to produce high communality (as in factor analyses) they say that we had better put our marbles on the more general variable. They are not alone in thinking this way; it is highly reminiscent of views expressed by Terman, McNemar, many of the British psychologists, and others.

The trouble is, I think, that this line of thinking takes us to the wrong

SOURCE. Reprinted from *Exceptional Children*, 1967, **33**, 317–318. By permission of the author and publisher.

ball park as far as the practical matters of instruction are concerned. Teachers are involved mainly in choices between curricula, teaching methods, special placements, and materials—with the aim of influencing achievement—not in making grand, long range predictions. A key point, as noted by Cronbach, is that ". . . since the general test predicts grades in every curriculum to about the same degree, it sheds no light on the decision"(s) the teachers must make (1965, p. 141). The Mann and Phillips discussion develops mainly from the framework of classical measurement theory; I'm proposing that a decision theory framework is much more relevant. In the latter frame what is required of a test is that it produce significant interaction effects with "methods," not high zero order predictions.

Highly g saturated tests have dominated the schools for years, and they have served quite well in making certain kinds of predictions. But precisely because they predict so much within methods, they are not very useful in choosing between methods, and it is the latter that must occupy teachers. Simple predictions might be of interest to psychometricians and to employment counselors, but are of minor import to teachers. Let it be clear that teachers must fractionate, to use the Mann-Phillips terminology. One cannot deal with the universe and teachers cannot teach all and everything at once. They are constantly called upon to make judgments about specifics and they will seek whatever minor helps test makers can give them. Everyone recognizes, I hope, that isolating any aspect of behavior is delusional if it fails to recognize the larger interactions and wholeness of behavior.

In a practical sense, I agree with Mann and Phillips that there are many problems in some of the newer approaches in special education. Sometimes excesses in diagnostics merely cover ignorance in methodology. Some techniques are sold before they meet any decent test. On the other hand, we should honor the people, such as those who have produced the ITPA, who carry through the very difficult work of evaluation.

Finally, it appears that Mann and Phillips posit general versus fractional approaches as competitive. I think this fails to see that the problems of general assessment and prediction may be quite distinct from problems of instruction. I have long believed that we can have our cake and yet eat it in this sphere of things; just as it is possible and useful to look carefully at highly specific language abilities and at the same time to look at a general language ability measure which might be generated at some second order level. It doesn't seem terribly important to me whether one considers the general factor to be primary or of a second order nature, so long as we test carefully for usefulness of each variable entered into the total system.

Reference

Cronbach, L. J., and Gleser, G. C. *Psychological tests and personnel decisions.* Urbana: University of Illinois Press, 1965.

27. THE FACETS OF EDUCATIONAL EXCEPTIONALITY: A CONCEPTUAL FRAMEWORK FOR ASSESSMENT, GROUPING, AND INSTRUCTION

HERBERT C. QUAY

It has long been recognized that current programs for exceptional children have at least two basic weaknesses. First, current grouping practices force the educator to deal with children who, while they may be somewhat homogeneous in certain intellectual, physical, and behavioral characteristics, are far from homogeneous in regard to abilities or disabilities crucial to classroom learning. One hardly need point out that cerebral palsy is a medical entity, mental retardation is a psychometric category, and emotional disturbance is a psychiatric-psychological classification.

At the same time, special education programs are rarely designed specifically to improve the academic competence of the child by the application of an instructional technology aimed at improving those aspects of the learning process in which the child may suffer a disability.

A number of approaches have been suggested as correctives. Stevens (1962) has given attention to the development of a taxonomy within the domains of educationally significant somatopsychological variation, educationally significant attributes of body disorders, and special educational procedures. His formulation is much broader than the approach

SOURCE. Reprinted from *Exceptional Children*, 1968, **35**, 25–32.
By permission of the author and publisher.

which will be proposed here in that his concept involves many factors outside the classroom (e.g., finance, modification of laws, etc.) and is not based on an analysis of the learning process and the range of individual differences relative to it.

Dunn (1968), in calling into question the current relevance of much special educational practice, argues for the need for developing both tests to measure a child's learning ability (as separate from learning acquisition) and techniques to determine whether special methods or materials will be required to teach him. At the same time, Dunn calls for the design of sequential step by step programs to move the child from where he is to where he needs to go.

"The first step would be to make a study of the child to find what behaviors he has acquired along the dimension being considered. Next, samples of a sequential program would be designed to move him forward from that point. In presenting the program, the utility of different reinforcers, administered under various conditions, would be investigated. Also, the method by which he can best be taught the material should be determined. Different modalities for reaching the child would also be tried. Thus, since the instructional program itself becomes the diagnostic device, this procedure can be called diagnostic teaching. Failures are program and instructor failures, not pupil failures. . . . This diagnostic procedure is viewed as the best available since it enables us to assess continuously the problem points of the instructional program against the assets of the child. After a successful and appropriate prescription has been devised, it would be communicated to the teachers in the pupil's home school and they would continue the procedure as long as it is necessary and brings results. From time to time, the child may need to return to the center for reappraisal and redirection [Dunn, 1968, pp. 12–13]."

The conceptualization offered here attempts to provide a framework for accomplishing what Dunn feels is necessary in both assessment and remediation.

Blackman (1967) has also recently called for the development of a school relevant taxonomy of the psychoeducational characteristics of the mentally retarded to go hand in hand with the description of school tasks "in terms of what psychological and educational 'muscle' a child requires in order to approach that task with a reasonable probability of success [p. 8]."

This paper is clearly directed toward a statement of an educationally relevant taxonomy, at least partially in the belief that the learning parameters to be described are involved in the learning of *any* school relevant task. While it is clear that certain modalities and functions within the framework to be proposed below may be differentially weighted as to their involvement in different tasks, it is not clear that any task can be learned with maximal effectiveness without manipulation of the parameters to be described below.

Finally, the author has suggested thorough study of children grouped according to current practices in terms of their learning characteristics and the peculiar demands which these might make on the instructional process in the hope that some educationally relevant homogeneities might appear (Quay, 1963; in press). While this approach offers some promise and it does not, at least at the outset, require regrouping of children along lines not currently acceptable by custom or by statute, its long range promise is not nearly as good as a more radical approach.

What is needed to produce a truly effective special education is the development of a conceptual framework which permits the assessment of exceptional children on educationally relevant variables, their grouping according to similarities of dysfunction on these variables and the development of a classroom teaching technology aimed at the correction of these deficiencies.

The elements of such a system should be those variables related to the learning process *which can be manipulated in the classroom*. While hypothetical constructs may be of value in the construction of theoretical explanations of learning, these are inferred from stimulus response relationships and they cannot be directly manipulated. While defective auditory association may help explain some facet of poor performance in the learning process, only the variables of stimulus, response, and reinforcement can be manipulated to improve auditory association. At least at the outset, then, assessment and remediation should be tied very closely to those facets of the classroom instructional process which can be varied in a systematic way.

The framework which is offered in this paper consists of a set of functions as related to certain modalities involved with the learning parameters of input, response, and reinforcement.

The interaction of these three components provides various areas in which a child may be said to have learning problems or to suffer a dysfunction of ability. Figure 1 presents this framework schematically. There are 41 cells, each of which represents the point of interaction of a function and modality with a parameter of learning; each of these cells also represents a possible condition of dysfunction which can require some intervention (remedial technology) for its remediation.

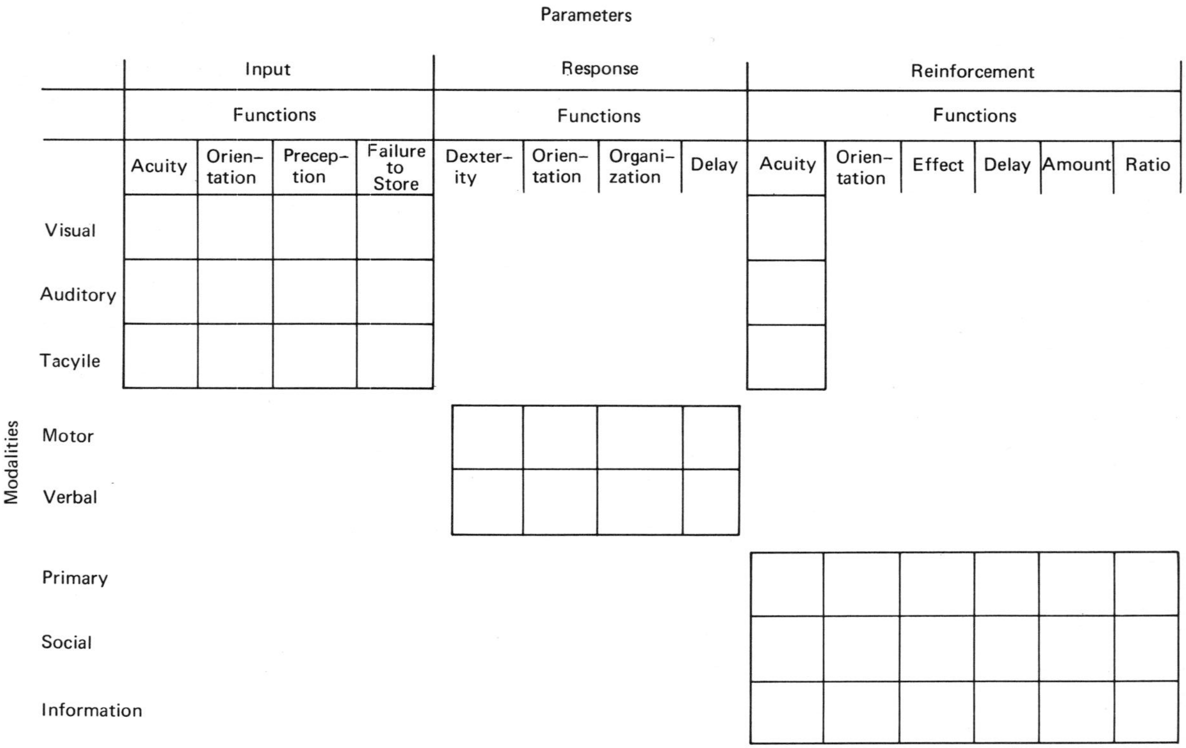

FIG. 1. *The parameters, modalities, and functions of classroom learning.*

DEFINITION OF THE FUNCTIONS

Acuity. It should be obvious that problems of sensory acuity may limit or obviate the use of certain receptive channels for stimulus presentation and for the presentation of reinforcing stimuli. We recognize that sensory acuity may be a complex matter, as in the case of the child who has a hearing loss for only certain frequencies in the speech range. However, poor acuity itself may be remediable to some extent under certain circumstances since acuity relates to the use of the modality for learning (Barraga, 1964).

Dexterity. The response counterpart of acuity is the ability, facility, and accuracy with which the child can make responses. The inability of the athetoid cerebral palsied child to make fine motor responses clearly precludes the attachment of such responses to *any* stimulus until the response mechanism itself can be improved.

Orientation. This refers to the basic necessity for the child to be oriented toward the stimulus in order for a response to the stimulus to occur. The hyperactive child who does not even look at his worksheet obviously cannot perceive its contents no matter how good his skills in the perceptual area. Neither can the child respond without orientation; he cannot write the spelling word on the page while looking out the window, nor can he respond orally to a question while talking to his neighbor. Finally, a reinforcer cannot operate unless orientation towards it occurs.

Perception. Orienting to (looking at) a blackboard and perceiving its content are not the same, even though orientation must precede perception. Perceptual differentiation (e.g., discriminating a B from a D) is dependent on both orientation and on the ability to attend to the relevant aspects of the stimuli to be differentiated. This ability to attend to the relevant dimensions of a stimulus is what is meant by perception. For example, studies of the mentally retarded have demonstrated that once they can be taught to attend to the relevant elements of the stimulus presentation, they are able to make the necessary discriminations as well as normals (Zeaman and House, 1963). Perceptual failure may occur due to figure ground reversal, as well as to apparent anomalies in the physical perceptual apparatus.

Organization. On the response side, it can be observed that certain children cannot bring together the components necessary to make a response. For example, some children have difficulty with the integration of the motor and the verbal systems necessary in describing an activity being carried out motorically.

Failure of Storage. This refers to the failure of the stimulus to be retained by the subject so that the stimulus response connection can be made and/or recalled. Ellis (1963), for example, proposes that the retarded suffer from a failure of the stimulus to leave a trace within the organism. Methods can be used to increase the probability that the information will be stored (Adams, 1967).

Delay of Response. Some children may be observed to be unable to inhibit the response to the initial element of a stimulus sequence which then interferes with the ability to respond correctly to the total sequence. The ability to delay in responding appropriately is clearly crucial to effective learning.

Effect. This refers to the capacity of a reinforcer of a certain type or quality to be actually reinforcing. Studies have shown, for example, that knowledge of results is relatively less effective as a reinforcer with lower class children as compared to middle class children (Terrell, Durkin, and Wiesley, 1959; Zigler and Kanzer, 1962), and that social reinforcement is very weak in its effect on hyperaggressive, unsocialized adolescents and young adults (Johns and Quay, 1962; Levin and Simmons, 1962). The failure of a child to respond to social reinforcers can present a serious problem in the classroom.

Delay of Reinforcement. While it has been well demonstrated that immediate reinforcement is most effective in promoting learning, the nature of school organization and society in general requires that some delay in receiving rewards be tolerated with learning still taking place. Research has shown that children differ in the ability to tolerate delay with variations related to both intellectual (Ross, Hetherington, and Wray, 1965) and personality (Mischel, 1966) dimensions.

Amount. The amount and quality of reinforcement necessary to fixate a stimulus response sequence can vary among children (Witryol, Tyrrel, and Lowden, 1965) and can present an educational problem if extremely large rewards are necessary to promote learning. The child who responds only to large doses of attention and praise makes heavy demands on teacher time.

Ratio. It is well known that the frequency with which the correct response is followed by a reinforcer can have a noticeable effect on acquisition and retention. In the classroom it is rare that every correct response can be followed by a reinforcer; children must learn to make a number of correct responses to receive a single reward. Children who do not respond to less than a 100 percent ratio of reinforcement clearly create a special problem.

THE MODALITIES

Sensory Modes. In the main, information reaches the classroom child through the tactile, auditory, and visual modes. Obviously, sensory impairment in the function of any one or more of these modalities will require special programming of the stimulus display. In addition, acuity impairment will require modification in the extent to which reinforcing stimuli can be delivered via the impaired modality.

Response Modes. All of the responses of the child can be seen as occurring through either the motor and/or the verbal mode. Impairment of the response functions of either mode will necessitate some remedial approach. For example, the child with expressive aphasia would be said to be handicapped in the dexterity function of the verbal response mode.

Reinforcement Modes. Rewards in the classroom are generally of the primary sensory (food or money—some preferred sensory or motor activity), social (teacher praise, peer approval), or information (knowledge of results) types. The author recognizes that it can be argued that knowledge of results is basically a social reinforcer, but since response to knowledge of results sometimes does not serve as a reinforcer to children who are responsive to direct praise, it has been kept as a separate mode. Failure of any of the reinforcement functions for any of the three modes will usually require some remediation before the child can function most effectively in the regular classroom.

ASSESSMENT

The framework offered above provides a clear-cut guide for the assessment of the exceptional child in terms of learning functions relevant to the classroom. Each of the 41 cells in Figure 1 represents a behavior which can be measured to yield a quantitative estimate for a given child. Measurement will need to be accomplished through direct observation of learning behavior (e.g., orientation, organization) (a) through the use of laboratory type procedures and "miniature situation" tests (e.g., effect and delay in reinforcement), (b) by means of psychometric procedures (e.g., verbal dexterity), and (c) through the employment of tests of sensory (acuity) and motor (dexterity) skills. While it is doubtful that truly adequate measures currently exist for the assessment of the behaviors of all 41 cells (failure to store is perhaps the best example), such tests can be devised because each cell is defined by some observable behavior or behaviors. In fact, such tests would make a much greater contribution to education—and psychology—than the majority of those devised to measure hypothetical constructs.

The framework, as a diagnostic and remedial guide, also has certain properties of a scale. For example, given a complete lack of acuity in a sensory modality, diagnostic study relative to any of the other functions for either input, response, or reinforcement need not be carried out. Given a serious failure of orientation, it is likely that additional diagnostic study would not produce valid results since lack of orientation precludes the operation of the other functions. At the same time, attempts at remediation of perception without correction of orientation failure would be futile. In the reinforcement parameter, questions of magnitude, delay, and ratio are irrelevant if the child fails to respond to a certain type reinforcer. For the child who does not find teacher praise rewarding, manipulation of its quantity and timing are not likely to be effective until his failure to respond to such social reinforcement can be corrected.

DEVELOPMENT OF A CLASSROOM TECHNOLOGY

An additional feature of the conceptual scheme is that it offers a guide to the development of a classroom technology for the modification of the various dysfunctions of the learning process. Since the variables of the framework are closely tied to the empirical facts of learning, procedures designed to facilitate the various functions which have been developed in the laboratory are now directly relevant to the special classroom. There is literature, for example, on the effect of various reinforcers on orientation in the classroom (Patterson, Jones, Whittier, and Wright, 1965; Quay, Werry, McQueen, and Sprague, 1966). Suggestions have also been made, based on experimental evidence, as to how the engineering of the stimulus display can favorably influence organization behavior (Scott, 1966). Many, many other examples could be cited. Further, since the functions of each of the 41 cells are defined behaviorally, they are open to experimentation in regard to remedial methodologies.

GROUPING FOR INSTRUCTION

The use of the proposed framework provides a basis for grouping children according to their special needs in terms of educationally relevant variables rather than according to characteristics related to hypothetical causes (e.g., minimal cerebral dysfunction) or according to variables of concern to fields other than that of education. Thus, children can be grouped because they have orientation defects which can be ameliorated by a particular classroom technology, or because they have defects in their capacity to respond to social reinforcers which can also be corrected. What is likely is that defects in a number of the functions will be correlated so that, for example, a group of children could be formed and placed in a classroom with a program designed to correct orientation, response delay, and reinforcement effect deficiencies, while another classroom might be directed toward helping children with problems in perception, organization, and verbal dexterity.

Ability and Disability. No doubt motivated at least somewhat by a despair of remediating disabilities, there has been considerable concern with capitalizing on abilities—"teach through strength rather than to weakness." While it may be obvious that in certain instances this can occur (e.g., the use of intact auditory modalities instead of impaired visual ones for both input and reinforcement), care must be exercised to see that intact but nonequivalent functions are not substituted in the hopes of circumventing disabled ones. Capitalization on unique storage ability (memory) cannot compensate for orientation failure; in fact, storage cannot occur in the total absence of orientation. Neither is it clear that reliance on unimpaired auditory storage, for example, will not leave holes in the child's achievement that would not be there had the capacity for visual storage been increased by judicious manipulation of the stimulus display.

At the same time it should be recognized that there is likely to be some point at which the disability is so severe that the function in question must be bypassed, either because of absolute necessity or because of cost efficiency considerations.

CURRENT CATEGORIES AND THE PROPOSED CONCEPTUAL FRAMEWORK

It is tempting to compare the profiles of hypothetical children who might be said to typify current diagnostic groups. This is difficult, however, since the abilities of many such children are not clearly understood in terms of the learning relevant functions of Figure 1. For example, the extent to which the retarded child suffers a failure in perception and/or storage is certainly not fully understood. One must also recognize that some cerebral palsied children may have a handicap in the perceptual area while others may not; some emotionally disturbed children suffer from orientation failure while others clearly do not.

With these problems in mind, Figure 2 has been prepared, indicating the functional areas in which certain of the current categories of exceptional children appear to experience difficulties. It is apparent that the profiles of particular groups, assuming that their classical characteristics are in fact correct, are quite similar and thus even now might be effectively combined for certain remedial procedures. For example, orientation dysfunction in both input and response parameters appears to be

Parameters

	Input Functions				Response Functions					Reinforcement Functions				
	Acuity	Orien-tation	Percep-tion	Failure to Store	Dexter-ity	Orien-tation	Organi-zation	Delay	Acuity	Orien-tation	Effect	Delay	Amount	Ratio
Visual		MR BD MCD	CP MR MCD	MR										
Auditory		MR BD MCD	CP MR MCD	MR										
Tactile		MR BD MCD	CP MR MCD	MR										
Motor					MR MCD CP	MR BD MCD	MR CP MCD	MR BD MCD						
Verbal					MR BD	MR BD MCD	MR	BD						
Primary										MR MCD		MR BD		BD
Social										MR MCD	BD	MR BD		
Information										MR MCD	BD	MR BD		

Legend: MR—Mentally Retarded
BD—Behavior Disorder
MCD—Minimal Cerebral Dysfunction
CP—Cerebral Palsy

FIG. 2. The parameters, modalities, and functions of learning and the characteristics of four groups of exceptional children. Legend: MR = mentally retarded; BD = behavior disorder; MCD = minimal cerebral dys-

common in children in the traditional categories of mental retardation, conduct (acting out) behavior disorders, and minimal cerebral dysfunction. Since this is a dysfunction at a basic level, its remediation must occur before one needs to be concerned with dysfunction of perception, organization, delay, and effect. Thus, children of all three categories might be placed *first* in a classroom with a remedial technology directed at improving orientation. The children with minimal cerebral dysfunction, the cerebral palsied, and the mentally retarded could then be grouped in a classroom oriented toward providing remediation for perception deficits while the conduct problem children would next require a program aimed at correcting dysfunctions in the reinforcement parameter.

CONCLUSION

The conceptual framework offered here has a number of advantages. In drawing upon the empirical facts of the learning process as they operate in the classroom, educationally relevant functions on which children differ widely are made the basis for diagnostic assessment, instructional grouping, and teaching technology. The current state of the art of diagnosis for educational purposes can clearly be improved by attention to these functions and by the development and refinement of measures of them. These same functions can also become the basis for a technology of instruction which can draw on laboratory procedures for effective stimulus display, response control and shaping, and reinforcer manipulation.

Obviously, we do not have a finished product. Additional research in learning will probably reveal functions which will have to be added to the scheme. Perhaps such research will also demonstrate that some of the current functions are special cases of more comprehensive parameters or are altogether irrelevant. Better diagnostic tools are also needed, especially in such functions as perception, effect of reinforcement, and failure to store.

Finally, one cannot help but speculate on the degree to which the entire educational process might be improved if the technology of teaching were directed toward the maximum utilization by normal children of their abilities in the various functions.

References

Adams, J. A. *Human memory.* New York: McGraw-Hill, 1967.

Barraga, N. *Increased visual behavior in low vision children.* New York: American Foundation for the Blind, 1964.

Blackman, L. The dimensions of a science of special education. *Mental Retardation,* 1967, **5,** 7–11.

Dunn, L. M. Special education for the mildly retarded—is much of it justifiable? *Exceptional Children,* 1968, **35,** 5–22.

Ellis, N. R. The stimulus trace and behavioral inadequacy. In N. R. Ellis (Ed.), *Handbook of mental deficiency.* New York: McGraw-Hill, 1963. Pp. 134–158.

Johns, J. A., & Quay, H. C. The effect of social reward on verbal conditioning in psychopathic and neurotic military offenders. *Journal of Consulting Psychology,* 1962, **26,** 217–220.

Levin, G. R., & Simmons, J. J. Response to food and praise by emotionally disturbed boys. *Psychological Reports,* 1962, **11,** 539–546.

Mischel, W. Theory and research on the antecedents of self-imposed delay of reward. In B. A. Maher (Ed.), *Progress in experimental personality research.* Vol. 3. New York: Academic Press, 1966. Pp. 85–132.

Patterson, G. R., Jones, R., Whittier, J., & Wright, M. A behavior modification technique for the hyperactive child. *Behavior Research and Therapy,* 1965, **2,** 217–226.

Quay, H. C. Some basic considerations in the education of emotionally disturbed children. *Exceptional Children,* 1963, **30,** 27–31.

Quay, H. C. Dimensions of problem behavior and educational programming. In P. S. Graubard (Ed.), *Children Against Schools.* New York: Follett, in press.

Quay, H. C., Werry, J. S., McQueen, M. M., & Sprague, R. L. Remediation of the conduct problem child in the special class setting. *Exceptional Children,* 1966, **3,** 390–397.

Ross, L. E., Hetherington, M., Wray, N. P. Delay of reward and the learning of a size problem by normal and retarded children. *Child Development,* 1965, **36,** 509–518.

Scott, K. G. Engineering attention: Some rules for the classroom. *Education and Training of the Mentally Retarded,* 1966, **1,** 125–129.

Stevens, G. D. *Taxonomy in special education for children with body disorders: The problem and a proposal.* Pittsburgh: University of Pittsburgh, Department of Special Education and Rehabilitation, 1962.

Terrell, G., Jr., Durkin, K., & Wiesley, M. Social class and the nature of the incentive in discrimination learning. *Journal of Abnormal and Social Psychology,* 1959, **59,** 270–272.

Witryol, S. L., Tyrrell, D. J., & Lowden, L. M. Development of incentive values in childhood. *Genetic Psychology Monographs,* 1965, **72,** 201–246.

Zeaman, D., & House, B. J. The role of attention in retardate discrimination learning. In N. R. Ellis (Ed.), *Handbook of mental deficiency.* New York: McGraw-Hill, 1963. Pp. 159–223.

Zigler, E., & Kanzer, P. The effectiveness of two classes of verbal reinforcers on the performance of middle and lower class children. *Journal of Personality,* 1962, 30, 157–163.

28. SPECIAL EDUCATION: A TEAPOT IN A TEMPEST

M. STEPHEN LILLY

The purpose of this article is to examine present policies and practices in the field of special education and to determine the extent to which present behavior patterns in the field are educationally based and relevant to school learning and behavior problems. The focus of this paper is on the child whose problems can be seen as relatively mild, those children traditionally labeled as educable mentally retarded, emotionally disturbed, behaviorally disordered, educationally handicapped, learning disabled, or brain injured. The one common characteristic among all these children is that they have been referred from regular education programs because of some sort of teacher perceived behavioral or learning problem. The ideas presented herein also apply to children with physical or sensory deficits, though the application is not as direct nor the problems as immediate as with the traditional groups mentioned earlier.

This article does not refer to children who have been called trainable mentally retarded, severely emotionally disturbed, multiply handicapped, or to children who are so obviously deviant that they have never been enrolled in any kind of normal school program. It must be recognized,

SOURCE. Reprinted from *Exceptional Children*, 1970, 1, 43–49.
By permission of the author and publisher.

however, that such children constitute a very small percentage of exceptional children, and that the real focus of the present controversy in special education is on that large group of children traditionally labeled mildly handicapped. It is with regard to these children that we as special educators have trouble justifying our practices both socially and morally, and this is the area in which we must spend considerable time and energy examining both our actions and our motives.

It is the position of this writer, based upon consideration of evidence and opinion from many and varied sources, that traditional special education services as represented by self contained special classes should be discontinued immediately for all but the severely impaired as delineated above. Supporting data from the various efficacy studies will not be reviewed in detail here, since these data are readily available to the concerned reader from several other sources. These studies have produced conflicting evidence concerning special class programs, with the weight of the evidence suggesting that special programs have produced little that is superior to what is produced in the regular class setting. To avoid exhaustive argument with regard to research design and confounding variables in these efficacy studies, let us accept the statement that they are inconclusive to date. It must be added, however, that in the true spirit of research they will be inconclusive forever.

Notwithstanding the integrity of the efficacy studies, concern with the adequacy of the traditional special education model has grown over the last decade. There are deficiencies in logic as well as product in our present practices, and once the efficacy studies cued professionals to the possible existence of problems, the logical inconsistencies of the model became more and more apparent. The question of logic in our special education model is examined in some detail by Reger, Schroeder, and Uschold (1968).

Let us share at this point a series of statements, dating from 1960 to 1969, all of which are statements of concern with the practices which are still most prevalent in the field of special education today. Most of these statements are from known and respected special educators, and one is from a federal judge in Washington, D.C. The latter statement served to abolish the track system in the schools of the District of Columbia, on the basis that it was by its very nature discriminatory. These are only eight of many such statements, both oral and written, which could have been chosen to represent what must be considered a bona fide movement in special education. The statements which follow are representative of the feelings of a large body of professionals and have yet to be seriously heeded by the majority of special education policy makers and practitioners.

"In a rare moment of candidness, a distinguished special educator recently remarked, during a meeting in which this writer participated, that special education isn't special nor can it, in many instances be considered education. Studies find that, insofar as measurable abilities are concerned, mentally handicapped children in special classes are very similar in development to those in regular grades. In fact, the earlier studies of Bennett and Pertsch found that retarded children in special classes did poorly in physical, personality, and academic areas as compared with retarded children in regular classes. Later studies by Blatt and Cassidy found few significant differences between those children in the regular classes and those in special classes. Notwithstanding the many obvious and valid criticisms of studies comparing special vs. regular class membership, it has yet to be demonstrated that the special class offers a better school experience for retarded children than does regular class placement [Blatt, 1960, pp. 53–54]."

❈   ❈   ❈

"It is indeed paradoxical that mentally handicapped children having teachers especially trained, having more money (per capita) spent on their education, and being enrolled in classes with fewer children and a program designed to provide for their unique needs, should be accomplishing the objectives of their education at the same or at a lower level than similar mentally handicapped children who have not had these advantages and have been forced to remain in the regular grades [Johnson, 1962, p. 66.]"

❈   ❈   ❈

"We seem to be possessed with categories and organizational designs which entrench the categories. Are we so sure that special classes, broken down into categories—slow learners, neurologically impaired, etc. are doing the job? While the process may be administratively convenient, there is no doubt that the procedure has made special education special, isolated it and in so doing perpetuated the isolationism and attending mysticism which has stood in the way of special education development [Fisher, 1967, p. 29]."

❈   ❈   ❈

"As to the remedy with respect to the track system, the track system simply must be abolished. In practice, if not in concept, it discriminates against the disadvantaged child, particularly the Negro. Designed in 1955 as a means of protecting the school system against the ill effect of integrating with white children the Negro victims of de jure separate but unequal education, it has survived to stigmatize the disadvantaged child of whatever race relegated to its lower tracks—from which tracks the possibility of switching upward, because of the absence of compensatory education, is remote [Wright, 1968, p. 210]."

*   *   *

"We are saying that grouping children on the basis of medically derived disability labels has no practical utility in the schools. Children should be grouped on the basis of their education needs, and these needs may be defined in any number of ways. The notion that simple labels, applied by high-status authorities from outside the school, should serve as a basis for grouping children is basically nothing more than a refusal to accept responsibility for making educational decisions. It is educational laziness [Reger et al., 1968, p. 19]."

*   *   *

"In my view, much of our past and present practices are morally and educationally wrong. We have been living at the mercy of general educators who have referred their problem children to us. And we have been generally ill prepared and ineffective in educating these children. Let us stop being pressured into continuing and expanding a special education program that we know now to be undesirable for many of the children we are dedicated to serve [Dunn, 1968, p. 5]."

*   *   *

"Special education is part of the arrangement for cooling out students. It has helped to erect a parallel system which permits relief of institutional guilt and humiliation stemming from the failure to achieve competence and effectiveness in the task given to it by society. Special education is helping the regular school maintain its spoiled identity when it creates special programs (whether psychodynamic or behavioral modification) for the "disruptive child" and the "slow learner," many of whom, for some strange reason, happen to be Black and poor and live in the inner city [Johnson, 1969, p. 245]."

*   *   *

"There has been no reliable evidence produced to indicate that differential benefits, either social or academic, accrue to regular students as a result of either the exclusion or inclusion of exceptional students in regular classes. However, even if differential effects were found favoring the former, a democratic philosophy would dictate that the most justifiable course of action in dealing with exceptionality would be the altering of classroom practices whenever possible, rather than the segregation of the deviant individuals. The rapid growth of special classes, in the face of lack of either supporting evidence or acceptable democratic social philosophy, has but limited justification [Christoplos & Renz, 1969, p. 373]."

It has been stated above that the majority of policy and decision makers in the field of special education have paid little heed to these straightforward statements of dissatisfaction with the status quo. As evidence for this statement, let us look briefly at the structure and operation of the two most powerful agencies in the field, the Council for Exceptional Children (a professional agency) and the Bureau for Education of the Handicapped (a government organization).

The Council for Exceptional Children is the largest professional organization in the field of special education. Its membership consists primarily of special education teachers, administrators, and college teaching and research personnel. It cannot be said that the Council is unaware of the tempest which is raging in its ranks; both the 1970 Convention program and recent activities of the CEC Policies Commission attest to the fact that the Council is paying attention to the concerns of its membership. This raises somewhat of a problem in itself, since the perennial top concern of the membership, as expressed in Delegate Assembly at the Convention, is more efficient and effective means of processing membership forms and renewal notices. Quite a far cry from the children we purport to serve.

While the Council is willing to consider the controversy over appropriate models for special education services, it operates in some areas as if the field were united and no disagreement existed. One such area, of crucial importance, is federal legislation. Consider the following four statements, made. in congressional testimony last year with regard to appropriations for special education:

"Of the 6,000,000 handicapped children in the nation only ⅓ are receiving special education services. Handicapped children are legally defined as 'mentally retarded, deaf, speech impaired, visually handicapped, seriously emotionally disturbed, crippled, or other health impaired. . . .'" It is difficult to imagine that $50 per child is too much to ask for. We hope that we will not have to tell the six million handicapped children of this country and their families that the federal government was unable to make this small investment [Geer, 1969, p. 176]."

✿   ✿   ✿

"It is expected that many of these children without appropriate
educational services may require institutionalization at a cost of
over $200,000 per child as opposed to an anticipated cost of
$20,000 for a complete educational program [Geer, 1969, p. 176]."

✿   ✿   ✿

"Each year that a learning handicapped child is denied the services
that are presently available to others, that child is being denied his
right to equal educational opportunity. No argument, however well
phrased, can avoid this conclusion. To the extent that failure of
the Congress to act now (on the Children with Learning Disabilities
Act of 1969) deprives even one child of the utilization of his
learning capabilities, Congress is derelict [McCarthy, 1969, p. 35]."

✿   ✿   ✿

"We have delayed long enough. It is time that acceptance be
given to the learning disabled child as a legitimate handicapping
condition and that procedures be created to extend educational
services to such children [Geer, 1969, p. 33]."

It is thus clear that while CEC is attending to the controversy in its
ranks on some fronts, it is ignoring it on others. While IMPACT sessions
are held in Chicago, legislative lobbying takes place which encourages
hardening of the categories and proliferation of services of dubious
value. At the same time, the categorical approach to CEC Divisional
structure is strengthened and expanded. While it is difficult to argue with
some of the emotional appeals made in the testimony cited above, the
logic is altogether refutable. With the seemingly sure rise in stature of
educational accounting principles the day of educational reckoning is
fast approaching, and when that roll call is taken, emotional appeals
will suddenly lose their longstanding credibility. If we are to change
our approach and our practices, as we must, the most opportune time is
yesterday and the next most opportune today.

The situation is much the same in the Bureau of Education for the
Handicapped (BEH). BEH is in a rather awkward position in that it
was created by an act of Congress, after much Congressional lobbying
concerning the distinctly differing needs of handicapped children. Likewise, the Division of Training Programs in particular has leaned heavily
on traditional special education categories for building its funding base.
A change at this time to a different framework would introduce two
problems of considerable potential impact. First, a change in the basic
structure of special education could indicate that the present funding
system is inadequate and inappropriate, and that this inadequacy was

apparent even while programs were being established and strengthened. The second concern is that such a move would introduce uncertainty into a reasonably stable system. At this time, educational accounting in BEH is fairly straightforward in terms of numbers and teachers and researchers trained, areas in which they are trained, and numbers of children needing and receiving special education services. Some of these accounting data are seen in the testimony of Geer cited above. When the system is changed however, and new special education models are put forward, the old accounting methods will be inappropriate and it will become more difficult to count numbers of children waiting and teachers needed.

While BEH certainly has problems in a changing education world (any governmental agency does), it is felt that the same conclusions apply here as were drawn in the discussion of CEC. That is, if change is needed, the time to change is now. More water under the bridge can only further pollute the stream. If changes are needed in the underlying structure of special education services—and that is the urgent message of this article—then these changes should be made as quickly and completely as possible. Further, the changes should not involve moving from one rigid system to another, but rather the new structure should be supportive of broad experimentation with a variety of new approaches to children with problems in school.

The most often heard remark in opposition to basic changes in special education says something to the effect that "You are trying to destroy the old system, and do not have anything adequate with which to replace it." This is closely allied to the familiar "throwing the baby out with the bath water" argument. These arguments ignore the growing body of literature on appropriate educational practices for children encountering problems regardless of their specific classroom setting. Reger, Schroeder, and Uschold (1968) have written a curriculum and materials book which can rival the older, traditional texts, but which advocates an overhaul of the self contained special education program and replacement with an approach which stresses each individual's learning and behavioral needs. These authors point out:

"The label applied to the child serves as a sanction for administrative action, meaning placement into a special class or into some other special program. The whole procedure tells us nothing about a child that we did not already know because nothing was added to our fund of knowledge about the child, and we have no information about what to do with the child after placement changes are made. Moving a child from one classroom to another is an administrative action; it is not an act of understanding or explanation [p. 16]."

If one is interested in new models to work from, the following are offered as only a few of a growing number of "less special" education models that are beginning to develop: The Educational Modulation Center (Adamson, 1969; Adamson & Shrago, 1969), Diagnostic/Prescriptive Teaching (Prouty & Prillaman, 1967; Vinagradoff, 1969), Project PLAN (Flanagan, 1967; Weisberger & Ramlow, 1968), Guaranteed Performance Contracting (Elam, 1970), Individually Prescribed Instruction (Glaser, 1966; Bolvin & Glaser, 1968), Teacher Moms (Donahue & Nichtern, 1965). These approaches are not meant to be inclusive, nor do they necessarily represent an ultimate system, either in isolation or in combination. They are listed here only to indicate that the "we don't have anything to substitute" argument no longer represents an adequate reason to postpone the rather frightening task of redefining our roles as special educators and tightening both the logical basis for and the accountability of our educational practices.

The remainder of this article will not outline an alternate model for special education services; this has been and is being done by educational practitioners with more expertise in program development than this writer. In addition, it is felt that this activity would not serve to convince dubious readers that we as special educators need to be concerned with internal change. Thus, an alternate model presented at this time would tend to reinforce the ideas of those readers who agree with the article thus far, and would be skipped over rather quickly by those who are not in agreement. In short, it would produce little or no positive action.

Instead of presenting an alternate model, the remainder of the article will present a new approach to defining exceptionality, an approach which in the opinion of this writer will, if accepted, begin to lead us out of the categorical web which we have spun. Traditionally, definitions of exceptionality have been child based, aimed at identifying basic deficits in children. Dunn (1963) offered a typical definition:

"Exceptional pupils are those (1) who differ from the average to such a degree in physical or psychological characteristics (2) that school programs designed for the majority of children do not afford them opportunity for all-round adjustment and optimum progress, (3) and who therefore need either special instruction or in some cases special ancillary services, or both, to achieve at a level commensurate with their respective abilities [p. 2]."

Kirk (1962) spoke of the exceptional child as having "discrepancies in growth" which make him different from the normal child only in terms of certain characteristics.

Once defined, exceptional children seemed to fall "naturally" into specified categories of deviance, though not so naturally that all authorities agreed on the exact nature of such categories. Nor did all categories share a common frame of reference. Mental retardation, for instance, was based on a supposed psychological deficit in the area of learning, while emotional disturbance and/or social maladjustment were said to have been a function of other psychological processes. In searching for commonalities among the categories of mild handicap, two emerged: (a) all were stated in terms of "problems within the child," and (b) all referred to less than adequate situations within the school setting. In short, it can be said that exceptionality is a psychological construct, created to make order out of chaotic classroom situations. The causative agents of such chaos were posited in children, and special education programs ensued. Eventually, as is often the case with psychological constructs, we ceased to regard exceptionality as an explanatory concept and it became as real as the mumps in children.

In order to return exceptionality to its rightful status as an explanatory concept, it must be made to adhere more closely to real school situations, that is, it must be removed from the child. Thus, it is suggested that we move from defining "exceptional children" to defining "exceptional situations within the school." The following represents a beginning in developing such a definition:

"An exceptional school situation is one in which interaction between a student and his teacher has been limited to such an extent that external intervention is deemed necessary by the teacher to cope with the problem."

This definition takes into account the actual procedure by which children have been labeled exceptional in the past. It posits as the basic problem a breakdown in the student-teacher relationship, with resulting disruption of normal routine. It does not specify the basic nature of the problem, nor does it specify the child (or the teacher) as the causative agent in any given situation. In essence, it demands a complete analysis of the classroom situation before statements are made concerning the nature of the problem and steps necessary to bring about a solution.

The implications of this definition of exceptionality are numerous, and must be explored in determining its viability. Acceptance of the definition would set new priorities for research, training, and school practices in special education. Most likely, it would signal the end of special education as we have known it. In its place, however, would emerge a system in which it is *not* assumed that all school problems are centered in the child and that removal of children from problem situations will be beneficial for everyone involved. Just what the new system would assume is negotiable, but at least it would be built upon a definition of exceptionality which is both truthful and realistic. Let us remove the onus of inadequate educational settings from the shoulders of its victims.

References

Adamson, G. The Educational Modulation Center: An overview. *Kansas Studies in Education*, 1969, **19**, 1–3.

Adamson, G., & Shrago, M. The educational team. *Kansas Studies in Education*, 1969, **19**, 4–8.

Blatt, B. Some persistently recurring assumptions concerning the mentally subnormal. *Training School Bulletin*, 1960, **57**, 48–59.

Bolvin, J. O., & Glaser, R. Developmental aspects of individually prescribed instruction. *Audiovisual Instruction*, 1968, **13**, 828–831.

Christoplos, F., & Renz, P. A critical examination of special education programs. *The Journal of Special Education*, 1969, **3**, 371–379.

Donahue, G. T., & Nichtern, S. *Teaching the troubled child.* New York: Free Press, 1965.

Dunn, L. M. (Ed.) *Exceptional children in the schools.* New York: Holt, Rinehart & Winston, 1963.

Dunn, L. M. Special education for the mildly retarded—Is much of it justifiable? *Exceptional Children*, 1968, **35**, 5–22.

Elam, S. The age of accountability dawns in Texarkana. *Phi Delta Kappan*, 1970, **51**, 509–514.

Fisher, H. K. What is special education? *Special Education in Canada*, 1967, **41**, 9–16.

Flanagan, J. C. Functional education for the seventies. *Phi Delta Kappan*, 1967, **49**, 27–33.

Geer, W. C. Testimony. *Hearings before the General Subcommittee on Education.* Committee on Education and Labor. Washington, D.C.: USGPO, 1969.

Glaser, R. The program for individually prescribed instruction. Paper presented at the annual meeting of the American Educational Research Association, Chicago, Illinois, February 1966.

Johnson, G. O. Special education for the mentally retarded—A paradox. *Exceptional Children*, 1962, **29**, 62–69.

Johnson, J. L. Special education for the inner city: A challenge for the future or another means for cooling the mark out? *The Journal of Special Education*, 1969, 3, 241–251.

Kirk, S. A. *Educating Exceptional Children*. Boston: Houghton-Mifflin, 1962.

McCarthy, J. M. Testimony. *Hearings before the General Subcommittee on Education*. Committee on Education and Labor. Washington, D.C.: USGPO, 1969.

Prouty, R., & Prillaman, D. Educational diagnosis: In clinic or classroom? *Virginia Journal of Education*, 1967, 61, 10–12.

Reger, R., Schroeder, W., & Uschold, D. *Special education: Children with learning problems*. New York: Oxford University Press, 1968.

Vinagradoff, V. The role and function of the diagnostic teacher. Paper presented at the annual meeting of The Council for Exceptional Children, Denver, Colorado, April 1969.

Wright, J. S. The Washington, D.C. school case. In M. Weinberg (Ed.), *Integrated education: A reader*. Beverly Hills: Glencoe Press, 1968. Pp. 207–213.

Weisberger, R. A., & Ramlow, H. F. Individually managed learning. *Audiovisual Instruction*, 1968, 13, 835–839.

29. A HIERARCHY OF EDUCATIONAL TASKS FOR CHILDREN WITH LEARNING DISORDERS

FRANK M. HEWETT

The child who fails to learn in school is communicating vital information about himself. He may be revealing his general intellectual limitations or some specific sensory or perceptual-motor handicap. He may be apprising us of the inadequacy of his previous schooling due to poor teaching methods or sporadic attendance. He also may be communicating an inability to cope with social and emotional stress which is manifest through poor concentration, comprehension, and recall in the classroom.

Seldom is such a child's message clearly understood and seldom is the explanation for his learning problem a simple and specific one. Constitutional, environmental, and psychological factors usually overlap, making it difficult for the educator to properly program the child according to his most basic needs.

In the search for remedial and educational guidelines, teachers have looked to the clinical psychologist, the educational psychologist, and the child psychiatrist for assistance. While these child specialists offer relevant generalizations regarding learning and behavior, their contributions are not always practical in the classroom setting. The battle strategies laid down by the military advisors in the tactical planning room may

SOURCE. Reprinted from *Exceptional Children*, 1964, 31, 207–214.

need alteration and clarification before they are useful to the field general on the front lines.

It is this gap between theory and practice that the concept of a hierarchy of educational tasks for children with learning disorders attempts to narrow. The basic assumption underlying the hierarchy holds that an effective educational program for children with learning disorders depends on the establishment of a point of meaningful contact between the teacher and the child. Such a point of contact is only possible when the child is experiencing gratification in the learning situation and the teacher is in control.

There is a wide range of types of gratification which the child may experience while learning (from a candy reward for each correct response to recognition for academic efforts by a place on the honor roll), and there are many levels of teacher control (from permissiveness in structuring to careful setting of behavioral limits and academic expectations). It is establishing this point of contact while providing appropriate student gratification and teacher control that is a crucial consideration for the teacher of children with learning problems. The normal achiever may be motivated by grades, competition with other students, and a variety of other social and intellectual rewards, but the nonachiever may be deterred from entering into the learning situation by these same factors. While normal classroom procedures may dictate that all students be held for definite academic and behavior standards, the child with a learning problem may have to be viewed within a broader educational frame of reference.

The theoretical framework to be presented in this paper has grown out of three years experience teaching hospitalized emotionally handicapped children and adolescents with learning problems at the Neuropsychiatric Institute School (NPI) at the University of California, Los Angeles. It is the result of a felt need on the part of the staff teachers for a set of working hypotheses with which to formulate realistic goals for their complex and highly variable students.

Meaningful contact and varying degrees of student gratification and teacher control are possible on seven educational task levels. These will be discussed following a brief historical review of the concept of a hierarchy of human development and behavior.

REVIEW OF HIERARCHIES

Hierarchies of developmental tasks and human motives are basic to the writings of Freud (Munroe, 1955), Erickson, Havighurst, and Maslow. Freud's psychosexual stages of development form such a hierarchy and presuppose mastery and gratification at each earlier level before an individual is free to devote his energies to succeeding stages. Thus, an individual who experiences a faulty oral stage of development may have to divert a disproportionate amount of his energies toward oral gratification during later years. In Freud's own metaphor, an army general is less likely to win a war if he must leave a number of his troops to deal with unfinished battles along the way.

Erickson (1950) and Havighurst (1952) have described developmental tasks of early and middle childhood, adolescence, and adult life. Learning a sense of trust in others, learning social and physical realities, building a wholesome attitude toward one's self, and developing a clear sense of identity are a few of the tasks to be mastered for successful ascension up the ladder of life.

Maslow (1954) has suggested that human motives arrange themselves in a hierarchy from the most basic biological needs for self-actualization. Beginning with body needs such as hunger and thirst and moving step by step through safety needs for self-preservation, love needs for approval of others, esteem needs for self-enhancement, and finally, at the top of the scale, self-actualization needs for realization of one's utmost potential, Maslow has constructed a hierarchy within which he attempts to explain all human motivation. Maslow postulates that successful achievement and satisfaction of higher level needs is dependent upon reasonable fulfillment of needs at the lower levels.

The hierarchy of educational tasks which makes up the subject matter of this paper represents an attempt to organize and formulate psychological principles of development into practical terms for the educator. Each level is concerned with the reciprocal tasks of student and teacher in the formation of a working educational relationship. In an ascending order, the hierarchy of educational tasks consists of primary, acceptance, order, exploratory, relationship, mastery, and achievement task levels.

PRIMARY TASK LEVEL

The most primitive level on which teacher and child may interact is the primary task level. Here, the teacher's task is to provide maximum gratification and to establish contact on the student's own terms, thus laying the groundwork for future interactions in which more control and direction may be exercised. This level is generally only applicable in cases of severe learning disability where the student is inaccessible to social controls or totally resistant to learning. The child's task is minimal at the primary level. The teacher may appeal to such basic needs as a desire for candy or money rather than to more complex social needs. It is at this level that operant conditioning work with severely regressed schizophrenics and autistic children is undertaken. Lindsley (1956), Ferster (1961), Isaacs (1960), and Weiland (1961) have demonstrated that such inaccessible individuals may take note of a teacher or therapist who has a piece of candy, gum or the like, pay attention and begin to learn or re-learn appropriate behaviors in order to obtain the desired reward.

Related work starting at the primary level has been done by Slack, (in a lecture to NPI Staff, 1963), who has shown how a desire for money may be an effective motivator for getting a school drop out with serious motivation and learning problems to learn to read. Slack approached such individuals and asked them to help him evaluate a teaching machine reading program. For their efforts these boys were given a penny for each frame of the reading program. In the course of acquiring $30 and exposure to a basic reading vocabulary, many of these boys actually learned to read. More important, many manifested a new interest in school and learning and continued their formal education. Similar methods have proven successful with inmates in state prisons.

In the NPI school, a two year educational program was recently completed with a twelve year old autistic boy who had never developed speech (Hewett, 1964). The goal of the program was to teach this withdrawn and unsocialized boy to read and write and thus enable him to communicate more appropriately with the environment. Candy gumdrops established the first point of contact between teacher and student. The boy paid attention and engaged in simple reading activities such as picture-word matching in order to obtain an immediate candy reward. Once this contact was established, the boy was given higher level tasks. This is an important characteristic of the hierarchy; while the teacher may initiate contact with the child on the lowest appropriate level, the eventual goal is to engage him in higher level tasks.

ACCEPTANCE TASK LEVEL

The second task level consists of acceptance tasks for both teacher and child. At this level, the teacher communicates complete acceptance of the child and attempts to establish the beginning of a relationship with him, still primarily on the child's terms. While the child may have perceived the teacher as an undifferentiated means to immediate gratification at the primary level, he now has the task of relating to the teacher as a social object. The child acknowledges the teacher's presence and responds more attentively to verbal interaction. This is only the very early stage of a genuine interpersonal relationship between teacher and child which will be the focus of a later level. At the acceptance level the teacher sets few behavioral limits and usually works on a one-to-one basis with the child. The student competes only with his own record and no grades are given. In addition, academic demands are minimal and the teacher's main goal is to make the child secure and successful in the learning situation. Toward this end a variety of activities such as playing games and taking walks may be utilized.

The child who refuses to get out of his parents' car and come into the classroom may be joined in the back seat by the teacher who initiates contact through reassurance and gradual building of an accepting relationship. At the NPI school, teachers often go on the wards and into the bedrooms of frightened withdrawn children who refuse to get out of bed and come to school. The teacher may sit on the bed next to the child and use a small projector to show him colored slides on the ceiling, or read him stories, or play simple games with him. The teacher who hopes to be successful with children who have serious learning problems and who are threatened by the prospect of further failure should be prepared to settle for the minimal but significant tasks on the acceptance level.

ORDER TASK LEVEL

Once the child feels accepted and is secure enough to form a limited relationship with the teacher, he is ready to be held for order tasks on the next level of the hierarchy. The teacher's task at this level is to increase her control and gradually impose structure, routine, and definite limits in the learning situation. Although academic deficiencies are still completely accepted, the student is now held for more appropriate behavior. He no longer works on his own terms and must accept certain conditions for learning. The work of Cruickshank (1961), Haring and Phillips (1962) suggests that well structured classroom environments facilitate learning among hyperactive and distractible students with learning problems. The concept of order and routine is basic to an effective learning situation for all children but particularly important for children with learning disorders whose erratic patterns of functioning in the classroom have contributed to their failure to learn. At the order level the teacher carefully judges the child's capacity for choice, presents him with small realistically attainable units of work and removes extraneous stimuli which are distracting in an effort to promote maximum gratification and success in the classroom.

At the NPI school, a resistant, nonconforming child who has failed to learn is often brought into the classroom for periods of ten to fifteen minutes a day. During this short period, the child's task is to function at the order level as a "student"—sit at a desk, follow simple directions and routines, and control his behavior. Longer periods are introduced as the student is able to tolerate them. During this time the child may be given certain order tasks to do such as sorting objects on the basis of size and color, puzzle making, or map coloring and labeling.

Recently a seventeen year old boy with a severe physical disability who had never learned to read was provided with an elaborate experiential reading program based solely on his great interest in rockets. The teacher spared no amount of effort in providing the boy with stimulating and interesting material. The boy, however, came to school when he pleased, would only work as long as he wished, and in essence set his own limits in the learning situation. Despite the ingenuity and total dedication of the teacher, the reading program was a complete failure. It was only after a staff conference during which the lack of limits and teacher control in the program were examined that a change was made. The boy was later told that an instructional program in reading was available for him but only at certain specific times. If he wanted to learn to read, he had to participate exactly as the teacher directed; otherwise, he did not have to come to school. The results were surprising. The boy showed up in class regularly and began to learn to read. He worked diligently and functioned on the teacher's terms. While for some students, an experiential or exploratory program, such as the one first tried with this boy, would be successful, it was necessary in this case to engage the student in tasks at the order level before learning could take place. Exploratory educational activities, to be discussed at the next level, are more likely to be successful once the student is functioning on the order-task level.

The task of maintaining order may be over learned by the rigid and obsessive-compulsive child with a learning problem. It will be the teacher's task to direct such a child's energies from, rather than toward, more order and routine. This is another characteristic within all levels of the hierarchy. It is the teacher's task to help students who display extreme behavior to achieve a healthier balance.

EXPLORATORY TASK LEVEL

Exploratory tasks are found on the next level of the hierarchy. Once the teacher and child have formed a beginning working relationship, they may explore the environment together. Now it is the teacher's task to introduce learning by offering the child a rich variety of multisensory experiences. The child's task is to reach out and explore the real world around him with his eyes, ears, hands, nose, and even his taste buds. It is the appeal that exploratory activities have for the child, not their appropriateness for his chronological age or grade level, that is important. The teacher assesses the sense modalities by which the child learns best. Where sensory and perceptual motor problems exist, particular attention is paid to making the child's learning experience as reinforcing as possible. The work of Kephart (1961) and others has stressed the importance of readying a child for more complex educational tasks by special emphasis on the basic perceptual motor components of learning; these are undertaken at the exploratory level. Concrete experiences are utilized as a basis for instruction. The stimulus value and impact of all materials is enhanced and immediate feedback is provided the child following each exploratory experience. Exploratory activities such as music, simple games, imaginative play, story telling and arts and crafts, are often useful in reaching a child who is not ready for academic instruction.

The Fernald (1948) method of kinesthetic word tracing and experiential story writing as a means of teaching remedial reading and spelling is an example of an educational program organized at the exploratory level. The child is given a highly reinforcing means of word learning which provides him with visual, auditory, and kinesthetic cues. In addition he writes a daily story in class about anything of interest to him. This combination approach which reinforces reading and spelling offers an opportunity for expression of personal interest through written expression and is a highly successful approach with children with learning disorders.

An eleven year old catatonic schizophrenic boy in the NPI school was carried to school in a rigidly immobilized state. After several weeks he interacted and cooperated with his teacher for the first time by pushing a lever which turned on a slide projector and exposed a series of colored pictures of prehistoric animal life in front of him. The boy was motivated by a strong personal interest in prehistoric animals. A teacher of sixth grade normal children observed this boy's daily level pushing interaction with the teacher and remarked that it was "interesting" but expressed concern because no regular sixth grade science curriculum in her school included the study of prehistoric life. Needless to say, the concept of a hierarchy of educational tasks and the necessity for establishing a point of contact with such a severely handicapped child was alien to her.

RELATIONSHIP TASK LEVEL

Relationship tasks are found on the next level of the hierarchy. The teacher has the task of increasing her value as a social reinforcer and forming a genuine interpersonal relationship with the child. This implies more than mutual acceptance which was the focus of the acceptance task level, for the interpersonal relationship now becomes an important source of motivation. The child is concerned with gaining the teacher's approval and recognition. The teacher expresses more personal interest in the child and uses social approval and disapproval more freely as a means of motivation and control. It is at this level that the child's peer relationships also are of greater concern to the teacher. Students with similar interests and needs may be paired and more group instruction may be utilized.

Since the child who has failed to learn in school has often been subjected to considerable social devaluation, the tasks at this level are of particular importance. The teacher who sets realistic academic goals for the nonachiever and who helps him achieve success resulting in deserved praise and recognition will be shaping positive academic and social attitudes which may have far-reaching implications. A relationship with an adult who objectively deals with one's shortcomings while communicating respect and acceptance may be highly significant to the child with a learning disorder who has had previous faulty relationships with rejecting parents and unreasonable teachers.

A bright thirteen year old boy in the NPI school who was deficient in all achievement areas, particularly long division, had adopted the position that he was far too intelligent to concern himself with mundane educational matters. He was going to design a computer that would solve all mathematical problems in order to prove his genius. This boy's fear of facing the reality of his educational needs was prompted by achievement-conscious parents who would not settle for anything but an all "A" report card. The teacher devoted almost an entire semester forming a relationship with this boy. The relationship was developed while working on science experiments at the exploratory level. The turning point occurred when the boy completed a simple electrical device with the teacher's help. He found he could diagram and explain its function mathematically. The boy explained to the teacher, "This is the first thing I ever made that worked and that I really understand." From this point on, the boy talked less and less of his grandiose and unrealistic aspirations and began to work on his existing school problems.

The five previously discussed levels are essentially readiness levels for formal academic work. They have been stressed more than will be the remaining two levels because their importance may be overlooked by the teacher who views the child with a learning disorder as primarily in need of remedial academic help. Not until the child has shown the capacity to handle the lower level tasks is he seen as really ready to undertake remedial work solely on the mastery level. While remedial work may be given on any level, the emphasis will not be on academic accomplishment but on more basic educational needs as implied by the hierarchy.

MASTERY TASK LEVEL

When the child is ready to deal with his academic deficiencies and concentrate on basic curriculum, mastery tasks on the next level of the hierarchy are undertaken.

The teacher's task at the mastery level is to help the student acquire essential information and understanding about the environment and to develop the intellectual and vocational skills necessary for social survival. The students learn reading, writing, and arithmetic since these skills are basic for all learning. The emphasis is on practical application of these skills to daily living. Intelligence and achievement testing are important at the mastery level. The teacher carefully assesses a given child's learning potential as well as his specific academic deficits before formulating a program on the mastery level. In addition, the use of progress tests and grading may be introduced.

Since the emotionally handicapped child with a learning disorder may have a marginal if not faulty reality orientation and limited resources for communication and social interaction, mastery skills are vitally important to him. One of the characteristics of emotionally handicapped children is that they often complete tasks on the hierarchy out of sequence. The schizophrenic child may learn to read, spell, and master number concepts while relating to the teacher on the primary level. Despite these academic gains, such a child may make no progress on the acceptance, order, exploratory, and relationship level. In the broadest sense, despite academic progress, the child is still suffering from a serious learning disorder and the teacher's goals should be set accordingly.

ACHIEVEMENT TASK LEVEL

Not a great deal needs to be said about achievement tasks which constitute the highest level on the hierarchy. The child who is consistently self-motivated, achieving up to his intellectual potential, eager for new learning experiences, and socially well-integrated in the classroom, is functioning on the achievement level. All teachers know the joy of working with such children. These are the children who have successfully completed all the tasks described on the lower levels and who are in a position to devote their energies to learning.

DISCUSSION

The staff teachers of the NPI school have found it useful to describe and program all students within the framework of the educational task levels on the hierarchy. The student's observed functioning level is plotted for each task shortly after his enrollment and an educational program is formulated for him. In the charting of these plans, the following considerations are made:

1. The most significant goals will be set on the lowest task levels where the student is either deficient or given to extremes. The chances that a student will be successful at a given task level are greatly increased if he is adequately functioning at all lower levels.
2. The educational program may be best instituted on a task level where the student is functioning reasonably well. This initial level may be above or below the level viewed as most in need of emphasis. Therefore, the schizophrenic overachiever may be reached initially on a purely academic and intellectual level with the more important tasks of the relationship and exploratory levels emphasized as soon as possible.
3. Once contact has been established with a student on a particular level, the teacher attempts to deal with unmet tasks on lower levels, and then to move up the hierarchy as quickly as possible.
4. Several task levels may be worked on concurrently and seldom will a teacher restrict an educational program to only one level. However, lower, unmet task levels will receive greater emphasis.
5. From time to time, students may regress in their functioning at a particular task level necessitating a reassessment of goals and a possible alteration of the educational program.

Table I provides an example of the description and program of Steven, an eleven year old boy who had refused to go to school for more than a year prior to hospitalization. The teacher's initial observations appear in the left column and her suggestions for the educational program in the right column. In the case of Steven, the basic task for teacher and student was set at the acceptance level. The teacher was most concerned with communicating an attitude of acceptance and helping this boy feel secure in the classroom at the expense of higher level tasks. While this was her major concern, the boy was held for some level of functioning with higher tasks.

Most children with learning problems are given tasks at all levels with the possible exception of the primary and achievement levels which are not applicable in the majority of cases. Once establishing contact at the

TABLE I

Hierarchy of Educational Tasks—Student Program

Student: Steven

Description	Program
	Achievement
Not functioning at this level	

Mastery

—Underachieving in all subjects.
—Claims can't do basic addition and subtraction which he has previously demonstrated.
—Will do some silent reading at approximately third grade level but has poor comprehension.

—De-emphasize academic accomplishments particularly in arithmetic and give easy third grade reading.

Relationship

—Becomes very anxious when singled out by the teacher for praise.
—Relates with other students only through provoking them to test classroom limits.

—Maintain distance both physically and interpersonally.
—Respect his preference to be dealt with as member of group.

Exploratory

—Demonstrates few interests.
—Holds back in all activities and claims no interest in anything.
—Has shown some interest in movie projector and how it works.

—Arrange to have science teacher let him experiment with an old projector.
—Start him on a simple electrical project when he seems ready.

Order

—Overcontrolled, rigid in his behavior
—Refuses to have haircut or remove his red jacket in the classroom.

—Arrange seating so he will not be next to volatile class members.
—Encourage some freedom of movement.
—Avoid discussion of jacket or haircut at present.

Acceptance

—Suspicious, guarded in relation to teacher.
—Withdraws when teacher approaches.
—Asks to work in study booth alone.

INITIATE CONTACT HERE
—Permit independent study in booth.
—Give small units of work and request he bring to teacher's desk.
—Approach initially in business-like but friendly manner.
—Attempt to find some simple classroom chore he might do for teacher while other students working.

Primary
Not functioning at this level.

Hierarchy of educational tasks

acceptance level, the teacher carefully weighed the factors of student gratification and her own control and initiated the program as described. Her educational plan was not a static one; it changed from day to day. The teacher increased her control step by step until after a six month period, she had the student functioning effectively on the mastery level. He was able to tolerate interaction with teacher and peers, explore the classroom environment more freely, and display a consistent level of performance in his class work.

It is hoped that this concept of a hierarchy of educational tasks may make psychological principles of development more meaningful to teachers and provide them with a measure of educational economy in understanding and adequately programing for children with learning disorders.

References

Cruickshank, W. *A teaching method for brain injured and hyperactive children.* New York: Syracuse University Press, 1961.

Erickson, E. *Childhood and Society.* New York: W. W. Norton Company, Inc., 1950.

Fernald, G. *Basic techniques in remedial school subjects.* New York: McGraw Hill, Inc., 1948.

Ferster, C., and De Meyer, M. The development of performances in autistic children in automatically controlled environments. *Journal of Chronic Diseases*, 1961, **13**, 312–345.

Haring, N., and Phillips, E. *Educating emotionally disturbed children.* New York: McGraw Hill, Inc., 1962.

Havighurst, R. *Developmental tasks and education.* New York: Longmann-Green and Company, 1952.

Hewett, F. Teaching reading to an autistic boy through operant conditioning. *The Reading Teacher*, 1964, **17**, 613–618.

Isaacs, W., Thomas J., and Goldiamond, I. Application of operant conditioning to reinstating verbal behavior in psychotics. *Journal of Speech and Hearing Disorders*, 1960, **25**, 8–12.

Kephart, N. *The slow learner in the classroom.* Columbus, Ohio: Charles E. Merrill Books, Inc., 1961.

Lindsley, O. Operant conditioning methods applied to research in chronic schizophrenia. *Psychiatric Research Reports*, 1956, **5**, 118–139.

Maslow, A. *Motivation and personality.* New York: Harper and Brothers, 1954.

Munroe, R. *Schools of psychoanalytic thought.* New York: The Dryden Press, Inc., 1955.

Weiland, H., and Rudnick, R. Considerations of the development and treatment of autistic children. In Ruth S. Eissler et al. (Editors), *The psychoanalytic study of the child.* Vol. 16. New York: International Universities Press, 1961.

30. LEARNING PROBLEMS

HOWARD S. ADELMAN

PART I: AN INTERACTIONAL VIEW OF CAUSALITY

In recent years, a great number of children with learning and behavior problems have been grouped under one or more of three labels: *learning disabled* (LD), *emotionally disturbed* (ED), *educationally handicapped* (EH). Despite all that has been written about these three groups, neither the nature nor the implications of the heterogeneity that exists in these populations has been widely discussed in the literature. In particular, little has been written about the likelihood that, in practice, the groups categorized as LD, ED, and EH include not only youngsters who actually have major disorders that interfere with their learning, but also youngsters whose learning and behavioral problems stem primarily from the deficiencies of the learning environment in which they are enrolled. The purpose of this article is (1) to discuss an interactional view of factors that determine school success and failure and (2) to relate this model to the heterogeneity that exists in the LD, ED, and EH populations.

Currently, at least as applied to youngsters in public school programs,

SOURCE. Part I is reprinted from *Academic Therapy*, Volume VI, No. 2, Winter 1970–1971; Part II is reprinted from *Academic Therapy*, Volume VI, No. 3, Spring 1971. By permission of the author and publisher.

the terms *specific learning disabilities, emotionally disturbed,* and *educationally handicapped* have been defined as follows:

The definition formulated by the National Advisory Committee on Handicapped Children identifies children with specific learning disabilities as "those who have a disorder in one or more of the basic psychological processes involved in understanding or in using language (spoken or written), which disorder may manifest itself in an imperfect ability to listen, think, read, write, spell, or do mathematical calculations. These disorders include such conditions as perceptual handicaps, brain injury, minimal brain dysfunction, dyslexia, and developmental aphasia." The number of youngsters who fit this definition has been conservatively estimated as ranging from 1 to 3 percent of the school population, or roughly five-hundred thousand to one million five-hundred thousand students.

While seriously emotionally disturbed children have been defined in a variety of ways, all definitions tend to characterize such children as manifesting moderate to severe maladaptive behaviors with reference to the society in which they live. The components of such definitions usually include references to hyperactivity or withdrawn behavior, emotional lability, oversensitivity to stimuli, short attention span, difficulties in interpersonal relationships, such as tendencies toward fighting and other active or passive-aggressive actions, and underachievement. Such behaviors are seen, of course, as resulting from severe emotional, other than neurological, impairment. The number of youngsters in this category has been estimated, variously, from 0.5 percent to 10 percent of the school-age population.

As described in the California Administrative Code, Title 5, Section 3230, an EH minor ". . . has marked learning or behavior disorders, or both, associated with a neurological handicap or emotional disturbance. This disorder shall not be attributable to mental retardation. The learning or behavior disorders shall be manifest, in part, by specific learning disability. Such learning disabilities may include, but are not limited to, perceptual handicaps, minimal cerebral dysfunction, dyslexia, dyscalculia, dysgraphia, school phobia, hyperkinesis or impulsivity." In California, approximately forty-three thousand children, 8/10ths of 1 percent of the public-school population were enrolled in EH programs in 1969–1970.

At present, the majority of youngsters who come to be diagnosed as LD, ED, or EH have already experienced some degree of failure in their efforts to perform as requested in the classroom. It is well-documented that such failure produces effects that can confound efforts to diagnose, reliably and validly, the cause of the problem. In fact, it may be that such youngsters are so-labeled primarily on the basis of assessment data, which reflect little more than the effects of the school failure. Thus, it seems likely that many youngsters who are diagnosed as LD, ED, or EH are so-labeled on the basis of inferences derived from data that are of questionable "post-dictive" validity.

Despite the lack of reliable and valid etiological data, many professionals have tended to act as if all youngsters who are labeled LD, ED, or EH are handicapped by an internal disorder that has caused the learning or behavioral problem. Unfortunately, this emphasis on the "disordered child" has tended to restrict the range of efforts designed to enhance our knowledge regarding the etiology, diagnosis, remediation, and prevention of school learning and behavioral problems.

There is a viable alternative to this disordered-child model. This alternative view emphasizes the dynamic nature of the process by which school skills are acquired. Thus, the model stresses that a given youngster's success or failure in school is a function of the interaction between his strengths, weaknesses, limitations, and the specific, classroom-situational factors he encounters, including individual differences among teachers and differing approaches to instruction. Stated differently, with specific reference to children who manifest school-learning or behavioral problems, or both, this interactional model suggests that such problems result not only from the characteristics of the *youngster,* but also from the characteristics of the *classroom* situation to which he is assigned.

The Youngster and the Classroom

Throughout the following discussion, there is frequent reference to the characteristics of the youngster and the program in which he is required to perform. Therefore, there is a need to be more explicit as to just which characteristics are of major relevance.

The important characteristics of the youngster are conceptualized as his behaviors, skills, interests, and needs as they are manifested in the school situation. In addition, of course, it is recognized that all youngsters differ from each other in terms of (1) development—in sensory, perceptual, motoric, linguistic, cognitive, social, and emotional areas; (2) motivation—defined in this instance as the degree to which a youngster views a specific classroom activity or task as meaningful, interesting, worth the effort, and attainable through an appropriate amount of effort; and (3) performance—emphasizing rate, style, extent, and quality as the major variables.

The important characteristics of the classroom situation include the personnel, goals, procedures, and materials that are employed in the school's efforts to provide effective and efficient instruction. Of particular relevance for the following discussion, these situational variables are seen as combining differentially to produce classrooms that vary critically in terms of the degree to which the program (1) allows for the wide range of developmental, motivational, and performance differences that exist in every classroom; (2) is compatible (does not conflict) with the fostering of each youngster's desire to learn and perform; and (3) is designed to detect current and potential problem-students and is able to correct, compensate for, or tolerate such deviant youngsters. This dimension may be conceptualized as the degree to which the program is personalized.

(Classrooms that are personalized usually have a wide variety of "centers," which are designed to foster and stimulate interest in learning; the teacher in such a classroom typically emphasizes individualized programs for each youngster, rather than a three-group, basal, text-oriented approach to instruction, and, in general, he attempts to minimize failure experiences, as well as tedious and boring activities.

It is recognized that many professionals do not feel that such personalized programs can be developed in regular-classroom programs that enroll thirty-five to forty students. Because of this factor, it should be noted that my colleagues and I have just completed a project that has successfully trained teachers of culturally disadvantaged youngsters to personalize classroom programs that contain large numbers of children.)

Formal Hypotheses and Implications

The nature of the interaction of the child and program characteristics, then, is seen as the major determinant of school success or failure. The hypothesized relationship between these two sets of characteristics and school success and failure can be stated formally as follows:

The greater the congruity between a youngster's characteristics and the characteristics of the program in which he is required to perform, the greater the likelihood of school success; conversely, the greater the discrepancy between the child's characteristics and the program characteristics, the greater the likelihood of poor school performance.

This hypothesis suggests that there are children whose school difficulties are due primarily to the fact that their classroom programs are not effectively personalized to accommodate individual differences. Therefore, as a corollary, it is hypothesized that the greater the teacher's ability in personalizing instruction, the fewer will be the number of children in her classroom who exhibit learning or behavior problems, or both; conversely, the poorer the teacher's ability in personalizing instruction, the greater will be the number of children with such problems. It is unknown how many of these learning-problem youngsters are diagnosed as LD, ED, or EH at some point in their schooling. However, with the increasing interest in these areas, it seems probable that the number of youngsters assigned to one, or more, of these categories is increasing.

More specifically, it is hypothesized that there are at least three types of youngsters with problems within each category. In addition to (1) youngsters who do have major disorders that predispose them to school difficulties, there are (2) youngsters who do *not* have such internal disorders, but who simply do not function well in nonpersonalized instructional programs, and (3) youngsters who do have minor disorders, but who, under appropriate circumstances, are able to compensate for such disorders in performing and learning school tasks, for example, if the instructional process is approximately motivating.[1] For the purposes of this discussion, the nondisordered children are referred to as Type I learning problems; the children with minor disorders are referred to as Type II learning problems; and the youngsters with major disorders, namely, those with specific learning disabilities and serious emotional disturbances, are referred to as Type III learning problems.

In contrast to this view, the majority of states with public-school programs for the learning disabled and emotionally disturbed, having established two discrete categories, tend to assume implicitly that each group consists of a different and relatively homogeneous population, while a few states, such as California, encompass both LD and ED youngsters under the rubric *educationally handicapped* and tend not to differentiate among youngsters when they are assigned to this label. Figure 1 summarizes three views of the LD, ED, and EH populations. The view being hypothesized here suggests that the majority of such youngsters are Type I and II learning problems and that only a small percentage actually come under the heading of *specific learning disability* or *seriously emotionally disturbed*. In this connection, it may be that a more fruitful use of the label *educationally handicapped* would be to employ this term for Type I and Type II problems and reserve the categories of *specific learning disability* and *seriously emotionally disturbed* for Type III problems.

(The question of what the actual percentages are for these three types of learning problems is an intriguing one. From personal experience, the Type III group appears to be only about 10 to 15 percent of the total group currently labeled LD, ED, or EH; it is recognized, however, that without empirical data, such an estimate is easily challenged.)

In summary, what these hypotheses and inferences suggest is: (1) that the populations currently labeled LD, ED, and EH each consist of

---

[1] The issue of compensatory mechanisms has not been well-studied, but there are many examples of highly motivated individuals who have overcome severe handicaps in their efforts to understand and to communicate with others.

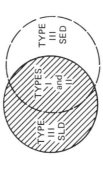

Majority view — Learning Disabled and Emotionally Disturbed students are categorized as separate populations.

Minority view — Learning Disabled and Emotionally Disturbed students are grouped together and categorized as Educationally Handicapped.

Hypothesized view — The Learning Disabled and Emotionally Disturbed populations are seen as overlapping and as consisting of three major subgroups of youngsters with learning problems

Type I   No disorder (problem results primarily from the deficiencies of the learning environment.
Type II   Minor disorder (problem results from deficiencies in both the child and the learning environment).
Type III Major disorder (problem results from the child's deficits and/or disturbance, i.e., a Specific
          Learning Disability — SLD — or Serious Emotional Disturbance — SED.

FIG. 1. *Three views of the learning-disabled, emotionally disturbed, and educationally handicapped populations.*

at least three major subgroups of youngsters with learning or behavioral problems, or both, ranging from those youngsters whose problem seems to stem primarily from the deficiencies of the learning environment to those who actually have major disorders that interfere with school learning or performance, or both; and (2) that there is a significant relationship between teachers' ability to personalize instruction and the type and relative proportion of the problem-youngsters who are likely to be found in these teachers' classrooms. Specifically, it is suggested that the more able the teacher, with reference to personalizing the classroom, the fewer Type I and II learning-problem youngsters will be found in his classroom. This hypothesized relationship is shown in Figure 2.

Type   I — No disorder (problem results primarily from the deficiencies of the
           learning environment).
Type II — Minor disorder (problem results from deficiencies in both the child
           and the learning environment).
Type III — Major disorder (problem results primarily from the child's deficits).

FIG. 2.   *The hypothesized relationship between teachers' ability to personalize the classroom program and the type and relative proportion of learning-problem children in the classroom.*

At this point, then, it is emphasized that, in actual practice, the populations labeled *learning disabled, emotionally disturbed,* and *educationally handicapped* have been, and probably will continue to be for some time, heterogeneous with regard to both etiology and appropriate remedial strategies. This state of affairs, of course, is detrimental to efforts directed at developing a comprehensive and meaningful body of knowledge with regard to such youngsters. Therefore, it seems reasonable to suggest that professionals who are concerned with developing such a body of knowledge need to devote ever-increasing effort to differentiating among the youngsters who are so-labeled.

PART II: A SEQUENTIAL AND HIERARCHICAL
APPROACH TO IDENTIFICATION AND CORRECTION

In the Winter 1970–1971 issue of *Academic Therapy*, I presented the
position that a given youngster's success or failure in school is a function
of the interaction between his strengths, weaknesses, limitations, and the
specific classroom situational factors he encounters. On this basis, it is
hypothesized that the learning-disabled (LD), emotionally disturbed
(ED), and educationally handicapped (EH) populations each consist
of three major subgroups of youngsters with learning or behavioral problems, or both. These subgroups include, at one end of a continuum, those
youngsters who actually have major disorders that interfere with learning (Type III learning problems), and at the other end of the continuum,
those whose problem stems primarily from the deficiencies of the learning environment (Type I learning problems); the third group encompasses those youngsters with minor disorders who, under appropriate
circumstances, are able to compensate for such disorders (Type II learning problems). In this article, a set of sequential and hierarchical teaching strategies, which involve a two-step process by which teachers can
identify and attempt to meet the remedial needs of the youngsters in
each of these three major subgroups, are suggested.

The interactional view of the nature of the heterogeneity that exists
in the LD, ED, and EH populations, which was described in Part I of
this article, has specific implications for classroom efforts that focus on
the diagnosis, remediation, and prevention of school problems. Based on
this view, specific teaching strategies for the diagnosis and remediation
of the three general types of learning problems described above have
been conceptualized and are presented in Figure 1.

Essentially, what is suggested is a two-step sequential process by
which the teacher (1) establishes a personalized learning environment,
and then, if necessary, (2) employs up to three sequential and hierarchical
remedial strategies in a sequence that is predetermined by the success or
failure of each attempted strategy. That is, after the first step has been
initiated, the teacher proceeds to the second step, for those youngsters
who continue to manifest occasional-to-chronic learning difficulty. The
three sequential and hierarchical strategies, which are included for possible use during this second step, represent three different levels of instructional focus. Level A emphasizes maintaining the focus on basic
school subjects. Level B emphasizes instruction of the prerequisites that
are needed before school subjects can be mastered. Level C attempts to
deal with any pathological behaviors or underlying process deficits that
may interfere with school learning.

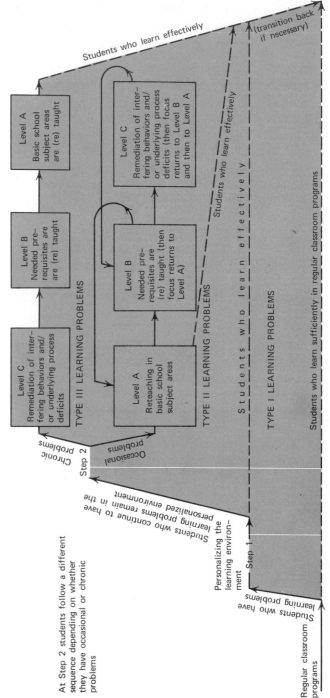

FIG. 1. *Sequential and hierarchical teaching strategies for the remediation of school learning problems.*

374

| | TYPES | | | | | |
| | Awareness and Attitudes | | Behaviors and Skills | | Content and Concepts | |
	Self	Others	Self	Others	Self	Others
L E V E L S — Basic School Subjects						
Prerequisites to School Learning						
Interfering Behaviors and/or Underlying Processes						

FIG. 2. *Levels and types of remedial instructional focus.*

It should be noted that no formal tests are employed to specify the etiology or level of remedial needs; assessment procedures are employed only to determine instructional needs at a particular step and level. In effect, both the youngster's type of learning problem and the level of his remedial needs are identified only after the impact of each teaching strategy becomes apparent. It will also be noted that most LD, ED, and EH teachers already employ these three levels of action in their classrooms; however, these teachers frequently have not conceptualized their procedures as discrete strategies and often employ them in a rather random manner. In contrast, what is being suggested here is that the approaches should be employed systematically, namely, sequentially and hierarchically. As may be seen in Figure 1, the following sequence of events is recommended.

Step 1

Those youngsters in regular-classroom programs who are doing poorly (as reflected by such factors as being assigned D or F grades) are provided with a new learning environment where the program is personalized, namely, where individual differences in development, motivation, and performance are accommodated and fostered and where a greater degree of deviation can be tolerated or compensated for. The establishment of a new environment is accomplished either by altering the regular-classroom program or, if necessary, by removing the youngsters to another classroom. The implementation of Step 1 should be a sufficient remedial strategy for the children who have been referred to above as Type I learning problems. (If Step 1 is successful, it suggests that if the youngster had been in such an environment from the beginning of his schooling, he might not have had difficulties. Therefore, with a view to prevention, such a classroom environment might prove to be a prototype for all regular classroom programs.)

Having established such an environment (Step 1), it should be possible, then, to identify all three types of learning-problem youngsters. Type I youngsters are those who are able to function effectively in the new learning environment; Type II youngsters are those who are able to function effectively in most areas of learning, but who have occasional problems, for example, memorizing such things as the times tables or some vocabulary words; Type III youngsters are those who continue to manifest pervasive learning or behavior problems, or both. Since the first step is sufficient for the Type I youngsters, the next step focuses only on Type II and Type III learning problems.

Step 2

During the second step of the sequence, the teacher may employ up to three teaching strategies. However, the sequence and level of instructional focus of these three strategies differ for Type II and III youngsters. That is, Type II youngsters begin at Level A and Type III youngsters begin at Level C.

When a Type II learning-problem youngster does have difficulty, the teacher must decide whether or not instruction can be delayed in that area, until a later time when learning might prove to be easier. If instruction cannot be delayed, then the next step in the sequential strategy is initiated (Step 2). The emphasis, at first, is on reteaching behaviors, skills, content, and concepts related to basic school subjects (Level A); Level B instruction is initiated only if reteaching does not succeed; and Level C efforts are initiated only if Level B instruction proves to be unfruitful. Thus, it may be seen that the simplest and most direct approaches are employed first and that all three levels of instruction may not be necessary in the remediation of the problem.

More specifically, when the teacher decides that instruction cannot be delayed, his efforts are directed toward reteaching in the area of immediate difficulty (Level A). Such reteaching is not a matter of trying more of the same, for example, more drill. Rather, it requires the implementation of qualitatively different instructional approaches. That is, if a youngster is having difficulty with arithmetic or reading, the teacher attempts procedures that range from simply using a different kind of general explanation, technique, or material (such as another example or analogy or a "concrete" demonstration) to the use of specialized remedial procedures (such as a kinesthetic approach).

If the teacher finds that reteaching in basic school-subject areas (Level A) does not work, then he assesses whether the student lacks a necessary prerequisite and, if he does, the teacher attempts to correct this deficiency (Level B). For example, if a youngster is having difficulty with reading comprehension, the teacher might find that the student has little awareness of underlying concepts, such as the relationship between the spoken and printed word, or the student may be deficient with regard to such basic educational skills as the ability to follow directions, answer questions, and order and sequence events. If the teacher is able to detect and correct such deficiencies, then he is in an improved position with regard to the remediation of the original problem.

However, if this remedial effort proves to be unfruitful, the teacher proceeds to the final strategy in the sequence (Level C), which involves the assessment and remediation of interfering behaviors or underlying process deficits, for example, behavioral, perceptual-motor, or linguistic problems. (There seems to be an unfortunate tendency for some educational, medical, and psychological specialists to begin at this level when working with any child who has been categorized as a school problem.)

It should be noted that when remediation at Level B or C is effective, there is, of course, still a need to return, sequentially, to the higher instructional levels. For example, if a student overcomes his basic problems at Level C, then the teacher is ready to reteach any necessary prerequisites that may not have been assimilated (Level B), and then, in turn, is ready to remedy the learning difficulty that originally set the entire sequence into motion (Level A).

In contrast to the Type II learning problem, the Type III youngster is characterized as manifesting pervasive learning or behavioral difficulties, or both. Thus, after the first step, the sequential strategies begin at Level C. That is, initially, efforts are made to assess and remedy either interfering behaviors or underlying process deficits, or both, and, as some success at this level is achieved, the sequence proceeds so that needed prerequisites and basic school subjects can be acquired. However, even with Type III learning problems, there are likely to be some areas where the disorder is not severely handicapping and where learning can proceed developmentally or, at least, where remediation can be focused more directly and simply on Level B or A. Therefore, it seems probable that these students' can pursue learning at several levels simultaneously. (For purposes of closure, it should be noted that, if necessary, any youngster who has been removed from his regular classroom can be transitioned back when he is once again learning effectively—see Figure 1.)

SPECIALIZED TEACHING TECHNIQUES AND MATERIALS

Thus far, the focus has been on a set of general teaching strategies, which may be employed, systematically, in efforts to remedy and prevent school learning and behavioral problems. Before concluding, it seems appropriate to reflect briefly on the role played by special techniques and materials in correcting the learning problems of Type I, II, and III youngsters. Every LD, ED, and EH teacher, of course, has a grab bag of such specialized approaches, many of which are based on specific theoretical formulations that emphasize such ideas as stimulus bombardment or modality isolation. Since many of these remedial rationales are based on theories that view learning problems as stemming from disorders residing within the youngster, such techniques and materials *and* their rationales may prove to be valid for youngsters in the Type III category and for some in Type II.

However, with reference to Type I and many Type II learning problems, the position taken in this article has been that the *disordered-child* view is inappropriate. Nevertheless, such specialized techniques and materials can play an important role in the programs of such youngsters. Specifically, a variety of alternative approaches allows the teacher to use, and the student to find, learning activities that not only are appropriate for the youngster's strengths, weaknesses, and limitations, but that are novel and exciting and have not become aversive—activities that facilitate, simultaneously, an increase in approach and a decrease in avoidance tendencies on the part of the student (and the teacher). For such youngsters, then, the impact of a particular technique and material is not seen as being dependent on the validity of the procedure's underlying rationale; rather, its effectiveness is viewed as being dependent on how successful the approach is in helping the teacher to maintain a student's attention and interest and, in general, to facilitate learning.

In conclusion, then, it is emphasized that the heterogeneity that exists in the LD, ED, and EH populations has specific implications for classroom practices. The procedures proposed here have been based on a set of hypotheses with regard to the nature of this heterogeneity, and it is felt that as these procedures are subjected to empirical investigation, we will be in a better position to understand the nature and scope of the problem with which we are confronted.

31. TEACHER-PUPIL ANALYSIS OF THE LEARNING PROCESS: LEARNING HOW BY KNOWING WHY

VIRGINIA L. BROWN

Special education stresses the availability of a variety of methodologies and materials for children who do not achieve in a regular educational setting. This emphasis is accompanied by the assumption that special class teachers will individualize instruction for these children by matching instructional procedures and materials to each child's learning characteristics. Special class teachers who attempt to meet this standard, however, are usually confronted with an instructional dilemma. The amount of time required by the task is rarely available to them, even if they have a thorough knowledge of all the factors.

The unrealistic demand which this approach makes on teachers is further compounded by a widespread misunderstanding that individualized instruction occurs only when a child is seated at an individual place with an infinitely replenishable supply of instructional materials and receives a great deal of individual instruction from the teacher.

Most current views regarding the best way to design and conduct individualized instruction tend to identify the teacher as the basic resource. It is the teacher who must analyze the learning process and engineer and execute a plan for learning. In short, current views appear to

SOURCE. Reprinted from *Teaching Exceptional Children*, 1969, 106–111. By permission of the author and publisher.

suggest that a special class teacher is expected to assume the role of classroom Guru.

Instructional technology may one day provide a definitive matching of method, material, and child. At present, however, most special class teachers, confronted with the limitations of time and resources, either do not attempt to individualize instruction or do so on a hit or miss basis. The few teachers who do provide effective individualized instruction often do so at a personal cost which goes beyond what might be considered reasonable.

AN ALTERNATIVE APPROACH

An alternative to traditional individualized instruction actively and systematically involves children in the analysis and formulation of the diagnostic-treatment process so that the teacher-Guru becomes the teacher-Guide. The Guide model was initiated at Peabody College as a part of Project Re-Ed in Nashville, Tennessee, as an attempt to modify the academic program for a special class of preteen boys categorized as behavior disordered. The Guide model is currently being extended in several programs for academically retarded and for educable mentally retarded children.

The rational for the Guide model may be as simple as, "letting children in on the teacher's secrets" or as sophisticated as an extension of what has been discussed as "Conveying Information About Expected Performance," (Gagne, 1965, p. 221).

An analysis of the procedures currently being utilized in the Guide model reveals five general stages. These stages involve the identification of instructional objectives by the teacher and guidance of the children in their analysis of, (a) the skills or facts they must learn, (b) ways to evaluate and record their progress, and (c) alternative learning strategies. Each stage receives elaboration according to the skill, creativity, and initiative of the instructional personnel who use the Guide model.

Stage One—Precise Teacher Identification of Instructional Objectives

This stage is deceptively simple. It involves the teacher's honest appraisal of the goals to be achieved by performing a particular task or during a specified period of time. Examples include:

1. Completing correctly an assigned page of a workbook.
2. Writing correctly each word the teacher calls on Friday at 10 a.m.
3. Finishing an assigned art project within a 25 minute block of time.
4. Copying correctly material from the chalkboard.
5. Oral reading of an assigned passage when called upon.

6. Playing for 20 minutes without fighting.
7. Reading from pages 79 to 89.

At this time, there should be no evaluation of the appropriateness of the activities assigned. The purpose at this stage of the process is to obtain a description of the teacher's expectation for the assignments given. In describing objectives, the use of general statements such as "to work on phonic analysis skills" should be avoided. A more specific description of the same objective would be, "to write in the correct beginning consonant blend for eight different word parts."

Descriptions of objectives should include the exact number of items to be completed during an assigned activity, and/or the exact amount of time allotted for the activity. The basis and utility of this stage of the process is clearly and simply delineated by Mager (1962).

Stage Two—Pupil Analysis of the Objectives of the Lesson or Activity

Group or individual discussion offers an opportunity to develop this stage of the procedure. The children are encouraged to ask such questions as:

1. What will the finished task look like?
2. What new information or process is being learned?
3. Does the teacher expect mastery, or are errors permitted?
4. Why is this a necessary step in learning to read, spell, etc.? (This question should be the focus at the remaining stages.)

In analyzing the requirements of a task, it frequently becomes necessary to separate expected behaviors which are skill oriented from those behaviors which might be called Teacher Pleasing Behaviors (TPB). In most instructional environments, pupils, whether in kindergarten or in graduate school, must rely on their intuition, or their ability to "psych out" the teacher, to identify the TPBs expected of them.

Some TPBs, such as, "working quietly when the teacher is occupied with another child or group," contribute to the orderly operation of the class. Others, such as, "having your name and the date written in the top right corner of all papers," are idiosyncratic to the teacher. Interestingly enough, once there is agreement between children and teacher about the identification of such behaviors, and a demonstration that not all expected behaviors are TPBs, the formerly reluctant worker cheerfully (or condescendingly) plays the teacher's game.

Stage Three—Discussion of the Evaluation Process

Evaluation should be distinguished from grading. A grade is an arbitrary value assigned by the teacher. Evaluation is a process which should involve self-improvement in performance. A graded paper is usually a forgotten paper. An evaluated paper is one which allows for correction by the learner. This means that answers should be available at the appropriate time for the child to review. Some teachers duplicate answers; others use master pages placed in a location convenient for the children. The emphasis is placed on learning rather than on "getting caught in a mistake."

An analysis of errors helps the child determine what else he needs to know, or be able to do, in order to attain the criterion performance. Most youngsters become adept at placing errors into several categories.

Carelessness. This type of error frequently accompanies work which, for a variety of reasons, is unchallenging. One source of boredom, for the older youngster in particular, is the low interest value of materials that are geared to their academic level and not to their interest level. Newer materials such as the *Reading Incentive Series: For the Reluctant Reader* (Summers, 1968) emphasizes provocative content at a readable level rather than word analysis drill. Hagaman, in a discussion of content interest in mathematics, a relatively unexplored field, also emphasizes the importance of interest level. Hopefully, both of these programs will receive more systematic attention in pre-service and in-service teacher education programs.

Another problem which contributes to the lack of challenge is the underestimation of the level of difficulty. Unless a program has been individually written for him, the child who can always get the right answers (although he doesn't always write the right answers!) is probably working at a level of difficulty which is too low.

A third source of boredom arises out of constant repetition of the same kind of task. Even adults tire of filling in blanks or of copying sentences verbatim. A task with a meaningless incentive will prove unstimulating to the child. Grades, for example, are of better consequence for some children than for others.

Incomplete Understanding of Expected Performance. The language of written and/or verbal directions may present difficulties to some children. Also, students may not actually be aware of all the requirements they were expected to fulfill. This source of errors can be greatly reduced by simplifying instructions and by encouraging children to ask for further clarification if they are uncertain of the task requirements.

Failure to Master Some Component Skill or Information. Identification of this source of error requires that pupils and teacher do a task analysis of the assignment. For example, the teacher and children might independently list all the possible ways in which this problem might be completed: $23 \overline{)349}$. They would then list every possible error point. (Was copying the example included?!) There should follow an interesting discussion of the different ways to approach the problem.

Another example of task analysis may be found in the area of handwriting. Poor performance is generally due to insufficiently monitored instruction in the exact mechanics of letter formation. In cursive writing, the connecting strokes are especially troublesome, yet their formation seldom receives supervised attention.

Overestimation of the Functional Level. Whether in terms of interest, difficulty, or cognitive level, children who are constantly faced with assignments which they are not capable of completing will make errors. At the cognitive level, for example, drawing inferences from the story read is much more difficult than finding "exactly what John said."

Inappropriate Time Requirement. Rates of performance are one aspect of individual differences. If a time requirement for task completion has been overestimated, children may have time for misbehavior or they may attempt a variety of tasks and overlook the accurate completion of the task at hand. If the specified time requirement has been underestimated, the child's slow working pattern may be misinterpreted as slow learning.

Stage Four—Presentation of Alternative Learning Strategies

At this stage, the children are encouraged by the teacher to explore new methods and materials, some of which are made accessible only by the teacher. As much attention is given to the process of learning as to the content. One boy immediately perceived that a new girl in class was having difficulty with a spelling assignment. When the boy asked how the newcomer studied, she replied, "I just keep spelling the words under my breath until I get them right." The boy taught the newcomer a visualization method and said, "If that isn't right for you, just let me know. We got lots more ways to learn how to spell the words."

The presentation of alternative strategies may be accomplished in one or more ways: (a) systematically introducing new techniques to the whole class; (b) teaching each child a different technique, and then letting the youngsters teach each other; (c) giving a child access to teacher's editions; and (d) letting the children suggest better strategies.

It is at this point that "knowing why" becomes an important aspect of "learning how." Discussion with children about methodology and content often encourages the teacher to question why some materials are used, or why some skills are so carefully taught. Many youngsters spend more time learning the rules of reading than actually engaging in reading behavior.

The consideration of individual preferences for the use of one method or material over another is possible when alternatives are available to the child.

Stage Five—Instruction Regarding Ways to Collect Data About One's Own Performance

The only requirement at this stage is that the student and the teacher agree on the goals of the instructional program, and that the child be able to show convincing data regarding his progress.

Various methods of data collection have been invented by children and teachers. The use of graphs, running accounts, stop watches, time clocks, marks on paper, etc., depends upon the resources available as well as on the functional level of the children involved.

BENEFITS OF USING THE GUIDE MODEL

What has been described is a straightforward technique of applicable research by the individuals most concerned with learning—the children themselves. The teacher-Guide model is a strategy which encourages individual modifications of the techniques used.

Certain side effects likely to occur as a result of the initiation of such a program are:

1. Both children and teachers become more skilled in sorting out those aspects of curriculum which are relevant/non-relevant to the attainment of specified objectives.
2. Objectives are clarified. An especially interesting phenomenon has been the consistent emergence of the dichotomy between learning process and performance goals, and Teacher Pleasing Behaviors.
3. Children and teachers have noticed improvement in the ability to identify potential instructional problems in novel situations, as in the classrooms of other children.
4. Failure behavior is quickly eliminated as red pencils become obsolete.
5. The use of time undergoes a change. One pupil engaged in the program asked to be excused from doing the daily spelling assignments if she could perform accurately on the Friday spelling test. This request was based on her desire to work on another project. Given permission to do so, she set about quite accurately analyzing the next five pages of her reading workbook. Upon completion of the task, she had identified several workbook exercises which appeared to have no meaningful relation to learning to read. After reviewing her conclusions with the teacher, the teacher began to have the child spend more time on the application of skills than on the completion of workbook exercises.

Teachers Interested in Using the Guide Model

Just as children tend to demonstrate clear preferences regarding methods and materials of learning, so do teachers. Undoubtedly, some teachers may prefer a more traditional approach to individualize instruction than that afforded by the Guide model. Teachers interested in attempting a departure, however, particularly if they fall into the following categories, may find the venture worthwhile: teachers who are uncertain as to what is best for every child; teachers who are willing to innovate new programs or change programs dictated by a textbook or a supervisor; teachers who do not enjoy being classroom Gurus; and teachers who possess a good sense of humor!

Readers interested in trying any of all aspects of the strategy described are requested to share their experiences with the author.

References

Gagne, R. M. *The conditions of learning.* New York: Holt, Rinehart, and Winston, 1965.

Hagaman, A. P. Word problems in elementary mathematics. *Arithmetic Teacher,* 1964, *11,* 10–11.

Mager, R. F. *Preparing instructional objectives.* Palo Alto: Fearon Press, 1962.

Summers, E. G. (Ed.) *Reading incentive series.* St. Louis: Webster Division, McGraw-Hill, 1968.

32. A PROPOSED MODEL FOR SELECTING, MODIFYING, OR DEVELOPING INSTRUCTIONAL MATERIALS FOR HANDICAPPED CHILDREN

E. EUGENE ENSMINGER

LEARNING DISABILITIES AND INSTRUCTIONAL MATERIALS

Although the decade of the sixties was marked with many significant achievements in the education of handicapped children, two of these achievements in particular will rank near the top of any listing of outstanding accomplishments. One of them was the heavy emphasis upon the development of instructional materials for the handicapped. The other was the renewed effort to develop diagnostic assessment devices with the purpose of prescribing appropriate educational experiences for the child.

Both of these movements have had a common educational objective, i.e. to provide the child who has a specific learning problem an appropriate and successful learning experience. However, a common rationale has not guided the development of diagnostic devices and the development of instructional materials. When instructional material and diagnostic development have occurred simultaneously, it has been within a limited range of educational experience needed by particular children who have specific learning deficits (Frostig et al., 1961; Frostig & Horne,

SOURCE. Reprinted from *Focus on Exceptional Children*, 1970, 1, 1–9. By permission of the author and publisher.

1964, Karnes, 1969). Even though a common rationale has not guided the overall development of diagnostic tests and instructional materials, most of these devices would appear to have their place in an educational program for a child experiencing learning difficulties if a common procedure were established in analyzing both types of information. Without a common procedure the classroom teacher currently finds it difficult to determine what materials to use based on diagnostic information to decide if materials are at all complimentary to one another. The teacher discovers many theoretical positions presented for teaching children with specific learning disabilities. (Cruickshank et al., 1961; Ebersole, Kephart and Ebersole, 1968; Johnson and Mykelbust, 1967; Kephart, 1960; Peterson, 1967) and many instructional materials for remedial teaching, but no logical system for combining the theories and the materials. The purpose of this article is to propose a system for teachers to use in analyzing instructional materials as well as for modification or development of materials for use with children possessing specific learning strengths and weaknesses.

Instructional Materials for the Handicapped

Perhaps the greatest single contribution to the instructional materials movement was the establishment of the Instructional Materials Center Network for Handicapped Children and Youth (Olshin, 1968). The Regional Special Education Instructional Materials Centers making up the IMC Network have had the effect of making materials available at the local level through the development of local IMC's.

While instructional materials are more readily available to the teacher today than they were a decade ago, the availability of materials for use with children still leaves much to be desired. In addition to availability, or *where* to locate materials, is the question of *what* materials to use for specific children. In other words, what rationale is to guide the teacher in selecting materials most appropriate for the learning characteristics of the child? It would seem that if a rationale for selection of materials were available, then the same rationale could be used for modifying materials, developing new materials, evaluating materials, and providing a diagnostic model as well.

Diagnostic Evaluation of the Learner

The second significant contribution of the 1960's to the education of handicapped children has been the renewed emphasis upon diagnostic testing as opposed to the previous use of tests to provide classificatory information (Kirk and McCarthy, 1961). This approach has emphasized the ferreting out of specific learning characteristics of the learner with the goal of prescribing educational activities to match the particular characteristics of the child. Although each diagnostic test has been developed upon a theoretical model (e.g., Frostig, 1961; Kirk, McCarthy and Kirk, 1969; Roach and Kephart, 1966) and each emphasized certain learning experiences related to educational achievement, none of the models is all-inclusive. Thus none of the models provides for adequate assessment for the entire range of learning characteristics of the child for subsequent educational programming. It should be emphasized that many of the diagnostic models have overlapping components, but they tend to look at only a narrow band of learning behavior. Thus, in order to adequately survey the learning behaviors of each individual child, many diagnostic instruments must be employed.

Many approaches to the analysis of test results have been proposed, and recommendations made regarding subsequent educational treatment. Some have followed the deficit approach in which the primary educational prescription is for purposes of increasing the efficiency of the child in the identified deficit area (Kirk and Bateman, 1962; Olson, Hahn and Herman, 1965; Kirk, 1966). This procedure provides for improving the educational deficit but does not give the teacher information on what to do for the child in other areas of instruction. The approach has generally treated the learner in a very fragmentary way, and the performance of the child in other learning areas receives less emphasis in planning the total educational program. Still other approaches have proposed that diagnostic tests should look not only at the deficits of the learner but also at his strengths (e.g., McCarthy, 1967). This technique utilizes all diagnostic information for prescribing a more complete educational program for the learning disability child but still doesn't tell the teacher what to do.

More specific procedures have been proposed which analyze each individual response made by the child as opposed to item classification deficit procedures (i.e., auditory decoding) for determining the starting point for remedial instruction. In some instances this approach to the analysis of a child's performance has utilized the subtest analysis technique in combination with classroom observation of the child's learning behavior. In the subtest analysis procedure, each subtest is reviewed and the child's response deficits are specified. Educational programming is then planned around the specific deficits identified by the analysis. When classroom observation is employed, the diagnostician can observe the child performing educational tasks and determine how the identified deficits found in subtest analysis correspond to classroom performance. The classroom observation approach uses the educational tasks provided by the curriculum as the diagnostic base. Subsequent educational programming is designed around the deficits the child demonstrates in a non-standardized educational setting (the classroom). This latter approach would appear to be one of the most practical techniques if a school system is fortunate to have enough educational specialists with an understanding of curricula and educational objectives as well as sufficient time for observation. Basing educational programming upon the child's response to educational tasks has the distinct characteristic of being more specific to the learning task and allowing the instructional program to teach those skills the child has not accomplished.

The task analysis procedure (observation of child when performing educational tasks) is a valuable procedure, but most teachers have difficulty in analyzing the various components of a task. In addition, no systematic procedure for determining the adjustment of the educational program for a particular child is available from one source to guide the teacher in this endeavor. A procedure for assisting the teacher in analyzing and prescribing for a specific learning situation is the modality approach (L'Abate, 1969; Wepman, 1967). The modality procedure considers both the stimulus presented to the child and the response made by the child. This approach is an input-output model (L'Abate, 1969) which emphasizes the visual and auditory inputs and the motor and verbal outputs. By describing the complexity of the stimulus and the response, the educational task can be modified to match the level of the learner on either end of this learning paradigm.

Genesis of the Modality Approach

Modality learning is based upon communication theory and has been applied to human learning through models proposed by Osgood (1957) and Wepman (1960). The educational application of these models can be found in the development of the Illinois Test of Psycholinguistic Abilities (McCarthy and Kirk, 1961). The Illinois Test of Psycholinguistic Abilities (ITPA) was first published in its experimental edition in 1961. This instrument was developed and published with the expressed intent of providing a diagnostic device that would stimulate remediation programs based on the diagnosis. Instead of classifying children, as was the practice with most earlier assessment devices, the emphasis was on identifying basic learning deficits with the goal of planning an educational program for remediation of the deficit. The 1961 experimental edition of the ITPA as well as the 1968 Revised Edition (Kirk, McCarthy and Kirk, 1969) categorized language along three dimensions. Language ability is viewed as being of two levels of organization (meaningful and non-meaningful language), three processes of assimilation (reception, association, and expression) and two channels of communication (auditory-verbal and visual-motor).

Channels of communication then refer to the manner in which a child receives sensory information and how he responds to that information. In the ITPA model, only two combinations of input-output were included. These two channels are the most common avenues of communication exchange, i.e. a child hears and then he speaks or a child sees and then he grasps, points, gestures, etc. Other combinations of input-output are possible as well as multiple input-output combinations, i.e. visual input and verbal-motor output. Wepman (1967) has referred to those channels as modalities or pathways of learning and has indicated that children are of certain learning types and thus they prefer certain input-output modalities for learning.

Current practice in many educational programs for children with learning disabilities is to prescribe remediation based on the child's strength or weakness in one of the learning channels. For example, if the child's strength is in the auditory-verbal channel the recommended approach to teaching reading is generally a phonetic-or linguistic-based approach. On the other hand, if a child has a basic strength in the visual-motor channel his visual strength is emphasized through the use of a whole word or sight word approach in teaching the child to read. As can be noted, however, the input modalities are of main consideration in the above examples rather than the output modalities. Although empirical evidence supporting such an approach to instruction is scarce, some evidence has been accumulated by L'Abate (1969) indicating support for the input-output approach as a diagnostic technique. The most important feature of the input-output procedure for instruction is that it requires the person doing the instructing to analyze the learning task in addition to the evaluation of the child.

A Model for Selecting Materials

With the great abundance of commercially prepared instructional materials currently available for the remediation of specific learning problems of children, it is indeed a difficult task for the teacher to determine what materials are most appropriate for a specific disability. In addition, producers of materials often advertise specific materials as being the solution to all of a child's problems when in fact they may be appropriate only for a certain level of development through which the child has already passed. Thus the absence of a clearly defined sequence for selecting instructional materials provides for more uncertainty because the teacher is left without a system for determining what instructional materials either precede, compliment, or follow any other instructional material. In addition, the teacher is left without a rationale for modification or development of materials when they are inappropriate for a child's level of functioning. This dilemma has provided for discontinuity in the educational programs for children with learning disabilities, and the absence of a comprehensible programming model for the teacher has lead to the perpetuation of a fractionated educational program.

Learning Stages

The Instructional Model presented in Figure 1 suggests a conceptual framework for evaluating the instructional experiences necessary for

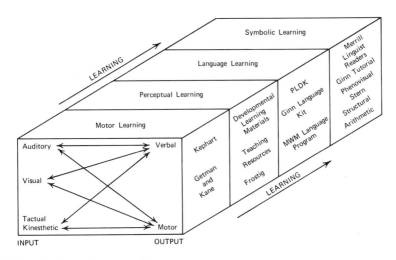

FIG. 1. *An instructional model.*

children to ultimately perform successfully in academic areas. This model suggests that two basic components must guide the teacher in planning a sequential program. First, the development stages of learning must be considered, with early learning being primarily of a motor nature while later learning is primarily symbolic. The four learning areas presented in this model are certainly not discrete since each level can be broken down into smaller stages. Each stage of development is also dependent upon experiences at a previous level or levels.

The Motor Learning stage in the suggested instructional model incorporates the gross-motor stage, the motor-perceptual stage, and the perceptual-motor stage described by Ebersole, Kephart and Ebersole (1968). Initial experiences of the child involve motor learning. Roach and Kephart's (1966) perceptual motor theory has emphasized the importance of early motor learning for the subsequent development of more complex learning. Basic to this theory are the early interactions of the child with his environment. These early interactions are largely of a gross-motor nature. Through motor exploration the child comes in contact with objects within his environment, and after repeated contacts he begins to gather basic perceptual information. This basic perceptual information is gathered through touching, handling and manipulating of objects in the child's immediate surroundings, and gross-motor responses provide perceptual information. The child progresses from the gross-motor stage to the motor-perceptual stage. As the child begins to depend on perceptual information for motor responding, the child progresses to the perceptual-motor stage. These early motor learnings will eventually allow the child to gain information perceptually without extensive motor experiences.

In addition to the perceptual information being associated with the tactual and kinesthetic experiences during the motor learning stage, the child establishes a common reference point for later interpretation of perceptual information. Through motor contact with objects in the environment the child establishes an internal awareness of his own body with respect to environmental information. This early information is accumulated through repeated motor movements and the tactual-kinesthetic stimuli received (feedback) through motoric exploration. The information input to the child in the early stages is essentially tactual and kinesthetic and the output is primarily of a gross motor nature. As perceptual information becomes meaningful, the motor responses of the child are controlled by his visual and auditory perceptions. When perceptual information leads to the same information as that received from motor exploration, the child has achieved the "perceptual-motor match" (Ebersole, Kephart and Ebersole, 1968).

Children with learning disabilities at the Motor Learning Stage may still need to gain basic perceptual information by additional motor exploration. Programs for training gross-motor and perceptual-motor skills have been published by Kephart (1960) in his book *The Slow Learner in the Classroom* and by Getman and Kane (1964, 1968). These programs emphasize the importance of the child gaining control of his own body in moving within his environment. As he gains control of his own body movements the child establishes a relationship to other objects with respect to orientation of his own body as well as time and space. Unless the child has achieved these basic learnings he will experience difficulties in tasks that are primarily of a perceptual nature.

The basic rudiments of perceptual learning occur in combination with motor learning. In many instances children first demonstrate their disabilities in school when a response must be made to perceptual information. Paper and pencil activities may be totally inappropriate, and the child may need to begin with activities involving large muscle action and real or replicas of objects, i.e. stacking large blocks (6" x 6" x 10") to match another stack of large blocks provided as a model. As the child becomes proficient at this task the model stack could be associated with a line drawing of the stack of blocks and the child would then stack the blocks to match the model stack and the line drawing. The next phase would be to remove the model stack of blocks so that the child could stack the blocks from the line drawing only. This procedure allows for Motor Learning while permitting the teacher to allow the response to remain constant as he modifies sequentially the complexity of the visual information. While the child is able to be successful at the motor level, the instructional program can take advantage of this strength and provide training in the visual perceptual area.

Chalkboard activities (Kephart, 1969) also permit the child to use large muscle activities for responding by tracing, copying or following stencils. Activities of this type refine the motor coordination skills while at the same time the perceptual skills are being sharpened.

The Perceptual Stage of the instructional model then continues from the simple to the complex with many of the more refined perceptual activities occurring at the child's desk. Perceptual training programs have been developed by Strauss and Lehtenin (1947), Cruickshank et al. (1961) and Peterson (1967) for using stencils, pegboards, cubes and parquetry blocks as the instructional media. An entire series of stencils, cubes and cube patterns, parquetry blocks and parquetry patterns have been produced and published by Developmental Learning Materials (1967). Materials for instruction at this stage are also available from Teaching Resources (Cheves, 1967; Dubnoff et al., 1968; Hatton et al., 1967). These provide perceptual training activities requiring finer perceptual skills as well as finer motor coordination skills while still permitting the child to manipulate objects for improving his perceptual skills.

When the child is successful at this level of perceptual learning, paper and pencil activities can be initiated using stencils of forms, tracing patterns, copying forms or reproducing simple forms from memory. As perceptual-motor skills are refined, the child can be presented materials like those developed by Frostig and Horne (1964). These materials provide training in eye-hand coordination, form constancy, position in space, figure-ground, and spatial relationships. When the child experiences difficulties with any of these tasks, the teacher can replicate these activities so that motor learning can occur. In other words the task can be made more concrete so that the child can motorically experience the activity by walking around the pattern traced on the floor or chalkboard.

Also occurring at the Perceptual Learning Stage is the acquisition of auditory skills. Auditory perceptual learning has received far too little attention in the form of commercially prepared materials. Auditory skills are of tremendous value when symbolic learning is introduced into an educational program. Reading is primarily the operation of transforming visual symbols into auditory symbols. The task of recognizing and discriminating sounds should be introduced into the educational program in a very consistent and systematic way in the child's early school experiences, if not before. Materials for auditory perceptual learning can be acquired from the Canadian Association for Children with Learning Disabilities in Toronto. The Knowledge Aids Division of the Radiant Corporation has recently published *Follow through with Sounds* that presents indoor and outdoor sounds. These sounds are on tape or records and pictures of indoor-outdoor scenes accompany the auditory materials. In almost all instances auditory skills can be simultaneously developed while training visual auditory perceptual skills. However, the educational program should provide training that emphasizes the acquisition of auditory perceptual skills. Many of the language development programs described below also provide experiences for auditory perceptual learning.

The Language Learning level of the instructional model suggests experiences that build upon motor learning and perceptual learning as well as to occur concurrently with the development of motor and perceptual skills. It could be argued that all learning, including the motor skills, is basically the acquisition of a language system. In all instances the child is learning to communicate with his environment, thus all learning is language learning only at different levels of stimulus and response complexity. Language development programs have essentially emphasized the production of Verbal Language. These programs stimulate language development through developing vocabulary, describing items, following directions, memory of visual and auditory sequences, classification of objects and words, listening, and productive thinking. Language learning is crucial to later success in symbolic learning and to the entire thinking process. It has been suggested that verbal learning controls behavior (Luria, 1961) and it has been demonstrated that children verbalizing while solving arithmetic problems improve their performance (Lovitt and Curtiss, 1968). These findings have implications for motor and perceptual learning, and suggest that they would be more efficient if the child described verbally what he does.

Commercial materials available for stimulating language development include the *Peabody Language Development Programs* (Dunn and Smith, 1965, 1966, 1967; Dunn, Horton and Smith, 1968). *The Ginn Language Kit* A (1965) and the *MWM Program for the Remediation of Language Learning Disabilities*, 1970. The *Peabody Language Development Programs* come in four different kits encompassing language development activities from pre-school through about third grade. Each kit treats the development of language from a global point of view and enough daily lessons are included in each kit to provide an academic year program. The MWM Program is a sequence of language activities based on the *Illinois Test of Psycholinguistic Abilities, Revised Edition*. The specific purpose of this program is to provide remediation activities for deficits shown on the ITPA although the authors emphasize that it is a development program as well as remedial program. Other language programs also have been developed using the ITPA as the model for developing activities (Karnes, 1969).

The fourth stage of the suggested instructional model is concerned with Symbolic Learning. Basic to successful symbolic learning are the learnings which occur at the motor, perceptual, and language levels described above. The symbolic learnings encompass those activities that are commonly thought of as academic. At this level, language symbols are acquired in the areas of reading, writing, spelling, and arithmetic. Many different reading programs are available and each is dependent upon the particular modality strengths of the child. The learning characteristics of the child must be considered when selecting a particular reading program. Reading programs that would appear to have merit in teaching the child with a symbolic learning disability are: The *Ginn Tutorial reading program* (Ellson et al., 1968) the *Sullivan reading program* (Sullivan & Buchanan, 1963), the *Merrill Linguistic Readers* (Fries et al., 1966), the *Phono-Visual Method* (Schoolfield & Timberlake, 1967), and the *Experience Approach to Teaching Reading* (Allen & Allen, 1966). An exemplary arithmetic program would be the *Structural Arithmetic Program* (Stern et al., 1952) which comes in three kits along with cubes, counting frames, and other concrete perceptual aids. The Science Research Associates (GCMP) arithmetic program (Thoburn & McCraith, 1962) with its accompanying drill tapes and overhead transparencies is also useful. The particular program used for a child with a learning disability should always be guided by the input-output dimensions described below.

Input-Output Systems

The second component of the suggested instructional model is the input-output systems of receiving and expressing information at any one of the developmental stages. The arrows on each of the various input-output combinations represent not only the fact that information is received and responded to but that feedback is received from the response which confirms or negates the accuracy of the information received. The input-output dimensions of the instructional model presented in Figure 1 highlights the importance of analyzing instructional materials with regard to the manner in which stimuli are presented and the responses expected from the child. Any combination of input and output is possible as well as any combination of inputs and outputs. Through this approach to analysis of instructional materials, the input-output dimensions of materials can be matched to the input-output dimensions of the learner. Although the ideal is for all modalities to be efficient in the process of learning, some children are found to have difficulties in processing information adequately through certain modalities. For these children, other sense modalities and response modalities may need to be used for instruction so their educational experiences can be successfully rewarding.

The implication of the input-output technique is that when children are having difficulties in responding to auditory stimuli it may be necessary to provide visual or tactual information to assist the child in making a response. On the other hand the child may be able to understand the stimuli but is unable to make the response expected of him. In this case, the type of response the child is to make may need to be altered. Using the example above, the child may be able to understand the auditory stimuli but unable to make the expected verbal response. By permitting a multiple-choice verbal response provided by the teacher, the child might be able to successfully complete the task. On the other hand, the child might be allowed to make a motor response by pointing to a picture which demonstrates that he understands the auditory stimulus. The child's successful responding with a motor response may not be the desired one but it does indicate that he understands. The teaching tasks then must be directed toward sequential training the verbal response system. The input-output technique then isolates the learning difficulty and allows for specific programming based on either an input or output dysfunction rather than the combination which can lead to confusion for the teacher and the child.

A final consideration to be made regarding the input-output component of the instructional model is the complexity of the input or output. Examples of types of input and output are presented in Table I. These are not considered to be inclusive but are presented here as examples of how the stimulus or response can be increased in complexity through the various modalities. To demonstrate how the stimulus complexity can

TABLE I

An Example of Input-Output Hierarchies

INPUT	
Auditory	Visual
1. Gross Sounds	1. Real Object
2. Speech Sounds	2. Replica or Model
3. Single Words	3. Photograph
4. Multiple Words	4. Line drawing
5. Single Directions	5. Abstract picture
6. Multiple Directions	6. Picture (missing parts)
	7. Symbols

OUTPUT	
Verbal	Motor
1. Yes or No	1. Walk toward
2. Labeling	2. Point
3. Phrase	3. Pantomime
4. Sentence	4. Trace
5. Sequence of Labels	5. Copy
6. Sequence of Ideas	6. Match objects
	7. Multiple Choice (2 or 3 item)
	8. Complete
	9. Order (series of letters)
	10. Write from recall

be utilized for programming, assume the child has been given three directions to follow and he is to respond by performing the tasks specified in the directions, i.e. pick up a book, close the door, and then stand on a chair. The child can do each of these tasks individually but he cannot remember all three when given as a multiple direction. The auditory input is too complex and thus the number of auditory directions will need to be reduced. The teaching task now demands the sequential development of a program to improve the number of auditory directions that can be given with subsequent successful execution by the child. The other input and output modalities can be modified in a similar manner. The input-output component of the instructional model adds a dimension of flexibility to any instructional material by providing a framework on which to modify the material for a child who is unable to learn through standard procedures.

In summary, the proposed model is not presented as a panacea for all instructional problems but it is presented as a model that can provide a frame of reference for making instructional decisions. The current state of the art in instructional materials continues to place a heavy demand upon the teacher to make adjustments in the educational program. The instructional model presented here demands that the teacher assume the responsibility for the child's failure to accomplish a task as a result of not adjusting the input-output functions of the instructional materials to match the input-output functions of the child. This paper has not considered a most crucial aspect of any learning experience—reinforcement. A systematic reinforcement procedure must always be employed to insure maximum learning in any instructional program.

Finally, it is hoped that material developers and publishers will ultimately provide instructional materials with suggested alternatives for adapting them to children having input or output deficits. The clinical teacher will always be necessary, but systematically developed instructional programs will be the only way of reducing instructional variability for the handicapped child.

References

Allen, R. V. & Allen, C. *Language experiences in reading.* Chicago: Encyclopedia Britannica Press, 1966.

Cheves, R. *Visual-motor perception teaching materials.* Boston: Teaching Resources, 1967.

Clymer, T., Christenson, B. M. & Russell, D. H. *Building pre-reading skills; Kit A, language.* Boston: Ginn and Company, 1965.

Cruickshank, W. M., Bentzen, F. A., Ratzeburg, F. H., & Tannhauser, M. T. *A teaching method for brain-injured and hyperactive children.* Syracuse, New York: Syracuse University Press, 1961.

Dubnoff, B., Chambers, I., & Schaefer, F. *Dubnoff school programs: Experimental perceptual-motor exercises.* Boston: Teaching Resources, 1968.

Ebersole, M., Kephart, N. C., & Ebersole, J. B. *Steps to achievement for the slow learner.* Columbus, Ohio: Charles E. Merrill Publishing Company, 1968.

Ellson, D. G., Barber, L. W., Harris, P. L., & Adams, R. B. *Ginn tutorial: A tutorial system.* Boston: Ginn and Company, 1968.

Fries, C. C., Wilson, R. G., & Rudolph, M. K. *Merrill linguistic readers.* Columbus, Ohio: Charles E. Merrill Publishing Company, 1966.

Frostig, M. & Horne, D. *The Frostig program for the development of visual perception: Teachers guide.* Chicago: Follett Publishing Company, 1964.

Frostig, M., Lefever, D. W. & Whittlesey, I. R. *Developmental test of visual perception.* Palo Alto, California: Consulting Psychologists Press, 1961.

Getman, G. N. & Kane, E. R. *Developing learning readiness.* New York: McGraw-Hill Book Company, 1968.

Getman, G. N. & Kane, E. R. *The physiology of readiness: An action program for the development of perception in children.* Minneapolis, Minn.: Programs to Accelerate School Success, 1964.

Hatton, D. A., Pizzat, F. J. & Pelkowski, J. M., *Perceptual-motor teaching materials, Erie program 1.* Boston: Teaching Resources, 1967.

Johnson, D. J. and Myklebust, H. R. *Learning disabilities: Educational principles and practices.* New York: Grune & Stratton, 1967.

Karnes, M. B. *Helping young children develop language skills: A book of activities.* Washington, D. C.: The Council for Exceptional Children, 1969.

Kephart, N. C. *The slow-learner in the classroom.* Columbus, Ohio: Charles E. Merrill Publishing Company, 1968.

Kirk, S. A. *The diagnosis and remediation of psycholinguistic disabilities,* Urbana, Illinois: Institute for Research on Exceptional Children, University of Illinois, 1966.

Kirk, S. A. and Bateman, B. "Diagnosis and remediation of learning disabilities." *Exceptional Children,* 1962, 29, 73–78.

Kirk, S. A. and McCarthy, J. J. "The Illinois Test of Psycholinguistic Abilities an approach to differential diagnosis." *American Journal of Mental Deficiency,* 1961, 66, 399–412.

Kirk, S. A., McCarthy, J. J., and Kirk, W. D. *Illinois Test of Psycholinguistic Abilities, revised edition.* Urbana, Illinois: University of Illinois Press, 1968.

L'Abate, L. "An input-output approach to psychodiagnosis of children, *World Journal of Psychosynthesis,* 1969, 1, 68–73.

Lovitt, T. C. & Curtiss, K. A. "Effects of manipulating an antecedent event on mathematics response rate." *Journal of Applied Behavior Analysis,* 1968, 1, 329–333.

Luria, A. R. *The role of speech in the regulation of normal and abnormal behavior.* New York: Pergamon Press, 1961.

McCarthy, J. J. and Kirk, S. A. *Illinois Test of Psycholinguistic Abilities, experiment edition.* Urbana: Institute for Research on Exceptional Children, University of Illinois, 1961.

McCarthy, J. M. Psychoeducational diagnosis—a derivative of classroom behavior. Unpublished manuscript, Community Consolidated School District 54, Hoffman Estates, Illinois, 1967.

Minskoff, E. H., Wiseman, D. E., Minskoff, J. G. The *MWM program for the remediation of language learning disabilities,* Chicago: Follett Educational Publishers, in press.

Olshin, G. M. Special education instructional materials center program. *Exceptional Children,* 1968, 34, 515–519.

Olson, J. L., Hahn, H. R., and Herman, A. L. "Psycholinguistic curriculum." *Mental Retardation,* 1965, 3, 14–19.

Osgood, C. E. Motivational dynamics of language behavior. *Nebraska Symposium on Motivation.* Lincoln: University of Nebraska Press, 1967.

Peterson, W. "Children with specific learning disabilities." In N. G. Haring and R. L. Schiefelbusch, (Eds.), *Methods in Special Education.* New York: McGraw-Hill Book Company, 1967, pp. 159–208.

Schoolfield, L. D. and Timberlake, J. B. *The phonovisual method.* Washington, D. C.: Phonovisual Products, 1967.

Sounds and Patterns. Chicago: Knowledge Aids Division, Radiant Corporation, 1968.

Stern, C., Stern, M. B. & Gould, T. S. *Structural arithmetic.* New York: Houghton Mifflin Company, 1952.

Strauss, A. A. and Lehtinen, L. E. *Psychopathology and education of the brain-injured child.* New York: Grune & Stratton, 1947.

Sullivan, M. W. and Buchanan, C. D. *Programmed reading.* New York: McGraw-Hill Book Company, 1963.

Thoburn, R. and McCraith, L. *Greater Cleveland mathematics program.* Chicago: Science Research Associates, Inc., 1962.

Wepman, J. M. "The perceptual basis for learning. "In E. C. Frierson & W. B. Barbe, *Educating children with learning disabilities.* New York: Appleton-Century-Crofts, 1967.

Wepman, J. M., Jones, L. V., Bock, R. D., and Pelt, D. V. "Studies in aphasia: Background and theoretical formulations." *Journal of Speech and Hearing Disorders,* 1960, 25, 323–332.

Woodcock, R. W. *Peabody rebus reading program.* Circle Pines, Minn.: American Guidance Service, 1967.

33. LEARNING THEORY APPROACHES TO CLASSROOM MANAGEMENT: RATIONALE AND INTERVENTION TECHNIQUES

HARVEY F. CLARIZIO and STEPHEN L. YELON

Today, more than ever before, there is acute concern about the mental health of children. Traditionally, we have modeled intervention efforts after the clinical concept of treatment. Dissatisfaction with the limitations of psychotherapeutic intervention (Levitt, 1957) together with the professional manpower shortage in the mental health field has led, however, to suggestions, e.g., Redl (1962), that we need new modes of treatment, closer to real-life situations, if we are to tackle children's problems more effectively.

When psychodynamic models were the preferred method of treatment, teachers were accorded at best a second-string status on the clinical team helping emotionally handicapped children. The increasing popularity of behavior therapy and other approaches based on learning theory now offers teachers opportunities for an integral role in the quest for better mental health for children. Indeed, it might well be the mental health specialist who will now assume the supportive role (Gallagher & Chalfant, 1966) in the "treatment" of children.

In the application of learning theory principles to the modification of

---

SOURCE. Reprinted from *The Journal of Special Education*, 1967, 1, 267–274. By permission of the publisher.

deviant behavior, the emphasis is on the changing of behavior with little attention devoted to the etiology of the behavior. Why should teachers focus primarily on the behavior rather than on its causes? There are several reasons:

1. First, teachers by virtue of their orientation are not trained to probe the causes of behavior that even mental hygiene specialists often consider obscure and uncertain. Hence, it is really helpful to ask the teacher to understand the causes underlying children's disturbed behavior?

2. Teachers in any case are rarely in a position wherein they can directly manipulate the causes so as to modify their influence on the child's classroom adjustment. For example, if the problem lies in the parent-child relations or in a brain lesion, there are few if any constructive intervention techniques that the teacher can employ. Yet the child's troublesome behavior persists and must be handled as effectively as possible when it occurs in the classroom.

3. Even in such occasional cases where the causes can be identified and manipulated directly, the maladaptive behaviors may persist. Thus despite the discovery and correction of the contributing role of poor vision and faulty child-rearing practices in a reading disability case, a pupil may continue to experience difficulty with his reading until attention is *specifically* devoted to his reading behavior, and unless he can experience success in this specific area, his mental health will continue to be impaired.

4. Behaviors or symptoms or habits may in their own right be incapacitating and disturbing, and current persisting symptoms may themselves be producing emotional disturbance (Franks, 1965) above and beyond the core disturbance from which the child is suffering. And, as research indicates (White & Harris, 1961), it is difficult to disentangle educational and emotional madadjustments in the school-age child (Gallagher & Chalfant, 1966).

5. There is little substantial evidence to indicate that if the teacher assists the child in modifying his behavior or symptoms, other undesirable behaviors will inevitably take their place in the manner of symptom substitution (Grossberg, 1964).

6. Finally, and most importantly, as already implied, the teacher most commonly has no resort other than to deal with the pupil's behavior as it appears in the here and now. As Lewis (1965) attests:

"If we cannot aspire to reconstruction of personality that will have long range beneficial effects, we can modify disturbing behavior in specific ways in present social contexts. This more modest aspiration may not only be more realistic but it may be all that is required of the child-helping professions in a society that is relatively open and provides a variety of opportunity systems in which a child can reconcile his personal needs with society's expectations of him."

Having argued that the teacher should be primarily concerned with behavior *per se* rather than with its causes, let us turn to techniques emanating from learning theory which have relevance to the modification of deviant behavior in the classroom (see Glossary of Terms on the next page). Although the techniques to be presented are discussed separately for the sake of clarity, it should be recognized that more than one of them may be operating at any given time in real-life attempts to modify behavior. Moreover, common to all of these techniques is the use of "systematic environmental contingencies to alter the object's responsiveness to stimuli" (Krasner & Ullman, 1965).

THE TECHNIQUES

Extinction. There is a growing body of research demonstrating that simple withdrawal of reinforcers can reduce or eliminate such troublesome behavior as excessive talking, tantrum behavior and academic errors (Warren, 1965; Williams, 1959; Zimmerman & Zimmerman, 1962). Extinction is not always, however, the most economic and effective means of producing behavioral change (Bandura & Walters, 1963). Certain cautions should be recognized:

1. Spontaneous remission—the return of undesirable behavior—may occur following the extinction trials, thus necessitating additional extinction sessions.
2. When behavior is maintained on a partial reinforcement schedule, removal of the reinforcers may actually produce an increase in the frequency and intensity of the deviant responses. Moreover, it is sometimes extremely difficult not to reinforce maladaptive behaviors in a school setting, since circumstances may be beyond the teacher's control. The aggressive youngster who kicks the teacher or a classmate cannot help but be reinforced by the look of pain on the victim's face. The needed cooperation of classmates in the application of extinction procedures may also be difficult to secure, so that by necessity the deviant behavior is established on a partial reinforcement schedule.
3. General observation suggests that certain behaviors do not diminish and disappear simply because reinforcers are withdrawn, and sometimes teachers cannot or will not wait long enough to permit the completion of the extinction process. These limitations are particularly

acute in situations in which emotional contagion is a distinct possibility. Behaviors seriously injurious to the self would also seemingly not lend themselves well to this technique. In brief, this method of behavior change has proven to be of value with acting-out as well as inhibited youngsters. Yet, its limitations suggest that other methods of behavioral modification are at times more economical and effective (see also Ausubel, 1957, Bandura, 1965).

Positive Reinforcement. Operant conditioning techniques constitute one of the main tools of behavior modification. In this technique, emphasis is placed on the response made by the individual, and only minimal attention is given to the stimuli eliciting the response. Essentially, the teacher presents a reward whenever the child emits the desired response. While teachers have been cognizant of the value of positively reinforcing "good" behavior, there is ample evidence to suggest that even "good" teachers not uncommonly reinforce undesirable behavior. One of the merits of the positive reinforcement technique stems from its applicability to antisocial youngsters as well as to withdrawn children (Bandura & Walters, 1963).

There has been a dearth of psychotherapeutic approaches designed for the conduct problem child, despite such pupils typically being the most disruptive of classroom procedures. The application of positive reinforcement principles to seriously aggressive children involves the manipulation of three variables: the schedules of reinforcement, the interval factor and the type of reward. With respect to the concept of reinforcement schedules, a distinction must be enforced between the acquisition and the maintenance of behavior. For the former, continuous or full-schedule reinforcement or reward after each appearance of the desired behavior is most effective, whereas for the latter, partial or intermittent reinforcement is most economical and effective. The interval variable merely refers to the passage of time between the production of a response and the presentation of the reward or reinforcer. The delay factor should usually be quite short initially, because acting-out children typically have difficulty in postponing gratification. Step by step, the interval can be lengthened as the child acquires more adequate behavioral controls.

The rewards for such pupils, at the start, may have to be tangible or physical in nature but should always be paired with verbal social reinforcers, e.g., "You handled yourself well in that situation today" (Quay, 1963). Gradually, the reinforcers can be shifted away from the concrete into language and other symbolic forms of reward until the child can respond satisfactorily to them. In deciding upon the most suitable reinforcers, consideration should be given to such factors as the child's developmental level and socio-cultural background.

The main unresolved question with the technique of positive reinforcement centers around the question of how to make the child initiate the response in the first place so that he can be rewarded (Franks, 1965). The technique of social modeling may well provide at least a partial answer to this problem (Baer, 1963; Ferster, 1961; Hewett, 1964; Slack, 1960; Wolf, Risley & Mees, 1964).

Modeling. Modeling is based on the premise that a child will imitate the behavior of others. Modeling is important in that children commonly acquire social skills through imitation of and identification with examples of socially approved behaviors presented by suitable models. School teachers thus have a unique opportunity to influence the behavior of entire groups of children. However, this technique has been typically overlooked in the management or modification of deviant behavior in schools. Modeling procedures may represent a more effective means than positive reinforcement of establishing new response patterns in children (Bandura, 1965). Moreover, a behavior pattern, once acquired through imitation, is often maintained without deliberate external reinforcement, because human beings learn to reinforce themselves for behaving in certain ways. Teacher training institutions have long recognized the importance of modeling procedures in the training of future teachers and, accordingly, attempt to provide adequate models in the form of critic teachers. However, attention should now be devoted to the teacher's use of modeling procedures in influencing the behavior of the pupils.

There are three effects of exposure to models: the *modeling effect*, the *inhibitory* or *disinhibitory effect*, and the *eliciting effect* (Bandura, 1965). Through the *modeling effect* children come to acquire responses that were not previously a part of their behavior. As noted earlier, modeling procedures may be considerably more economical in establishing new responses than the method of operant conditioning based on positive reinforcement, especially when a combination of verbalizing models and demonstration procedures are used. The strengthening or weakening of inhibitory responses already existing in the observer (the *inhibitory* or *disinhibitory effect*) can also be accomplished through modeling procedures. Children, for example, who see a model punished or rewarded for aggressive behavior tend to decrease or increase their aggressive behavior accordingly. The *eliciting* or *response facilitation effect* refers to the teacher's eliciting responses that precisely or approximately match those exhibited by the model. Thus, observation of the teacher's response provides discriminative clues that trigger similar responses already in the pupil's behavior repertoire. This eliciting effect is distinguished from the modeling and the disinhibiting effects in that the imitated behavior is neither new nor previously punished.

The probability that a child will imitate a model is a function of several variables. Modeling is partly dependent upon the reinforcing consequences of the model's behavior. Thus, if a model is rewarded for his socially approved behavior, the likelihood that the observer will behave in a socially approved manner is increased. Other factors include the process of attending to the model's behavior, e.g., previous training in observation, and various environmental stimuli, e.g., the complexity of the stimuli (Baldwin, 1967; Bandura, 1962b; Bandura & Hutson, 1961; Bandura & Kupers, 1964; Bandura, Ross & Ross, 1963).

Punishment. Aversive conditioning or punishment is an intervention technique which has been used primarily to discourage undesirable behavior. This technique consists in the presentation of either physically or psychologically painful stimuli or the withdrawal of pleasant stimuli when undesirable behavior occurs. The use of punishment as a technique for behavioral modification has been contraindicated for the following reasons:

1. Punishment does not eliminate the response; it merely slows down the rate at which the troublesome behaviors are emitted.
2. This technique serves notice to stop certain negative behaviors; it does not indicate what behaviors are appropriate in the situation.
3. Aggressive behaviors on the teacher's part may provide an undesirable model for the pupil.
4. The emotional side effects of punishment, such as fear, tenseness and withdrawal are maladaptive.
5. Punishment serves as a source of frustration which is apt to elicit additional maladaptive behaviors.

Some psychologists, who are currently reconsidering the concept of punishment, contend that it can have a beneficial effect if applied to specific responses rather than to general behavior (Marshall, 1965).

Teachers, whatever their motivations, use verbal reprimands and other forms of correction in their approach to classroom management, and the judicious use of punishment as an intervention technique is most likely necessary in that it is impossible to guide behavior effectively with positive reinforcement and extinction alone. As Ausubel (1957) asserts, "It is impossible for children to learn what is *not* approved and tolerated simply by generalizing in reverse from the approval they receive for the behavior that *is* acceptable." Thus, punishment of specific responses can have an informative and beneficial effect. A particular positive value that may accrue from the use of punishment is that undesirable behaviors are held in abeyance, thus permitting the teaching of desirable modes of behavior through such intervention techniques as social imitation or positive reinforcement. Although punishment techniques have been used primarily with acting-out pupils, they have also been found to be of value in certain cases of withdrawn behavior (Bandura, 1962a; Church, 1963; Lovaas, 1965; Meyer & Offenbach, 1962; Redl, 1965; Sears, Maccoby & Levin, 1957; Solomon, 1964).

Discrimination Learning. Children sometimes engage in maladaptive behavior because they have transferred behaviors acceptable in one setting to a second setting where these behaviors are considered inappropriate and maladaptive. Thus, for example, the child who is overly dependent upon his mother may behave in a very dependent way toward his teacher. Such cases of inappropriate generalization can sometimes be remediated through the use of discrimination learning. Essentially this process consists of labeling given behaviors as appropriate within a specific environmental context. The teacher in the above case, for example, may inform the child in a nonpunitive way that she is not his mother but his teacher and that as such she will require him to become more self-reliant. This labeling by the teacher makes the child more aware of both inappropriate and appropriate behaviors. Interestingly, children do not always have to be able to express such discriminations verbally in order to achieve "insight" into their behavior. It is rather required, to insure effective results, that appropriate responses be rewarded and undesirable responses discouraged. Discrimination learning thus may be of service in conjunction with most other techniques in managing conduct and personality problems in the classroom (Ayllon & Michael, 1959; Barrett & Lindsley, 1962; Brackbill & O'Hara, 1958; Penny & Lupton, 1961; Stevenson, Weir & Zigler, 1959).

Desensitization. Desensitization as an intervention technique has been used principally with the fearful and phobic child. The basic objective is to have the child achieve a relaxed response in the presence of what were previously anxiety-producing stimuli. To accomplish this relaxed response, the subject is encouraged to perform approximations of previously punished acts within non-punishing or actually rewarding situations. Or through gradual exposure to the feared object or situation, a subject may become able to perform a formerly feared act or approach the feared object in a relaxed manner (Bentler, 1962; Garvey & Hegrenes, 1966; Jersild & Holmes, 1935; Lazarus, 1960; Wolpe, 1958).

CONCLUDING REMARKS

As evidenced by our discussion of the limitations of each technique, we do not envision management techniques emanating from learning theory as a panacea, but these intervention techniques do have certain potential advantages:

1. The fruitfulness of these techniques in modifying human behavior has been demonstrated in laboratory settings as well as in natural settings.
2. They are consistent with the teacher's role whereby she must reflect cultural expectations and set standards for her pupils' academic and social behavior.
3. Behavioral approaches offer specific and practical techniques for use in day-to-day classroom problems. While teachers already use some or all of these techniques, they frequently do so intuitively or inconsistently thereby reducing their efficacy.
4. These techniques enable the teacher to strive toward more realistic and obtainable goals relative to their pupils' mental health.
5. One of the most important attributes of these techniques is the fact that they can be taught to teachers. While there are few if any teacher training institutions currently offering didactic and practice training in such techniques, one can envision the time when teachers will acquire such skills through laboratory courses taken in conjunction with their formal course work or through in-service meetings and workshops.

Glossary of Terms

Behavior Therapy: A therapeutic process in which the primary goal is to change overt behavior rather than to re-structure an individual's personality makeup. The process uses principles of learning for its methodological source.

Extinction: The decrease and eventual disappearance of a response learned under conditions of reinforcement when the reinforcement is withheld.

Reinforcement: Whatever serves to maintain the occurrence or increase the strength of a response, e.g., food, water or the avoidance of punishment.

Partial reinforcement: A condition in which subjects receive reinforcement only at various time intervals or after a certain number of responses.

Positive reinforcement: Much the same as reinforcement, i.e., *presenting* a pleasant stimulus when a response occurs, as opposed to negative reinforcement where an unpleasant stimulus is *removed* when a response occurs.

Modeling: A condition where the behavior to be acquired is demonstrated for the learner.

Punishment: A condition where a learner is made to feel uncomfortable by being presented an unpleasant stimulus, e.g., the infliction of pain by hitting, and/or a condition where a pleasant stimulus is withdrawn so that the learner is made to feel discomfort, e.g., having threats withdrawn.

References

Ausubel, D. *Theory and problems of child development.* New York: Grune & Stratton, 1957.

Ayllon, T. & Michael, J. The psychiatric nurse as a behavioral engineer. *Journal of Experimental Analysis of Behavior,* 1959, 2, 323–334.

Baer, D. Effect of withdrawal of positive reinforcement on an extinguishing response in young children. *Child Development,* 1961, 32, 67–74.

Baer, D. Social reinforcement and behavior change. *American Journal of Orthopsychiatry,* 1963, 591–633.

Baldwin, A. Theories of child development. *Critique of social learning theory,* Chapter 16. New York: Wiley, 1967.

Bandura, A. Punishment revisited. *Journal of Consulting Psychology,* 1962, 26, 289–301(a).

Bandura, A. Social learning through imitation. In M. Jones (Ed.), *Nebraska Symposium on Motivation,* Lincoln, Nebraska: University of Nebraska Press, 1962. Pp. 211–269(b).

Bandura, A. Behavioral modification through modeling procedures. In L. Krasner & L. Ullman (Eds.), *Research in behavior modification.* New York: Holt, Rinehart & Winston, 1965.

Bandura, A. & Hutson, A. Identification as a process of incidental learning. *Journal of Abnormal and Social Psychology,* 1961, 63, 311–318.

Bandura, A. & Kupers, C. The transmission of patterns of self-reinforcement through modeling. *Journal of Abnormal and Social Psychology,* 1964, 69, 1–19.

Bandura, A., Ross, D. & Ross, S. Imitation of film mediated aggressive models. *Journal of Abnormal and Social Psychology,* 1963, 66, 3–11.

Bandura, A., & Walters, R. *Social learning and personality development.* New York: Holt, Rinehart & Winston, 1963.

Barrett, B. & Lindsley, O. Deficits in acquisition of operant discrimination and differentiation shown by institutionalized retarded children. *American Journal of Mental Deficiency*, 1962, 67, 424–436.

Bentler, P. An infant's phobia treated with reciprocal inhibition therapy. *Journal of Child Psychology and Psychiatry*, 1962, 3, 185–189.

Brackbill, Y. & O'Hara, J. The relative effectiveness of reward and punishment for discrimination learning in children. *Journal of Comparative and Physiological Psychology*, 1958, 51, 747–751.

Church, R. The varied effects of punishment on behavior. *Psychological Review*, 1963, 70, 369–402.

Ferster, C. Positive reinforcement and behavioral deficits of autistic children. *Child Development*, 1961, 32, 437–456.

Franks, C. Behavior therapy, psychology and the psychiatrist: contribution, evaluation and overview. *American Journal of Orthopsychiatry*, 1965, 35, 145–151.

Gallagher, J. & Chalfant, J. The training of educational specialists for emotionally disturbed and socially maladjusted children. In *N.S.S.E. yearbook 1966: social deviancy among youth*. Chicago: University of Chicago Press, 1966. pp. 398–423.

Garvey, W. & Hegrenes, J. Desensitization techniques in the treatment of school phobia. *American Journal of Orthopsychiatry*, 1966, 36, 147–152.

Grossberg, J. Behavior therapy: a review. *Psychological Bulletin*, 1964, 62, 73–88.

Hewett, F. Teaching reading to an autistic boy through operant conditioning. *The Reading Teacher*, 1964, 17, 613–618.

Jersild, A. & Holmes, F. Methods of overcoming children's fears. *Journal of Psychology*, 1935, 1, 75–104.

Krasner, L. & Ullman, L. *Case studies in behavior modification*. New York: Holt, Rinehart & Winston, 1965.

Lazarus, A. The elimination of children's phobias by deconditioning. In H. Eysench (Ed.), *Behavior therapy and the neuroses*. New York: Pergamon Press, 1960. Pp. 114–122.

Levitt, E. E. Results of psychotherapy with children: an evaluation. *Journal of Counseling Psychology*, 1957, 25, 189–196.

Lewis, W. Continuity and intervention in emotional disturbance: a review. *Exceptional Child*, 1965, 31, 465–475.

Lovaas, I. Building social behavior in autistic children by use of electroshock. *Journal of Experimental Research in Personality*, 1965, 1, 99–109.

Marshall, H. The effect of punishment on children: a review of the literature and a suggested hypothesis. *Journal of Genetic Psychology*, 1965, 106, 108–133.

Meyer, W. & Offenbach, S. Effectiveness of reward and punishment as a function of task complexity. *Journal of Comparative and Physiological Psychology*, 1962, 55, 532–534.

Penny, R. O. & Lupton, A. Children's discrimination learning as a function of reward and punishment. *Journal of Comparative and Physiological Psychology*, 1961, 54, 449–456.

Quay, H. Some basic consideration in the education of emotionally disturbed children. *Exceptional Children*, 1963, 30, 27–31.

Redl, F. Crisis in the children's field. *American Journal of Orthopsychiatry*, 1962, 32, 759–780.

Redl, F. The concept of punishment. In N. Long, W. Morse & R. Newan (Eds.), *Conflict in the classroom*. Belmont, Calif.: Wadsworth, 1965.

Sears, R., Maccoby, E. & Levin, H. *Patterns of child rearing*. Evanston, Ill.: Row Peterson, 1957.

Slack, C. Experimenter-subject psychotherapy: a new method for introducing intensive office treatment for unreachable cases. *Mental Hygiene*, 1960, 44, 238–256.

Solomon, R. Punishment. *American Psychologist*, 1964, 19, 239–253.

Stevenson, H., Weir, M. & Zigler, E. Discrimination learning in children as a function of motive-incentive conditions. *Psychological Report*, 1959, 5, 95–98.

Warren, A. All's quiet in the backroom. Paper read at the Council for Exceptional Children, Wichita, Kans., Oct., 1965.

White, M. & Harris, M. *The school psychologist*. New York: Harper, 1961.

Williams, C. D. The elimination of tantrum behavior by extinction procedures. *Journal of Abnormal and Social Psychology*, 1959, 59, 269.

Wolf, M., Risley, T. & Mees, H. Application of operant conditioning procedures to behavior problems of an autistic child. *Behavior Research and Therapy*, 1964, 1, 305–312.

Wolpe, J. *Psychotherapy by reciprocal inhibition*. Stanford, Calif.: Stanford University, 1958.

Zimmerman, E. & Zimmerman, J. The alternation of behavior in a special classroom situation. *Journal of Experimental Analysis of Behavior*, 1962, 5, 59–60.

Index